JEWISH SOCIETY
THROUGH THE AGES

JEWISH SOCIETY
THROUGH THE AGES

Edited by

H. H. BEN-SASSON and S. ETTINGER

SCHOCKEN BOOKS - NEW YORK

First SCHOCKEN edition 1971
Second printing 1973

Copyright © UNESCO 1969

Library of Congress Catalog Card No. 77-148836

Manufactured in the United States of America

This book was originally published in a slightly different form under the auspices of UNESCO, as a special number of the *Journal of World History*, whose general editors are Guy S. Métraux and François Crouzet. The book was prepared with the support of the Memorial Foundation for Jewish Culture, New York, and with the cooperation of the Israel National Commission for UNESCO, whose chairman, Dr. Moshe Avidor, provided liaison between the editorial staffs.

CONTENTS

CONTENTS

CONTRIBUTORS

BEN-ZION DINUR
Emeritus Professor of Modern Jewish History at the Hebrew University, Jerusalem.

R. J. ZWI WERBLOWSKY
Associate Professor of Comparative Religion at the Hebrew University, Jerusalem.

HAYIM TADMOR
Associate Professor of Assyriology at the Hebrew University, Jerusalem.

YITZHAK F. BAER
Emeritus Professor of Medieval Jewish History at the Hebrew University, Jerusalem.

MENAHEM STERN
Associate Professor of Jewish History at the Hebrew University, Jerusalem.

DAVID G. FLUSSER
Associate Professor of Comparative Religion at the Hebrew, University, Jerusalem.

E. E. URBACH
Professor of Talmud and Midrash at the Hebrew University, Jerusalem.

SHMUEL SAFRAI
Senior Lecturer in Jewish History at the Hebrew University, Jerusalem.

S. D. GOITEIN
Emeritus Professor of History of Islam and Muslim Peoples at the Hebrew University of Jerusalem; Visiting Professor of Arabic at the University of Pennsylvania.

I. TWERSKY
Head of the Department of Jewish Studies at Harvard University; Visiting Professor at the Hebrew University, Jerusalem.

H. H. BEN-SASSON
Associate Professor of Jewish History at the Hebrew University, Jerusalem.

HAIM BEINART
Associate Professor of Jewish History at the Hebrew University, Jerusalem.

CECIL ROTH
Formerly Emeritus Reader in Jewish Studies, Oxford University, Visiting Professor, Queens College and the City University of New York. Died 1970.

S. ETTINGER
Associate Professor of Jewish History at the Hebrew University, Jerusalem.

JACOB KATZ
Professor of Jewish Social and Educational History at the Hebrew University, Jerusalem.

MOSHE MISHKINSKY
Research Fellow in History of the Jewish Labor Movement at the Hebrew University, Jerusalem.

LLOYD P. GARTNER
City College of the City University of New York.

S. N. EISENSTADT
Professor of Sociology at the Hebrew University, Jerusalem.

JEWISH SOCIETY
THROUGH THE AGES

BEN-ZION DINUR

JEWISH HISTORY—ITS UNIQUENESS AND CONTINUITY

T HE articles in this collection all deal with social life and thought
in different periods of Jewish history from early Israel down to
our own time. In order to place those aspects of historical life in
their true perspective we have to make some preliminary remarks on
the general framework of Jewish history, its uniqueness, continuity
and the different periods into which it falls.

I

It is commonplace to say that the character of every nation shows
itself in the course of its history and is evident in its historical consciousness. External sources—the evidence of other nations—are useful to establish such matters as a nation's first appearance in history.
This applies to the date of the Patriarchs and the origins of the Jewish
people. The references to the *Habiru* and the problem of their identity
with the Hebrews, as well as the occurrence of the name *Israel* in the
Marneptaḥ Stela are certainly important. However, a nation's account
of its origins unquestionably encapsules its own tradition on its uniqueness as understood by its earliest generations, and thus every testimony
of a people about itself has a special value as a source for the internal
processes governing its life. There is no doubt that for the distinctive
traits of Israel, the people's own testimony on its origins (the stories
about its ancestors) must be regarded as the primary source. According to the Bible we may recognize four basic features that distinguish
the Jewish people from the outset: they are (1) ethnic, (2) religious, (3)
social, and (4) territorial.

(1) The ethnic feature is attested not only by the tradition on the
common origin of mankind and the distinct position of the Jewish people
within this family of nations—an early tradition preserved in the Bible
(Gen. 11: 10-32, which serves as a continuation of 10: 1-32)—but also
by ethnic consciousness: the people refused to intermarry with their
neighbours, the inhabitants of Canaan. In spite of friendly relations

and treaties between Israel and her neighbours, there was no treaty of intermarriage with any of the adjoining people. Ethnic specificity is also attested by the patterns of national growth and the nomenclature used for them: the people are called "Children of Israel", and as a whole it is the "House of Israel", while its parts are the "tribes of Israel" and its heads the "elders of Israel". These names ascribing the people to its eponymous ancestor are found above all in the stories and traditions about the period down to the foundation of the kingdom.

(2) The second distinguishing feature is religious. The stages of religious development are symbolized in the Bible by three figures from Israel's early history: Abraham, Jacob or Israel, and Moses. Abraham is called, even in prophetic times, the "father of the people"; the people are "the offspring of Abraham, my friend". Relating the people to Abraham is usually connected with faith rather than ethnic identity. Israel is "the people of the God of Abraham" (Ps. 47: 9; 2 Chr. 20: 7). Abraham "believed the Lord and he reckoned it to him as righteousness" (Gen. 15: 6). God tried him time after time and he always stood the test. There are about twenty references in Genesis to God's appearing to Abraham. God made a covenant with Abraham and promised to give the Land to his descendants, and to remember the covenant and the promise. In these traditions, even for his pagan neighbours Abraham was "a prince of God" (Gen. 23: 6) and a prophet (Gen. 20: 7). God had chosen Abraham, "knew" him and appointed him, "to keep the way of the Lord": "for I knew him that he will command his children and his household after him and they will keep the way of the Lord and to do justice and judgment" (Gen. 18: 19). Several other passages in the Bible should be referred to Abraham's position as a "Prince" of God, the head of a religious community. The words "the men of Abraham's house" (Gen. 17: 23), "the souls that they had gotten in Ḥaran" (Gen. 12: 5) are understood by early commentators as referring to those whom Abraham had won over to his faith, i.e. proselytes. Later tradition (Jub. 11-12, the early *Targums*, the *Talmud* and *Midrash*) tells stories about Abraham fighting against idolatry and the worship of graven images and propagating the belief in the one God; it also relates how God miraculously saved him from his enemies. It may be assumed that these stories go back to early traditions for even Isaiah speaks of the God "who redeemed Abraham" (29: 22).

The second stage in the religious development of Israel is associated with the figure of Jacob or Israel. The struggles between Isaac and Ishmael, and between Jacob and Esau for blessing and birth-right, are struggles for the heritage of Abraham. The stories about the beginnings of Israel and all the direct and indirect references to the name "Israel" and its use, form one self-contained unit, a historical tradition representing the people's testimony about itself. According to this tradition the name "Israel" symbolizes the growing awareness of religious uniqueness and the emergence of a particular section of the descendants of Abraham that was faithful to his heritage. The new religious feature that shaped the heritage of Abraham and became the symbol of "the tribes of Israel", was one of struggle and activity on behalf of this uniqueness born of faith—the special divine relationship of Israel—and it is expressed in the saying God "fought for you". According to this early tradition the Land became the patrimony of the Children of Israel because they were faithful to the religious heritage of Abraham; it was this fact that entitled them to the promise that they should inherit the Land. Jacob was zealous in rejecting strange gods, and God renewed the covenant with him. This early tradition reflects the historical reality of "the first Israel", i.e. a religious community or brotherhood of that part of the "seed of Abraham" that appeared under the name of "Israel".

The third and decisive stage in the religious development of the people is the exodus from Egypt and the revelation on Mount Sinai. Early tradition regards the people's liberation from slavery, its wanderings in the desert and the establishment of the religious covenant on Mount Sinai as one chain of events through which the Children of Israel became the "nation" of Israel, the "congregation" of the Children of Israel or the "assembly" of the Children of Israel.

The tribes became a nation and the nation, welded together by its religious uniqueness, became a congregation and an assembly, the "assembly of the Lord". At this stage God made himself known to His people by this name—the God of their fathers, who had led them out of Egypt and given them the Torah and commandments by which they were to live, and had brought them to an ever-lasting pinnacle as "a kingdom of priests and a holy people". This, according to the tradition, was a divine mission accomplished by Moses, the servant of God, prophet and messenger, the greatest of the prophets: "for there arose not a prophet since in Israel like unto Moses" (Deut. 34: 10). The divine Law was given to Israel through Moses and is therefore called the "Law of Moses". This religious uniqueness is characterized above all by monotheism, not only in the sense of denying the existence of other gods but in the sense that God does not stand for any natural force and is not governed by any law of nature; and it has stamped its unique imprint on the nation throughout its history and its external as well as internal struggles.

(3) The distinctive social feature of early Israel is marked by its being a "congregation". A congregation is a social entity which comes into being and develops mainly as the result of a common will and not, like the family or tribe, by natural processes. Its members live in one place, but what distinguishes them is a common faith and common

beliefs, a way of life, will; ideas and aspirations. The basis of this
entity lies in man rather than in a place; its aim is not so much to maintain the organizational unit as the aspiration to change reality, to create
a more desirable social reality than the existing one. The idea of the
organization is prior to its existence. The social system of early Israel
was not, therefore, as is usually maintained, simply patriarchal: alongside the "elders", heads of houses or fathers and "heads of families",
other elements were active in directing and shaping affairs: the princes
of the congregation and heads of the congregation, "assembly and
congregation", prophets or messengers and judges or saviours. This
social order was of a specific character which greatly influenced the
history of Israel and the fashioning of the individual in Israel.

(4) The territorial element. The nation began with Abraham's arrival
in Palestine. The early tradition contains many stories about Abraham's
wanderings all over the Land, how he received divine revelations in
many places and built many altars; how both he and Isaac dug wells
and how envious neighbours filled them up. We also hear about "the
Land of the Hebrews" (Gen. 40: 15), apparently the area from Ḥebron
to South of Beer-Sheba, in which they dwelt. Likewise many Hebrew
place names that point to particular types of cultivation (Bethlehem—
literally "the House of bread", Beth ha-Kerem—"the House of vineyard", Gath Rimmon—Pomegranate press, Beth Thapuah—"The House
of Apple") are evidence of the Hebrews' being rooted in Canaan. To
the Children of Israel whom famine had driven to Egypt and who were
slaves there for several generations, Canaan was still the land of their
fathers and their own country; they continued to long for it until finally,
under the leadership of Moses, they left Egypt to go there.

This short survey of early tradition of Jewish historical consciousness shows, that decisive features of its formation were neither the
tribal element nor nomadism. Without claiming for itself autochtonous
roots in its cherished Land or political greatness or even uninterrupted
personal freedom (remembering always the house of bondage), it stresses
the historical processes of its becoming, stage by stage, the "People
of the God of Abraham", "the House of Israel", His Children and tribes
till, with the Law of Moses, it became a "Congregation", chosen by its
God for an appointed spiritual task, and destined to retake the Land of
its Fathers. Truly, a new chapter in human historical consciousness.
Such an involved and unusual historical conception could not arise but
out of a rich cultural legacy.

The unique features present at the very beginning bear witness to
the fact that the people already embodied ancient historical principles
based on religious and social opposition to the kingship system prevailing in Babylon, the Fertile Crescent, Northern Syria and the Nile
Valley. It was the combination of a society that knew how to fight

while being peace-loving and a nucleus that aspired to create a new religious and social reality, that had left the land of its birth to find a country in which it might realize its aspirations, which had had to bear a bitter period of slavery and had succeeded in renewing the religious covenant, in becoming united through it and conquering its country— it was this which determined the character and history of Israel. In considering the continuity of Jewish history we must always bear in mind the lasting influence of the unique character of the nation at its birth.

II

One can only understand the changes in social life, which form the true subject matter of history, by being aware of the unchanging elements; one can only discern what is new by looking at the elements of continuity. For every historical event is determined by the interaction between these two forces. On the other hand, historical continuity consists of an endless process of change, of cause and effect, throughout the ages, while society zealously preserves its life and guards its independence.

(1) The ethnic feature. In spite of the religious ban on intermarriage designed to prevent the penetration of idolatry, intermarriage was common throughout antiquity and in the first centuries of the Middle Ages. When the Children of Israel conquered Canaan the country was inhabited by diverse tribes and nations and the Bible tells us that the Children of Israel "settled among the Canaanites, Hittites and Amorites and Perizzites and Hivites and Jebusites. And they took their daughters to be their wives, and gave their daughters to their sons" (Judges 3: 5). The destruction of Samaria and Jerusalem and the exile of the Northern tribes of Israel and a large part of Judah led to the decline of the Jewish population and the growth of the gentile communities; the result was an acceleration of the process of intermarriage which continued after the exiles returned from Babylon. The battles waged by Ezra and Nehemia against those who had married foreign women are evidence for this fact. Certainly the dispersal of the Jews outside Palestine and the popularity of proselytism to Judaism in many countries added new ethnic elements to the Jewish stock. The marked religious character of the Jewish family caused the proselytes to be absorbed in the family and to be considered "children" or "seed" of Abraham, who was "the glory of the proselytes"; the sense of common origin became their heritage too. After Christianity and Islam became dominant their adherents strictly forbade intermarriage with Jews. Even the many instances of mixed marriages in the recent past have not

undermined the sense of ethnic identity in present day pluralistic society; for some of them, the problem of identity became one of the
major ingredients of their intellectual life.

(2) Religious development. The sense of religious uniqueness grew
apace and had a decisive influence on all aspects of life, individual
and communal. One of the first Jewish philosophers, Sa'adya Gaon,
who lived in the first half of the 10th century, went so far as to say:
"Our nation is a nation by virtue of its religion alone". The Law mi-
nutely regulated the life of the Jew from the day of his birth until
the day of his death and his burial. It included dietary laws and laws
governing the purity of the family; it laid down how he was to bring
up his children in the fear of Heaven and how to teach them the Torah;
how to rest on the Sabbath and how to celebrate the festivals. Needless
to say, there were detailed regulations about the forms of community
worship in the synagogue and the procedures of study in the schools and
academies. The early "houses of the people" (Jer. 39: 8) had become
"houses of prayer" and "meeting places" (Ps. 74: 8) and finally "houses
of assembly" i.e. synagogues. The service consisted of prayer and the
reading of portions of the Torah, accompanied by translation, commentary and homiletic interpretation. From this arose the rich literature
of *midrashim*, biblical commentaries and homiletic interpretations. An
important part of the prayer was formed by the reading of Psalms and
piyutim (liturgical poems). More than thirty thousand such poems—
from the pen of over two thousand writers, and dating from the destruction of the second Temple until the middle of the nineteenth century—
have come down to us. In oriental communities religious poetry for
every occasion of life continued to be written until the last generation.

The decrees of Ezra and Nehemiah which proclaimed the Torah as
the official way of life of Judaea made its study and the observation
of its commandments the focus of education. The last part of the statutes of Artaxerxes addressed to Jerusalem and the province of Yehud
authorized Ezra to teach the laws of God "to them that know them not"
(Ezra 7: 12-26). Thus in the time of Ezra, Levites were appointed who
"helped the people to understand the law": so "they read from the
Book from the Law of God clearly, and gave the sense and caused them
to understand the reading" (Neh. 8: 7-8). Among the Levites there were
also "scribes" (2 Chr. 34: 13) who taught the people, especially the
Pentateuch (Bab. Talmud, Baba Bathra, 21: 2). It is from this time that
the academies existed as permanent institutions headed by famous
scholars. They taught not only "the fear of God" but also "the Law of
the Most High", searched out "the wisdom of all the ancients" and were
"occupied with the prophets of old" (Ecclus. 39: 1-3). In addition they
were the depositaries of secular lore and learning about the "signs of
heaven according to the order of their months" (Jub. 4: 17) and "every-

thing that takes place in heaven... set in order each in its month" (Enoch 2: 1) and they advanced this lore. The esteem in which physicians and pharmacists were held (Ecclus. 38: 1-8) makes it probable that medicine and pharmacy were among the subjects taught in the academies. The rich literature of *Halakhah* and *Agadah* (law and lore), of Mishnah and Talmud and science (Shmuel the astronomer, Asaph the physician etc.) was the legacy of these academies, which in various forms survived throughout the ages. Parallel to this activity ran the reaction to, and absorption of, changing external challenges and influences, starting with Canaanite influence on Israel, especially the worship of Baal, that had been connected with the transition from a pastoral way of life to agriculture and with the beliefs and worship of other peoples with whom the Jews came into contact. Naturally contact with new cultures produced a questioning ferment and called forth spiritual efforts to come to terms with them, to take over what seemed kindred elements and to reject the rest. Thus there were struggles first with Persian dualism, then with Hellenistic and Roman culture, with Christianity and Islam, and finally with the philosophical currents of the recent past. Throughout the ages there arose a variety of trends and schools, parties and sects, academies and assemblies; they preached to the many and organized the select few, they expounded early texts and infused new meanings; they produced violent turmoil and drew adherents. Seers, prophets and their disciples, nazarites and ascetics, sages and scribes, faithful adherents of the Torah and Hellenizers, Pharisees and Sadducees, Essenes and Zealots, Tanaites and Amoraim, Rabbanites and Karaites, philosophers and mystics, Cabbalists and Ḥassidim, moralists and reformers—the common factor between all these is the religious ideal and the struggles for, and within, its framework.

(3) The social organization of the Jewish people displays a surprising stability in view of the long period of time covered by Jewish history and the great political changes that took place. According to evidence preserved in the Bible, Israelite society was organized in parallel structures: there were the families at whose head stood the "elders"; next, the cities, headed by nobles; and finally there was the assembly, the whole people gathered in "houses of the people" at the city gates, near the Temple and elsewhere. The heads of the people in the cities acted as judges too. During the Second Temple the cities' autonomy was extended. This applied equally to the city councils and the assemblies of citizens. They had the right to make ordinances for themselves, to maintain external security by building walls, appointing guards, etc., to establish law courts and synagogues and to supervise the observation of religious law. Even in later periods every place that contained at least ten adult male Jews became the seat of a "congregation" with all

the duties of a true city: it had to establish a synagogue, provide for the education of children, support the aged and see that the religious commandments were properly kept. Jewish autonomy was a result of the fact that Jews everywhere organized their public life according to their own laws and customs. The privileges granted by kings and emperors, including the right to have their own law courts, were merely the recognition of an existing state of affairs. The Jewish community— its organization, leadership, tasks, institutions and officers—was a mirror of Jewish social life. The persistence of its institutions and problems, even in their outward form, merits special attention on the part of historians.

(4) Territorial element. The attachment to Eretz-Israel persisted in two ways. First, the Land of Israel was regarded as the country destined for the Jewish people; it was the people's duty to settle and develop it, and to fight for Jewish rule and freedom there. Secondly, the Land of Israel was holy. It was the seat of the divine presence and hence it was incumbent on Jews to ensure that it was always a seat of learning and faith. Spiritual movements, new trends in Judaism hoped for their acceptance by the guardians of Jewish presence in the Holy Land.

In the 1370 years that spanned the period from Joshua's conquest to the Bar Kokhba revolt, the people of Israel showed their readiness and ability to defend the freedom of their country against neighbouring tribes and distant empires alike: they fought against Canaanites and Philistines, Moabites and Ammonites, Idumaeans and Aramaeans, Assyrians, Babylonians, Persians, the Hellenistic kingdoms and all the might of Rome. Even after the fall of Betar, Hadrian's triumph was not complete. He had the Temple Mount ploughed up, obliterated the name of Judah from the land, prohibited Jewish settlement there and banned the observance of Jewish law, which he regarded as a denial of his victory. But the Jews were willing to be martyred for their faith, and their passive resistance finally compelled the Romans to cancel their edicts and permit Jewish settlement once more. The last Jewish revolt of antiquity took place under Heraclius, the last Byzantine emperor to rule Palestine, in 614 C.E. Twenty thousand Jews fought against him. At the time of the first crusade the Jews of Jerusalem were the first to man the walls in the city's defence and the last to be beaten. In 1100 Haifa was a Jewish fortress conquered by Tancred only after bitter fighting.

The devotion of the Jews to their country is shown most clearly by the constant struggle for Jewish settlement there. A hundred years after Hadrian had laid it waste to the last olive tree, confiscated most of the land and reduced the Jews to leasing it from the emperor, we hear of a discussion among the sages of Tiberias on whether most of the agricultural produce of the country was to be considered as coming from

Jewish land or not. The revolt of Sepphoris included not only Galilee but part of Judaea and the Negev.

Eilat was still a Jewish city at the time of Mohammed. Every single city in the country had Jewish inhabitants, as we learn from archaeological remains, particularly inscriptions, and written documents. The Emperor Heraclius's punitive measures caused many Jews to flee to neighbouring countries, especially the deserts between Palestine and Arabia. According to the Armenian bishop Sebaeus, who was a contemporary of these events, thousands of Jewish refugees served in the Arabian armies that conquered Palestine.

With the Moslem conquest many Jews came to the country not only from the South but from the rest of the Diaspora, and some went to live in Jerusalem once more; the Jews hoped for the Redemption, went up to the Temple Mount in large throngs to celebrate the festivals and even erected booths there on the Feast of Tabernacles. Their expectations were however disappointed. For in the wake of the conquest and for many years afterwards Arabs came to settle in Palestine and were given the confiscated Imperial land. Thus in fact the returning Jews were deprived of their land. The permanent settlement of the Arabs in Palestine and their building works, which constituted their chief activity in the early period, were viewed by the Jews as a calamity. Moreover, the conquerors aspired to adopt the sanctity of Jerusalem and to take over the Jewish claims to the country. At first they shared possession of the holy places, i.e. Jerusalem and Hebron, with the Jews; later they ousted the Jews completely. Thus they gradually limited Jewish access to the Temple Mount. In the Jewish literature of the period—the *Pirkei de Rabbi Eliezer* and the liturgical poems by Kalir and his followers—we find echoes of these "deeds of Ishmael in the Land of Israel". The Jewish reaction took the form of a powerful Messianic movement at the beginning of the eighth century; it was led by Abu 'Issa and spread to many countries especially Central Asia. Its aims were to come to terms with Christianity and Islam by recognizing the validity of Jesus' and Mohammed's prophetic mission to the gentiles; to spread Judaism to the pagans (in Khwarezm and Khazaria) and to conquer the land of Israel. A contemporary Christian author, Daniel the Copt, even relates that Meruan II was planning to re-establish a Jewish commonwealth at the time of the civil wars of the Caliphs.

The attachment to Eretz-Israel is also attested by the fact that up to the time of the crusades the office of *nasi* (Patriarch) remained in fact the pivot of Jewish communal organization in Palestine. The *nasi* was the supreme religious authority, the acknowledged representative of the community, the highest judicial magistrate and the head of the great Rabbinic academy of Jerusalem; his office was considered a "remnant of the House of David". Even after the office fell into abeyance efforts were made to restore a supreme religious authority in the Land of Israel by other means. The crusades, which in the eyes of the Jews were a battle between Christians and Moslems for the inheritance of Israel, inaugurated a period of intensified Messianic expectation and immigration to Palestine. Jews were the victims of violent persecutions, libels and measures of extermination designed to make them abandon their faith: the principle underlying these measures was "let us cut them off from being a nation". The martyrs went to the scaffold courageously proclaiming the unity of God and the election of Israel.

All this convinced the Jews that the Redemption was at hand. They regarded martyrdom as a renewal of the ancient covenants made by Abraham and Moses with God; their agony represented "the birth pangs" of the Messiah, who would shortly come. The devastating wars between Christians and Moslems confirmed the ancient promise that the land of Israel would not tolerate strangers but would wait for her sons. The Messianic fervour of the people seized the whole Diaspora, from Kurdistan to Cordova, from the Yemen to Bohemia, from Fez and Cairo to Lyons and Sicily. In spite of the dangers, immigration to Palestine continued. It even became a point of doctrine with the sages, for it was said that a prior condition for the Redemption was the return of prophecy, and that could only come about when the *élite* of the people, longing for the redemption and striving for spiritual purification, would go up to the Land of Israel. Judah Halevi, the greatest Jewish poet of the Middle Ages, expounded this view in his "Khuzari" and made it the theme of much of his poetry; he left for Palestine in the early forties of the twelfth century but died on the way. At the beginning of the thirteenth century three hundred renowned rabbis came from France, England and probably also from Italy. They were followed, after the havoc wrought by the Mongolians, by Moses Nachmanides of Gerona, one of the greatest sages of his time, commentator, mystic, jurist, theologian and poet. One of his disciples, who himself moved to Palestine, wrote: "Now many people take courage and eagerly go up to the Land of Israel". This intensive immigration restored the *Yishuv* (Jewish population of Palestine) after the wars of the crusaders.

The maintenance of the *Yishuv* required constant economic and political effort. The small, desolate and impoverished country could not support a sizable city population, whilst administrative and political conditions prevented the Jews from engaging in agriculture and severely limited their opportunities as craftsmen. The serious efforts made in the sixteenth century, after the expulsion of the Jews from Spain, to develop Jewish endeavour in Safad, Tiberias and the surrounding areas met with failure—or rather, their work was simply destroyed. Hence constant aid from the Diaspora was an important factor in the country's economic life and its beneficiaries were not only the Jews. The Jewish population was an unfailing source of income to the various local rulers and magnates. To a certain extent the survival of the *Yishuv* depended on the maintenance of equilibrium between the local rulers' fanatic desire to reduce and humiliate it as much as possible and their calculation, confirmed by long experience, that it was better not to kill the goose that layed the golden eggs. But this would not have sufficed in times of stress without the protection of communities abroad. It was their constant endeavours in Cairo and Constantinople that led to the intervention of the central government in favour of the *Yishuv*. Thus the survival of the *Yishuv* in the face of violence and opposition was the result of unceasing exertions on the part of anonymous individuals as well as organized communities. It was thanks to these that the country was not abandoned and that the Torah was not forgotten there. Of course the success of their efforts depended in part on external circumstances, i.e. the governments of the time; but the effort itself was an essential part of the Jewish people's unique relationships to its land.

The special position of the Land of Israel is also shown by the remarkable continuity of its culture. In spite of the changing composition of the *Yishuv* brought about by repeated waves of immigration, its traditions remained relatively constant; so did its internal organization, whilst governments came and went; its religious authority in the Diaspora remained supreme in the face of external opposition and internal disputes; and the harsh conditions of life, the paucity of opportunities for immigrants did not lead to a lowering of cultural standards. This is most clearly shown by the high level of Jewish learning and the extent to which Hebrew was the language of communal life and scholarship. Above all the uniqueness of the Land of Israel expressed itself in the quality of Jewish life there. At all times and from all countries it was the most committed Jews that came to Eretz-Israel. Hence life there was more stubbornly and faithfully Jewish than anywhere else. The *Yishuv* was always—though to varying degrees—the focus of religious tension, the centre of great religious upheavals and, above all, of Jewish creativity. The Mishna, the Jerusalem Talmud, legal and homiletical *midrashim*, the establishment of the masoretic Biblical text and its vocalization, the creation of the genre of *Piyutim*, the beginnings of Hebrew grammar, of Jewish philosophy, the polemics between Karaite and Rabbinic Judaism, messianic movements, the polemics against the work of Maimonides, Lurianic Kabbalah in the sixteenth century, Sabbatianism in the seventeenth and Ḥassidism in the eighteenth—this list is enough to show the central importance of the Land of Israel in Jewish life.

The four major elements listed above are not the only ones to carry and express the continuity of Jewish history and culture. I would like to dwell on two more factors:

(5) The linguistic factor. One of the consequences of the minority status of the Jewish people not only abroad but also in Palestine, was that Hebrew was no longer the only living language of the Jews.

Nevertheless it would be a mistake to suppose that it became a dead language or that it ever lost its place in Jewish consciousness as *the* language of the Jews. The scope of its use was reduced but it remained the language of communal affairs, of religious writings, of Law and the courts, of Torah, literature and science. It was also the medium of conversation between Jews from different countries; a Jew who could not speak Hebrew to his fellow Jew was a rare phenomenon. In Palestine Hebrew continued to be a spoken language for a long time; in many other countries it was spoken in the Rabbinic academies and *Yeshivoth*. Moreover, Jews introduced many Hebrew elements into the foreign languages they spoke, so that these acquired a Jewish character and Jewish vernaculars came into being. Hebrew elements in them were not confined to religion, to family, communal and legal matters or even to economic and social matters with a Jewish bearing. It is characteristic that they extended also to ethical and emotional aspects of life and that they included conjunctions and adverbs expressive of a distinctly Jewish pattern of thinking. The most eloquent testimony to the importance of Hebrew is to be found, however, in the enormous number of books written in Hebrew; they were copied, printed and circulated abroad in large numbers, thus helping to maintain the unity of Jewish intellectual life throughout the world.

(6) The political element. With the loss of their independence and the dispersion, the Jews ceased to constitute a political entity. If they took part in politics it was generally as individuals, though sometimes their Jewishness played a decisive role. A sense of a Jewish political entity may be said to have existed in only two fields: a lively interest in the fate of the Land of Israel, and the help extended to fellow-Jews in other countries when they were persecuted. Every change in the fortunes of Palestine produced a Jewish reaction in the form of intensified Messianic expectations, immigration, political programmes and attempts at colonization. This happened during the dynastic wars between Ummayads and Abbasids; at the beginning of Fatimid rule in Palestine; at the time of Saladin's victory and again after the Muslims yielded Jerusalem to the crusader emperor Frederic II; finally when Don Yosef *Nasi* rose to eminence at the court of Suleiman the Magnificent and Salim II. Similarly the concerted Jewish action to help brethren in distress were made at all times and in every country. One of the earliest instances is that of Ḥasdai ibn Shaprut who used his political influence to help the Jews in Toulouse. In more recent past—the intervention of Moses Montefiore and Adolph Cremieux with Mohammad Ali of Egypt after the Damascus blood libel, and the efforts of Jewish bankers at the

end of the nineteenth century to help their persecuted brethren in Rumania and Russia. With regard to the Damascus affair there is some basis for the opinion voiced at the time that the blood libels and the ensuing pogroms were part of a plan to frustrate projects of large-scale Jewish settlement in Palestine. But one of the results was a general Jewish awakening and the formation of a world-wide organization, the Alliance Israélite Universelle, to defend Jews suffering from persecution.

III

On the basis of the foregoing remarks I propose to take the following assumptions as the point of origin for a division of periods of Jewish history.

(1) The history of Israel should be divided into two main periods: Israel in its homeland and Israel in dispersion.

(2) The second of these periods should begin with the Muslim conquest of Palestine. Until then, the history of Israel is essentially that of the Jewish people living in its own country, notwithstanding the fact that the dispersion started much earlier. (From Roman and Byzantine times we have the names of more than three hundred Jewish communities outside Palestine.) The second period is characterized by the continuity of Israel as a distinct entity even while it was displaced in its own country by another nation, which formed the majority there.

(3) In spite of the fact that the homeland, in which Jewish life had been stamped with its own distinctive character, had become the fixed abode of another people, the Jews even abroad tenaciously clung to their way of life and their close ties with their ancient country; though scattered they maintained their spiritual unity.

(4) As the turning points of the second period we must regard those events which affected the whole Diaspora or at any rate most of it, including its spiritual life, as well as the fate of the Land of Israel and the Jewish people's relationship to it.

Accordingly, we may divide the history of Israel into twelve periods, six belonging to "Israel in its homeland" and six to the time of the Dispersion.

I. Israel in its homeland (C. 1400 B.C.E. - 636 C.E.)

(1) The beginnings of Israel, the conquest of the country and the settlement of the tribes (ca. 1400-1040 B.C.E.).

(2) The United kingdom, the kingdoms of Israel and Judah (ca. 1040-586 B.C.E.).

(3) The Babylonian exile, the return to Zion and the Persian province of Yehud (586-332 B.C.E.).

(4) Hellenistic rule: Ptolemies and Seleucids, religious persecution and revolt; the Hasmonean kingdom (332-63 B.C.E.).

(5) The Roman conquest, the Herodian dynasty and the revolts and wars against Rome (63 B.C.E.-135 C.E.).

(6) The restoration of the *Yishuv* and of the *nasi*, the struggle against Byzantine persecution (135-636).

II. Israel in Dispersion (636-1948)

(1) The predominance of the Diaspora and its unity (636-1096). The Arab conquest and the "arabization" of Palestine; the expansion of the Diaspora, the founding of a pattern of Jewish organization there, the supremacy of the *nasi* and "heads of the dispersion", the *Yeshivoth* of Babylonia and Palestine; Messianic movements and religious opposition.

(2) Crisis and martyrdom (1096-1496).

The crusades, the persecutions in Europe and the destruction of the communities in Palestine; the systematic oppression of European Jewry; the increase of fanaticism and religious coercion in Muslim countries; persecution, libels, forcible conversion, expulsion and mass martyrdom in Christian countries; religious revivals, messianic movements and immigration to the Land of Israel to bring about Redemption.

(3) Expulsion and Resettlement (1496-1700).

Continuing religious persecution in Central Europe; the rise of the Polish and Ottoman communities; further large-scale immigration to the Land of Israel and attempts to make it a religious centre once more; the persecution of 1648/49; the Sabbatian Messianic movement and its failure.

(4) Tolerance, growth and concentration, integration, assimilation, spiritual impoverishment, internal division (1700-1881).

The end of persecution, the growth of the Jewish population and its concentration in cities and small towns; the integration of Jews in the economy of their countries; changes in political structure; civil and political equality for Jews; cultural assimilation and a shrinking of Jewishness; social and cultural division, prolonged internal conflict and the emergence of new trends and movements: Hassidism and *Haskalah* (enlightenment), "Science of Judaism", reform movement, forerunners of Zionism.

(5) Antisemitism, intensification of Jewish activity and the Holocaust (1881-1947).

Revulsion against exile and renewed settlement in the homeland; social and national awakening of the Jewish masses and the great migration; racial antisemitism, attempt at extermination of the Jewish people.

(6) The struggle for independence, the establishment of the State of Israel and the beginnings of the "ingathering of the exiled" (from 1947).

SELECTED BIBLIOGRAPHY

1. S. RAWIDOWICZ, ed., *The Writings of Nachman Krochmal* (2nd ed., London and Walham, Mass., 1961) in Hebrew. See also Solomon SCHECHTER, "Nachman Krochmal and the 'Perplexities of the Time' ", *Studies in Judaism*, First series, pp. 46-72.

2. H. GRÄTZ, *Die Konstruktion der jüdischen Geschichte, 1848* (Berlin, 1936).

3. S. DUBNOV, *Jewish History, an Essay in the Philosophy of History* (Philadelphia, 1903).

4. S. W. BARON, *A Social and Religious History of the Jews* (2nd ed., New York, 1952), pp. 3-32.

5. S. W. BARON, *History and Jewish Historians* (Philadelphia, 1964), pp. 5-106.

6. F. BAER, *Galut* (New York, 1947).

7. I. ABRAHAMS, E. R. BIRAN, C. SINGER, eds., *The Legacy of Israel* (Oxford, 1927).

8. B. DINUR (Dinaburg), "Israel nella Diaspora", *La Rassegna mensile dei Israel* (April, 1948), pp. 17-29, 77-91.

9. L. W. SCHWARZ, ed., *Great Ages and Ideas of the Jewish People* (New York, 1956).

10. D. BEN-GURION, ed., *The History of the Jews in their Land* (London, 1966).

R. J. ZWI WERBLOWSKY

MESSIANISM IN JEWISH HISTORY

THE least that can reasonably be asked of a writer on messianic ideas and messianic movements in Jewish history is to provide an adequate definition of the term "messianism" whose history is to be described. Alas, it is easier to give an account of the historical developments than to define the term itself which seems to mean all things to all men—or at least, to all theologians. In fact, messianism is often said to be an essential and characteristic feature of Judaism from which it was then transmitted also to other religions and civilizations.

No doubt the word derives etymologically from Hebrew and semantically from Jewish tradition, and the term indicates that in the course of Jewish history there arose a complex of ideas and expectations and an attitude to the time-process and to the future which borrowed their name from the politico-religious and cultic-national vocabulary of Israelite Kingship. The Hebrew noun *mashiah* (messias), from the verb *mashah* "to anoint", means "the anointed one" in general and (in later Judaism) "the anointed one" in particular, i.e. the ultimate redeemer, the expected king of the Davidic line who would deliver Israel from foreign bondage and restore the glories of its Golden Age. In Biblical Hebrew the adjective or noun *mashiah* is used of material objects as well as of consecrated persons, such as High Priests and Kings. The latter would also be described as "the Lord's anointed", the title expressing the charismatic character and divine sanction of their office as well as the inviolability of their status. In exilic and post-exilic usage, the term "anointed" could denote anyone with a special mission from God—prophets, patriarchs, and even a gentile king like Cyrus the Mede (Isaiah 45: 1). The Old Testament does not speak of an eschatological messiah and we look in vain for even traces of messianism in many books of the Bible, including the Pentateuch. Even the "messianic" passages containing prophecies of a future Golden Age under an ideal king, do not use this word as a technical term.

Nevertheless, beliefs and ideas that could later be subsumed under the heading "messianism" were gradually taking shape under the stres-

ses and disillusionments of Israelite history. No doubt the tribes that
crossed the Jordan with Joshuah and conquered the Land of Canaan
had neither cause nor use for messianic beliefs. They were, after all, the
generation not to whom a promise was given but in whom the promise
to the Patriarchs was being fulfilled. This fulfillment reached its apogee
in the King of Victory, David, and the King of Peace, Solomon, and in
retrospect this double reign appeared surrounded by a halo of divine
blessing and invested with the significance of a "normative" and ideal
paradigm of history consummated. It is difficult to imagine the champion of pure theocracy and author of the violently anti-monarchic dia-
tribe found in I Samuel 8 waxing enthusiastic over the idea of a messianic king. Evidently the growth of the messianic idea presupposes the
establishment of an Israelite kingship ideology, and the expectation of
a divinely operated tide in the affairs of Israel did not grow out of
nothing. It seems to have crystallized round certain ideas drawn from
the ancient Near-Eastern mythologies. Reading the biblical books and
particularly the Book of Psalms, we cannot fail to detect mythological
overtones, echoing archaic notions of creation as a victorious divine
battle against the forces and monsters of chaos, and of the cyclical renewal of nature as a re-enactment or reaffirmation of this archetypal
event. This old mythology contains an element of genuine universalism,
since it is concerned with creation, i.e. with the world as such, but it was
transformed in the context of the Israelite theology of covenant and
election. Even as God had smitten the heads of Leviathan on the waters,
so also will he (represented by the tokens of his presence: the Ark of the
Covenant, and his anointed King, the present and "pre-eschatological"
Messiah) smite the historical representatives of evil, death and destruction. But whereas the pattern of nature is cyclical and that of early
Israelite history, as told in *Joshuah* and *Judges,* was repetitive (idolatry-
tribulation-repentance-relief), later history became oppressively monoto-
nous and unrhythmical. The present was unmitigated oppression and
rule of wickedness. Slowly but thoroughly the significant features of the
cyclical pattern were transferred to the linear, once-for-all dimension of
history. There had been one cosmic victory in the beginning. What mattered now was not the annual repetition of this event but the day of the
Lord, that is, the final victory at the end of history. The establishment of
the Israelite kingship ideology and its interpretation as part of God's
eternal covenant with His people, are reflected in the accounts given in
the historical and prophetic books of the Old Testament and in the
Psalms. As actual reality and the careers of the historical kings proved
more and more disappointing, the messianic kingship ideology was pro-
jected on the future. With the declining national fortunes of Israel, the
notion developed of an eschatological change for the better. The greater
the contrast between the unsatisfactory present and the imagined future,

the more thoroughly utopian the quality of this future. Whilst much of the early Biblical eschatology (and especially that drawing on the historical books with their idealized view of the reigns of David and Solomon) is restorative, looking forward to better times, that is, to a restoration of the good old times in a relatively near, or at least historically accessible future, other trends—partly influenced by the more radical and universalist style of prophetic hyperbole—were more utopian in outlook (e.g. Isaiah 2). The expected future was not merely better; it was totally and absolutely different. It not only restored an original happy state but was to bring about something that was completely and fundamentally new. In some forms of apocalyptic eschatology the expected change was not an event *in* history, but something *outside* history.

But whether in history or outside it, fully developed messianism represents a decisive transformation of the notion of time. For time and the time process are now held to be directed to a final event or consummation. This *eschaton* is not necessarily the fulfilment and achievement of the forces and dynamisms at work *in* the process of history (as e.g. according to the messianic version of the modern evolutionist view that history is progress); it may also be conceived as the final victory *over* history, a victory which abolishes a history which is essentially negative. But either way, there is a directedness in the time process and a peculiar tension which is expected to find its discharge in the decisive consummating event. Hence the adjective "messianic" has been applied, with greater or lesser justification, to various types of nativistic, utopian, millenarian (chiliast) and apocalyptic ideologies and movements. Marxism, too, as is well known, has frequently been described as "messianic" because of the eschatological structure of its doctrine.

For the student of Jewish history the problem of messianic movements is historical rather than purely phenomenonological, i.e. the question is not so much one of deciding whether or not a certain movement deserves the epithet "messianic", but rather one of describing the continuity of messianic belief and expectation as it manifested itself in the events and crises of Jewish history.

Whilst the Old Testament period laid the foundations of Jewish messianism, the last two centuries of the second Temple Period bear witness to a variety of established or emerging messianic beliefs and to an active messianic ferment. The developments that brought this about are, in part, still obscure. We do not know enough about the extent, nature and impact of the disillusionment that followed the very partial and inadequate fulfilment of the high-pitched hopes focussed on the return to Zion of the Babylonian exiles (see Deutero-Isaiah). A similar contrast and tension between sanguine expectation and sobering reality must have characterized the period following upon the successful Maccabean revolt, 165 B.C. The analysis of modern "messianic" movements (nativistic, millenarian, revitalization, cargo cults, etc.) in primitive societies, suggest that these are to a large extent connected with the stresses and tensions of an acculturative situation. Perhaps Jewish history at the end of the Second Temple Period has not been sufficiently studied from the point of view of the acculturative crisis as a decisive factor in the wider situation of foreign (i.e. Roman) domination. At any rate, there is evidence of the proliferation of both messianic beliefs and messianic movements, as well as of an increasingly "messianic" character of the various national risings, though as regards the latter our sources are not clear and explicit enough. It is easier to describe the history of messianic ideas as they evolve in the several sects and circles whose theological literature has by chance been preserved, than to gauge the messianic character of e.g. an uprising or a revolt of which we only know the date or the name of its leader, or a few other incidental details. Thus, the Maccabean insurrection against the Seleucid policy of enforced Hellenization seems, on the evidence of the Book of Daniel, to have had messianic overtones, though it can hardly be described as a fully messianic movement. Messianic ideologies and acutely eschatological movements proliferated after the Hasmonean period, and several main types emerged. At times alternative or even mutually exclusive ideas and beliefs existed side by side, without anyone apparently bothering to arrange them in a logical and coherent system. This was attempted only later by the medieval theologians desirous of harmonizing all ancient, and hence venerable and authoritative, texts and traditions with some degree of consistency. Ideas and hopes were current about a glorious national restoration under a victorious military leader, or through a miraculous intervention from above. The ideal redeemer would be a king—the Lord's anointed—from the line of David, or a Heavenly Being referred to as "Son of Man". Redemption could thus mean a better and more peaceful world, or the utter end and annihilation of "this age" and the ushering in, amid catastrophe and judgement, of a new era, and of "a new Heaven and a new Earth". As a matter of fact, this catastrophic element remained an essential feature of the dialectic of messianic utopia: ultimate salvation was accompanied, or preceded by destruction and by the terrors of the "birth pangs" of the messianic age. In fact, this catastrophic aspect became so much part and parcel of the messianic complex that in later periods, the occurence of particularly cruel persecution and suffering was frequently regarded as heralding the messianic redemption. This was not merely wishful thinking, a defence mechanism to make suffering bearable, but an application to concrete historical situations of one of the traditional dialectical patterns of messianic belief. The terrors of these pre-eschatological birth pangs were taken so seriously that more than one Talmudic Rabbi would affirm his traditional hope in the advent

of the Messiah with the qualifying rider: "Let Him come, but I do not
want to witness it".

The chaotic welter of these ideas is visible not only in the apocryphal
books of the Bible but also in the New Testament writings, and particularly in their accounts of the diverse attitudes towards Jesus adopted
by his disciples and by the various groups in Jerusalem. The ministry
of Jesus has to be seen in the context of a messianic complex that included such ideas as the coming of Elijah, the Son of David, the Son of
Man, deliverance from the yoke of the Gentiles, and the ushering in of
a new age. It was a period that saw the activity of many messianic
leaders, as we learn from Josephus and from *Acts*, 35-37. The original
biblical tradition of thinking about the future in social, collective and
historical terms was now further complicated by the emergence (or
absorption) of new patterns of thought. The increasing preoccupation
with the destiny of the individual together with the demand for a satis-
factory account of the ways of divine justice in meting out reward and
punishment, produced the notion of the resurrection of the dead. (This
Pharisaic doctrine was also affirmed by Jesus as against the Sadducees
who rejected it). There also was the notion of an immortal soul that
would go to its heavenly reward (or alternatively eternal punishment),
after its departure from the body. The tension between these incompat-
ible traditions, and more particularly between the spirituality of the
doctrine of immortality and the materiality of the doctrine of resurrection, is well expressed by the compromise solution, also found in
Paul, according to which the soul ultimately returned to a spiritual or
"glorified" body. These ideas are relevant here because it is important
to emphasize that the doctrine of immortality (as many mystery-cults
and religions of salvation attest) lifts individual eschatology out of the
historical messianic context. The course of history as such becomes
irrelevant to the fate and destiny of the individual. In the later development of Judaism the tension between the two tendencies remains discernible and it seems that historic sense and messianic fervour are related in inverse ratio to the strength of the philosophical or mystical
preoccupation with the fate and progress of the spiritual soul.

We have thus at least three strands making up the thread of eschatology: the "messianic" era of national restoration, and possibly of universal peace; the new *aion* of God's kingdom, including the resurrection
of the dead; and the celestial hereafter in which the soul eternally enjoys
the blessed vision. But even the first two varieties leave scope for further
varieties and subdivisions. It goes without saying that the eschatology
of the new *aion* is more radically utopian than the expectation of a future
that knows no new heaven and new earth but rather a peaceful dwell-
ing, on this earth, of every man under his vine and under his fig tree
(Micah, 4: 4). Also the nature and function of the messianic personality

that is at the centre of the decisive changes is conceived differently in the different trends. The messiah may be the presiding figure in what is essentially a messianic situation without being its main cause or agent. This would seem to be the Pharisaic and Rabbinic view of the matter, and one which is clearly indebted to at least one major strand in Biblical literature: a Davidic king rules over the House of Israel, and his rule is the tangible symbol of the restoration of the Golden Age. There is nothing to indicate that he, or his actions, military or otherwise, would bring about the desired new dispensation. Even for Jeremiah the glorious future is simply a matter of Israel's faithfulness to God's Law for "if ye do this thing indeed, then shall there enter in by the gates of this town, Kings sitting upon the throne of David, riding in chariots and on horses, he and his servants and his people" (Jeremiah, 22: 4). On the other hand, the personality of the messiah may be more central, its character and function more clearly outlined and—consequently—a stronger personal bond to it on the part of the believers may be deemed to be essential. The small Jewish messianic sect composed of the disciples and followers of Jesus of Nazareth is a case in point. Considerable light has been thrown on the kaleidoscopic variety of Jewish messianic beliefs during the end of the Second Temple Period by the discovery in the Judaean Desert of the library of the congregation of the New Covenant (also known as the "Dead Sea Sect"). The sect is remarkable among other things for envisaging a future presided over by two anointed heads: a Davidic king and (superior to him) a messianic High Priest of the House of Aaron. It seems obvious that here the messianic pair functions as a sign and symbol of the perfect social order—as envisaged already in the prophecy of Zachariah concerning Zerubbabel and the High Priest Joshua—rather than as bringing about this order by their messianic ministry.

The reference to the Qumran Covenanters may serve to turn our attention to yet another point of interest for the sociology of messianic sects. Biblical eschatology was a collective, ethnic-national affair, since the nation (or its faithful remnant) was the bearer of the religious calling and promise. Membership in the messianic community is ascriptive: "and Thy people shall all be righteous: they shall inherit the land for ever, the branch of My planting, the work of My hand, that I may be glorified" (Isaiah, 60: 21). On the other hand membership in the congregation of the New Covenant of the Qumran Sect, is elective rather than ascriptive or, to be more exact, elective-charismatic in an ascriptive framework: the chosen ones are the Children of Light from the House of Israel. This elective conception completely ousted the ascriptive one in the development of the Christian church.

The messianic beliefs affirmed and cultivated by Pharisaic and later Rabbinic Judaism (or "normative" Judaism, as it is frequently called) thus emphasized the more restorative ethnic-national and historical elements. Evidently, after the destruction of the Temple, the Ingathering of the Exiles and the rebuilding of the Temple were added to the messianic programme of an ideal future. Nevertheless, a strong apocalyptic current continued to flow and to crystallize in eschatological legends and prophecies describing the sufferings preceding the messianic advent, the War of Gog and Magog, the wreaking of vengeance on the gentiles, and the building of the New Jerusalem. Many of the Jewish patriots who participated in the great revolt against Rome in 66-70 AD surely believed themselves to be fighting in the eschatological battle that would be followed by the reign of the messiah. Both the revolt of 115-117 and the uprising led by Bar Kokhba, 132-135, were probably influenced by messianic hopes and speculations. Whether Bar Kokhba himself entertained any messianic pretensions is doubtful though Rabbi Akiba, one of the leading rabbinic masters of the age, considered him as such and applied to him the prophecy (Numbers, 24: 17): "There shall come a star out of Jacob and a sceptre shall rise out of Israel". The messianic character of the revolt seems, however, to be confirmed by an interesting development in Jewish eschatology that took place after the death of Bar Kokhba. There arose the concept of a second messianic figure, the Warrior Messiah of the House of Joseph (or Ephraim), who would precede the triumphant Messiah of the House of David but would fall in the battle against Gog and Magog. It should be noted that this Messiah of the House of Joseph is not a suffering messiah; he is a warrior-martyr. To the extent that a ministry of suffering is mentioned in Jewish apocalyptic texts or legends, it is ascribed to the messiah of the House of David during his hidden period, i.e. before he manifests himself in triumphant glory. Referring to the aforementioned two sides of Jewish apocalypse—catastrophe and messianic triumph—the Messiah of the House of Joseph may perhaps be said to represent the catastrophic aspect of the expected redemption. In many apocalyptic texts, which later became part and parcel of the popular messianic belief among the Jewish masses and even among the learned, this catastrophic stage included wars, plagues, famine, and other social and cosmic upheavals, such as licence, heresy, a general defection from God's law, earthquakes, hailstorms, etc. The important point about most of these mythological notions is that they assume a radical discontinuity between our present age and the messianic reign. There is no smooth transition from the one to the other but rather a violent break marked by violent upheavals and catastrophes, after which, behold, all things shall be made new, or at least very different.

As the above brief sketch has indicated, by the time the Jewish people embarked on its long and gruelling history as a people in exile, dispersed, humiliated, despised and often physically threatened and persecuted, it was already equipped with messianic beliefs and hopes that were too axiomatic to be questioned. No matter what the details of the historic genesis of the messianic idea might be, and no matter what emphasis would be placed by different thinkers at different periods on the various aspects of this idea (physical-political or more spiritualized; popular-mythological or philosophical-rationalist; restorative or utopian; national or more universalist; catastrophic or more gradual; focussed upon a personal messiah or upon a messianic era, etc.) the messianic dimension was a permanent and ever-present feature, at times latent, at times manifest, of Jewish history. Whilst the messianic quality of certain movements and insurrections in the Second Temple Period and immediately afterwards may still leave room for discussion and for correction in matters of detail, subsequent history is much more unequivocal in this respect. The messianic idea had been firmly established both on the popular, and on the more theological level. The unending experience of oppression and humiliation, persecution and bondage, far from leading to disintegration and despair, kept the messianic orientation alive and gave to eschatological hope as well as to actual movements of liberation, revolt, social protest and religious revival, a fixed, dogmatic point of reference. There is thus a close connection between the generally accepted and practically axiomatic messianic belief on the one hand and messianic movements on the other. No doubt the existence of the former by itself was not sufficient to precipitate social movements, but it certainly provided a permanent potential and a latent structure within which historic dynamisms, revivals and responses to particular situations could take shape and articulate themselves. In their turn many of these messianic revivals had significant repercussions on messianic ideology, often by way of stimulating a restatement of belief that would safeguard orthodoxy and the institutions of society against the inevitable disillusionment and consequent despair, as well as against the heretical and antinomian dangers inherent in any messianic explosion. At other times the relationship would be less apologetic, and in the course of the development of a messianic movement the concomitant theology would change and adjust to the facts and pressures of the historical situation. Among the dangers of potential heresy that were felt to be inherent in actual messianism, there is one that in a Jewish context is particularly significant. Antinomianism is a feature that is well known in many movements of redemption and salvation, but in an historical tradition based on obedience and fidelity to a divine law conceived as a supreme expression and vehicle of the relationship of the people to its God, its critical significance is even greater. Certain ancient rabbinic utterances (e.g. the statement that in the messianic era all ritual prohibitions would be suspended, or references to the "Halakhah [the law] of the messianic age") seemed to harbour explosive

charges and to invite dangerous speculations. There was an inner logic
to these antinomian potentialities. After all, the "yoke" of the law,
whilst beloved, light and sweet on the conscious level, undoubtedly
represented on the unconscious level the symbol of a life circumscribed
and limited on all sides. It thus functioned as the internal counterpart
(both from the point of view of individual experience, and in the social
life and organization of the Jewish communities) of the outer limitations and restrictions imposed by life in exile and by subjection to a
hostile, gentile environment. If the messianic advent meant freedom,
shaking off the yoke, and the making of all things new and different,
then it is not surprising that the possibility of untramelled, antinomian
freedom should also manifest itself now and then.

One other point deserves to be mentioned at this juncture. Jewish
messianism, for the greater part of its history, retained its national,
social and historical basis whatever the universalist, cosmic, or inner
and spiritual meanings accompanying it. One may, perhaps, speak of
a spiritual deepening of the messianic idea in the history of Jewish
religious thought, but these allegedly more "spiritual" elements never
replaced the concrete, historical messianism ; they were merely added
to it. Jewish apologists tended to view Christian accusations of a "carnal" understanding of messianic deliverance as a compliment. To them
it seemed that a certain type of spirituality was merely an escape into
a realm where one was safe from the challenges of historical reality
whose tests one evaded. "Humankind cannot bear very much reality",
and hence it tries to evade the crucial tests. If messianic redemption has
a spiritual dimension, then according to the Jewish theologians and
mystics it must be the inner side of a process that manifests itself essentially in the outer sphere of historical facts.

The corollaries of this are obvious. Messianic movements are by
definition doomed to failure in the historical sphere. If they wish to
remain messianic, they either have to relinquish the historical sphere or
to spiritualize themselves, or else to admit failure and to postpone the
hope for consummation to a more successful future. The vitality and
reality of the messianic idea among the Jews is attested by the fact that
messianic outbreaks, revivals and movements were an almost permanent feature of their history. Most of these movements were limited in
time and space; very few of them embraced the whole Jewish people
or left a prolonged and noticeable aftermath. As a rule what happened
was this: somewhere a prophet, a precursor, or a messianic pretender
would arise, proclaim that the end of days or the redemption of Israel
was at hand, and launch a movement limited to a smaller or larger
area. In the usual course of things, none, or few of the initial promises
could be fulfilled. Reports at first eagerly believed turned out to be un-
true, the messiah disappeared or was killed, and the movement petered

out. But for an occasional temporary chronicler or letter-writer, not even an echo of many of these movements would have reached us, and it is more than probable that there were many such movements which left no trace at all and are unknown to the modern historian. There is no need here to give a catalogue of messianic movements, or of the names of messianic pretenders and prophets, or of the many messianic revivals in Jewish history that testify to acute or latent millenarian expectations and longing. Many of these movements did not result in actual eschatological outbreaks though they bear eloquent witnesses of the existence of a messianic ferment. Lists of these names and movements can be found in any Jewish encyclopaedia or work on Jewish history. Nevertheless, a word seems to be in order here on the significance of these "pseudo-messianic" movements, for they are the tragic and moving witnesses of the powerful sway of messianic hope and belief over the Jewish people throughout their historic existence. As the philosopher Franz Rosenzweig once put it: belief in the advent of the messiah would be no more than an empty phrase if false messiahs did not constantly arise in whom this belief might assume reality and shape. The false messiah exists as long as does the genuine hope in the true messiah, and he divides every generation in which he appears into two camps: those who have the power of faith to believe and hence to err, and those who have the power of hope not to err but rather continue to endure until the advent of the true redeemer. The former were perhaps the better Jews, the latter were the stronger Jews. Of course, messianic movements are not to be accounted for solely in terms of messianic doctrines, eschatological beliefs and traditional hopes. Whilst facts require ideas and social symbolism before they can assume cultural shape and historical reality, it is no less true that beliefs and doctrines require a specific constellation of facts in order to pass from potentiality to actuality. The historian, faced with the aforementioned catalogue of messianic movements, will therefore always ask what factors precipitated a messianic outbreak at a certain place and at a certain time. He will want to know in what circles the movement originated, in what groups it spread, and who were its spokesmen and propagators as well as opponents. He may, to give just one random example, wonder why several pseudo-messiahs appeared in the 11th and 12th centuries in Western Europe, and particularly in Spain, or why Persia proved during a certain period such a fertile hotbed of messianic sectarianism—from Abu Issa al-Isfahani and his disciple Yudghan in the 8th century, to David Alroy in the 12th. Abu Issa, who proclaimed himself the messiah of the House of Joseph, duly fell in a futile battle against the Abassid forces against which he marched with his ten thousand followers, while David Alroy—known to many from Disraeli's fanciful novel—staged a revolt against the sultan. Sabbetai Zevi (see below),

on the other hand, fought only with the mystical-magical weapons of
the Kabbalah. Social tensions, class distinctions, the common fate of all
Jews as a despised and persecuted minority in a hostile environment,
sharing the same culture, all these played their role and would have to
be examined for each messianic movement individually.

To do justice, however, to the strength of messianic dynamism in
Jewish history one has to take into account not only the acute messianic outbreaks centred on the figure of a messianic prophet, pretender
or precursor, but—as has been hinted above—also the many movements
that were less obviously and blatantly millenarian but whose inspiration and strength derived from messianic sources. Thus, the phenomenon
of smaller or larger groups of Jews leaving their countries of origin
in the Diaspora to settle in the Holy Land was not infrequent. Of course,
one can settle in the Holy Land in order to live, to pray and to die
there, without any messianic overtones. But in point of fact many of
these movements were inspired by messianic motives, though not necessarily by the belief that the messiah had appeared and was calling
his followers to leave the lands of exile and move to the Promised Land.
Very often the motivation was "pre-eschatological" and seemed to
assume that a life of prayer and ascetic sanctification in the Holy Land
would hasten the advent of the Messiah. This notion of actively hasten-
ing the advent of the Messiah is of considerable interest and seems to
point to a curious tension in the Jewish soul as it reacted to the experience of exile. An ancient rabbinic source comments on the Song of
Songs, 2: 7: "I charge you, O ye daughters of Jerusalem, by the roes
and by the hinds of the field, that ye stir not up nor awake my love
till he please", by saying: "Four charges are contained in this verse:
Israel should not revolt against the kingdoms of this world; they should
not force the end; they should not divulge their mystery to the nations of the world; and they should not go up [to Eretz Israel] in a
great mass". Whatever the historical experience that led to this unequivocal rejection of all messianic activism, the temptation was evidently there and had to be guarded against. The only activism that
was admitted was of a spiritual kind. In the words of the Talmud, if
Israel would do penitence for one day only, they would immediately
be redeemed, as it is written (Psalm 95: 7): "Today if ye will hear His
voice". Spiritual activism, when all realistic and practical outlets are
closed, easily turns into magical activism, and Jewish legend knows of
Kabbalist masters who decided to force the messianic advent by means
of extreme mortifications, special meditations and kabbalistic incan-
tations. These legends, the best known of which is that concerning Rabbi
Joseph della Reyna, usually end with the kabbalist adept falling a prey
to the daemonic powers which he had meant to vanquish.

The appearance of such legends in the late mediaeval kabbalist context is no accident, for kabbalism is an essentially activist, viz. "theurgic" type of mysticism. In the form that it assumed in Galilee in the 16th century under the influence of the kabbalist Rabbi Isaac Luria, it interpreted exile and redemption in terms of a cosmic—or rather divine—drama, in which God himself was involved. According to this strangely "gnostic" myth, a primordial catastrophe or "fall" occurred as the divine light-essence externalized itself with a view to creating the world, and divine sparks fell into chaos. These sparks of divine life, imprisoned and "exiled" in chaos, sustain the life of the daemonic realm. Israel's exile and suffering merely reflect on the external, historical and material level, the more fundamental mystery of God's exile and suffering. Redemption means the liberation of the divine sparks from the defiling embrace of the daemonic powers, no less than the liberation of Israel from its subjection to the gentiles. Indeed, the latter process would follow as a natural consequence from the former, which it was Israel's true and mystical calling to bring about by a life of piety and holiness. This is spiritual activism at its most extreme, for here God has become a real *salvator salvandus*. But to the Jew Israel's exile became meaningful because it was seen as a participation in the profounder exile of God, and God Himself required Israel's active participation in the redemption of Himself and His people. It is not surprising that in this kabbalistic system the personality of the messiah played a relatively minor role. He was not so much a redeemer as a sign and symbol that the redemptive process had been achieved. In fact, the messianic doctrine of Lurianic Kabbalah comes close to the structure of an evolutionist scheme.

This kabbalistic system provides the background of one of the most remarkable messianic episodes in the course of Jewish history. In spite of its uniqueness it is, however, sufficiently representative of the various forces at work in Jewish history and of the interaction of external and internal factors to deserve a brief account here. I am referring, of course, to the messianic movement that grew up around the person of Sabbetai Zevi of Smyrna.

With the expulsion of the Jews towards the end of the 15th century first from Spain and then from Portugal, a new phase had begun in Jewish history. The magnitude of the sufferings seemed to indicate the birth pangs of the messianic age as foretold by tradition. False messiahs arose and disappeared but still salvation tarried, and new and greater sufferings followed instead, reaching their climax in the Chmelnitski massacres. Tens of thousands of Jews perished in these massacres between 1648 and 1658 in Poland and Lithuania, which represented a peak of Jewish suffering unparalleled until the 20th century. But now at least every single Jew knew without any doubt that the Messiah was coming, for he had to come. The Kabbalah flourished at this period and within a short time gained complete control of Jewish thought and piety mainly because of its strongly eschatological orientation. The kabbalists focussed all their religious fervour and asceticism, their power of prayer and meditation, on the imminent redemption. It was, indeed, from the circle of kabbalists that the messiah did come. The beautiful and fascinating youth from Smyrna soon succeeded in bewitching a group of friends and (after some initial difficulties and even, like Mohammed, flight from home) finding rich adherents. Soon he also had his prophets. It was not long before Sabbetai was venerated as "our Lord and King", and homage was paid to him from Cairo to Hamburg, from Salonika to Amsterdam. With very few exceptions, the sceptics kept their doubts to themselves and no longer dared to speak out. When things seemed to the Sultan to be going somewhat too far he had Sabbetai imprisoned, yet the belief in the messiah went on growing. After all, everyone knew that the messiah must suffer for a time before revealing himself with miracles in all his power and glory. Sabbetai lived like a king in captivity, receiving embassies and assigning the provinces of his future kingdom to his relatives and friends, until the Sultan summoned him and gave him the choice between death and Islam. From the Palace, a short time afterwards, there emerged no longer the Rabbi Sabbetai Sevi but Mehemet Effendi. Later, as he continued to make trouble, Sabbetai was exiled to Albania where he died alone in 1676.

Now only did the well-nigh incredible happen: betrayed and disillusioned, Jews had once more to choose. Many of them who had believed, and indeed believed not only with an easy faith without works, but selling or flinging aside their property and chattels to go and meet the messiah, now recognized with a heavy heart that history had once more given its verdict. There was no change in the world and no salvation; they had to go on waiting. But not all were prepared to submit themselves to the verdict of history. They had experienced salvation themselves; they had felt the thrill of renewal and change within their hearts. The inward experience was too powerful, it could not be annulled or invalidated even by history. In this way there arose a Sabbatian heresy and a Sabbatian theology which finally led out of Judaism and vanished, at least as far as the Jewish people is concerned. It would lead us too far to pursue further the extremely complex and psychologically fascinating development of the Sabbatian sect. Of more immediate interest to our present analysis of messianism is the analogy in certain respects with Christianity. Since history proved a disappointment there grew up a theology and a paradoxical mystical belief which turned the rational stumbling block into its very corner stone. Both Christianity and Sabbatian theology owe part of their emotional appeal to their very paradoxicality. Because the messiah had abdicated so unexpectedly there arose the belief in his resurrection and return and— in later Sabbatianism—also in his reincarnation. Since salvation was not manifest to those who saw with eyes of flesh, a distinction was made between an invisible redemption, accessible only to the eye of faith, and the final consummation in which all things would become manifest and the redemption, wrought by the messiah, would clearly be visible to all. Because the messiah had ended his earthly career in disgrace, a theology evolved which explained how this disgrace actually represented the climax of his messianic ministry. One of the main differences between the Christian and Sabbatian theologies is the nature of the messianic paradox. In the case of Jesus of Nazareth it takes on a form that might be called metaphysical. Jesus accepts the disgrace of death for the sake of redemption. For Sabbatianism the paradox is of a more moral kind. Sabbetai accepts worse than death, namely the disgrace of sin, and of the worst sin at that, apostasy. Sabbatians believed that the process of salvation had begun in the inner, spiritual layers of the cosmos, but that our visible, tangible and material world would finally be caught up, too, in this process. Then salvation would be visibly manifest and complete. This theology was the way, perhaps the heroic way, of escape for those who maintained the overriding validity of their inward experience over and against what seemed to be the judgement of external history. But Israel as a whole reacted in the old and well-tried way. The world was not changed and hence Sabbetai Sevi was an imposter like all his predecessors. Since then, "auto-messianism", as Martin Buber has called it, declined steadily. A few more minor convulsions in the wake of the Sabbatian movement and personal messianism ceased to be a real possibility and thus a real danger. The spiritual revival movement in 18th century Polish and Ukrainian Jewry, known as Hassidism, seems to have brought about, at least to some extent, a neutralization of the explosive possibilities of utopian and apocalyptic messianism by teaching a way of redemption through mystical inwardness. Whilst Hassidism may therefore be said to have provided an answer to the challenge of the Sabbatian aftermath in traditional religious terms, other and more modern versions were slowly coming to be enunciated by a European Jewry that was seeking and gradually finding its way to religious liberal reform and civil emancipation. It is not difficult to show that these modern ideologies, even if they were not messianic movements in the strict sense, had certain messianic overtones or, at least, consciously made use of traditional messianic terminology. No doubt these progressive liberals, or later socialists, did not think in terms of Armageddon, or a heavenly Jerusalem descending from above, or the Son of David riding on a donkey, but civil liberties, equality before the law, increased human welfare, universal peace and all-round ethical and human progress, appeared to them transformed with a biblical halo and as the true essence of the traditional messianic hopes. The messianic dimension, in many cases unconscious, of the Jewish national revival which began in the 19th century in Europe, developed into the Zionist Movement and culminated in the establishment of the State of Israel in 1948, is even more obvious. Of course, Jews rarely ask the literalist questions so congenial to Christian fundamentalist minds. They do not, as a rule, inquire, whether this or that historical event is the "fulfilment" of this or that Biblical prophecy, even though some religious circles nowadays speak of "the beginning of the sprouting of our redemption". But although there is no question of fundamentalist messianism or apocalyptic eschatology, there can be no doubt of the presence of messianic undertones. The end of the Exile, the return to the Promised Land, the re-establishment of Israel as a Jewish commonwealth, the experience of "completeness" connected with the return to the ancestral soil and with the somewhat Tolstoyan ideal of manual labour and the socialist ideal of justice and equality (as attempted by the kibbutz movement) — all these, whilst not strictly "biblical", nevertheless could not but strike responsive chords in the Jewish soul.

In fact, even the most secularized Jew realized that the certainties enunciated in the Scriptures and the reality of his own experience somehow coincided. Both operated, as it were, on the same experiential wavelength. The fact that the birth of the State of Israel took place in the aftermath of a tragedy which even in Jewish history is unparalleled, the cold-blooded murder by the Nazis and their accomplices of six million Jews, and amid toil, sweat and heroic struggle for survival, seemed to make actual modern history conform to the almost archetypal notion mentioned above of a double-faced messianism composed of catastrophe on the one hand and redemption on the other. Contemporary history is notoriously more difficult to study than that of past generations. Consequently, the history of the religious, apocalyptic and mystical messianism of ancient, mediaeval and early modern Jewish history has been written more or less satisfactorily, whilst a thorough and authoritative analysis of the messianic elements in the religious thought and the national and social movements of late modern and contemporary Judaism is still outstanding. Yet it is a significant fact that Jewish messianism seems to be passing through something like a crisis. For close on two thousand and five hundred years the Jewish people have waited for a better king or for better times, for a glorious restoration or for a new heaven and a new earth. Their theologians and mystics expanded this notion of redemption from exile, suffering and persecution to include redemption from sin and from all evil. The Return to Zion and the Ingathering of the Exiles would be a redemptive consummation because it seemed beyond the range of natural possibilities and hence in no way less miraculous and supernatural than the conquest of sin and evil and the realization of complete communion with God. In fact, both would come together. By the middle of the 20th century a largely secularized Jewish people found itself in an unprecedented situation within a secularized world. That which many generations had prayed and hoped for, or rather believed in with that stubborn faith that springs less from fanaticism than from a profound inner certainty, had come to pass, and yet nobody would be bold enough to speak of a messianic consummation, even though some might speak of a messianic beginning. There is as yet no peace on the borders, and both individual man and society as a whole know that they are still far removed from that wholeness and completeness which traditional utopianism had associated with the messianic age, notwithstanding the more rational and anti-apocalyptic statement of one ancient Rabbi, to the effect that the only difference between exile and the messianic age would be Israel's freedom from gentile domination. It seems that precisely because the Zionist Movement has realized so many—though not all—of its aims, and fulfilled so much of the dynamism of Jewish history, that its immense achievement renders the absence of a messianic consummation even more glaring. It has posed the question of messianism anew, for realization is the strongest enemy of hope, even as the life of hope is the most eloquent witness to the truth that realization is still outstanding. But if the past holds any clue to the future, it would seem to suggest that the present crisis of messianism will lead to a new reinterpretation rather that to the total abandonment of a complex symbol that for millenia has served as the expression of the Jew's unshakeable conviction of his national identity, religious destiny, inalienable promise and absolute certainty of a future for himself bound to that of mankind.

H. G. FRIEDMANN, art. "Pseudo-Messiahs", in *The Jewish Encyclopaedia*, vol. X, pp. 251–255.

H. GRESSMANN, *Der Messias* (1929).

J. KLAUSNER, *The Messianic Idea in Israel, from its Beginnings to the Completion of the Mishnah* (1955).

S. MOWINCKEL, *He That Cometh. The Messianic Concept in the Old Testament and later Judaism* (1956).

J. SARACHEK, *The Messianic Idea in Medieval Jewish Literature* (1932).

G. SCHOLEM, *Major Trends in Jewish Mysticism* (1961), Index svv. Messiah, Messianic, Messianism.

Id., *Sabbatai Sevi and the Messianic Movement during his Lifetime* (1957) (in Hebrew; Engl. translation in preparation).

Id., "Zum Verständnis der messianischen Idee im Judentum", in *Eranos-Jahrbuch*, XXVII (Zurich, 1960); "Toward an Understanding of the Messianic Idea in Judaism," in *The Messianic Idea in Judaism* (New York, 1971).

A. H. SILVER, *A History of Messianic Speculation in Israel* (1958).

R. J. ZWI WERBLOWSKY, "Crises of Messianism", in *Judaism*, VII (1958), pp. 106–120.

M. ZOBEL, *Der Messias und die messianische Zeit in Talmud und Midrasch* (1938).

HAYIM TADMOR

"THE PEOPLE" AND THE KINGSHIP IN ANCIENT ISRAEL: THE ROLE OF POLITICAL INSTITUTIONS IN THE BIBLICAL PERIOD [1]

A. Introduction

THE special interest displayed by twentieth century historical research in social phenomena has found an ample expression in the study of the ancient Near East and of the history of Israel in the Biblical period. In these areas, previously dominated by philological, political and theological approaches, a new line began to make its appearance. Undoubtedly, the credit for this new direction in research goes to Max Weber and his *Das Antike Judentum,* published posthumously in 1921. That work, however, was based mainly on secondary sources and occasionally on some unsound postulates prevalent among the Biblical critics in his day and on rather arbitrary analogies between the Biblical and ancient Greek societies. Albrecht Alt, who was influenced to no small extent by Weber's methodology in the sociology of religion, further developed this line of research, particularly in the area of political theory and the study of institutions in ancient Israel. His work, and that of his disciple Martin Noth, still remain the basis for further research in these fields.[2]

[1] The nucleus of the present study was a paper "The 'General Assembly' in Ancient Israel: An Aspect of 'Primitive Democracy'", read before the *XIIIe Rencontre Assyriologique Internationale* in Paris, July 1964 devoted to the question of *Vox Populi.*
The following abbreviations have been employed:
Enc. Miqr. = *Encyclopaedia Miqra'it* (Encyclopaedia Biblica, in Hebrew), vols. I-V, Jerusalem, 1950-68.
JAOS = *Journal of the American Oriental Society*
JNES = *Journal of Near Eastern Studies*
RA = *Revue d'Assyriologie*
RB = *Revue Biblique*
VDI = *Vestnik Drevnei Istorii*
VT = *Vetus Testamentum*
[2] A. ALT, *Die Staatenbildung der Israeliten in Palästina* (Leipzig, 1930), *(Kleine Schriften,* II, [München, 1953], pp. 1-65); "Das Königtum in den Reichen Israel und Juda", *VT,* I (1961), pp. 2-22 *(Kleine Schriften,* II, pp. 116-34); also available now in English translation: *Essays on Old Testament History and Religion* (Oxford, 1966), pp. 173-259); M. NOTH, *Die Geschichte Israels* (Göttingen, 1950), English translation from the 2nd ed., London, 1958 [henceforth: NOTH, *History*]; "Gott, König, Volk im Alten Testament", *Zeitschrift für Theologie und Kirche,* XLVII (1950), pp. 151-191, *Gesammelte Studien zum Alten Testament* (3rd edition, München, 1966), pp. 188-229. English translation by D. R. Ap-THOMAS, from the 2nd ed.: *The Laws of the Pentateuch and Other Essays* (Edinburgh and London, 1966), pp. 145-178.

A marked revival of research in the society and institutions of the Biblical period took place after 1943, when Thorkild Jacobsen called the attention of scholars to "democratic" terms and concepts in the authoritarian world of ancient Mesopotamia.[3] Since then, this field of research has broadened, and scholars pointed to similar phenomena in Seleucid Babylonia, as well as among the Hurrians and the Hittites, in Ugarit (Ras-Shamra), in Nubia, and even in ancient China.[4] It is in this context that the situation in Israel during the Biblical period has been considered, particularly in the tribal-patriarchal society, before the rise of the monarchy, and typological comparisons have been made between early Mesopotamian institutions and similar ones in Israel.[5] In recent years, more detailed studies of some specific institutions in Ancient Israel have been published[6], culminating in Roland de Vaux's most valuable synthesis.[7]

The political institutions in Ancient Israel during the conquest of Canaan, the period of the Settlement and the time of the Judges, have been studied at length by a number of scholars,[8] and we shall not revert

[3] Thorkild JACOBSEN, "Primitive Democracy in Ancient Mesopotamia", *JNES*, II (1943), pp. 159-172. See also I. M. DIAKONOFF, *UDI* (1952), No. 2, pp. 13-37; and G. EVANS, *JAOS*, LXXIX (1958), pp. 1-11.

[4] A list of the relevant works appears in I. M. DIAKONOFF, *UDI* (1963), No. 1, pp. 21-22. See also: V. V. IVANOV, *UDI* (1957), No. 4, pp. 19-36; *ibid.* (1958), No. 1, pp. 3-15 (on the assembly among the Hittites); M. L. HELTZER, *ibid.* (1963), No. 1, pp. 36-56; N. B. IANKOVSKAIA, *ibid.* (1963), No. 3, pp. 35-55 and, more recently, A. F. RAINEY, *The Social Structure of Ugarit* (in Hebrew), (Jerusalem, 1966), pp. 104-105 (on the autonomy of the community in Ugarit).

[5] C. U. WOLF, "Traces of Primitive Democracy in Ancient Israel", *JNES*, VI (1947), pp. 98-108; R. GORDIS, "Democratic Origins in Ancient Israel—the Biblical '*Edah*", *Alexander Marx Jubilee Volume* (New York, 1950), pp. 369-388.

[6] J. van der PLOEG, "Les 'nobles israélites'", *Oudtestamentliche Studiën* IX (1955), pp. 49-64. W. McKANE, "The '*gibbor hayil*' in the Israelite Community", *Transactions of the Glasgow University Oriental Society*, XVII (1959), pp. 28-37.

[7] *Les Institutions de l'Ancien Testament* (Paris, 1958-1960), I-II. English translation: *Ancient Israel, Its Life and Institutions* (London, 1961), (henceforth: de VAUX, *Institutions*). Of the studies that have appeared subsequently, specific reference is made of: J. L. McKENZIE, "The Elders in the Old Testament", *Analecta Biblica*, X (1959), pp. 388-400; G. EVANS "'Gates' and 'Sities': Urban Institutions in Old Testament Times", *Journal of Religious History*, II (1962), No. 1, pp. 1-12; E. A. SPEISER, "Background and Function of the Biblical *Nāsi*", *Catholic Biblical Quarterly*, XXV (1963), pp. 111-117; K. H. BERNHARDT, *Das Problem der altorientalischen Königideologie im Alten Testament* (Leiden, 1961); J. LIVER, "Kingship" in *Enc. Miqr.*, IV, cols. 1080-1112 (in Hebrew); A. MALAMAT, "Kingship and Council in Israel and Sumer: a Parallel", *JNES*, XXII (1963), pp. 247-253; *idem*, "Organs of Statecraft in the Israelite Monarchy", *The Biblical Archaeologist*, XXVIII (1965), pp. 34-50; G. EVANS, "Rehoboam's Advisers at Shechem, and Political Institutions in Israel and Sumer", *JNES*, XXV (1966), pp. 273-279. On the problem of '*am ha-ares*, see the literature quoted in footnote 39, below.

[8] NOTH, *History*, pp. 83 ff.; J. BRIGHT, *A History of Israel* (Philadelphia, 1959) [henceforth: BRIGHT, *History*], pp. 142 ff.; H. M. ORLINSKY, "The Tribal System of Israel and Related Groups in the Period of the Judges", *Oriens Antiquus*, I (1962), pp. 11-20; A. MALAMAT, J. LIVER, E. A. SPEISER in B. MAZAR, (ed.), *The Patriarchs and the Judges*, "The World History of the Jewish People, First Series: Ancient Times", vol. II (Tel-Aviv, 1967) [in Hebrew], pp. 219-262; 197-300.

to that subject here. In the present study we shall attempt to demonstrate the dynamic and changing character of the political bodies, particularly those which express the sovereignty of the people. Accordingly,
we have chosen to limit our investigation to the period of the monarchy,
a time when these bodies were hard-pressed by centripetal tendencies
and their authority was giving way to that of the kingship. We submit
that, despite the centralized character of the united kingdom in the
period of David and Solomon, and despite the well-rooted royal tradition in the separate states of Judah and Israel, the sovereignty of the
people—as expressed in its institutions—did not cease, but continued
to express itself—though in changed forms—until the fall of the two
states and even thereafter.

We shall define a number of basic concepts which we have to employ.

The usual term used to denote the entire people as the bearer of
political, military, or cultic-ceremonial authority are: "Israel", "all
Israel", "the people of Israel", and "congregation" ('edah or qahal).
Of these, "Israel", "the people of Israel" or in shortened form "the
people"—ha-'am—denote not only the totality of the tribes but any
part of them—whatever their number—acting on its behalf. The assembly
of the people termed: ha-'edah = "the congregation" (or "the congregation of Israel", "the congregation of YHWH", etc.), denotes for the
most part the gathering for purposes of war and worship; the use of the
term 'edah is mainly ancient, gradually disappearing in the period of the
kings. Qahal (or qehal Yisrael, qehal YHWH, qehal elohim [i.e. of the
Lord], etc.) as its name signifies, is another term for an assembly. Unlike
'edah it did not become obsolete in the period of the monarchy and after
the return from the Babylonian exile it became the regular term for the
"assembly of the people". The "elders"—(zeqenim)—"the elders of
Israel", "the elders of Judah"—were the heads of the clans, the notables
by their familial-social or economic status. Their authority, which was
considerable in the pre-monarchial period and included powers of
adjudication and leadership, was naturally curtailed after the monarchy
established its own institutions, but they are still mentioned several times
in the course of the history of Israel and Judah.

The connecting link between the ancient tribal organization of Israel
and the centralized monarchial regime of David and Solomon was the
kingdom of Saul, the last of the judges and the first of the kings. However, very little is known of the governing organs during his reign. The
main posts in the newly created administration were alloted—as it appears—to the King's kinsmen from the tribe of Benjamin. On the other
hand, in David's time we find a highly-developed officialdom, seemingly
springing from nowhere, which included new positions and new persons,
some of them non-Israelites (II Sam. 8: 16-17, 20: 23-26). This officialdom was composed of (a) the generals of the army—Joab, "in command

of all the army of Israel" and Benaiah ben Jehoiada, commander of the Cherethites and the Pelethites, the Philistine mercenaries who served as the King's bodyguard and (b) the chief ministers in the civil administration, most of whom—as B. Mazar indicated[9]—were apparently Canaanite in origin: the "recorder" *(mazkir)*, the royal herald, on the pattern of the Akkadian *nāgiru*, the "secretary" i.e. the scribe—*sopher*, who was by the nature of his office in charge of correspondence with the neighbouring countries; and the officer "who was over the levy", i.e. in charge of the corvée. In addition, there were the "stewards" *(sarim)* of David's property—the officers in charge of the crown lands and of the various economic branches of the royal establishment (I Chron. 27: 25-31). This was evidently a kingdom with new and effective instruments of government, which for the most part were foreign to the political tradition of Israel.

We are now confronted by an astonishing phenomenon. The vigorous royal government with its complex of officials and its extensive personnel sustains a most serious shock towards the end of David's reign: the revolt of Absalom and the revolt of Sheba ben Bichri which stemmed from it. Both rebellions, which almost succeeded in overthrowing David's rule, revealed the extent of the power vested in the people and the vitality of their institutions. Since that was a crucial point in the history of the early monarchy and especially as there is no reason to doubt the reliability of the source which describes it (II Sam. 15-20, recorded not long after the events occurred—perhaps by eye-witnesses)—we shall make it a point of departure in the present study.

B. *The Rebellion of Absalom: the role of "The men of Israel"*

Coming to consider the episode of Absalom's revolt, we are confronted with a basic question: why did the people extend wide support to Absalom and abandon their king completely? One can hardly be satisfied with the answer of the ancient biographer who attributes Absalom's success to his personal charm: "And Absalom used to rise up early, and stand beside the way of the gate: and it was so, that when any man had a suit to come before the king for judgment, Absalom call to him and say: 'From what city are you?' And when he said: 'Your servant is of such and such a tribe, in Israel'. And Absalom would say to him: 'See, your claims are good and right; but there is no man deputed by the king to hear you'. Absalom said moreover: 'Oh that I were a judge in the land! Then every man with a suit or cause might come to me, and

[9] B. MAISLER (MAZAR), *Bulletin of the Jewish Palestine Exploration Society*, XIII (1946/46), pp. 105-114 (in Hebrew); see also, R. de VAUX, *RB*, XLVIII (1939), pp. 394-405.

I would do him justice'. And whenever a man came near to do obeisance
to him, he would put out his hand, and take hold of him, and kiss him.
Thus did Absalom to all Israel who came to the king for judgment; so
Absalom stole the hearts of the men of Israel" (II Sam. 15: 2-6).

What, then, were the forces that supported Absalom? From the
description of the revolt it becomes apparent that most of the people
supported Absalom, while David was left with "his servants" (15: 14)—
the courtiers—and his regiment of loyal mercenaries (*ibid.*, 18). The royal
structure he had established, with all its officials and with all its army,
seemed to crumble and disappear. When he finally took steps to fight
Absalom, David was compelled to organize an essentially new army
(I Sam. 18: 1), apparently of the men of Gilead, the only district in his
kingdom which remained loyal and extended him broad support.

The forces arrayed behind Absalom are generally designated "the
elders of Israel"—*ziqnei Yisrael*—and "the men of Israel"—*'ish Yisrael*
(lit. "the man of Israel"). At the very beginning of the revolt David is
told: "The hearts of the men of Israel are after Absalom" (I Sam. 15: 13);
when David flees from Jerusalem and Absalom comes to the city "all
the people, the men of Israel" will come with him (16: 15); it is before
the king "and all the elders of Israel" that Ahitophel gives his advice
about how to capture David (17: 4), and it is before Absalom "and all
the men of Israel" that Hushai the Archite gives his advice to the contrary. Absalom "and all the men of Israel" cross the Jordan in pursuit
of David (17: 24). Absalom's camp is referred to in shorter form as
"Israel"—"So the people (i.e. David's army) went out into the field
against Israel" (18: 6). It is clear that "the elders of Israel" and "the men
of Israel" are not used synonymously, but that there is a clear distinction
between them. Whereas the king and the "elders of Israel" accepted the
advice of Ahitophel, "the men of Israel" rejected it. This, then, was a
higher authority, which could overrule the decision of the elders; "the
men of Israel" constituted a broader body than the elders not only in
name but also in substance. Whom did "the men of Israel" encompass
in this case? It cannot be assumed that the reference is to the heads of
the clans or to the tribal notables, since these seem to be identical with
"the elders of Israel", or at least the two overlaped to a large extent.
The comprehensive definition of the concept "the men of Israel" is clearly emphasized, for example, in the words of Hushai the Archite (16: 18):
"and this people, and all the men of Israel". Now, the only body before
which David was likely to have fled from Jerusalem with his professional
army when news of the rebellion reached him—could only have been the
army; we will thus not err in proposing that "the men of Israel" was
the army of Israel. This assumption explains why "the men of Israel"
accompanied Absalom when he entered Jerusalem, and why it was that
body (rather than "the elders of Israel") that later crossed to trans-Jor-

dan to fight against David: "Absalom passed over the Jordan, he and all
the men of Israel with him" (17: 24). On the basis of this distinction, we
can understand the contrast between the nature of the counsel of Ahitophel—the moving spirit behind Absalom's revolt—and that of his rival,
Hushai the Archite—David's "fifth column". Ahitophel's advice—"Let
me now choose out twelve thousand men, and I will set out and pursue
David tonight" (17: 1)—was meant to give an all-tribal expression to
the war against David, since the intention was—one thousand men from
each tribe. Ahitophel's aim was a quick action to capture David alone
without touching the people who were with him (17: 2). But Hushai the
Archite likewise offered military-tactical arguments against this advice
and urged that "all Israel be gathered to you from Dan to Beersheba,
as the sand by the sea for multitude" (17: 11) and that this reinforced
army be used to attack David and his camp and to destroy all his supporters (*ibid.*, 12). We know, of course, that it was Hushai's advice that
was taken, but it is worth noting some fine distinctions in the wording:
Absalom's army which was fighting David's army is called simply
"Israel" (18: 6) or "the people of Israel", whereas David's army is referred to as "the servants of David": "And the people of Israel were
smitten there before the servants of David" (18: 7). The contrast here is
clear and sharp: David and his "servants" versus the whole people of
Israel, including the tribe of Judah. Indeed, there is no basis for the
assumption that the tribe of Judah took no part in Absalom's revolt and
remained neutral throughout. Moreover, it is inconceivable that Absalom
would have been crowned in Hebron—the sacred city of Judah—without
that tribe's active co-operation or consent. And only on the assumption
that Judah participated in the revolt together with the other tribes of
Israel it is possible to explain the appointment of Amasa, a Judahite and
a relative of the king, as Absalom's general (17: 25). However, when
Judah appears in opposition to Israel after the suppression of Absalom's
revolt we find the "men of Israel" as a body distinct from "the men of
Judah" (19: 43-44, 20: 4). Clearly, the term "the men of Israel" appears
here in the narrow sense of the army of the "ten tribes", just as the term
"Israel" denotes in the Biblical books sometimes the entire people, including Judah, and sometimes Israel alone, to the exclusion of Judah.

What was the actual composition of "the men of Israel"? We have no
definite knowledge as to the structure of David's national army. The
sources speak mostly of his professionals: (a) the *gibborim* i.e. the "champions" or "the mighty men" and (b) the Philistine mercenaries: the
Cherethites and the Pelethites and the 600 warriors from Gath (II Sam.
15: 18). However, we can hardly doubt the existence of a conscript army
that was assembled in major wars during David's reign. Such army is
mentioned explicitly in the battle against the Arameans: "Now when
Joab saw that the battle was set against him before and behind, he chose

of all the choice men of Israel, and put them in array against the Arameans" (II Sam. 10: 9). It is a fair assumption that when the people were
called to arms in David's times, it was on a family basis, as was the customary procedure in the tribal society of Israel in which the family unit
was identical with the military one. In that case, the term "'eleph"—i.e.
a thousand—still played a vital role in David's conscript army, as it did
in the early days of Israel. The basic meaning of 'eleph is family or tribe,
but it also means the military unit which the family or the tribe sets up.
Theoretically, this unit consisted of "1,000 men", but actually the number might have been much smaller.[10] When the people were recruited
to the army, on the tribal-familial basis, they were assembled "by their
thousands". Under such a recruitment system, based on the 'eleph unit,
the local-tribal leadership would naturally retain a large measure of influence. And it is quite likely that the chiefs of "the thousands" and
even the chiefs of the hundreds—the sub-units of the 'eleph—came from
the stratum of the local leadership and not from the professional military
officers who rose by their own merit.[11] It is, then, this system of recruitment to the people's army in the time of David that enabled Absalom to
launch his rebellion. The inherent connection between the military structure and the tribal-familial pattern is manifested in the participation of
both institutions in Absalom's revolt: "the men of Israel"—the people's
army based on the family-unit—and the "elders of Israel"—the representatives of the people according to the patriarchal-territorial structure.
The two were just different expressions of a single social entity.

A brief examination of the use of the term "the men of Israel" in the
sources of the pre-Davidic period would seem to strengthen the suggested
explanation.

(a) In Joshua 9, the Gibeonites, who had formerly belonged to the
area of Jerusalem, turn to Joshua and "the men of Israel" and ask for a
treaty of protection with them. In this story "the men of Israel" is identical with the "congregation" of Israel ('edah), whose "princes"—nesi'im
—make the covenant and swear in its name. "The men of Israel" in this
case would denote the tribal league in its military capacity.

(b) In Judges 9, "the men of Israel" offer the kingdom to Gideon,
after his victory over the Midianites, and there is reason to suppose that
here too the reference is to warriors (just as "the men of Ephraim" in
Judges 12, who are opposed to Jephtah the Gileadite, are the fighting
men of Ephraim, and "the men of Judah" whom Saul assembles [I Sa-

---

[10] G. E. MENDENHALL, Journal of Biblical Literature, LXII (1958), pp. 52-66;
de VAUX, Institutions, Eng. tr., pp. 225-226.

[11] Y. YADIN, who has made a detailed study of the method of recruitment and
the structure of the army in the time of David, went even further and suggested that
the tribe (i.e. the heads of the tribe) determined the service of the sub-units in time
of war: Y. YADIN, The Scroll of the War of the Sons of Light Against the Sons of
Darkness (Oxford, 1962), pp. 49-53 and 83-86.

muel 11: 9] in order to fight against the Ammonites—are the fighting men of Judah).

(c) The nature of the term "the men of Israel" becomes particularly clear from the story of the war launched by the tribes of Israel against the tribe of Benjamin, recounted in Judges 19-20. The "congregation" assembles at Mizpah, on the border of Benjamin, and chooses by lot 10 percent of all the fighting men: "ten men of a hundred throughout all the tribes of Israel, and a hundred of a thousand, and a thousand out of ten thousand". From this point on, this selected army is referred to as "the men of Israel" (20: 11) or "Israel" or "the children of Israel" (*ibid.*, 23-24) or "all the people" (*ibid.*, 26-30). It is unlikely that these variants stem from different sources; they appear rather to be stylistic variants. Only at a later stage in the story, when there is a discussion how to prevent the tribe of Benjamin from being annihilated, after most of its men had fallen in battle (21: 16), do the "elders of the people" make their appearance. Here, too, the distinction is preserved between "the elders" on the one hand and "the men of Israel"—on the other. For the purpose of our discussion it is not necessary to consider the question of the historical reliability of these stories; admittedly, the degree of historicity of some of them is not at all clear, especially, as there are grounds for the assumption that they were composed or edited—whether for etiological or, more likely, for polemical purposes—in the reigns of David and Solomon. The essential factor for our purpose is, that the term "the men of Israel" is used in these stories in the very military sense in which it appears in the narrative of Absalom's revolt.

The only source where "the men of Israel" is not necessarily used in a military sense is I Kings 8: 1: "Then Solomon assembled the elders of Israel, and all the heads of the tribes, the leaders of the fathers' houses of the people of Israel, before king Solomon in Jerusalem, to bring up the ark of the covenant of the Lord out of the city of David... And all the men of Israel assembled themselves to king Solomon... And all the elders of Israel came, and the priests took up the ark..." This is the last mention of "the men of Israel" in the historical books of the Bible, as well as the last occurrence of the "heads of the tribes" and of the *nesi'im* ("leaders", "princes") taking part in public affairs during the period of the monarchy. It is very likely that the editor here intentionally employed older terms in order to set his story against the background of the tribal institutions in their broadest sense. It follows that the appearance of "the men of Israel" in the context of Absalom's rebellion is in fact the last use of this term in an authentic historical framework.

We now turn to another aspect in the story of Absalom's rebellion—the very appearance of "the men of Israel" and "the elders of Israel" as consultative body to the king. This phenomenon evokes special interest, since it is a complete innovation as compared with the custom followed in the time of David. Neither of the two terms is mentioned even once in the historical narratives describing David's kingship, nor is there the least hint that the king ever had to resort to the counsel of the people; his rule was based on the ramified officialdom—"the king's servants"— and on the professional army. Consulting the warriors and the elders was by no means a symbolic act or a casual change in the decision-making procedure initiated by Absalom. It was, we submit, the very essence of the rebellion. The radical transformation that occurred in Israel with the establishment of the centralized monarchy, the supplanting of the tribal-patriarchal institutions by royal ones, thus impinging upon the traditional leadership, the aloofness of the king from the people and the fading of the image of the king as a "judge" (shofet) to whom any citizen could come to obtain justice—these dynamic changes which occurred within a few decades aroused an ever-increasing resentment which came to the open in the revolt of Absalom. It is against this background that the support offered to Absalom by heterogeneous tribal institutions should be considered. The elders, "the men of Judah" and "the men of Israel"— all united in one stream which expressed itself in a paradox: the autocratic prince, the scion of a royal family also on his mother's side (II Sam. 3: 4), who could hardly have the least attachment to popular institutions, and who acted as if he were king even during his father's lifetime, has won the full sympathy and support of the traditional leadership who hoped to find in him their redeemer. And indeed, in no time Absalom revived the authority of the bodies latent since the days of Saul. Even then, their voice—particularly that of "the elders of Israel"—was heard only in moments of anarchy and of breakdown of royal authority: when Saul died and later, when his son Eshbaal was assassinated. By letting the elders and the warriors play active roles in deliberations of vital importance, Absalom's action seems to be a subtly planned demagogic move. One might well doubt whether this new arrangement would have been retained had Absalom succeeded in routing his father in battle. In any case, a monarch whose sovereignty is limited by tribal assemblies or by councils of elders is a phenomenon so far unattested in Israel in the Biblical period nor in the neighbouring kingdoms, large or small.

Absalom's revolt failed, and with it the hope of his supporters to set back the clock and to revive the authority of the ancient institutions. It might have been expected that after this defeat David's position would be strengthened and that he would even assume more centralized powers than in the past. But things turned out differently. Since the rebellion itself revealed the weakness of the regime and emphasized the strength of the people's institutions, David felt necessary to follow a new course. He did not return to Jerusalem as a victor at the head of his army, but made a decision which was destined to determine the fate of the united kingdom of Israel. We deduce this new policy of David from the wording of the message he sent to the elders of Judah: "Why should you be the last to bring the king back to his house—when the word of all Israel was come to the king?—You are my kinsmen, you are my bone and my flesh; and why then should you be the last to bring back the king? And say to Amasa: 'Are you not my bone and my flesh? God do so to me, and more also, if you are not commander of my army henceforth in place of Joab. And he swayed the heart of all the men of Judah, as the heart of one man; so that they sent word to the king: Return, both, you and all your servants." (II Sam. 19: 12-16).

It transpires, that David here is trying to repeat old tactics which had previously helped him become king of Judah and Israel. At that time, after the death of Saul, he won over the elders of Judah and particularly those of southern Judah by defending them against the Amalekites and by sending them part of the booty (I Sam. 30: 26-31); then he went up to Hebron where "the men of Judah" annointed him king. Only after a few years, upon the death of Eshbaal son of Saul, did "all the elders of Israel"—the representatives of the "northern tribes"—ask David to extend his rule over Israel (II Sam. 5: 1-3); so after he made a covenant with them in Hebron "before the Lord", he was annointed king over all Israel, uniting, to use Alt's expression, in his personality Judah and Israel under a single crown. Now, confronted with the breakdown of the united kingdom he had created, David set himself to consolidating his position through the tribal institutions of Judah in the hope that these might serve as a springboard for strengthening his authority over "all Israel". This explains David's preference for Judah and the tribes of the south not only in his hints, "you are my bone and my flesh, why then should you be the last to bring back the king?", but also in a deliberate act: the appointment of Amasa of Judah, the commander of "the men of Israel" in Absalom's army, in place of Joab. A clear expression of the preference of Judah was the symbolic act of the king's crossing the Jordan when the "men of Judah" brought the king and his household over the Jordan (II Sam. 19: 41). Upon their arrival to welcome the king, the "men of Israel" discovered, to their consternation, that they were late. The argument of the "men of Israel", according to the story, was that "We have ten parts in the king", while the "men of Judah" maintained: "The king is near of kin to us" (19: 43). The story ends with the obscure statement: "And the words of the men of Judah were fiercer than the words of the men of Israel" (19: 44). It now became evident beyond any doubt that David was indeed closer to Judah and that henceforth he would maintain a closer attachment to its tribal institutions, thus disturbing the equilibrium of his kingdom. The anger of "the men of Israel" expressed itself in the revolt led by Sheba ben Bichri, of the tribe of Benjamin, who called for the overthrow of the House of David. His slogan, "We have no portion in David, neither have we inheritance

in the son of Jesse", which concluded with the cry, "every man to his
tents, O Israel!" (II Sam. 20: 1), expresses the essence of his rebellion.
As at this stage the rebels had no other candidate to replace David, whose
rule they had just denounced, the actual implication of the revolt was
therefore either the temporary abolition of the monarchy, or at least a
period of anarchy until a new king would be chosen. It is thus under-
standable why David regarded this new crisis as more serious than the
rebellion of Absalom: "Now will Sheba ben Bichri do us more harm
than did Absalom" (20: 6). David set out to suppress the rebellion in
its rise. He first tried to mobilize "the men of Judah" for battle, but
Amasa, who was assigned this task, failed to carry it out. David had no
choice but to rely on his loyal army, the *gibborim*, and on the Philistine
contingent, under the command of Joab and Abishai his brother, who
were now urgently dispatched to pursue Sheba ben Bichri. When the
rebel was turned over by the citizens of Abel beth-Maacha, in Northern
Galilee, the revolt ended, and the people returned "every man to his
home" (20: 22).

The privileges extended to Judah have not been abolished after the
last rebellion was quelled. Moreover, there is reason to believe that in
Solomon's time Judah was not included among the twelve administrative
districts (I Kings 4 : 7-19) and was therefore exempt from the obligation
of supplying produce for the king's court and possibly from other reve-
nues imposed on the tribes of Israel[12]. Yet, the special position of Judah
within the kingdom did not cause an immediate rebellion of Israel; the
economic prosperity of the state, the political successes, and the years of
peace and stability that marked Solomon's reign kept the internal equilibrium. In the second half of his reign however, when the political and the
economic conditions had deteriorated and the levies (mobilization and
corvée) had increased, a ferment began, which developed into a real revolt.[13] Jeroboam, an Ephraimite, one of the king's officers in charge of
the corvée labourers of "the house of Joseph", "lifted up his hand against
the king" (11: 27). But this revolt—of which a variant version is preserved in the Septuagint—failed. Jeroboam fled to Egypt and found refuge with Shoshenq, the founder of the 22nd dynasty and an enemy of
Solomon. It was only upon the death of Solomon (928 B.C.E.), when his
son Rehoboam ascended the throne, that the movement of rebellion was
revived and assumed greater dimensions. The assembly of "all Israel"

---

[12] Following B. MAZAR, *Bulletin of the Israel Exploration Society*, XXIV (1960),
p. 13 (in Hebrew): Y. AHARONI, *The Land of the Bible* (London, 1966), p. 279; and
Z. KALLAI, *The Tribes of Israel* (Jerusalem, 1967), pp. 38 ff., (in Hebrew). A different
view is held by W. F. ALBRIGHT, *Archaeology and Religion of Israel* (Baltimore, 1942),
p. 141; and BRIGHT, *History*, p. 200. On the other hand, A. ALT (*Kleine Schriften*,
II, p. 89) and M. NOTH (*History*, p. 211) are undecided on the question whether
Judah was exempted from taxation.
[13] B. MAZAR in *Enc. Miqr.*, I, cols. 711 ff.

at Shechem—the ancient centre in the Mount of Ephraim—to crown Rehoboam (II Kings 12) expresses a later and advanced stage of this ferment.

C. The Assembly at Shechem: the Covenant and the Dynastic Principle

We may well assume that the very fact of chosing Shechem instead of Jerusalem for the coronation ceremony and the fact that the king had to appear there before the assembly testifies to the authority wielded by the institutions of the people in time of crisis. Moreover, "all Israel" in assembling aimed not at the formal coronation ceremony as such, but intended to make the coronation conditional on the introduction of reforms. This was expressed in the ultimatum: "Now therefore lighten the hard service of your father, and his heavy yoke upon us, and we will serve you" (12: 4). Rehoboam was called upon to proclaim certain ameliorations specified in advance, quite in the manner of the Akkadian mīsharum-act, which the early Babylonian kings in the second millennium would proclaim upon assuming the throne.[14] The specific reform in this case concerns the corvée, which, as has been noted, constituted a heavy burden at the end of Solomon's reign and which the people regarded as a severe infringement upon the freeholder. Judah, which was not especially affected by this levy, did not participate in the ferment. The assembly (qehal Yisrael in 12: 2) which conducted the negotiations with Rehoboam thus represented only the northern tribes, headed by Jeroboam, who had returned from Egypt. At first, it appeared that the result would be compromise. Rehoboam's coming to Shechem and the participation of Jeroboam, the leader of the previous rebellion, in the assembly indicated the young king's willingness to listen to the people and to do their will. But it was already too late (12: 18), for the advice of those of Rehoboam's counsellors who favoured an authoritarian monarchy prevailed. The "old men" and the "young men"—not permanent councils of any sort—indicate two opposing tendencies which stemmed from two political traditions, both groups being officials and courtiers of the king. The "old men" (zeqenim) were the veteran officials "that had stood before Solomon", i e., who had served him (in accordance with the meaning of the same idiom in Akkadian).[15] They witnessed the struggle

---

[14] These proclamations of mīsharum were intended mainly for the remission of debts and were essentially limited in nature. See in detail : F. R. KRAUS, Ein Edikt des Königs Ammi-ṣaduqa von Babylon (Leiden, 1958), pp. 194-209; J. J. FINKELSTEIN, "Some New Mišarum Material and Its Implications", Studies in Honor of Benno Landsberger (Chicago, 1965), pp. 234-246. A practice related to mīsharum was the andurārum (Hebrew deror), and see J. LEWY, Eretz Israel, V (1958), English section, pp. 21-31.

[15] ina pān uzuzzu "To stand before somebody", i.e., to do court service; and cf. A. L. OPPENHEIM, JAOS, LXI (1941), p. 258; W. von SODEN, Akkadisches Handwörterbuch (Wiesbaden, 1963), p. 409.

between the king and the people's institutions at the time of Absalom's revolt and still remembered David's successful diplomacy in reaching a compromise with the people; they therefore advised Rehoboam to yield to the assembly at this time of crisis, if only for the moment: "...and speak words to them, when you answer them then they will be your servants for ever" (112: 5). Yet, the "young men" (*yeladim*, lit. "the children"), those young courtiers of Rehoboam "who had grown up with him, and stood before him" (12: 8), and who had been reared in the authoritarian-centralized tradition, saw in the very demand of the assembly for reforms a serious affront to the sovereignty of the young king and an encroachment upon the royal prerogatives.[16] These groups of officials are not typologically similar to the institutions of "the elders of the city" and "the young men of the city" in ancient Mesopotamia,[17] which serve as classical example of "primitive democracy."[18] The story deliberately employs here the terms "young" and "old" because it is coached in the style of those wisdom tales which stress the polarity between the "child"—i.e. the young man—who lacks experience and the wise old man. From its style and language one can deduce that the story was composed by the same scribes who compiled the rest of Solomonic history—i.e. "the book of the acts of Solomon" (I Kings 11: 41).[19] This circle, which portrayed Solomon as the father of wisdom in Israel, regarded the conduct of his pretentious son as an act of outright foolishness: by not heeding the advice of his veteran, experienced officials and by accepting that of the arrogant "*yeladim*", he brought calamity upon his kingdom and was heavily punished for his folly.

The same assembly of "all Israel" at Shechem that deposed Rehoboam—using the slogan of Sheba's revolt (12: 16)—enthroned his Ephraimite adversary. The designation of that assembly by the old tribal term *ha-'edah* (20: 20) can hardly be accidental. And indeed, the infamous innovations Jeroboam introduced—the shrines of YHWH at Dan and Beth-El, the festival in the eighth month, and the appointment of priests "from among all the people" (12: 25-33)—were essentially the restoration of ancient traditions which had been prevalent in Israel prior to the establishment of the monarchy.[20] He was even careful not to establish a single capital city—a symbol of centralized government—but had his

---

[16] I. MENDELSOHN, *Bulletin of the American Schools of Oriental Research*, CLIII (1956), pp. 17-22; A. ALT, *Kleine Schriften*, III (München, 1969), pp. 348-372.

[17] A different opinion is held by A. MALAMAT, *JNES*, XXII (1963), pp. 247-253. But see the cogent critical remarks of G. EVANS, *JNES*, XXV (1966), pp. 273-279.

[18] *JNES*, II (1943), 165 ff.; see, however, the remarks of S. N. KRAMER, *RA*, LVIII (1946), pp. 152-156.

[19] See more recently: J. LIVER, *Biblica*, 48 (1967), pp. 96-99.

[20] W. F. ALBRIGHT, *From the Stone Age to Christianity* (Baltimore, 1940), pp. 228-230; B. MAZAR, *Enc. Miqr.*, 1, cols. 715; H. TADMOR, *ibid*, III, cols. 773 ff.; S. TALMON, *UT*, VIII (1958), pp. 48-58; BRIGHT, *History*, pp. 217-218.

seat first in Shechem and afterwards in Penuel and Tirzah (I Kings 12: 25, 14: 17). In this, too, he may have been returning to earlier customs, and it may further indicate the influence exerted by the separatist, tribal-territorial forces that had raised him to the kingship.

We come now to consider the theory which in recent years has gained support among scholars, namely that the purpose of the assembly at Shechem was to make a covenant with the king and, moreover, that the status of the monarchy in Israel was based on a covenant between the king and the people.[21] This theory, is, in effect, an extension of Alt's views on the specific character of the monarchy in Israel and Judah. Alt, who studied in 1930 and again in 1951 the ideological aspect of the monarchial institutions in ancient Israel, put forward the hypothesis— one that has been widely accepted in Biblical research—that in its inception the monarchy in Israel was charismatic while that in Judah was dynastic. According to this view, every king of Israel was chosen only for his lifetime, the concept of a dynastic monarchy being foreign to the spirit of Israel until the time of Omri. Only after Omri established Samaria as his capital with a special constitution of its own—like Jerusalem —and created "the personal union between the city state of Samaria and the national state of Israel"—did the dynastic idea take root in Israel. "It was self-evident that in the new city of Samaria, after the death of its founder, his authority should pass by law to no one but his descendants; and if the king of Samaria was also king of Israel it was virtually inevitable that the government of the kingdom of Israel should be included in the inheritance of the royal house, so long as the affairs did not—as in the exceptional case of Jehu—reverse their normal course".[22] This view requires some far reaching modifications. Every king in the ancient Near East reigned "by the grace of God", that is, his authority was charismatic, even though this was an already "routinized charisma".[23] In Egypt, the king was considered a god, while in ancient Sumer, Babylonia and Assyria the king was regarded as having been chosen by the gods, even it he had succeeded to the throne legitimately—and certainly if he had usurped the throne or founded a new dynasty. In fact, in Babylonia, and apparently in Assyria too, the gods re-confirmed the king in his office each year during the New Year festival, in the Spring, as if "choosing" him anew. The formal nomination of the king by the gods— carried out, in effect by the priest or the prophet—was thus an established principle in the theory and the practice of kingship in Mesopotamia as

---

[21] G. FOHRER, *Zeitschrift für die alttestamentliche Wissenschaft*, LXXI (1959), pp. 1-22; A. MALAMAT, *The Biblical Archaeologist*, XXVIII (1965), pp. 35-37.

[22] A. ALT, *Kleine Schriften*, II, p. 124, quoted from R. A. WILSON's translation of ALT's selected works: *Essays on Old Testament History and Religion*, p. 249.

[23] M. WEBER, *The Theory of Social and Economic Organization* (paperback edition), (New York, 1964), p. 366.

60 HAYIM TADMOR

well as in ancient Anatolia and in Ugarit;[24] in this respect there was
nothing unique about the kingship in Israel or Judah. And as for the
dynastic principle, here too, Israel was not different from other kingdoms of the ancient Near East: none of them recognized a monarchy
that was not hereditary. True, from time to time there were interruptions
in the order of succession or changes of dynasty, but the dynastic principle as such was never questioned in any of the kingdoms we know of,
large or small. No king—even a usurper who ascended the throne by
force—believed that he would reign temporarily, but trusted that he and
his sons would reign "forever". In Israel, Jeroboam, Baasa, Omri, and
Menahem ben Gadi founded dynasties and were indeed succeeded by
their sons, if only for a year or two. The cessation and the destruction
of their dynasties within one or two generations resulted not from any
particular ideology, but from the social and political upheavals of their
time.

Furthermore, there is no evidence to support the hypothesis that as
far as the dynastic principle was concerned, Samaria was different from
the rest of Israel. It was not designed as a separate entity—a city-state
within a state—but as a capital, the king's city, on the pattern of royal
cities or new capitals built in the ancient Near East by ambitious kings
who wished to demonstrate, in this manner, their sovereignty and independence. Thus, for example, in Assyria Ashurnasirpal II built Calah
(Nimrud), and Sargon II built Dur-Sharrukin (Khorsabad).[25] Unlike
the citizens of the ancient temple-cities, the inhabitants of these new cities
received no special privileges.[26] Even Jerusalem—which according to
Alt's hypothesis served as the prototype for Samaria—has never been a
corpus separatum with the kingdom of Judah, and David was never
regarded as "king of Jerusalem", but as king of Judah and of Israel.
From the references to the "inhabitants of Jerusalem" as separate from
the "men of Judah" (e.g. Isaiah 5: 3) one should not infer that its inhabitants had a separate constitution or enjoyed special status—just as such
an inference would be unwarranted in the case of Constantinople, despite
its sacred and honoured position in the Byzantine empire, or in the case
of Moscow in the Russian empire.

[24] R. LABAT, *Le caractère religieux de la royauté assyro-babylonienne* (Paris,
1939), pp. 95-117; H. FRANKFORT, *Kingship and the Gods* (Chicago, 1948), pp. 231-
248; O. R. GURNEY, "Hittite Kingship", in S. A. HOOKE, ed., *Myth, Ritual and Kingship* (Oxford, 1958), pp. 114-119; J. GRAY, *The Legacy of Canaan* (Leiden, 1957),
pp. 160 ff.; A. R. RAINEY, *The Social Structure of Ugarit*, pp. 22 ff. (in Hebrew).
    [25] D. D. LUCKENBILL, *Ancient Records of Assyria and Babylonia* (Chicago, 1927),
II, pp. 63 ff. Sargon states, in this and in similar inscriptions, that the land on which
the new city was built was purchased from the legal owners at the full price—exactly
as in the case of Omri in Samaria (II Kings 16: 24).
    [26] W. F. LEEMANS, *Symbolae van Oven* (Leiden, 1946), pp. 36-61; H. TADMOR,
*City and Community: Lectures delivered at the XII Convention of the Historical
Society of Israel* (Jerusalem, 1967), pp. 189-203 (in Hebrew).

As we have indicated above Alt's concept on the nature of the kingship in Israel has led to the view that it was based on a covenant between the king and the people, renewed whenever a new king assumed the throne. This view, however, cannot be accepted. Only twice—as attested —were covenants concluded between the king and the people: once, between David and the elders of Israel at Hebron, when having already been king of Judah, he became king of all Israel (II Sam. 5: 3). Another covenant—as reported—was made between the people and the seven-year-old king Jehoash (II Kings 11: 17),[27] who was hidden for six years in the house of Jehoiada, the High Priest, after Athalia had "destroyed all the royal family" (11:1). Both cases are exceptional, the result of extraordinary circumstances. In the first case—the Davidic dynasty was established, in the second it was restored. In no other time had the kings of Judah made covenants with the people nor is there any evidence that the kings of Israel, including Jeroboam, ever did so.

In fact, covenants between the people and the king are not attested in the ancient Near East. Entirely different is the Assyrian "loyalty oath" to a new king, the adē [28] which the officials, the courtiers and the vassal kings were required to take, particularly if the order of succession was irregular. Thus, for example, Sennacherib made his people swear an oath of allegiance ("over water and oil") that they would remain loyal to Esarhaddon his son who, by his own admission and according to independent testimony, was not the first-born.[29] Similarly, when Esarhaddon, in his lifetime, divided his kingdom between his two sons, Ashurbanipal and Shamash-shum-ukin, he made all the palace officials, the army and "all the people of Assyria small and great" as well as the vassal kings, take an oath that they would not revolt against his heirs nor support anyone who might attempt to violate the order he had determined.[30] Upon Esarhaddon's death the queen-mother hastened to impose an oath of loyalty upon Ashurbanipal's brothers, the state officials and the people.[31]

It may perhaps be conjectured—though no proof exists—that also in Judah and in Israel the court officials took an oath of loyalty to the king. Attention should be drawn to the term pasho'a, lit. "to transgress"

[27] The text says: "And Jehoiadah made a covenant between the Lord and the king and people that they should be the Lord's people, and also between the king and the people." On the question whether this was one or two separate covenants see A. MALAMAT, The Biblical Archaeologist, XXVIII (1965), p. 37; M. NOTH, The Laws of the Pentateuch and other Essays, pp. 115-116. The religious character of this covenant—which resulted in the abolition of the Baal worship in Jerusalem—is rightly stressed by J. LIVER, Enc. Miqr., IV, cols. 1090 ff.
[28] E. J. GELB, Bibliotheca Orientalis, XIX (1962), pp. 161-162.
[29] R. CAMPBELL THOMPSON, The Prisms of Esarhaddon and of Ashurbanipal (London, 1931), p. 11, lines 50-51.
[30] D. J. WISEMAN, "The Vassal-Treaties of Esarhaddon", Iraq, XX (1958), pp. 5-7.
[31] ibid., 7-8; H. LEWY, JNES, XI (1952), pp. 282-285 and esp. note 92.

—identical with the Akkadian *haṭû*—the technical term denoting the violation of a loyalty-oath on the part of the vassal.[32] *Pasho'a* is used when a vassal king, like Mesha the Moabite, or a vassal state, like Edom, rebels against the suzerain (II Kings 1: 1; 3; 8: 23). It is therefore significant that *pasho'a* is used in the story of the assembly of Shechem: "So Israel rebelled (lit. 'transgressed') against the House of David" (I Kings 12: 19). Accordingly, in the opinion of the author, or the editor of that story, the status of the tribes in relation to David was that of vassals towards their sovereigns. This ideology, though it takes for granted the existence of a covenant between the Davidic dynasty and the people, considers the king as the senior partner; and thus, does not allow for the view that the people were legally entitled to nullify the covenant whenever they felt this was justified.

D. Kings and People in Israel and Judah

The rest of our study is concerned with the extent of the authority exerted by the people in crowning kings in the separate states of Israel and Judah. Indeed, the contrast between the status of the monarchy in Israel and that in Judah is striking: whereas the latter was ruled for over 400 years by a single stable dynasty, which cultivated an ideology of sanctity that surrounded its founder and that emanated to all of his successors, the ruling dynasties in Israel had short lives, and were replaced every few generations in cruel revolts. The paramount tension among the tribal-territories in Israel, the social and class contrasts within the kingdom, and the vitality of the bodies traditionally opposing authoritarian monarchy—all combined to create a natural background for violent interruptions in dynastic continuity. In theory, the people remained the ultimate source of the royal authority, and it was they who had to give their approval to the usurper, the founder of a new dynasty. But in practice it was the army, in effect the commanders of the army, who produced the new king from among their own number. In other words, the army officers became now the source of authority, i.e. "the people". Thus, Nadab, Jeroboam's successor was killed in a military camp in time of war against the Philistines, when he and "all Israel were laying siege to Gibbethon" (I Kings 15: 27). His murderer, Baasa, of the tribe of Issachar, who was properly crowned by the same body—"all Israel"—annihilated all the House of Jeroboam; though not explicitly stated in the chronicle, it is very likely that he himself was an army commander. Baasa's dynasty was likewise destroyed in a military *coup d'état*, by Zimri, commander "of half his chariots" (I Kings 16: 9), but the latter did not win the support of the people. The army which was again encamped at Gibbethon, made haste to crown Omri, the commander of

---

[32] *The Assyrian Dictionary* (Chicago, 1956), volume IV, p. 157 b.

the army. While Omri's military camp is called "all Israel" (ibid., 16: 16), we read in a following passage (ibid., 21-22) that a competitor to Omri arose—Tibni ben Ginath—who was chosen king by a different part of the people (perhaps the army brigade that was encamped in the north); and that only four years later Omri triumphed over his rival. Jehu, who overthrew the house of Omri, was likewise an army general and was crowned by his fellow officers in a military camp, at Ramoth-gilead, during the war against the Arameans (II Kings 9: 13). It is not stated whether the army took part in the coup d'état against Zechariah, the last of Jehu's dynasty, but it seems that Menahem, who came to the throne in the following coup, relied on the support of the army when he exacted from gibborei ha-ḥayil the sum of one thousand talents of silver "to give to the king of Assyria" (II Kings 15: 20).[33] Pekah the Gileadite, who overthrew Menahem's son was also an army commander—a shalish ("the third man in the chariot", "captain", ibid., 25). According to the chronicle (ibid.), he was aided only by fifty Gileadites, but it may be that in this period the real influence had passed to the noblemen from the Gilead. The power of the military commanders manifested in the surprising fact that during the last four years of Samaria—from the imprisonment of Hoshea, its last king, by Shalmaneser V king of Assyria in 724/3, and to its final conquest by Sargon in 720—it was they, as far as we can judge, who managed the affairs of Samaria, without even producing a king from their midst.[34]

The growth of the authority of the army was the outcome of repeated military coups, which occurred in times of crises, generally as the result of a defeat suffered by Israel. The House of Jeroboam was destroyed after sustaining heavy defeats, one at the hands of Egypt—in the campaign of Soshenq [35]—and the other by Judah—when Abijah, Rehoboam's

---

[33] It follows that the gibborei ha-ḥayil numbered 60,000, and such a large number certainly does not reflect the owners of large estates alone, as has sometimes been assumed, but the majority of those who went out to battle. The concept gibbor ḥayil—"a mighty man of valour"—is close in meaning to 'ish ḥayil, i.e., a qualified soldier (cf. S. E. LOEWENSTAMM, Enc. Miqr., II, cols. 397 ff.). Yet it carries also a social connotation, since those who bore the burden of military service were mainly the independent farmers, the freeholders, who may even have been required to equip themselves. The classical example of a gibbor ḥayil holding a respectable social position in his city is Boaz (Ruth 2 : 2). Gideon (Judges 6 : 12) and Jeroboam I (I Kings 11 : 27) were likewise gibborei ḥayil. The military-social character of the term is evident from II Kings 24 : 14-16, which enumerates the people exiled to Babylonia in 597—the élite of Judah: 7,000 gibborei ḥayil, 1,000 craftsmen and the smiths and the royal officials and courtiers. Despite the importance of the gibborei ha-ḥayil within the military organization, one should not attribute to them so decisive a role in the Israelite society as does MAX WEBER, who regards them as the "full citizens or political peers" (Ancient Judaism, tr. and ed., Hans H. Gerth and Don Martindale [Glencoe, Illinois, 1952], pp. 13-23, 432 n. 16) and cf. J. van der PLOEG, "Le sens de gibbôr ḥail", RB (1941), pp. 120-125.

[34] H. TADMOR, Journal of Cuneiform Studies, XII (1958), pp. 35 ff., and n. 110, p. 35.

[35] B. MAZAR, UT, Suppl. IV (1957), pp. 57-66.

successor, conquered southern Ephraim including Beth-El (II Chron. 13: 15-19). The House of Baasa was destroyed after sustaining a defeat at the hands of Ben-Hadad I, king of Damascus, who conquered parts of the Galilee (I Kings 15: 20) [36], while the House of Omri was liquidated after a series of grave military set-backs: the rebellion of Mesha the Moabite, the failure of the military campaign against Moab (II Kings 3), and the crushing defeat sustained by Israel at the hands of Hazael, king of Damascus, at Ramoth-gilead. Nothing is known of the circumstances surrounding the fall of the House of Jehu (747 B.C.E.). Yet, the rise and fall of the kings of Israel after that, must be viewed against the background of the political and military decline of Israel, which followed the glorious reign of Jeroboam II (784-748)—a decline which resulted from the ascendancy of Judah under Azariah (Uzziah) and from the menacing, sudden growth of Assyria under Tiglath-Pileser III, the founder of the Assyrian empire.

In these dynastic changes the sources always stress the role of *the prophet:* no royal house was ever established or was deposed without the accordance with the word of the prophet. Thus, the House of Jeroboam rises to kingship and is overthrown in fulfilment of the prophecy of Ahijah the Shilonite (I Kings 11: 29-39; 13: 7-11). The House of Baasa is deposed conforming to the prophecy of Jehu ben Hanani (*ibid.*, 16: 1-4). While no prophecy is mentioned in connection with the rise of Omri, his destruction is prophesied by Elijah (I Kings 21: 21-22) and is carried out by his disciple Elisha (II Kings 9: 1-9). We even find a uniform pattern, repeated by almost every prophet on the eve of the downfall of a dynasty (e.g. I Kings 14: 10; 16: 4; 21: 24), which may be, as some assume, a literary pattern superimposed on the text by a late editor,[37] or, what is more likely, an integral part of the original prophetic narrative [38]. In any event, we should not doubt the historic role of prophets in the ninth century B.C.E., in the political and religious upheavals of their time. The resort of the prophets to the ideology of a holy war—and hence their attachment to the army of Israel—is clearly revealed in the days of Ahab. The prophets objected to the peace the king had arranged with Ben Hadad and forcefully insisted that he should fight against Aram (I Kings 20: 42). Elisha even goes along with the armies of Israel and Judah in the futile campaign against Moab, which bears the mark of ḥerem, a holy war (II Kings 3: 16-19). As he is about to die he encourages the king of Israel to fight against Aram "until you have made an end of them" (II Kings 13: 17). This close link between the prophet and the army is evident, in particular, in the crowning of Jehu in the battle-

---

[36] This war took place in the 26th year of the reign of Asa, king of Judah (and not in the 36th year, as in II Chron. 16 : 1), which, accordingly, was the last year of Baasa's reign. See our remarks in *Enc. Miqr.*, IV, col. 297.

[37] A. JEPSEN, *Die Quellen des Königsbüches* (Halle [Saale], 1956), pp. 76-101.

[38] Cf. J. LIVER, *Enc. Miqr.*, IV, cols. 1137 ff.

field. Thus, these early prophets were not merely faithful preservers of old tribal ideals, they were an active element exercising real influence upon the society of Israel and its army.

We have so far discussed the role of the people and the army of Israel in the making of kings. We shall now examine briefly the role of the elders. The historical sources contain no evidence that "the elders of Israel", as an institution, possessed any authority in the selection or in the approval of the king. Only in time of grave national emergency did the king take the step of seeking their support. Ahab summons "all the elders of the land" (I Kings 20: 7) in order to decide whether he should submit to the ultimatum of Ben-Hadad II, of Damascus. A few decades later, at the time of the siege of Samaria by Ben-Hadad III, the elders seek a prophecy of salvation from Elisha (II Kings 6: 32). At this time of crisis they supported the king and did not advocate a change of dynasty. In Judah, too, the "elders" are mentioned only on a single occasion, when Josiah assembles "all the elders of Judah and Jerusalem" and "all the men of Judah and all the inhabitants of Jerusalem" and "all the people, both small and great" (II Kings 23: 2) for covenant—the conclusion of the far-reaching cultic reforms.

There is one instance which epitomizes the decline of "the elders" in the kingdom of Israel, namely the story of Ahab and Naboth's vineyard (I Kings 21). The elders of Jezreel were compelled by Jezebel to play a central role in the staged trial designed to convict Naboth, on the basis of false testimony, and to execute him so that the king might acquire the vineyard. The elders, though they had the authority to try capital cases, could no longer be the bearers of justice. Henceforth, it is the prophet, who represents the interests of the freeholder and it is he who accuses the king of Israel of murder, demanding that Ahab and his sons be punished. Only when the royal institutions collapse the elders assume their initial importance and appear again as leaders of the people. This is attested first in the Babylonian exile (e.g. Jer. 29: 1) and later in Judah, in the Persian period (Ezra 6: 7).

In the last section of the present study we shall deal with the political institutions in Judah.

As in Israel, so in Judah the necessity to resort to the people or their representatives arose only when the normal order of succession was disrupted. However, the terminology here is different. The body that chose or endorsed the king was 'am ha- areṣ, lit. "the people of the land". [39]

---

[39] Of the extensive literature on the problem of 'am ha-ares, special mention should be made of the basic work of E. WÜRTHWEIN, Der 'amm ha' arez' im Alten Testament (Stuttgart, 1936); and R. de VAUX's recent article,"Sens de l'expression 'peuple du pays' dans l'Ancien Testament et le rôle politique du peuple en Israël", RA, LVIII (1964), pp. 167-172. To the detailed bibliography given on p. 172 of the latter article, there should be added: E. W. NICHOLSON, Journal of Semitic Studies, X (1965), pp. 59-66; and S. TALMON, Beth-Miqra', XXXI (1967), No. 3, pp. 28-45 (in Hebrew).

Its first occurrence as an institution is in the first crisis of the Davidic
dynasty: in the rebellion against Athalia, when '*am ha- areṣ* participated
in the coronation of the boy Jehoash (II Kings 11: 14). Later on, "the
people of the land" slay the murderers of Amon and crown Josiah
(II Kings 21: 24), and when the latter is killed they crown Jehoahaz
his son, who was not in the direct line of succession (II Kings 23: 30).
In a similar situation, when Amaziah was smitten by the king of Israel
and later killed, "all the people of Judah" made Azariah king (II Kings
14: 21). We fully agree with the scholars[40] who consider "all the people
of Judah" synonymous with '*am ha-areṣ*. It is not known what was the
procedure by which '*am ha-areṣ* acted, nor how many actually participated in the nomination of the king. It seems that here, like in Israel,
those who acted—many or few—were regarded as acting by the authority
of the people. In principle then, there is no difference between "all the
people" who crowned Omri in the camp, "the men of Israel" who crowned
David anew and '*am ha-areṣ* who crowned Josiah.

The term '*am ha-areṣ* has a long history and its meaning has undergone transformation. By its very name it denotes the population of a
country or a city-state and so we find '*am ha-areṣ* in Byblos or *nišē māti*
—lit. "the people of the land"—in Assyria. It carries the same meaning
in early Biblical contexts. When purchasing the cave of Machpelah from
Ephron the Hittite, '*am ha-areṣ* refers to the inhabitants of Hebron who
had assembled at the gate of the city as a council: "Abraham rose and
bowed to the Hittites, the people of the land" (Gen. 23: 7). In the story of
Joseph '*am ha-areṣ* refers to the inhabitants of Egypt: "Now Joseph was
governor over the land, he it was who sold to all the people of the land"
(Gen. 42: 6), while in the story of the spies '*am ha-areṣ* refers to all the
inhabitants of Canaan: "... and do not fear the people of the land, for
they are bread for us" (Num. 14: 9). In all these cases the term naturally
denotes the indigenous population, the non-Israelites. The latter are
designated by their tribal-ethnic name "Israel", "the children of Israel"
or simply "the people", hardly ever in connection with their country. [41]
The writers of the early historical narratives of the tenth-ninth centuries, as well as the great literary prophets of the eighth century have not
used this term to designate Judeans or Israelites. It is in the sources of the
sixth and the early fifth century, especially in the books of Jeremiah and
Ezekiel that '*am ha-areṣ* becomes the accepted term for the population
of Judah. "And I, behold, I make you this day a fortified city, an iron
pillar, and bronze walls, against the whole land, against the kings of

[40] Cf. WÜRTHWEIN, *op. cit.*, pp. 25 ff.; de VAUX, *op. cit.*, p. 169.

[41] More recently: A. BESTERS, *RB*, LXXIV (1967), pp. 5-23.

[42] Especially in the legal part of Ezekiel 45 : 16-22; 46 : 3-9. '*am ha-areṣ* of Leviticus 4 : 27, listed in conjunction with the "annointed priest", the '*edah*, as a whole, and
the *nasi'* (*ibid.*, 3; 13; 22)—is in the spirit of the latter usage of the term, as it means
simply "any one of the people" (who commits a sin, etc.).

Judah, its princes, its priests, and the people of the land" (Jer. 1: 18); and similarly Ezek. 22: 26-30. Clearly the following categories are excluded from 'am ha-areṣ: (1) the king (or the "ruler"—nasi"); [42] (2) nobles (sarim); (3) priests; (4) prophets. In other words, anyone who was not connected with the monarchy or its functions, with the temple or with prophecy—was considered "the people of the land". [43]

Since 'am ha-areṣ meant "the populace, the people", the poorest population was rendered by the term dalath 'am ha-areṣ "the poorest people of the land" (II Kings 24: 14) or dalath ha-'areṣ "the poorest of the land" (Jer. 40: 7). These, presumably landless tenants, or owners of a small piece of land of their own received the lands of the exiles by virtue of a decree of Gedaliah the governor, with the consent of the Babylonian authorities (Jer. 39: 10; 40: 10). On the other hand, the term 'am ha-areṣ itself was relegated more and more to the richer sector of the population, as inferred from their participation in the ceremony of the release of slaves at the time of emergency (Jer. 34: 19) [44] and from Ezekiel's denunciations of "the people of the land" as those "who have oppressed the poor and needy" (Ezek. 22: 29).

With the collapse of Judah the ethnic map of the country has changed: only the poorest of the land remained, while the majority of the original "people of the land" went into exile. At the same time Judah's neighbours settled in parts of the now desolate territory. At the beginning of the return from Babylonia, i.e. after 539 B.C.E., the prophets Haggai and Zechariah still used the expression 'am ha-areṣ in its traditional—but now anachronistic—sense, as it had been used by Jeremiah and Ezekiel: "Yet now take courage, O Zerubbabel... take courage, O Joshua, son of Jehozadak, the high priest; take courage, all you people of the land" (Hag. 2: 4); and: "Say to all the people of the land, and the priests" (Zech. 7: 5). But afterwards, in the second half of the fifth century, 'am ha-areṣ already indicated the gentiles or those whom Ezra and Nehemiah considered gentiles: the neighbouring peoples around Judah, and the Samaritans. "Then the people of the land discouraged the people of Judah"... (Ezra 4: 4). But more often the term is used in the plural: 'ammei ha-areṣ or 'ammei ha-araṣot "peoples of the land" or "of the lands" (Ezra 9: 1; 10: 2; Nehemia 9: 30). This use is in the spirit of the old connotation of 'am ha-areṣ—as it appears in the Pentateuch. [45] The

---

[43] I. D. AMUSIN, UDI, 1955, No. 2, p. 18; R. de VAUX, Institutions, (Eng. tr.), pp. 70-73.

[44] This was a unique episode in the history of the kingdom of Judah: a covenant made by Zedekiah during the siege of Jerusalem with all the sectors of society to free the Hebrew slaves. This release carries precisely the same connotation as the Babylonian andurārum, and see above note 14; cf. also M. DAVID, Oudtestamentische Studiën, V (1948), pp. 63-79.

[45] Y. KAUFMANN, History of the Religion of Israel, IV/1 (Tel Aviv, 1956), pp. 184 ff. (in Hebrew).

further development in the derogatory connotation of this term, in the period of the Mishna and the Talmud, when 'am ha-areṣ came to denote peasants, especially in the Galilee, who do not observe the Rabbinic laws, is chronologically beyond the scope of this study.[46]

To sum up: We have observed that the intervention of the people in affairs of state occurred only in times of emergency and crisis. In the kingdom of Judah, notable for its dynastic stability and for a high degree of identity between the early tribal structure and the monarchy, the people's institutions convened and acted only sporadically—when the dynastic continuity was disturbed and when there was danger that anarchy would prevail and the social stability would be undermined. In the northern kingdom these institutions functioned much more frequently. And when powerful social groups, such as army commanders, decided upon questions of state, they derived their authority from "the people", and drew their power from the people's traditional institutions.

[46] S. W. BARON, *A Social and Religious History of the Jews* (New York, 1952), I, p. 278, and n. 36 on p. 414. It should be added, that 'am ha-areṣ never was the designation of the Samaritans (I. D. AMUSIN, *UDI*, No. 2, pp. 30-35). The Talmudic sources clearly differentiate between "the 'am ha-areṣ" and the *kuti* (a Cuthean, i.e., a Samaritan).

YITZHAK F. BAER

SOCIAL IDEALS OF THE SECOND JEWISH COMMONWEALTH

The Mishnah as an historical record of social and religious life during the Second Commonwealth

I

THE current image of the great historic epoch of the Second Jewish Commonwealth is largely the creation of Christian historians and theologians. These drew mainly upon extraneous sources such as Josephus, the Apocrypha and the New Testament. Thus evolved the theory accepted by most scholars, that Jewish society established itself under the tutelage of Persian, Hellenistic and Roman rulers in the form of a "Temple-State", which for a while, under the Hasmoneans, assumed the outlines of an Hellenistic principality. Under such conditions, it was claimed, the religious life and faith of the Jews developed amidst a struggle of several political and religious sects. This process is supposed to have reached its consummation after the destruction of the Second Temple, with the establishment of a normative and definitive religious system. Normative Judaism thus came to be regarded as a religion limited to the narrow confines of the Halakhah, the historical foundations of which remained shrouded in mist.

This presentation of the historic epoch under consideration could grow out from a disregard of the intrinsic sources of Judaism. It is remarkable that even most competent scholars in the field of history and religion, not excepting Jewish scholars with an excellent command of the Talmud, have failed to treat Jewish source material in accordance with critical methods universally applied to the study of Roman and Greek history. The marks of inadequate historical training are yet evident, even in the work of outstanding modern commentators of the Mishnah, who suffer from an insufficient grasp of the documentary significance of the rulings of early masters of the Halakhah.

The Mishnah furnishes us with a system of Halakhot, which constituted the inner basis of social and political life in the Land of Judea and Eretz Israel during a period beginning with the rise of Hellenism until after the destruction of the Second Temple. Strictly speaking, several Halakhot in the Mishnah are ascribed to Tannaim who lived in the post-Temple era; however, these are presented principally as ancient oral traditions, of which different versions have been handed down. Moreover, even when such Halakhot are interpreted by the Tannaim each according to the light of his own reason, the substance of their assertions no doubt grew from traditions rooted in the historical reality of a much earlier period. We are on less firm historical ground in the evaluation of the early origin of rabbinic pronouncements contained in the Baraita and Tossefta and Midreshë Halakhah, wherein each pronouncement must, after close historical scrutiny, be adjudged on its own merits. The Mishnah, on the other hand, ought to be regarded as essentially a self-contained body of laws and a living historical source, reflecting the social and religious aspirations of our forebears during the period of the Second Commonwealth.

Our principal record of the incipient stirrings of the renascent Jewish community under the royal aegis of Persia, is found in the books of Ezra and Nehemiah. Fragments of the reawakened religious activity of this period are still retained in the traditions embedded in the Mishnah. It is, however, during the Hellenistic period preceding the Hasmonean revolt, during the inner struggle against the Hellenizers and external pressure of religious persecution, and lastly during the reign of the Hasmonean princes, that the essential foundations of the Mishnah were laid. Details of the change wrought in Israel during the transition from Persian rule to the seizure of power in Egypt and Syria by Hellenistic monarchs, have receded from our view. However, both the style and contents of several Halakhot place their origin and sanction in this early period, when the borders of "Eretz Israel" did not really extend beyond those of Judea under Persian rule, with such minor adjustments as were effected by the Ptolemies. The "Eretz Israel" of the earlier Halakhah was in fact synonymous with Judea, an autonomously administered territory, but part of the Hellenistic empire; in the Jewish conception—a domain of sanctity set apart from the profane regions surrounding Israel, viz. the Land of the Gentiles (Eretz ha-amim) in the comprehensive terminology of the Halakhah. Judea of the Hellenistic period was a province of "Syria"—in Mishnaic parlance—viz. "Syria and Phoenicia" or "Syria", more particularly the southern part of Syria, an administrative region controlled by officers of the Hellenist rulers of Egypt. The "Medinat Hayam" (sea-coast) of the earlier Halakhah refers to the "Paralia", a region comprising the Hellenized Phoenician towns of the sea-coast. After the conquest of these territories as well as considerable sections of Ptolemaic and Seleucid Syria by the Hasmonean kings, the original significance of these notions became largely obscured. Indeed, latter Halakhic authorities, endeavouring to elucidate the political concepts of an earlier age were hard put in attempting to harmonize these with an historical scene, which had undergone radical change. Such was the limited geographic and political framework within which the Halakhah arose and its course of development paralleled the extension of Ḥasmonean power.

The laying of the earliest foundations of the Mishnah must therefore belong to an earlier period than has been generally conceded. The developments which took place on Eretz Israel soil between the early formative stage to the final maturity of Mishnaic Halakhah, certainly constitute one of the grandest chapters in Jewish as well as world history. The earliest phase of consequence in this drama actually coincided with the creation of the basic Halakhic tenets of the Mishnah. This process opens with the rise of the Hellenistic empires of the Ptolemaic and Seleucid dynasties and it extended down to the eclipse of Ḥasmonean rule in Eretz Israel.

The full Jewish and human significance of this epoch will not be realized unless it is viewed in terms of an encounter between Jewish monotheism and the polytheistic religion of classical Greece and of the Hellenistic epoch. The increasing inroads made upon the very core of Judaism by the Hellenizers, coupled with the great religious persecutions of Antiochus Epiphanes, spelled the peak of this contest. Whatever their violence, these upheavals could not, for any length of time, retard the unfolding of Jewish faith and the Halakhah. The Maccabees restored the integrity of the traditional framework of Judaism, which had suffered encroachments at the hands of traitors and foreign persecutors. The social and religious foundations of the Jewish commonwealth could thus withstand the vicissitudes of political change during the latter period of the Second Commonwealth. Though of overriding interest, the cardinal religious issue involved in this situation cannot be gone into within the limits of this article, except insofar as it illustrates the humanizing influence upon the social order, effected by the monotheistic faith of Judaism and the means chosen by the latter for implementing ideals regarded as utopian within the context of the realities of antiquity.

Prior to any further elaboration, a general description of the character of Jewish society and spiritual leadership during the Second Commonwealth is, however, called for. It has already been mentioned that the Mishnaic Halakhah arose within the limited confines of a small semiautonomous country, which succeeded in retaining its peculiar character in spite of being subordinated to the rationally conceived administration of Hellenist potentates. In several of its basic traits the society which gave rise to Mishnaic Halakhah reminds us of the "polis" of classical Greece—of the ancient city-states with their centrally placed sacred shrines. The kinship of the emergent Jewish society of the Second Commonwealth with the Greek "polis" expressed itself both in an affinity of basic structure as well as through ties of a more direct form.

The ancient cities of the classical period, whether situated on the Greek mainland, on the Aegean Islands, or in the Near East, continued to exist in Hellenistic times, retaining in some form the traditions of the classical era. The heritage of the "polis" was likewise perpetuated by Greek settlers in the colonies founded on territories conquered by Alexander the Great and his heirs. Such were the intermediate channels, through which entire sections of Greek municipal law filtered through into Judea and were subsequently incorporated into Mishnaic Halakhah.

The influence of classical Greek law can be discerned in several chapters of Mishnaic Halakhah—concerning the status of citizen and stranger, the constitution of the family, the laws of inheritance, legal and economic prerogatives of married women, laws relating to damages and injuries, the regulations of neighbourly relations, etc.

In some chapters of the Mishnah, we seem to behold the outlines of a small Hellenistic townlet. The Halakhot of the Mishna Demqi, ch. 2, 4-ch. 5, fit the life of a capital city, namely Jerusalem, and remind us of the social order and administration of the city of Athens during its period of decline. Thus, we meet in several Mishnaic Halakhot Greek concepts in their original form, extracted from the legal terminology of classical Greece. The influence of the Latin language, on the other hand, is both rare and insignificant. Evidently, the Mishnah also contains rudiments traceable to the heritage of the ancient East. Essentailly, however, the Halakhah and the social structure which evolved from it, owe their existence to ideals which both the rabbis and the public at large spontaneously derived from the Biblical and prophetic heritage. Properly, the Halakhah must thus be classed as one of the most original and magnificent products of the Hebrew genius.

The spiritual leaders of Jewry strove to follow in the footsteps of their illustrious mentors from the Biblical scene and thus they contributed to the solution of religious and social problems raised by the encounter with Hellenistic civilization. The early Halakhah refers either to the "Men of the Great Assembly", or to interdictions proclaimed by the "Scribes" and known as "Divrë Soferim". Their origin may be dated to the beginning of the Hellenistic period. In the main, Halakhic development sprang from a close union between the "Ḥakhamim" and broad strata of the entire population. Thus was the Halakhic lore studied and orally transmitted to posterity—a unique process, peculiar to the history of Jewry.

The laws and customs of all the nations of antiquity at first constituted an oral lore, committed to memory in a rhythmic style and thus conveyed to succeeding generations. In the seventh century B. C. the

Greeks committed their system of laws to writing in an effort to protect the population from the despotism of oligarchies. Among the Jews the axiomatic position of the written Torah had by then been established. The novel laws and Halakhic rulings of the Second Commonwealth, finally sanctioned as "Oral Torah" beside the Mosaic "Written Torah", achieved their consecrated status through the very act of being transmitted orally. From the very earliest this method of studying Halakhah by heart has served as an effective instrument of popular education and as such it has survived in the Talmudic academies down to our own days.

The character of the Judean Commonwealth was determined by the Ḥakhamim whose origin was not restricted to a single class, who maintained a close association with the popular strata of the community.

The oral method of study and transmission of the Mishnah is attested by certain rhythmic elements in the structure of the Mishnah, by the recurrence of modes of expression—not always in the proper context, by archaisms which the latter transmitters of Halakhah already found difficult to understand, and by mutually inconsistent passages. These characteristics could hardly be accounted for in a work transmitted through a literary medium.

A study of the mode of development and transmission of the Halakhah inevitably brings to light the character of the small state which rose at first in Judea and subsequently expanded during the Ḥasmonean period.

As long as the Temple existed and the inner autonomy of the Jewish state was not altogether extinct, the essential traits of the commonwealth could not really be affected, even after the transfer of political power into the hands of Herod and his heirs and of the Roman procurators. Through all these vicissitudes the Jewish commonwealth retained the features of a popularly based and Sage-directed polity, wherein the burden of determining law and custom was equally shared by broad sections of the nation and the spiritual and political leadership. This state was not far removed in character from that of the polis of Greek classical times; its political ideals were close to those of the philosophers of those times.

We are thus in a position to reject as unhistorical the allegation that the "ancestral tradition" (παράδοσις τῶν πατέρων)—subsequently known as "Oral Torah"— had been abrogated by despotic rulers, on account of the conflict of rival religious sects (Sadducees and Pharisees). In fact, sectarianism only became rife in the last generations before the destruction of the Second Temple. The Ḥasmonean monarchs derived their mandate solely as representatives of a popular and Ḥakhamim inspired polity. Prevalent theories about the decisive role of the priesthood in the control of the affairs of state may likewise be discarded on the same grounds. The Temple service did, of course, confer upon the priests certain ritual as well as moral obligations, e. g. scrupulous maintenance of purity of stock, through strict attention to family descent and adherence to the laws of ritual purity—more especially when partaking of sacrificial food. There were, no doubt, privileges too: the various offerings due to the priests, the prerogative of heading the Sanhedrin— if deserving, the ceremony of blessing the people and so forth. Moreover, the priests naturally possessed traditions of their own concerning the sacrificial laws and other matters relating to the Temple. Nevertheless, essentially in this sphere too the study and development of the Halakhah pursued its normal course under the Ḥakhamim, who ensured proper adherence to Halakhic norms in the Temple service. As to the laws and rules of Divine Worship and sacrifice in the Temple, the priests followed the interpretation of the Ḥakhamim; prayers, in one of the Temple halls, were said in the words and order set by the "Men of the Great Assembly". In principle the priests performed their service as representatives of the people, not unlike the officials of a great commonwealth, such as classical Athens with its numerous altars. Theirs, however, was a unique and highly exalted status requiring stricter adherence to the norms of ritual and moral sanctity.

The Ḥakhamim can be generally identified with the Ḥaverim— members admitted under certain conditions to the "fraternity" (Ḥavura). The Ḥaverim were strict observers of the laws, specially the provision of tithes and ritual purity. Thus they shunned contact with the plebeian "Am Haaretz" whose observance of these regulations was open to doubt. There is a certain resemblance between the Mishnaic Ḥaverim and the Pythagoreans, who avoided the open streets and public baths, being apprehensive of contact with the masses, whose ritual state of purity was dubious. From earliest time the Ḥakhamim impressed upon the people the ritual necessity of washing hands prior to the partaking of unconsecrated food.

During the festivals the multitude of pilgrims were all regarded as Ḥaverim—"Kol Yisrael Ḥaverim"—having cleansed themselves and the vessels they carried, by lustration, before entering the Temple and eating of the sacrificial food. According to the Mishnah, (Ḥagiga II, 7) a distinction was made between four grades of ritual purity, members of the higher order avoiding contact with the lower one, which they regarded as ritually unclean. Those adhering to the fundamental laws of ritual purity called themselves "Perushim" (i.e. separated from ritual uncleanness). Opponents of the Ḥakhamim have been led to employ this term in abusive sense: "Pharisees" (Josephus, New Testament), signifying a religio-political party, which in reality never existed.

A fourfold classification of ritual purity is likewise found among the Essenes ('Εσσηνοί), who ordained lustration for anyone of a higher order coming into contact with members of a lower grade. Besides stressing rigorous observance of ritual purity the Essenes shared a communistic way of life. Private property was totally renounced and their livelihood was derived from manual labour performed in common.

As distinct from the membership of orders recognizable by external forms of conduct, the Mishnah also refers to circles of Ḥassidim, whose very designation denotes an orientation towards the inner virtues of religion. In the words of the Mishnah (Berakhot V, 1): "The Early Ḥassidim (man of piety) used to wait for an hour and then pray, in order that they might direct their heart to God."

The preceding short survey should serve the purpose of outlining the political and religious factors underlying the social forms and ideals to be investigated in the following chapters.

II Agrarian Foundations of the Commonwealth

Jewish society of the Second Commonwealth was based largely on agrarian foundations which were laid in Judea during the Hellenistic and early Ḥasmonean era. The social and economic conceptions of this period, in many respects approximating those of ancient Greece, retained their authority also in later times.

Such was the basic situation. It is borne out inter alia in the legal sphere—in the laws of damages and injuries (Nezikin). If a man caused damage or injury to his neighbour in any of the four chief actionable causes enumerated in the Mishnah, the restitution must come out of "the best of his land"; "in the choice of land" (Baba Kamma I, 1-2; Baba Meçia IX, 3; Gittin V, 1). Jews were generally assumed to be farmers, hence the stipulation: "If a man lent money to his fellow he may not take a pledge from him except only by an order from the court... and he must give back the pillow for the night-time and the plough during the day-time" (Baba Meçia IX, 13).—A ruling found, as seems, in the laws of Gortyn and those of several other cities of the Greek mainland. As in Greece, staple food consisted mainly of cereals and fruits and other produce of the land (cf. Peah VIII, 5-7; Ketuboth V, 8; Baba Meçia VII, 1-5; Maaseroth II, 7-8). Meat was consumed solely in connection with the sacrificial obligations of every Jewish man and woman, of which the paschal lamb was an outstanding example. Brief mention must here be made of the laws relating to heave-offerings and tithes, of the feasts connected with the harvest, the Sabbatical year and regulations for the provision of food during that year—as will be amplified anon.

With the exception of the unique clan of the Rekhabites, no nomadic elements dating from the Biblical era have survived into the

period of the Second Commonwealth. Indicative of the earliest layers
of the Mishnah, no doubt, is the following Halakhah: "They may not
raise small cattle in the Land of Israel, but, they may raise them in Syria
(viz. in the province of Syria, to the north of Judea), or in the wilder-
nesses that are in the Land of Israel." (Baba Kamma VII, 7.) Such enactments are typical of the preoccupations of an agrarian society wherein
the low standing and detestation of the shepherd[1] equals that of the
tax collector (Τελώνης) of Hellenistic times: "For shepherds, tax collectors and revenue farmers it is difficult to make repentance." (Tosefta
Baba Meçia, Chapter VIII; Baba Kamma 94 b.) It is to the early generations of the Hasmonean monarchy, prior to its territorial expansion,
that Josephus is referring in his apologetic work (Contra Apionem I,
60): "Indeed, we dwell in a land which does not verge upon the sea and
thus we do not enjoy the benefits of trade ('εμπορία), nor have intercourse with strangers; however, our cities are far removed from the sea
and we are tillers of the good soil which is our heritage."

Further evidence of the agricultural structure of the country may be
gathered from the rules pertaining to the return of found objects, listed
in Chapter II of the tractate Baba Meçia. Among articles allowed to be
kept by the finder, being public property (the original owners having
despaired of regaining such and thus renounced all claim), are the
following (II, 1): "wool shearings which have been brought from their
country (of origin)", viz. from beyond the borders of Judea and "stalks
of flax and strips of purple wool", viz. expensive clothing material,
beyond the reach of the ordinary citizen. An ancient tradition preserved
by R. Simeon b. Eleazar adds the following articles of commerce
('εμπορία) need not be proclaimed. "This Halakhah refers to goods imported from abroad. Articles belonging to this class were regarded by
the Halakhah as owner-less property, being unfamiliar to the population. Likewise in his state Plato prohibited the import of "franckincense
and similar perfumes, used in the service of the Gods, which come from
abroad (ξενικά), and purple (πορφύραι) and other dyes which are not
produced in the country, or the materials of any art which have to be
imported (ξενικῶν τινῶν εἰσαγωγίμων) and which are not necessary, no
one should import them" (Nomoi, 847 c).

"For he (the legislator) has nothing to do with laws about shipowners
and merchants and retailers and innkeepers and tax collectors and mines
and moneylending and compound interest and innumerable other
things—bidding good-bye to these, he gives laws to husbandmen and
shepherds[2] and bee-keepers, and to the guardians and superintendents
of their implements" (ib., 842 d).

---

[1] See inscription of Heracleia (southern Naxos) published by L. ROBERT, *Hellenica*,
VII (1949), 161s; *Zion*, VII, 49; VI, 125.
[2] Differing from the early Halakhah.

It is precisely this image of an archaic state, which is conjured up by several Mishnaic Halakhot. On the basis of the written Mosaic law, the Mishnah prohibits the taking of interest on money loans granted to fellow Jews, or the stipulation of speculative clauses suspect of an element of interest. Indeed, in no other law book of antiquity do we find such meticulous care to avoid even the least trace or shadow of interest, in the relations between man and fellow man (Baba Meçia V). At first, the only form of commerce allowed was barter: "Movable property acquires other movable property" or "movable property acquires coined money, but coined money does not acquire movable property." The chief means of acquiring the right of possession was by an act of "drawing" an object towards oneself. "Thus if the buyer had drawn fruit into his possession from the seller but had not (yet) paid him money, neither may retract; but if he had paid him money but had not (yet) drawn the fruit into his possession from the seller, either may retract." However, mention is made in the Mishnah of an ancient imprecation invoked against one who does not honour his word even when the acquisition of the fruit had not been rendered final by "drawing". (Baba Meçia IV, 1-2.)

The outlines of a Judean owner of a typical medium size estate emerge in the Halakhot of the tractate Peah. The Biblical laws of charity relating to gleaning, the forgotten sheaf and the corner of the field, are here applied by the Mishnah under the novel conditions of a later period.

From the Mishnah (Peah IV, 1-5) it is evident that in accordance with prevalent Halakhah the landowners used to lay open the fences surrounding their fields and vineyard, during certain hours of the day. The landowner supplied the needy, or he allowed them to "forage" (i.e. take their due by force) in his possessions. This Halakhah is reminiscent of the customs of the Greek plutocracy. The story is told of Athenian Cimon, that being endowed with great munificence, he ordered the removal of the fences (φραγμούς) which enclosed his lands, so that needy strangers as well as citizens might help themselves to the fruits of the soil. Furthermore, he declared his house open to all the poor, providing them with a daily light meal. Similar deeds have also been attributed to Pericles[3]. These measures, no doubt, were largely due to political considerations, yet we may trace in them the elements of a primitive communistic economy which persisted even in later times among certain Greek tribes. In his "Politics" (II, 5) Aristotle considers the question whether it is to the advantage of the state for both the land and its produce to be in communal possession. Alternatively, joint ownership would be restricted to either land or produce. He concludes that it is preferable to retain private property, but out of generosity grant the privilege of usufruct to the public at large.

[3] PLUTARCH, *Cimon* c. 10; *Pericles* c. 9; ARISTOTELES, *Ath. Politeia* 27,3.

In the Mishnah too, there is clear evidence of the view that the laws of gleaning, the forgotten sheaf and the corner, imply an underlying idea that the national territory belongs to the public as a whole.

Beside the laws of Peah, the Mishnah mentions the practice of renouncing parts of an estate. Tracts not actually constituting the "corner" of the estate could be proclaimed "public property" under the principle of "Hefker" (Peah I, 3; I, 6). According to the school of Shammai it was possible to renounce only for the benefit of the poor, whereas the school of Hillel defined Hefker as total abandoning for rich and poor alike, as practiced on the Sabbatical year (Peah VI, l'Eduyot IV, 3). Indeed, the Sabbatical law meant that all the territories of the land of Israel and their produce passed into public ownership, as "Hefker". It is to the implications of this principle that our attention must below be directed.

Beside the poor man's regular share of the crop during harvest seasons, due to him under the law of Leket, Shikkha, and Peah on the very ground harvested, there was also a three-yearly allocation of Ma'aser 'Ani (Poor man's tithe) from the threshing floor. There was a difference of opinion among Tannaim of the post-Temple era as to the details of these provisions (Peah VIII, 5). Additional care was exercised in respect of the itinerant poor. They were provided with a loaf of bread which sufficed for two meals and were also entitled to cost of lodging. Three meals were supplied on a Sabbath. Each locality boasted of a "Tamḥui" (public kitchen) from which the poor received two meals daily. There was also the "Kupah" (alms box) for the disbursement of benevolent funds on the Sabbath Eve (Peah VIII, 7). Thus arose the charitable institutions of the Jewish people, a national characteristic ever since. Foreign as these customs were to the Greek and Roman frame of mind, they had an abiding impact upon the nature of the Christian "caritas".

Sabbatical-year law is an outstanding instance of the manner in which the ideals of the written Torah were preserved in the social and political framework of the Second Hebrew Commonwealth.

Judah Maccabaeus and his men, belaguered in 163 B.C. on Mount Zion, had—according to Macc. I—to cope with an additional problem in their stand against the Syrians, due to the fact that this was 'the seventh year' (Sheviith), 'the year of letting go' (Shemittah), and there was not enough of food reserves; this throws a light upon the views of the early rigorous school of thought as to the keeping of Shemittah Law. Essentially, the original significance of the principle of "Hefker" is derived from the laws of the Sabbatical year. On the seventh year all the lands and their produce were abandoned and thus turned into public property of rich and poor alike (Peah VI, 1). For the period of an entire year private property was annulled. The early Halakhah expresses it thus: "In the Sabbatical year a man opens his vineyard and tears down the fence" (in the version of the Tosephta quoted in the Biblical commentary of Báal Haturim). Thus also Maimonides, in the section of his Code dealing with the Sabbatical and Jubilee years (IV, 24): "Anyone who encloses his vineyard or erects a fence around his field during the Sabbatical year, has violated a positive commandment of the Torah, so also one who gathers his produce into his house. On the contrary, he must renounce everything, and all are equal in their rights everywhere." A language akin to that of the early Halakhah is used by Philo ("Concerning the Commandments" II, 104): "The legislator enjoined that no area be fenced in during the Sabbatical year, to allow free passage into vineyards, olive groves, and the like, so that rich and poor alike may enjoy the produce thereof."

Historically, these Halakhot must be viewed in juxtaposition with the more extreme social schemes of the Greek philosophers. They may even be compared with the constitution of the closed oligarchic society of the Spartans whose "ancestral tradition" (Πάτριος Πολιτεία) was being revived during the very period of the 3rd century B.C.E. when laws of Peah and the Sabbatical year received their Halakhic formulation.

Though based on earlier traditions, the present version of the Mishnah in the Tractate Shebiith displays a tendency towards mitigating, as it were, the rigorous approach of antecedent authorities. An attempt is made to meet the needs of a state and its considerations of political reality, without however revoking the written Torah or earlier Halakhah. The basic definition of Sabbatical Halakhah, as presented in the Mishnah, were formulated during the Hasmonean era. Transmitted through the customary oral channels, this tractate presents the aspect of a self-contained and logically arranged law, the work of a state legislator guided by the counsel of the Hakhamim. At the same time, however, traces of the earlier Halakhah are retained.

The agricultural methods discussed by the Mishnah in the tractate Shebiith resemble the means employed at the time in most southern European countries as well as in the Near East. Several passages particularly refer to the tilling of the soil in the Judean mountains, e.g. in the tractate Peah (II, 2), wherein Biblical language is employed by the Halakhah: "If any hill top can be hoed with a mattosk, 'even though the oxen cannot pass over with the plough'" (Isaiah VII, 25). The rhythmic alliterative prose, particularly conspicuous in the tractate Shebiith, emerges as a natural background to the teamwork, customary among primitive farmers. Evidently, these Halakhot arose together with the work itself, the rhythmic beat of the toil accompanying the mental endeavour of learning by heart. Thus were the Halakhot committed to memory and delivered into the keep of later generations.

Our present version of the Mishnah, however, does not mention the abolition of the fences of field and vineyard. On the contrary, several activities connected with the preservation of private property are sanctioned. It is precisely the pulling down of a fence which is disallowed on the grounds that it constitutes an improvement of the field (cf. Mish. Shebiith III, 6-9).

And just as Mishnaic Halakhah allowed the preservation of what constituted the limits of private land property, so it was anxious to provide the entire population with an equitable allocation of food, in spite of the interdiction on harvesting, during the Sabbatical year. The autonomous warring commonwealth of the Ḥasmoneans was unable to continue the policy of general abandonment of land, instituted on the authority of earlier rigorists. It had to concern itself with providing the people with food during the seventh year as well. A series of enactments thus came into being, but were apparently removed from the orally studied Mishnaic collections and preserved in the Tosefta alone. Following is an extract from the latter: "At first the emissaries of the Beth Din would visit the towns. Whoever brought fruit (viz. cereals and other produce of the soil) in his hands, the emissaries would take it from him and give him enough for three meals. The rest was deposited in the stores of the town. At the time of the fig harvest the emissaries of the Beth Din would hire workers who hoed them and made fig cakes. These were put into barrels and deposited in the stores of the town. At the time of the grape harvest the emissaries of the Beth Din would hire workers, etc. At the time of the olive harvest the emissaries of the Beth Din would hire workers who picked the olives, packed them into the press, inserted them into barrels and deposited them in the stores of the town. From there an allocation was made on Shabbath eve to each according to his household."

This text must be understood as an enactment, as an administrative provision from the days of the Ḥasmonean commonwealth, when the judicial authorities could proceed with a strong hand.[4] At first "all the fields passed into the possession of the Beth Din", i.e. into the hands of the supreme authority of the state, being either the Sanhedrin or another body vested with State powers and acting in agreement with the Ḥakhamim. Through a network of officers the grain was collected everywhere and from everybody, as were figs, grapes and olives. Cereals and other produce of the soil were suitably processed and stored up in public depots, wherefrom each family received the necessary weekly allocation, every Sabbath eve. Beside the "emissaries of the Beth Din", charged with gathering the produce of the Sabbatical year and preparing it for distribution, there were also other officials in

---

[4] Cf. Saul LIEBERMAN's excellent treatment of this subject, *Tosefta Ki-feshutah*, I (1955), 582.

charge of public affairs during the Sabbatical year. Noteworthy, among the latter are the ones mentioned in Mishnah (Shekalim IV, 1): "The guardians of the seventh year aftergrowths of the Sabbatical year receive their pay from the Terumah of the Temple Treasury-Chamber." The following is added in the Tosefta (IV, 7): "Guardians are to be posted in the towns adjoining the border, that the gentiles may not trespass and plunder the fruits of the seventh year."

The Sabbatical-year laws give us an interesting insight into the history of nutritional problems and policies of antiquity. In the more progressive Greek cities, such as Athens, the nourishment of the population was in the care of the state. The polis would help its people in times of distress and scarcity. It took care to have reserves of grain to distribute to the needy population. The employment of public granaries (θησαυροί) was developed to the point of perfection by the administrators of Hellenistic Egypt—which, no doubt, drew upon the traditional experience of ancient Egypt.

Although the chief concern of the Ptolemaic monarchs was with the financial interests of the state, the administrative techniques they employed yet exercised a noticeable influence upon the type of Halakhah previously quoted from the Tosefta.

In comparison with the sophisticated bureaucracy of a great empire, the administrative apparatus of the Jewish state was, no doubt, rather unassuming. Moreover, the early halakhic authorities, who conceived the above-mentioned enactments, strove to emulate the ancestral spirit of austerity in public matters, as indeed in the entire conduct of their lives.

A chief characteristic of the political machinery of the Jewish state was the tendency to dispense with writing and with the service of a vast bureaucracy. Though a few Halakhot of an administrative nature such as these have survived, they yet enable us to determine the character of the "Medinat Haḥakhamim" (i.e. sage-directed polity) and its position within the political structure of antiquity.

Basically, Jewish social and political patterns displayed an affinity with those of closed societies of the Spartan or Cretan type, whose constitution inspired the utopian schemes of Plato and other philosophers. Among the latter we find a realization of the principle that all members of the civilian community are entitled to an equal share of the land and its produce. It was customary for these oligarchic countries to collect the fruits of the land for use at the communal meals (συσσίτια) of members of the ruling sect. This practice became a permanent element in their constitution. However, this privilege was largely confined to members of the oligarchic families.

In the case of the Jews, on the other hand, it was during the seventh year alone that the communal principle was applied to the soil and its products. But once in practice, at fixed six-yearly intervals, the lofty theocratic and social ideal was fully realized. For the period of a whole year the citizens of the Jewish state renounced all productive work upon their fields, abandoned their produce and handed it over to the public authorities. In turn they received their meagre food rations from the representatives and leaders of the people viz. the Ḥakhamim or public officials acting on their behalf. Thus they realized in the second Temple days the biblical injunction (Lev. XXV, 23): "The land shall not be sold absolutely, for the land is mine, for ye are strangers and sojourners with me."

According to the written Torah the Sabbatical laws of fallowing are followed by those of the Jubilee year: "It shall be a jubilee unto you: and ye shall return every man unto his family." (Lev. XXV, 10.) There is a tendency among Biblical scholars to represent the Jubilee laws as an utopian design which was never put into practice. Furthermore, modern students of the Talmud have assumed on the basis of a rabbinic tradition originating after the destruction of the Temple, that the Jubilee laws were likewise not in operation during the Second Commonwealth. A closer analysis of the Mishnah in the tractate Arakhin should, however, lead to a more positive conclusion in this matter. The substance of the Mishnah in this tractate deals with the rules of dedication to the Temple treasury of movable or landed property. In the last chapters the Mishnah discusses the effects of the Jubilee laws upon the dedication of land to the Temple viz. the validity or otherwise of such an act during the Jubilee year.

Evidently, these last chapters ought to be regarded as no less historically relevant than the preceding ones. The return of every man to his possession and family presupposes a necessary link between land and family. This bond between family and land survived throughout the Second Commonwealth, even though, during the transition from the Persian to the Hellenistic period, the constitution of the family underwent developments which may not be known to us in detail.

The Bible distinguishes between "a field of his possession" and a "field of his purchase" (Lev. XXVII, 16-22). In the Mishnah too, this distinction is made and actually applied to the laws of dedication. Such differentiations bear the unmistakable imprint of reality during the Second Commonwealth, no less than in Biblical times. Moreover, in Greece too, the law distinguished between the heritage (kleros) of a family, distributed during the settlement of a tribe or redistribution of land (γῆς ἀναδασμός) and acquired land.

A similar degree of historical relevance must be imputed inter alia to all the pronouncements of the Mishnah of the laws defining the rights of the Temple authorities in the collection and realization of property dedicated to the Temple. The powers and formulas wielded by the priests in this sphere, do not accord with the Biblical source and must thus be attributed to a later period. The points raised in the Mishnah of the tractate Arakhin in connection with the Jubilee laws are neither to be found in the written Torah, nor can they be construed as resulting from later dialectics of an academic nature. They clearly belong to the historical reality of the Second Commonwealth, when the Jubilee laws were put into actual practice and the "fields of possession" truly reverted to the original owner in accordance with Biblical injunction. The underlying idea of such a dispensation could be none other than the desire to retain a modicum of equality in the distribution of lands, not unlike the Platonic ideal elaborated in the "Laws". Such projects could not survive many generations, inasmuch as the "utopian" elements failed to endure for any length of time. This would account for the fragmentary state of the Jubilee laws found in the Mishnah.

The treatment of the remaining Jubilee laws in Mishnah Arakhin VII, 1 - IX, 2, based on Lev. XXV, 1-25, is logically followed by Arakhin IX, 3 et seq.: "If a man sold a house from among the houses in a walled city"—based upon Lev. XXV, 29: "And if a man sells a dwelling-house in a walled city." That these laws were in actual operation during the Second Commonwealth is hardly open to doubt. The Mishnah indeed mentions in this respect a well-known enactment ordained by Hillel (Arakh. IX, 4). In a further Mishnah (IX, 6) we find a description of the structure of a "dwelling-house in a walled city". By way of illustration the Mishnah refers to names of citadels and fortified villages which would place these in the reign of Alexander Jannai-Jonathan[5] (103-76 B.C.). Similar fortifications, it should be noted, were also built by the Greeks for defensive purposes. The subject-matter discussed in this chapter thus clearly emerges as an integral element in the historical reality of the Second Commonwealth.

III. Laws of the Sanhedrin

The instances of civil law cited above (p. 72) indicate how the Ḥakhaïmim and Jewish public were instrumental in assimilating Greek laws into the halakhic traditions of the "Ḥakhamim".

It is to the nature of the Sanhedrin and its conduct in the sphere of criminal law, that we must now turn in our endeavor to illustrate the

---

[5] He is designated on his coins "Yehonathan the King" (Hebrew), "of the King Alexander" (Greek), and on those stamped in later years of his reign we have "Jonathan the High Priest and the Council of the Jews" (Hebrew); see Leo Kadman-Aryeh KINDLER, *Coins of Palestine throughout the Ages* (Tel-Aviv, 1963), p. 18. Such descriptions of his office on coinage come as decisive evidence against attaching any historical value to the legend included in the Babylonian Talmud, *Tractate Kiddushin*, Fol. 66a. As to the fortifications raised by this hasmonean ruler, see JOSEPHUS, *Bellym*, I ff., *Ant.*, XIII, p. 390.

significant correlation of the Jewish and Greek traditions. An approach akin to the legal notions of the Greeks may, in fact, also be detected in the laws on the function of the Sanhedrin (Jewish Supreme Court).

Most non-Jewish scholars have hitherto subscribed to the theory that the Sanhedrin, depicted in the Mishnah as a political and legal institution, did not in fact exist during the Second Commonwealth. It was dismissed as a figment produced by retrojecting the image of the academic Sanhedrin set up by the council of Ḥakhamim at Yabneh (after the destruction of the Second Temple). This notion is countered by elements of positive law found in the Halakhot of the Sanhedrin, which demonstrate that the very constitution and function of the Sanhedrin doubtless belong to historical reality.

The term Sanhedrin (συνέδριον) is found in the annals of classical Greece as well as subsequently, especially with reference to the supreme institutions of the federative leagues. In its function as supervisor in the maintenance of law and order and as a supreme political and administrative authority, the Jewish Sanhedrin resembled the Athenian Areopagus, as depicted in the period of its pristine grandeur.

However, though structurally the Sanhedrin rather resembled the council of Ḥakhamim of Yabneh, Usha or Tiberias, its political, administrative and judicial powers indubitably place it in the politically sovereign period of the Second Commonwealth. Spiritually members of the Second Commonwealth had many points in common with the philosopher-statesmen of the Platonic ideal state.

In the opinion of Plato, the solution of contemporary problems depended upon the affairs of state being entrusted into the hands of philosophers. On several occasions he even sought to convert his ideals into reality. But, in this case too, it was among the Jews, that the utopian aspirations materialized into historical fact. This occurred during the Second Commonwealth when Eretz Israel came to be a Ḥakhamim-directed state. However, in contrast to Plato's aristocratic ideal, the ranks of the Jewish supreme political and administrative authority, viz. the Sanhedrin, consisted of "Talmidei Ḥakhamim", drawn from all the social strata. These sages were nurtured in the study of the Halakhic lore, and in turn made their own contribution to its unfolding. The Sanhedrin or Great Beth Din, consisted of 71 members and was seated in the "Chamber of Hewn Stone" in the Temple "near the altar". It presided over all matters of religion and law, and "from thence issued Torah to all Israel".

It is chiefly to the Sanhedrin as supreme judicial authority that our attention will now be given.

"The Sanhedrin was arranged like the half of a round threshing-floor, so that they might see one another... Before them sat three rows of disciples of the Sages, and each knew his proper place. If they needed to appoint (another as a judge), they appointed him from the first row, and one from the third came into the second; and they chose yet another from the congregation and set him in the third row. He did not sit in the place of the former, but he sat in the place that was proper for him." (Sanhedrin IV, 3-4.)

In the traditional account of the Tannaim and Amoraim, the composition of the Sanhedrin followed the procedure ascribed in the Bible to Moses (Num. XI, 16-17): "And the Lord said unto Moses, gather unto me seventy men of the elders of Israel... and take them unto the Tabernacle... and I will come down... and I will take some of the spirit which is upon thee...".

The ordination of members of the Sanhedrin thus appears to have been regarded as an act of transferring pneumatic powers (Siphre, Num 92; Philo, de gigantibus 24-25). Such was the spiritual soil in which the judicial procedure of the Mishnah in criminal cases was grounded. Concerning the details of the Halakhah, here all belongs to the domain of real life. Each statement expresses a sense of moral responsibility and appears in several parts in bold contrast to the customs and laws prevalent then in Greece and Rome. The procedure of the Jewish Beth Din was decidedly archaic and formal in character. The legal procedure is oral only; no written documents are brought as evidence (or proof). In the Courthouse of Israel there is no room for lawyers and advocates. Evidence was taken from two witnesses, who were put to the test "in examination and enquiry" (Mishnah Sanhedrin IV, 1). However, underlying this formalism was a keen ethical sense striving for an objective determination of facts. The only evidence admitted in the Sanhedrin was that of a Jewish freeman. Slaves were disqualified from giving evidence (Mishnah in Jerushalmi Sanhedrin III, 3, and explicitly in Mishnah Rosh Hashana 1, 8; also cf. Tosefta, Sanh. 24 b). This stood in contrast to the repulsive practice current in classical Greece, whereby evidence would be extracted from slaves against their masters by means of torture (tormenta, βάσανος), totally absent in Jewish practice. From the very outset the judicial procedure of the Sanhedrin tended towards finding argument in favour of the accused. Among Greek and Roman officers, on the other hand, this inclination was generally absent. The Mishnah Sanhedrin (V, 4) declares: "If their (the witnesses) words were found to agree together they begin (to examine the evidence) in favour of acquittal. If one of the witnesses said, 'I have somewhat to argue in favour of his acquittal'... they silenced him", for once the examination of witnesses has run its course, the witness has no right to intervene in the deliberations of the court. Similarly, if one of the disciples, sitting before the Sanhedrin, wished to argue in favour of conviction, he was likewise silenced. But if on the other hand: "One of the disciples said, 'I have somewhat to argue in favour of his acquittal'; they bring him up (to the seat of the Sanhedrin) and set him among them and he does not come down from thence the whole day. If there is aught of substance in his words they listen to him. Even if the accused said, 'I have somewhat to argue in favour of my acquittal', they listen to him; provided there is aught of substance in his words". This prerogative is retained by the accused to the very last moment before death.

Never, on the other hand, have the Hakhamim considered the possibility of extracting confessions from the mouth of the accused, or influencing him towards admitting his guilt. Self-confession, having no legal standing, has therefore never been mentioned in the laws of the Sanhedrin, in marked opposition, it would seem, to the legal principles of Greece and Rome.

In Roman law the accused was interrogated by various methods with a view to forcing a confession. In fact, Roman criminal law followed the rule: "confessus pro iudicato est"[6]. From this Roman principle, medieval jurists deduced that an admission of guilt on the part of the accused constituted the "queen of testimonies" (Regina Probationum).

As stated before, the sole basis for the conduct of a trial was the evidence of two witnesses. These would be tested by "examination and inquiry" (Sanhedrin IV, 1-5; V, 1-3), viz. the court would investigate

[6] Cf. R. MOMMSEN, *Römisches Strafrecht* (1899), pp. 437–438. It is likewise in the traditions of Roman criminal procedure that we are led in the account of the interrogation of Jesus by the High Priest before the Sanhedrin, as told in the gospel of Mark. In the first stage of the trial evidence is invited against the accused, the court taking note of testimonies and denunciations. Upon further investigation, several utterances of the witnesses are invalidated, having contradicted each other. Finally, the High Priest rises, intent upon eliciting an admission of guilt (confessio) from the accused. At first, the latter remains silent; but when asked a second time he fully confesses to his Messianic mission. Thereupon the High Priest proclaims: "What need we any further witnesses?", and the Sanhedrin unanimously condemns him to be guilty. The legal procedure presumed by the author of this gospel story conforms to the Roman pattern, with which he was, no doubt, familiar from the trials of Christians by Roman officers. His story fails to show the slightest trace of conformity to Jewish law. Neither is it possible to maintain the veracity of the gospel account by arguing that the Jews condemned Jesus in contravention of their law, having recourse to "emergency provisions". The real nature of such provisions is expressed in the following opinion of R. Eliezer b. Jacob (B. Sanhedrin 46 a: Yebamoth 90 b): "I heard that even when not in agreement with the Torah Beth Din may impose flagellation and punish; not, however, for the purpose of transgressing the words of the Torah but in order to make a fence for the Torah." It is evident that the case in question deals with the meting out of punishment, harder than stipulated by law and not with any change in legal procedure. The non-acceptance of admissions of guilt (confessio) uttered by the accused is fundamental to the legal principles of Halakhah; the confession of the accused, moreover, does not even come up for consideration at court. Neither is it tenable to assume that a later Beth Din could alter a sacred and codified Halakhah deriving from early authority, and accept a foreign course, the purport of which it could hardly grasp. Cf. my article in *Zion* 31 (1966). Of a different opinion is the apologetical article of Ḥaim H. COHN, "Reflections on the Trial and Death of Jesus", *Israel Law Review Association*, 1967.

whether their statements agreed as to the time and place of the act in question. There was also the possibility of refutation of witnesses by proving an alibi (Hazamah), if the evidence was denied and contradicted by a pair of opposing witnesses claiming: "How can ye testify so, for lo, ye were with us that same day in such a place" (Makkoth I, 4). Likewise proof was required of the witnesses "that they had warned the accused prior to his criminal act" (Hathraa: Sanhedrin V, 1; VIII, 4; X, 4; Makkoth I, 8-9)—a stipulation which may have originated within the narrow confines of a small townlet, where all inhabitants knew one another personally and where the designs of fellow men were similarly known to all. No oath was demanded from witnesses, needless to say neither from the accused. The witnesses "were inspired with awe" (Sanhedrin IV, 5) instead. To get at the core of the sense of the "inspiring with awe" formulas quoted in the Mishnah, we should look to the oath formula current in Greece. In murder cases brought before the Areopagus court of Athens, the accuser, the accused and the witnesses had to take an awe-inspiring oath in front of animal sacrifices brought to the gods of oath. This oath was not intended to serve as judicial proof; its importance was sacral only. The accused gave his case in the hands of heaven; he proclaimed, "that if his oath was lying, let there be a curse of perdition on himself, on his progeny, on his house and family". Comparison with this enables to understand the formula of admonition to the witnesses before the Jewish Court: "Know then that capital cases are not like monetary cases. In civil suits, one can make monetary restitutions and thereby effect his atonement; but in capital cases he is held responsible for his blood (sc. the accused's) and the blood of his (potential) descendants until the end of time." The court would then proceed to add a general rule: "For this reason Adam was created as unique in the world, to teach that if any man has caused a single soul to perish, they impute to him in Heaven as though he has caused a whole world to perish; and if any man saves alive a single soul, they impute to him as though he had saved alive a whole world." (Sanhedrin IV, 5.) Thus we meet the supreme court of the Second Commonwealth in the role of an educational institution, proclaiming a universal humanitarian message to the immediate public as well as to future generations.

All in all, the legal procedure of antiquity was brief. In the Platonic version of the "Apology", the accused Socrates complains to the Athenians for not having accepted the legal practice current in other Greek states, whereby criminal cases were not concluded in a single day, but were accorded several days. In the Mishnah, on the other hand, it is written: "In capital cases, a verdict of acquittal may be reached the same day, but a verdict of conviction not until the following day." (Sanhedrin IV, 1). Subsequently (*ib.* V, 5) this principle is reemphasized and reasons for the postponement of the verdict are adduced in solemn prose and a rhythmic style, reflecting the deep sense of responsibility animating all pronouncements dealing with this subject. Thus: "If they found him not guilty, they set him free; otherwise, the trial adjourned until the following day, whilst they go about together in pairs, they practise moderation in food, drink no wine the whole day, and they discuss the matter (theoretically) throughout the night, and early on the next morning they came to court." Only then was the final decision arrived at and the verdict proclaimed.

The deliberations proceeded entirely by memory, as was also the custom in ancient Athens. There were, however, aspects peculiar to the Jewish Beth Din: "Before them (i. e. the Sanhedrin) stood the two scribes of the judges, one to the right and one to the left, and they wrote down the words of them that favoured acquittal and the words of them that favoured conviction." (*ib.* IV, 3.) Moreover, at the last session, the judges could either confirm their views, expressed during the first session, or alter the verdict from "guilty" to "innocent"; but they could not condemn one whom they held to be innocent in the previous session. If the judges erred in the matter, then "the scribes of the judges must put them in remembrance". Finally, "they take a vote" (*ib.* V, 5). The final verdict was not committed to writing, nor was the evidence given by the witnessed written down. Viewed as a whole, the procedure of the Sanhedrin is certainly a unique phenomenon in the history of law. In it we find a manifestation of monotheistic faith and an affirmation of the eternal value of each individual human soul. In the words of the Mishnah (*ib.* IV, 5): "The Holy One, blessed is he, has stamped every man with the seal of the first man, yet not one of them is like his fellow." It must, on the other hand, be admitted that cases involving the alien were apparently not brought before the Sanhedrin. Concerning the resident stranger (Ger Toshav) see further on.

The execution of the "four forms of capital punishment" of the Beth Din wask no doubt cruel. So, indeed, was all capital punishment of antiquity, as at all times. The means of execution in ancient times were influenced by prevalent religious motives. It was not to cause degradation to the human body, created as it was in the image of God[7]. Needless to say, the condemned was at no time subjected to cruel abuse, prior to execution, an accepted practice among the gentiles.

In Jewish law, the death penalty also applied to idolatry or to the act of seducing to idol worship, to a whole town condemned for idolatry and to blasphemy. For the most part, these laws may date to Ḥasmonean times. Also punishable by death were sexual relations of an adulterous or incestuous nature. The desecration of the Sabbath was likewise a capital offence, though no such verdict has come really to our notice except for Ḥasmonean times. In the case of the "rebellious

[7] Cf. A. BÜCHLER, *M.G.W.J.* 50 (1906).

and stubborn son", the law may, in fact, have been applied by earlier generations, who, side by side with Plato, held the opinion that "the death of the ungodly is a benefit to them and a benefit to the whole world" (Sanhedrin VIII, 5).

Of great general interest is the law of "The elder that rebels against the decision of the court" (Sanhedrin XI, 2-4). He is a sage who stands on his opinions against the Halakhah accepted and rendered statutory by the "Great Beth Din which is in Jerusalem". According to one tradition he is put to death during one of the festivals, so as to fulfil the verse: "and all the people shall hear, and be afraid" (Deut. XVII, 13). According to another version he is executed without delay and the message is written and dispatched far and wide by means of messengers, that the person in question has been condemned to death by the Beth Din. This Mishnah reflects the powers of the Sanhedrin as supreme legislative body and final arbiter in judicial as well as ritual matters affecting the commonwealth during the various stages of Halakhic development. From the "Laws" of Plato, we learn that a similar institution may also have existed in Greece or is to be explained as an utopic fiction of the great philosopher. It might also be noted in this context that the law of "The ox that is to be stoned (is judged) by three and twenty" (Sanhedrin I, 4), too has its analogy in Greece and among the Germans, where an animal guilty of manslaughter was condemned to death by sacral procedure. Minor infractions, not calling for the death penalty, were punished by flogging (Malkoth). Furthermore, it is stated: "If a man was scourged a second time, the court must put him in a pillory... If a man committed murder, but there were no witnesses, they must put him in a pillory" (Sanhedrin IX, 5)—by all appearance but a temporary infliction. The remaining material of this Mishnah is but latter-day addition. The mishnaic "kipa" is but a corruption of Κύφων i. e. "pillory" or "block".

Already in the written Torah we are taught to differentiate between acts committed unwittingly or wittingly, between intention and deed. In the Mishnah we find additional stipulations and definitions, which are paralleled in Cretan and Athenian laws of the 5th and 4th centuries B. C. E., as in the writings of Plato. "If a murderer had struck his fellow with a stone or with (an instrument of) iron, or if he had forced him down into the water or into the fire and he could not arise out of it, and he died, he is guilty. If he pushed him (and he fell) into the water or into the fire and he could arise out of it, and yet he died, he is not guilty." (Sanhedrin IX, 1.) "If he had intended to kill a beast and killed a man, or an alien and killed an Israelite, or an untimely birth and killed an offspring that was likely to live, he is not culpable" (Ib., ib. 2.)

"If a man caused fire to break out at the hand of a dead-mute, an imbecile or a minor, he is not culpable by the laws of man, but he is

culpable by the laws of Heaven.[8] If he caused it to break out at the
hand of one of sound senses, this one is culpable", as it was declared
that "there is no agent for an illegal act". "If one brought the fire and
then another brought the wood, he that brought the wood is culpable",
etc. (Baba Kamma VI, 4.) In matters such as these, no difference is felt
between Greek and Jewish dialectics.

This process of reasoning assumes added significance in regard to
the laws of a man "who killed a soul unwittingly" (Makoth Chapter II).
These constitute a revealing chapter in the legal development of human
society at large. Formerly, the disposal of an homicide, whether inten-
tional or inadvertent, was left to the judgement of the family of the
slain. Mosaic law was among the first to circumscribe the prerogative
of blood vengeance, held by the representative of the slain's next of kin.
Accordingly, the community or Beth Din were charged with taking the
final decision in the matter. In the view of the Mishnah it is for the
Beth Din to decide whether the slayer had acted with malice afore-
thought or otherwise. If the act was unpremeditated, the slayer was
exiled to one of the cities of refuge already existing in Biblical times
as also in the reconstituted Second Hebrew Commonwealth. The reservations of modern scholars notwithstanding, this socalled utopian
scheme has twice in Jewish history been translated into social and political reality.[9] Already in ancient Egypt outlaws could seek refuge
within the precincts of temples. The confines of the sanctuaries were
marked by inscriptions engraved upon stone pillars and surrounding
temple walls. In classical Greece and Hellenistic countries, there was
an accepted right of asylum (asylon, asylia) in cities and states dedicated to a deity (e. g. Dionysus or Apollo). No one was to be harmed in
these places. In Attica no cities of refuge were specifically set aside and
a person found guilty of unpremeditated homicide was condemned to
leave his homeland and go into exile (Φεύγειν) beyond its borders.
For the very presence of the murderer, so the Greeks believed, caused
the land to be polluted. In Eretz Israel of the Biblical era as well as
during the Second Commonwealth, a whole network of cities of refuge
was set up, granting asylum to homicides, as has been pointed out.
These were sanctified cities in a Holy Land.

Both the elaborate Attic legal code (or the Platonic "Laws"—based
on the legal traditions of the philosopher's home country), as well as
Mishnaic Halakhah—based on the written Torah, did not altogether
abolish the law of blood revenge. Rather did it effect a compromise, as
it were, between the avenger and the state. The blood avenger was not

[8] This is a legal concept, the like of which is found in Greece too, see also note.
[9] Cf. Y. F. BAER, "The Historical Foundations of the Halakha," *Zion*, XVII (1952),
pp. 13 ff.; idem, *Israel among the Nations* (Jerusalem, 1955), 68 ff.; B. Z. DINUR, "The
Religious Character of the Cities of Refuge and the Ceremony of Admission into
Them," *Eretz Israel*, III (Jerusalem, 1954), pp. 135–146.

allowed to harm the shedder of blood until the latter was brought before a Beth Din. Two "Talmidei Ḥakhamim" were delegated by the Sanhedrin to escort the unwiting manslayer to his city of refuge and protect him "in case anyone attempted to slay him on the way". The emissaries of the Beth Din were instructed to appeal to the blood avenger in a certain set style indicated in the Mishnah by the words: "and that they might speak to him" (i.e. the blood avenger). According to the Baraita (Sanhedrin 10b.; Tosefta III, (2)5), the following appeal is made to the blood avenger: "Do not treat him after the manner of shedders of blood; it was but in error that he had a hand in it." A reference may here be discerned to an accepted formula, akin to that of the Greek pacification appeal employed by the murderer in his address to the next of kin of the murdered.

If the murderer departed beyond the confines of his sanctuary and was subsequently found by the blood avenger, the latter had the right to kill him. This prerogative was retained by the avenger at all events: "That for the avenger it is a matter of obligation (to strike); for everyone else, a matter of option" in one opinion, and according to another authority: "the avenger of blood has the right" (Makoth II, 7) to do so. The verdict of exile to a city of refuge did not apply solely in the case of a feud where both parties were Jews, but also to the resident stranger (Metoikos). In other words, the Jewish commonwealth was willing to extend its protection also to strangers whose terms of residence in the land of Israel were defined in a specific covenant. The conditions included acceptance of certain moral obligations implied in the monotheistic creed (the Seven Noakhian laws). "A resident alien need not go into exile save only because of (another) resident alien", says the Mishnah. More than this we cannot determine with any degree of certainty. In the opinion of later commentaries, the verdict of exile also applied to a Jew who has unwittingly killed a resident stranger. According to another opinion a resident stranger who has unwittingly killed a Jew, was not sent into exile but put to death. This view need not, however, be accepted. It is possible that he was compelled to leave the country. Such, in fact, was the legal course pursued by the Attic state in all cases of involuntary murder. Needless to say, much depended on the nature of political circumstances, such as the degree of Jewish ascendency at any specific time.

In summation, this article—as far as space here allows—goes to prove that it is unthinkable, that the Halakhot of the Mishnah can be interpreted as the product of purely theoretical considerations. The very character of the halakhic matters dealt with in this article attests, that they could not have evolved in midair, as it were, but must be placed upon the terra firma of the historical scene to which they properly belong.

MENAHEM STERN

THE HASMONEAN REVOLT AND ITS PLACE IN THE HISTORY OF JEWISH SOCIETY AND RELIGION

IN the fourth decade of the second century B.C.E., a time when the political fate of the Mediterranean world was decided by the victory of the Roman Republic over Macedonia in the Battle of Pydna (168 B.C.E.) and by its political intervention in Egypt, tremendous events took place in Judea, the results of which were destined eventually to determine the spiritual and religious character of both the Near East and Europe.

The events in Judea were unusual in the history of ancient times in that they involved the total religious persecution of an entire nation, and whatever its original object may have been it soon turned into a war of religion and an ideological clash. It was regarded in this light by the persons who were active at the time of the crisis itself, and this is how its significance was understood by those Jews and non-Jews who were influenced by the experiences of the persecution and of the revolt which came in its wake.

The decrees of Antiochus IV Epiphanes (175-164 B.C.E.) against the Jewish religion were issued at a time when the prestige of the Seleucid dynasty had already waned considerably. The defeat suffered by Epiphanes' father, Antiochus III, at the hands of the Romans, and the peace treaty that terminated the war, curtailed the area of the kingdom and reduced its military potential. When Antiochus IV, after a struggle, secured his hold over Antioch, he found himself the king of a power which, though still strong, was smaller in size than it had been, less wealthy, and the prestige of which was impaired. Whenever an important political matter came up, it now, like the other states of the Hellenistic East, had to take into account the reaction of the Roman Republic.

Throughout his reign, Antiochus displayed vigorous activity in the political and military spheres, with the aim of strengthening the power of his kingdom. In Asia Minor he maintained close relations with the kingdoms of Pergamum and Cappadocia, while the ancient Greek cities of Megalopolis, Olympia and, above all, Athens, all benefited from the king's munificence. From the military point of view, the first years of his reign were colored by the tension, which had become traditional, in his relations with Ptolemaic Egypt, and it was the southern border of the kingdom on which Antiochus focused his military efforts. The tension developed into an armed conflict which, in 169-168 B.C.E., raised Antiochus to the peak of his success, before the intervention of Rome put all his achievements to nought From the very first, the period of Antiochus' reign was marked by an attempt at recovery and by feverish organizing within the Seleucid kingdom. Since the country had lost part of the manpower resources which had been at its disposal in Asia Minor, the king attempted to fill the gap by exploiting to the full the potential still available. Even if there is some exaggeration in the view of those scholars who lay great stress on Antiochus' role as the founder of new Hellenistic cities, he at any rate did more than his immediate predecessors to transform ancient eastern cities here and there into Greek *poleis*. The numismatic evidence supports the theory that he encouraged the participation of the cities in his kingdom in the endeavour to revive its power.

In view of Palestine's geographical position as a borderland between the Seleucid kingdom and Ptolemaic Egypt and as the main base for Antiochus' military campaigns in the Nile valley, and considering that Palestine was then at the height of a process of Hellenization which found expression in the development of Hellenistic patterns of city life, it is not to be wondered that the situation in this country was a matter of major concern to the king. The Hellenization of the East did not leave untouched the Jewish population of Palestine nor Judea itself. The protracted Greek rule in Judea, the patterns of the Ptolemaic and Seleucid regimes, the material achievements of Hellenistic civilization in finance, agriculture and city-building combined to produce far-reaching changes in Judea too. It should be noted that the Jewish population both in Judea and in other places was surrounded by a Gentile population which, although variegated in its ethnic composition, in the period of Greek rule did get a sort of uniform leadership of a Hellenistic character. And whereas previously it was the Jewish group that had been conspicuous for its unity, there now began to crystallize an upper class, Hellenistic in its way of life, which was gradually to absorb the ranks of leadership and culture throughout Palestine and to leave room only for the finest nuances which would distinguish between the earlier ethnic elements. The gravest danger that threatened Judaism in this period of expanding Hellenism, before the persecution launched by Antiochus, was not the absolute liquidation of the Jewish way of life in the country—for even in other places in the East and among populations of a less cohesive and less vibrant spiritual character than the Jewish nation at that time, Hellenization generally did not succeed in completely assimilating the masses of the rural population, but in effect remained the possession of the minority. The danger which to no small degree lurked in Judea, as in other places, was that here too the same split would take place between the ruling classes and the general run of the population, which would lead to the fusing of the former with the ruling Hellenic class and doom the others to a long period of relative stagnation and spiritual and cultural sterility.

Among the leading advocates of Hellenization in Jewish Palestine was the House of Tobiah, a distinguished family from trans-Jordan whose greatness can be traced back as far as the biblical period and whose representatives, at the time of Ezra and Nehemiah, were the main opponents of the latter's religious-political orientation and served as allies of Sanballat. Tobiah's sons also played an important role under the Ptolemaic rule; Joseph ben Tobiah became one of the most important individuals in Palestine, and even in Judea itself. The House of Tobiah was linked by marriage with the high-priestly dynasty, the House of Zadok. The high-priestly family was divided among itself. Whereas the high priest Onias III was ready to fight for the preservation of the traditional order in Jerusalem, his brother Jason attempted to effect fundamental changes in Judea. And, like the House of Tobiah, his viewpoint was more all-Palestinian than Judean. His ambition was to fuse Jerusalem, which he was reorganizing, into the Hellenistic urban society of the Seleucid kingdom; for example, he sent a sum of money on behalf of Jerusalem to be used for the worship of the Tyrian god, Hercules (Melkart). Especially extreme in their devotion to Hellenism and in severing themselves completely from Judaism in all its forms were the priests of the course of Bilga. One of them, Menelaus, in the course of time became the chief executor of Antiochus' policy in Judea.

The atmosphere in Jerusalem was replete with tension even before Antiochus IV ascended the throne and bloody riots broke out in the streets. From the time he came to power, Antiochus IV intervened actively in the affairs of Judea, and it was at his order that Onias was deposed as high priest and his brother Jason given the office. With the king's approval, Jason introduced far-reaching reforms in the government of Jerusalem and in its social order. Their purpose was to transform Jerusalem into a *polis* to be known as Antioch. Its establishment entailed the penetration of Hellenistic public and cultural institutions into the life of the Jewish capital.

Foremost among these institutions was the gymnasium—a hallmark of every Hellenistic city and the center of its cultural life. While there is no reason to believe that Jason introduced the worship of heathen gods into Jerusalem, the very presence of the gymnasium was a serious affront to the feelings of the Jews who were faithful to their religion, since the atmosphere of the gymnasium was basically Greek and idolatrous, being connected with the worship of Hermes and Hercules. It was not long before the gymnasium replaced the Temple as the focus of social life in Jerusalem. With great bitterness, the Second Book of Maccabees describes how the priests deserted the Temple service in order to witness competitive games in the gymnasium.

Jason did not hold long his position as high priest and as leader of the *polis* of Jerusalem. When war broke out with Egypt, Antiochus did not consider him loyal enough, and he was succeeded by Menelaus, who did not belong to the high-priestly family. The latter's status as high priest necessarily derived from the will of the king and went against Jewish tradition, a fact which also constituted a guarantee of his loyalty. A new page was thus opened in the history of the relations between the Seleucid kingdom and the Jewish nation. The high priest, who previously had represented the Jewish people before the king, now became the representative of the king in Judea, something of a commissioner of Antiochus and his right-hand man in executing his policy among the Jews.

Antiochus' battle campaigns in Egypt were closely connected with what was taking place at the time in Judea. Upon his return from one of his expeditions against Egypt, the king, with the support of Menelaus, plundered the great treasures of the Temple, thus arousing the wrath of the Jews, who regarded this as a serious infringement of their rights and a deliberate attack on all they held sacred. In 168 B.C.E., during Antiochus' last campaign in Egypt, rumors spread in Judea about the death of the king. Jerusalem revolted, and Jason, the deposed high priest, returned to the city and temporarily assumed control. After Antiochus' return from Egypt, Jerusalem was re-conquered by the Seleucid army. It was decided to punish the Jews for the rebellion and to insure the effective control of the city in the future. Foreign settlers were brought into the city, and these were joined by the extreme Hellenists of Menelaus' party. No decrees were yet issued against the Jewish religion. But the very control of the city by heathen settlers and extreme Hellenists, who differed from them very little, defaced the Jewish character of the holy city entirely and gave it the appearance of an idolatrous city swarming with pagan worship.

The foreign settlers of course brought their idols along with them. Many of the Jews who were loyal to the faith of their fathers and who were accustomed to regard Judea as a land not to be defiled by heathen cults could not reconcile themselves to the new state of affairs in Jerusalem. They abandoned their city and fled to the deserts east and southeast of Jerusalem or to the provincial towns northwest and west of the city.

The decisive step was taken in 167 B.C.E. In that year the Jewish religion was outlawed and the observance of its precepts strictly forbidden. We cannot accept the view that the decrees applied only to the narrow administrative boundaries of Judea, which covered only the small area between Beth-el to the north and Beth-zur to the south and between Jericho to the east and the Lod lowland to the west, and which encompassed only a small part of the Jewish population of Palestine. Even if the edict was originally intended to apply only to Judea, the extension of the territory involved stemmed naturally from the presence of a large Jewish population in the districts adjacent to the Judean border. The sources themselves testify to the imposition of the decrees also outside Judea. In fact, even Modi'in, the cradle of the revolt and the birthplace of the Hasmoneans who responded with the force of arms to the attempt to enforce the king's edict in their town, was located in the toparchy of Lod, which was included in Samaria. And from Antiochus' instructions to the administration of Samaria, it can clearly be seen that the king's religious policy also applied to that district. The Samaritans who lived in Shechem were not affected, not because they were outside Judea, but because they made a declaration in which they affirmed that they were different from the Jews and were willing to follow the Greek customs. There is hardly any doubt that the royal orders were also applied to the other Jewish population centers: in Galilee and trans-Jordan and in the territories of the Hellenistic cities. It is less clear to what extent the decrees affected the Jews living in the Seleucid kingdom outside Palestine, such as those in Antioch, the capital.

The royal decrees had a number of aspects. For one thing, the observance of the precepts of Judaism was forbidden. In particular, we hear of the desecration of the Sabbath, of the prohibition of circumcision and of the burning of Torah scrolls. In addition, the Jews were required to take part in the pagan worship, to offer sacrifices on the high places, and to eat forbidden foods, particularly pork. Pagan altars were set up in various cities of Judea, on which swine and other forbidden animals were sacrificed. Sacrifices were also offered in the streets and in the entrances to the houses. Furthermore, the Holy Temple in Jerusalem was desecrated and was converted into a temple of the Olympian Zeus. The feast of Dionysus was celebrated in the capital of Judea, and the Jews were compelled to take part in a procession in honor of the god, adorned with wreaths of ivy. It appears that a place for the goddess Athena was also designated in the new cult of the city of Jerusalem. Nor did the worship of the kings, which was well organized in the different parts of the Seleucid kingdom, including the non-Jewish districts of Palestine, leave Judea untouched. Each month, on the date of the king's birth, the Jews were dragged along to take part in the sacrifices. Many scholars have come to the conclusion that the new cult that was forced on Judea was not a Greek cult but an oriental one, that the Olympian Zeus after whom the Temple in Jerusalem was now called was actually Ba'al Shamem, and Dionysus simply the translation of the Arabic god, Dusares. As far as the Jewish reaction is concerned this of course does not make the slightest difference, since Judaism with its monotheistic character and its special national tradition made no distinction between one foreign cult and another. Hundreds of years after polytheism and idolatry had been extirpated from Judean soil it was inconceivable that Ba'al Shamem or Dusares would have any more attraction for the inhabitants of Judea than Zeus and Dionysus of the Greeks. In any case, the sources speak unmistakably of the penetration of Hellenic cults. In the official documents (*Antiquities*, xii, 263; II Maccabees, 11: 24) mention is made in this context of the Hellenic customs, and the same is true of the historical narrative in II Maccabees (see, e.g., 6: 9). Moreover, it should be kept in mind that at this period, unlike at the final stages of the ancient world, the terms "Hellenes" and "pagans" did not overlap. It is also doubtful that the description of sexual licentiousness in the Temple court (6: 4) refers to cultic prostitution typical of Oriental idolatry, rather than to plain debauchery without any cultic significance.

What the motives were for Antiochus' decrees has often been a subject of wonder. Since polytheism is essentially not exclusive and does not profess conversion designed to redeem souls, which is typical of the monotheistic religions in their development, its representatives had no religious pretext which, as a matter of principle, might spur them to force their beliefs and their cults on others. On the other hand, it is obvious that even a polytheistic government might find it necessary, either for the good of the state or to protect the public weal for which it was responsible, to issue a ban on certain cults and customs within the area of its authority and to require its subjects to show honor to the gods of the state and to maintain its cults. It appears, therefore, that considerations of this sort, rather than Hellenic missionary zeal, are what dictated the new policy of Antiochus. It is true that Antiochus developed a special personal attachment to the Olympian Zeus, an attachment which is also borne out by the numismatic material. But there are no grounds for assuming that this attitude led him to diminish the stature of other cults, whether Greek or Oriental. There is not the slightest allusion in our sources to any attempt on his part to resort to religious coercion among his subjects belonging to other nations throughout his kingdom. Only the Jewish religion suffered persecution at his hands—and with furious wrath. Apparently the continued state of tension and disturbances in Judea and the stubborn resistance of the Jews to the changes in government and society which were imposed on the initiative or with the aid of the ruling power convinced him that it was the loyalty of the Jewish masses to their religion that was forging their resistance to his policy. It is also likely that his conflict with the Jews led him to develop a deep personal antipathy to the Jewish religion and way of life, these being so foreign to his world view. This combination of political considerations and his personal revulsion for the militant and exclusivist Jewish monotheism go a long way in explaining the fanaticism with which Antiochus conducted his war against Judaism. It is also certain that the decrees ordering the Jews to adopt certain customs and cults, in addition to the prohibition he issued against the observance of the precepts of Judaism, were not the expression of any enthusiasm for the idea of religious conversion, but served as a further means for the suppression of Judaism. Antiochus was regarded by his contemporaries as an unusual person, and he never hesitated to do the unusual and the unexpected. He also considered his scheme enforceable, since the extreme Hellenistic circles under the leadership of the high priest, Menelaus, collaborated with him on all points. Menelaus in any case had nothing to lose from the abolition of the traditional Jewish cult or from the eradication of all the institutions of the Jewish society. In the eyes of the Jews faithful to their religion Menelaus to begin with was a usurper who had burst into the Temple and ousted the high-priestly family from its position. Other Hellenists might perhaps lose much as a result of Antiochus' policy and of the abolition of the class preeminence of the Jerusalem priesthood and the penetration of a foreign elite into Jerusalem. But Menelaus' circle in any case severed its ties with the traditional society of Jewish Jerusalem. The complete consent of this circle to the king's course of action misled the latter into thinking that all the members of the Jewish upper classes were ready to give him their consistent support against the elements hostile to the kingdom, who came mainly from the lower classes.

The execution of the policy was assigned to the royal administration and the army commanders in Judea. The orders were carried out with ruthless harshness. Anyone found in possession of a Torah scroll was executed. Mothers who circumcised their infant sons were killed and the babies hung by the neck. Many were killed for refusing to be contaminated by forbidden foods, while others were burned to death in caves where they had gathered in order to observe the Sabbath.

The royal policy and its cruel enforcement led to a reaction quite the opposite from that which the king and his counsellors had expected. Contrary to their hopes, the great majority of the nation remained faithful to their ancestral religion, and the members of the various classes showed a firm resolve to suffer whatever was imposed upon them rather than submit to the royal decree. The enthusiastic devotion of the Jews to their faith was a phenomenon possessed of deep roots. The prophets of the Lord at the time of Elijah who were killed at the command of Jezebel may perhaps be regarded as the first martyrs of the Jewish religion. Martyrdom was also involved in the fate of individual prophets in Judea at the time of the First Commonwealth. But now for the first time in the history of mankind do we witness martyrdom on a mass scale, and the resistance of the saintly and the pious at the time of the persecution served as an example to both Jews and non-Jews in all generations to come.

The martyrdom was accompanied by eschatological tension. The feeling grew, at least in certain circles, that the unparalleled suffering heralded the destruction of the evil kingdom and the realization of the visions of the end of days. As against the spirit of Hellenization and the threats of the Seleucid government there were forged the ideals of the faithful Jews, the Hasidim. It should be noted, however, that despite the eschatological ferment and the yearning for the end of days, no messianic movement arose in Judea at the time of the persecution and no seers or prophets emerged to proclaim the kingdom of the House of David. When the Hasmoneans came to the fore in launching the Jewish rebellion they performed their deeds as a priestly family profoundly loyal to the Jewish religion. Its adherents regarded it as a family to whom the deliverance of Israel had been entrusted at this time of confusion and terror. However, many also felt that the rule of the Hasmoneans would continue only until the reappearance of a prophet.

Even though the Jewish religion found itself in critical situations before, it would seem that never had the danger of extermination been as great as at the time of the bloodthirsty persecution by Antiochus Epiphanes. At the time of the persecution, the bulk of the Jewish population was concentrated in the territory governed by the Seleucids, both in Palestine and outside it. True, there were Jews also living beyond the boundaries of the Seleucid kingdom: in Egypt, Cyrenaica, Asia Minor and other parts of the Middle East which at that time were gradually being severed from the Seleucid center. But it is doubtful whether the spiritual or material resources of these Jewish groups were adequate to enable them to maintain the character of Judaism and the revealed monotheistic religion in the event of the destruction or the effacement of the nature of the Palestinian center. The later development of the Jewish nation and the consequences this had for world history were insured by the struggle of the Hasmoneans and the resistance displayed by the inhabitants of Judea in that fateful decade of the second century B.C.E.

The outcome of the struggle between the Seleucid kingdom and the Jews was no doubt determined by a variety of factors, both external and internal. Yet a cardinal role was played by the spiritual development which fashioned the image of Jewish society in Palestine in the generations following the return from Babylonia. The ideals which crystallized in Jerusalem and Judea in the centuries that preceded the decrees of Antiochus had penetrated the broad classes of the nation. The Torah had been absorbed into the daily life of the tens of thousands of Judean farmers and was regarded by them as a *sine qua non* of their existence. This spirit, which was not restricted to the priests or to other exclusive circles, also inspired the rebel troops with enthusiasm and confidence. Even among the upper classes only a minority, the circle of the sons of

Tobiah and Menelaus, stuck with Antiochus to the end. The moderate Hellenists, on the other hand, when the moment of decision came, put their talents and experience at the disposal of the Hasmonean leadership and aided them in the prosecution of the war and in forming ties with foreign powers.

As a result of this state of affairs it soon became obvious that, although the Hasmonean revolt was in a sense also a civil war, without the active intervention of the armies of the Seleucid kingdom the struggle would undoubtedly end with the victory of those faithful to Judaism. Even the weight of the Hellenistic population in the cities of Palestine outside the borders of Judea was not enough to counterbalance this situation.

Step by step Judea, under the leadership of the Hasmoneans, advanced towards freedom. Judah Maccabee succeeded in repelling a series of attacks launched by Antiochus' generals. The Temple was purified and the Seleucid government, even while Antiochus was still alive, recognized the right of the Jews to observe their religious customs. Judah's successors, Jonathan and Simeon, followed his ways and included in the sphere of their political and military activity various parts of Palestine and southern Syria. Demetrius II, king of Syria, officially recognized Judea's freedom (142 B.C.E.) and the Great Assembly which convened in Jerusalem two years later recognized the Hasmoneans as a dynasty of ethnarchs, high priests and military commanders in Judea (140 B.C.E.). There now began the process of the conversion of all of Palestine into Judea, which led to the integration of the islands of Jewish population throughout Palestine into the Hasmonean state of Judea, the assimilation of the non-Jewish rural population into the Jewish nation, and the cancellation of the influence of the Hellenistic cities in Palestine.

The Hasmonean revolt can, of course, be regarded as one of the events characteristic of the awakening of the East as a whole and its rising up against the Hellenistic hegemony. Just as the Parthians rebelled against the Seleucid kingdom as early as the third century, and just as there was a long series of revolts by natives in Egypt beginning at the end of that century and prophecies as to the destruction of detested Alexandria (the Potter's Oracle), so did the Hasmonean revolt too represent an important link in the process of the disintegration of Hellenistic rule. It can even be argued that the liberation of Judea was bound to come about even without the decrees and the rebellion, since other parts of Syria, Phoenicia and Palestine were later liberated gradually from Seleucid rule. On the other hand, it should be pointed out that Egypt, despite the ferment and the insurrections, never threw off the yoke of Hellenistic rule but immediately came under the sway of Rome. And even throughout the entire area of Syria, Phoenicia and Palestine, Judea was in fact the first to succeed in freeing itself from subjugation to the kingdom (the Nabateans had never been subject to the authority of Hellenistic kings). Thanks to the success of its rebellion, Judea thus became an active factor which accelerated the process of the disintegration of Seleucid Syria and perhaps of the liberation of other peoples and cities within the kingdom. However, the cities at any rate were Hellenistic in character, and in this context we cannot speak of conscious cooperation between Judea and the other oriental elements. Just as Ba'al Shamem was no closer to the heart of the Jews than was the Olympian Zeus, so there was no love lost between Judea and the Idumeans, for example. It should be stressed, however, that as a result of the Jewish victories and the integration of the bulk of Palestine into the Judean state not only was the advance of Hellenistic urban civilization in the country arrested for a long period, but also the struggle over the religious and ethnic character of the majority of the country's rural population ended with a victory for the Jews. The name Judea assumed a broad connotation and was used by Gentiles to refer to all of Palestine: "The interior of the country, as far as the Arabs, between Gaza and the Anti-Lebanon is called Judea", wrote the Greek geographer Strabo, a contemporary of Augustus *(Geog.* xvi. 2. 21). This situation did not change even with the Roman conquest in its early period.

The Hasmonean revolt did not break out as the result of any preconceived plan. Its standard-bearers did not go out to battle either to give dominion to new ideals or to establish the Kingdom of God on earth. As already noted, the revolt was not accompanied by any messianic movement which swept the nation, despite the eschatological atmosphere which pervaded some influential circles. Neither was the revolt nourished at first from a real evaluation or feeling that the time had now come to realize by the force of arms the long-standing hopes that nestled in the hearts of the Jews, including those of moderate views, like Ben Sira, for the restoration of Israel's glory. No view crystallized or was advanced that, as a matter of principle, any rule of this world must be resisted, a view that typified the Zealots and the Sicarii towards the end of the Second Commonwealth.

The Hasmoneans raised the standard of rebellion in Modi'in, and large numbers of Hasidim and other faithful Jews joined them because the situation had become unbearable and there seemed to be no other way to insure Judaism's survival. It was only after the initial successes of the Jews that they began to carry out the ancient wish to sever all ties with the heathen rule and to create changes in Judea and Palestine. The tremendous achievement of the revolt was the saving of the Jewish nation and religion. However, the changes that took place in the political situation and in the conditions that prevailed in Judea brought about a social and religious reshuffle, put an end to tendencies that had been strong in

Hellenistic Jerusalem, strengthened other trends, and gave birth to new ideas.

The tension caused by the reforms of Jason in the days of Antiochus, and by the persecution and the revolt soon expressed itself in a serious split among the ruling classes in Judea. The failure of the king's policy led to the liquidation of Menelaus, who served as a scapegoat for the defeat, while many of his adherents were also degraded. Menelaus' followers, headed by the House of Bilga, suffered a decline in prestige, and they were held in disgrace for a long time. But it is characteristic of the development of Jewish society in the generations that followed, generations which no longer knew idol-worship, that one of the descendants of that priestly house who lived in the generation of the destruction of the Temple sacrificed himself amidst the flames of the Temple, which was burned by the Romans (*The Jewish War*, VI, 280). The old high-priestly house of Joshua ben Jehozadak, suffered greatly from the upheaval and the revolt. This family, which had become a sort of ruling dynasty in Judea, was not consistent in its attitude towards the great problems of religion and society. Alongside Simeon the Just and Onias III, who was executed in the days of Antiochus—personalities who typify faithful Judaism—we find in this family individuals who strengthened their ties with the House of Sanballat and the House of Tobias and who expressed the policy of integration with the ruling classes of non-Jewish Palestine. It is no mere chance that the brother of Onias III, Jason, led the opposition against him. Jason himself died far from Judea, and we are unable to trace further the history of the ancient high-priestly line in Judea. On the other hand, a glorious political future awaited the descendants of Onias in Egypt, where they served as statesmen and generals under the Ptolemaic dynasty. They built a temple to God in Egypt, and they also aided Hasmonean Judea in the critical times of Alexander Yannai. The activities of the House of Tobias, which in pre-Hasmonean Judea had been more influential than any other non-priestly family, came to a complete end, and we hear nothing further of any remnant of this line in the history of the Jewish people. Together with it many of its supporters were also undoubtedly truncated from the national body.

On the other hand, the revolt brought new elements to the fore of Jewish society, elements which supported the Hasmoneans and who had not previously played a conspicuous role in the public life of Jerusalem —and at the end of the Second Commonwealth there were families, like that of the historian Josephus, who could look back on the days of the revolt as the beginning of their greatness.

These new elements assumed their place in the leadership, in the Temple, and in the Sanhedrin—which had inherited the place of the pre-Hasmonean Gerusia. Among the new elements who were active in government and society under the Hasmonean rule there were also families and individuals who stemmed from the border areas of Palestine, including proselytes of the type of Antipater the Idumean. The integration of a part of the upper classes of the non-Jewish Palestinian population into the ruling class of Judea thus took place in a form different from that anticipated in the age of expanding Hellenization. However, alongside the revolutionary change, there was also a factor of continuity that made itself felt. As we have already emphasized part of the upper strata of the priesthood and the leadership of Jerusalem also joined the Hasmoneans in their struggle against the heathen rule. Typical of this circle were the priests of the House of Hakotz. The latter had already played a central role in financial administration at the time of the Persian rule. It was one of them, Johanan, who obtained confirmation of the rights of Jerusalem and its traditional form of government from the Seleucid authorities. And his son Eupolemos, together with another priest, Jason ben Elazar, signed the treaty between Judea and the Roman Republic (161 B.C.E.) as emissaries of Judah Maccabee. The Hasmoneans themselves were an important priestly family attached to Jehoiarib, one of the outstanding priestly courses, and their victory in no way ended the group superiority of the priestly class in Judea.

But although the priesthood maintained its place of honor—and to some extent also its hegemony—in the life of Judea until the end of the Second Commonwealth, the unique development in Judea, and one of historical significance for many future generations of Jewish society, was the rise of the sages."'And the rough he-goat is the king of Greece...' (Dan. 8: 21)—that is Alexander of Macedon who ruled twelve years—until now the prophets prophesied in the holy spirit, from now on turn your ear and hear the words of the sages" (*Seder Olam Rabbah,* ch. 30). The status of the sages had its roots in the pre-Hasmonean period. However, it appears that as a result of the ideological polarization in the period that preceded the revolt and in the wake of the revolt itself the image of the sage changed considerably and a serious split occurred between the classes of the priestly leadership of Jerusalem and the sages: a process of democratization of the last-mentioned class began. The study of the Torah ceased to be the exclusive province of the priests, and anyone who was qualified and who wished to strive for "the crown of the Torah" could now do so. True, the number of priests among the sages during the Second Commonwealth continued to be large, but the study of Torah and the development of Halakha, which shaped the character of life, worship, government and law in the State of Judea, attracted the cream of the nation's spiritual powers. Alongside the priests, and even to a greater degree than them, the outstanding Torah scholars in this period are the sages who sprang from various classes of the Jewish population of Palestine and the dispersion. Moreover, even the descendants of proselytes occupied a place in the first rank of the sages. To be a disciple of Aaron was more important than to be of the seed of Aaron. There is a world of difference between the sage as portrayed in Ecclesiasticus and the sage that we know during the later generations of the Second Commonwealth.

The sages constituted the backbone of the principal religio-social stream of Judaism in the period of the Second Commonwealth: the Pharisee stream which left its mark on the entire internal history of Judea and which also laid the foundation for Talmudic Judaism. The Pharisees carried on the trend which had begun at the time of Persian rule, and their immediate predecessors were the groups of Hasidim who risked their lives in the days of the persecution and the revolt. To be faithful to the Torah and to help it penetrate every corner of life were the fundamentals of Pharisee thought. This Torah went far beyond the framework of the Written Law; it encompassed the living tradition of the Halakha as the Pharisee sages continued to cultivate it in accordance with their premise that the Torah is obliged to find a suitable answer to all the questions that come up in life, in all their details. The answers given in the Pharisee circles, which sometimes were opposed to the simple interpretation of the Written Law, embraced all aspects of religion, worship, law and social life. In the legislative activity, the general tendency of the Pharisees was to humanize the criminal law, while in theological questions they took the middle road between the idea of predestination and the belief in absolute freedom of choice, two conflicting conceptions which had gained currency among other circles in the same period. The Pharisees also believed in the immortality of the soul and in individual reward and punishment after death, and they shared the eschatological beliefs of the rest of the nation. The socio-spiritual activity of the Pharisees under the leadership of the sages preserved the character of Judaism as a living religion. The Pharisee leaders were also the chief spokesmen of the proselytizing movement throughout the Diaspora.

The influence of the Pharisees extended far beyond their direct adherents: most classes of the nation were actually attached to the Pharisees and regarded the Pharisee sages as their natural leaders and the Pharisee Halakha as the natural expression of the Jewish religion.

The chief adversaries of the Pharisees in the Hasmonean period were the Sadducees, who only accepted the sanctity of the Written Law and denied the authority of the Pharisee rabbis. They took issue with the Pharisees on many matters connected with the Temple service, the criminal law, and daily life. The Sadducees also denied the popular beliefs, which were widespread in those times, in the resurrection of the dead and in angels. Socially they represented mainly the Jewish upper classes—the priests, those of distinguished or wealthy families, and in general those elements which had ruled Judea in the generations preceding the revolt. Yet they did not join Menelaus and the Tobiads, but gave their support to the Hasmoneans in the struggle against Seleucid rule. Even their name Sadducees (Hebrew: *Zedukim)* seems to derive from their close connection with the high-priestly families named after Zadok—"the Sadducees having the confidence of the wealthy alone but no following among the populace, while the Pharisees have the support of the masses" *(Antiquities,* xiii, 298).

At first the Hasmonean house was carried on the waves of national-religious enthusiam. It was esteemed by many as a line to which the salvation of Israel had been entrusted. But from the very start there were elements making for disunity, since the supporters of the Hasmoneans were not all of a piece. It was not always possible to find a common language for the pious Hasidim and the representatives of the priestly aristocracy which had joined the Hasmoneans. At first the Hasmoneans were the natural leaders of those circles who had been represented and influenced by the Pharisees. Until the time of John Hyrcanus it was the Pharisee Halakha that officially determined the law and practice of the Judean State. A split between the Hasmonean house and the Pharisees appeared for the first time during John Hyrcanus' rule, and it widened under his heirs, until peace was again restored during the reign of Queen Alexandra.

One feature was common to all of the streams which played a role in the socio-religious development between the Hasmonean revolt and the destruction of the Temple: the deep loyalty of all parts of the Jewish nation in Palestine to monotheism, as expressed in the Jewish revealed religion and Torah. After the failure of the Hellenist extremists to adapt the beliefs and rituals of the outside world for themselves, no one questioned the exclusive sway of the religion of Israel among the Jewish nation. Individuals, particularly from among the upper classes in the countries of the Hellenistic dispersion, occasionally abandoned the religion of their fathers, and here and there one discovers instances of religious syncretism. But Palestinian Jewry itself remained unflinchingly loyal to their ancestral creed, and idolatry was no longer one of the sins that could be imputed to it. A general remark along these lines can already be found in the Book of Judith (8: 18)—"For there arose none in our age, neither is there any of us today, tribe or kindred, or family, or city, which worship gods made with hands, as it was in the former days"—and such an evaluation would be doubly true of the later generations of the Second Commonwealth. No Hellenistic king after Antiochus Epiphanes dared to renew decrees of the type issued by him. Also the Roman authorities, for the most part, observed the utmost caution when it came to the Jewish religion, knowing full well that any material religious affront to Judaism would touch off a serious conflagration in Palestine and even in the Jewish settlements in other parts of the empire. The readiness of the Jews to sacrifice their lives rather than violate the precepts of the Torah became in itself an historical factor of the first order. From the days of the persecution by Antiochus, martyrdom became one of the hallmarks of Judaism, and from Judaism it was taken over by the religions that drew from its source. The stories of the martyrs of the time of Antiochus—the episode of Elazar the priest and of the mother and her seven sons—which were recounted and adapted in many forms, served as an inspiration to the various branches of Hellenistic Jewry, just as they heartened the Christians in the generations that followed.

In certain circles the ideal of martyrdom in its various forms was associated with eschatological hopes. For these, the very phenomenon of martyrdom was a sign that the End of Days was approaching. It was this faith in the eschatological significance of the events of the day that gave the martyrdom its justification. Among the expressions of the eschatological yearnings of those times was the literature unique to the Second Temple period, the apocalyptic writings in the creation of which the period of the persecution by Antiochus constitutes one of the most important stages. The visions of Daniel, which were written at the very time of the suffering "such as never was since there was a nation even to that same time" (12: 1), began a new chapter in the history of Jewish literary-religious creativity.

The Hasmonean revolt was, in effect, the only one of the many rebellions of the Jews under Greco-Roman rule that ended in a Jewish victory, in the throwing-off of the foreign yoke, and in the restoration of the independence of Judea. This fact, together with the realization that these were events that had saved the Jewish religion from extermination, helped to perpetuate the events in Jewish tradition down the generations. Their memory is preserved in Hanukkah, the most important of the Jewish holidays which are not rooted in the Jewish Canon, and in the prayers connected with it, which extol the victory of the few over the many. In times of demoralization and persecution the significance of the events of the period of Mattathias and Judah Maccabee grew always greater. Also as a war of national liberation, the rebellion served as a symbol for future generations.

DAVID G. FLUSSER

THE SOCIAL MESSAGE FROM QUMRAN

THE Jewish religion is based on the concept of righteousness, and the unity of the purely religious and the social content of Judaism has resulted in two world religions, Christianity and Islam, developing from its roots. Thus, the Jewish social approach to life was not only one of the most important causes of the birth of these two great religions, but also through them the Jewish social heritage is manifest in modern culture.

Although the importance of the Jewish social message for modern man is well known, it can be shown that there was a Jewish-Christian impact upon modern society at many points where a Graeco-Roman influence is assumed. We do not want to minimize the cultural and social heritage of Greek and Roman thought, but sometimes, especially in modern political and social thought, when scholars quote Greek and Roman sources, they view them, unconsciously through a prism of Christian ideas, although some of these actually originated in Judaism.

The most important source of these ideas is of course the Old Testament, which became a Holy Book of Christianity. The other source, the New Testament, stems from later Judaism. Ancient Christianity tended to learn from the spiritual achievements of Hellenistic Judaism, and the Jewish roots of the teachings of Jesus and of the Mother Church of Jerusalem are well known. This tendency of Christianity, which finds expression especially in the first three Gospels, reveals a close affinity with the common Jewish non-sectarian tradition, which was then mainly represented by the Pharisees. Their prominent interest in social justice found its way into the Gospel of Jesus and, through the New Testament, into our modern social approach.

This question deserves to be studied in its entirety, but our present task is more limited. A new Jewish source of modern political and social throught has been discovered in the ancient Scrolls of Qumran in the vicinity of the Dead Sea. Most scholars rightly point out that these are remnants of the literature of the ancient Jewish sect of Essenes, already known from other sources. This discovery, together with a renewed study of historical sources about the Essenes, especially the Jewish historian Flavius Josephus, paves the way for a clarification of the roots of some modern social ideas and behaviour, which were unknown until the discovery of these venerable Hebrew documents. It is not only from the historical point of view that a knowledge of the roots of social and political ideas is important. If we know the origin of an idea, we can better understand the idea itself, because the original tendency of an idea often persists in its later manifestations.

In antiquity the community of property of the Essenes was famous. The existence of this institution is now confirmed by the Scrolls. It is probable that this communistic way of life originated in the strict observance of ritual purity by the sect; its members were forbidden to have contact with outsiders. This practice could lead to the maintenance of common warehouses and, since coins can transmit ritual impurity, even to community of wealth. Another source of the Essenes' community of wealth was their idealization of poverty. According to their ideology the poor man is closer to God than the rich man. Thus, a member of the sect, who has no private property, is more acceptable in God's eyes. But the economic communism of the Essenes was also based upon their dualistic theology. They believed that mankind is divided by Divine predestination into the blessed lot of God and the cursed lot of Belial. A permanent hatred exists between these two camps, and in the end, in the eschatological future, which is at hand, the wicked man and spirits will be annihilated, while the preordained elect ones will receive their recompense. According to this theology, the Sons of Light are the Essenes themselves, and the Sons of Darkness are their enemies—both other Jews and the Gentiles. Naturally, this strict belief of the Essenes in a double predestination serves in their ideology as a theological basis for their feeling of election, while the dualistic trend is a justification for their strong separatist tendencies. Although we know both from Josephus and from their own literature that the Essenes also lived in closed groups in many places in Palestine, their separatist outlook led many of them to think that they had to leave the habitations of the sinners and go to the wilderness. Thus it was that the Essene centre in the Judaean wilderness in Qumran was founded. The dualistic theology served the Essenes as the motive for their revolutionary isolation which could easily lead to the community of property, for which, as we have seen, there were also other causes. Consequently, Essene ideology was connected with their form of organization and their form of organization with their social message.

The present writer agrees with the many scholars who find a connection between the Dead Sea Sect and John the Baptist. It seems that John was directly influenced by the Essene teachings, but that he did not remain in the sect because of doctrinal differences. Evidently he declined to accept the view that salvation should be restricted to members of a sect and conditioned by the acceptance of a harsh discipline. According to John the Baptist there was only one condition for salvation—baptism—and his theology of baptism was similar to or even identical with that of the Essenes. Thus, the Baptist did not demand of the persons he baptized that they leave their position in society and separate themselves from their former way of life. The crowd asked him: "Then what are we to do?" He replied: "Let everyone who possesses two shirts share with him who has none and let him who has food do likewise." (Luke 3, 10-14). The Essenes maintained the community of property in a closed sect, while John the Baptist asked his adherents to share their goods with paupers.

The discovery of the Dead Sea Scrolls has shown that there are Essene elements in Jesus' message, the synoptic Gospels being the main channel through which Essene social doctrines have influenced modern thought. It seems that Jesus knew these motifs as they were modified by John the Baptist. Like the Baptist, Jesus did not ask his followers to leave their actual social frame and did not preach the community of property. All that he said was that if a man wanted to be perfect, he had to give his property to the poor and follow him. (Matthew, 19, 21). What Jesus wanted from his close group of adherents was not economic communism, but almost absolute poverty.

The situation changed after his death. Community of property was introduced in the Mother Church of Jerusalem, and the descriptions of this institution in the Acts of the Apostles had a great impact upon Christian revolutionary movements from the Taborites in Bohemia until modern times.

Most of these Christian groups rightly felt that there is a genuine connection between the community of property and the appreciation of poverty as a religious value and thus, unknowingly, they restored the original link between these two concepts, which existed in the Essenes' social message. Essene influence upon the social structure of the Christian community of Jerusalem can be detected even in the Essene terminology found in the Acts of the Apostles. Moreover, the influence of medieval and modern Christian communistic sects upon modern socialistic movements has been the subject of considerable scholarly research. Thus, not only were the Essenes precursors of these modern socialist movements, but there is even an historical connection between modern socialism and the ancient Jewish sect, whose writings have now been discovered.

The ideal of poverty meant for the Sect that wealth is an impediment to salvation. Its members pray: "...And Thou hast not placed my support on unjust gain and with wealth [gained by violence] my [heart desireth

not]. And carnal intent Thou hast not assigned for me... [And the so]ul
of Thy servant abhoreth we[alth] and unjust gain and with choicest plea-
sures [it] does not desire" *(Thanksgiving Scroll* X, 22-30). We find
already in the Scrolls the phrase "poor in spirit" (see also Matthew 5, 3),
which means "poor endowed with the Holy Spirit". This was evidently
also the meaning of the term as used by Jesus. Like the Essenes, Jesus
thought that it is difficult for a rich man to enter the Kingdom of Heaven.
Like the Essenes, Jesus too brought the message of salvation to the poor,
the mourners, the persecuted, the meek and the simple. The sect's influence on this ideology of poverty is clear from another saying of Jesus':
"No one can serve two masters: either he will hate one and love the
other, or else he will stand by the one and despise the other—you cannot
both serve God and the Mammon" (Mt. 6, 24). This saying is not only
replete with Essene phraseology, but it also reflects the Essene dualistic
tendency. In Essene thought the contrast is between God and his lot and
Belial and his lot, an idea we find in Christian form in 2nd Cor. 6, 14-16:
"Keep out of all incongruous ties with unbelievers. What have righteousness and iniquity in common, or how can bright associate with darkness?
What harmony can there be between Christ and Belial, or what business
has a believer with an unbeliever? What compact can there be between
God's temple and idols?..." In Jesus' saying the dualistic tendency is
weaker: instead of the contrast between God and Belial, there is here
only the contrast between God and wealth (Hebrew: mammon). Through
the Gospels, the Essenes' positive evaluation of poverty and the simple
life and their essentially negative attitude towards wealth influenced
Christianity and thus became a part of modern social thought.

Jesus not only refused to accept the Essenes' sectarian community of
wealth, but he expressly opposed their economic separatism. The Essenes' "Sons of Light" restricted their economic ties with the environment
to a minimum. "No one must be united to him (i.e. to a non-sectarian) in
his possessions and his property, lest he load upon him guilty sin. But he
shall keep far away from him in everything... No one of the men of the
community must... either eat or drink anything of their property, or
accept anything whatever from them without paying for it... For all those
who are not reckoned within His covenant, they and everything they
have must be excluded. The man of holiness must not lean on any works
of nothingness, for nothingness are all who do not care for His covenant.
For all those who spurn His word, He will destroy from the earth, for all
their doings are pollution before Him and impurity clings to all their
property" (Manual of Discipline V, 13-20).

As we have said, the social doctrine of Jesus was also influenced by
the teachings of some Jewish Pharisaic circles, who represented non-
sectarian Judaism and were naturally opposed to the Essene doctrine of
hatred. Judaism from its very beginnings was not only a national religion

but, because the God of Israel is the creator of the world, a universal religion: God is not only the King of His people, but His Kingdom is over the whole humanity. At the time of the Second Commonwealth, a period noticeable for theological thought, two ideas emerged simultaneously: the idea of Jewish "ecclesiology" and the universal approach to humanity. A non-Jew who observes the basic moral commandments is according to Jewish doctrine just as eligible for salvation as Jews by birth and proselytes. Thus is was logical that those Pharisaic circles which did not oppose the opening of the door to proselytes also developed the sublime idea of mutual love between men which they regarded as the essence of the Mosaic Law—and the concept of love of God instead of mere fear for the Creator. This approach of the "Pharisees of Love" was wholeheartedly accepted and developed by Jesus. This notion is surely in strong contrast to the ideology of hatred of the Essenes, who in opposition to the broader concept of non-sectarian Judaism, developed a separatist ecclesiology, according to which there is no salvation outside the Essene Church, not even for other Jews.

Jesus, who followed and developed the doctrine of love from contemporary Judaism, naturally opposed the Essenes' economic separatism. He said: "The sons of this world are wiser in their own generation than the sons of light. And I tell you, make for yourselves friends from the mammon of unrighteousness" (Luke 16, 8-9). The "wealth of unrighteousness" is equivalent, in the language of the Sons of Light from Qumran to "the wealth of unrighteousness", i.e. of the non-Essenic society. Thus Jesus shared the Essenes' positive attitude toward poverty and their suspicion of wealth, but because of his precept of unrestricted love he opposed their economic attitude and did not accept their economic communism. But in the subsequent development of Christian society in the Middle Ages and in modern times, not only was the Essenes' positive evaluation of poverty and their opposition to wealthy classes accepted by some Christian groups but, as we have said, the economic communism of the early Mother Church of Jerusalem, as known from the Acts of the Apostles, was sometimes combined with the ideal of poverty by these later Christian groups and thus assumed the original revolutionary impact which it had in the ancient Jewish sect of the Essenes.

Jesus's message was influenced in some points by the *social* doctrines of the Essenes. The Hellenistic Church, as represented especially by Paul and John the Evangelist, did not accept this social approach, but through different channels it became acquainted with the Essene dualistic *theology* of predestination. This theology operated in the sect especially to strengthen the adherence of the member to the sect: he had to prove his election by his conduct and his obedience to the rules of the sect, the sect being regarded as a holy body politic, separated from the world. It can be shown that the concept of double predestination, which occurs in a weakened form in some writings of the New Testament, originated in Essenic ideology. Insofar as it is accepted, this concept has a similar social function in Christianity as it did in the sect. The central point could not be accepted by the Church, namely, the idea of mutual hatred between the Sons of Light and the Sons of Darkness which, according to Essene opinion, was not only preordained by God, but also a commandment binding on the sectarians. A precept of hatred towards the surrounding environment is the opposite of Jesus' precept of love, whose roots lie in the Pharisaic doctrine. A Christian cannot be commanded by his faith to hate a fellow-man, but he can affirm that others hate him as a Christian.

If Christianity could not accept the Essene doctrine of hatred, it was deeply influenced by some Essene views about the necessary reactions to the surrounding world which emanated from this doctrine of hatred. Not only was the hatred between the Sons of Light and the Sons of Darkness, according to the sect divinely preordained, but also the Day of Wrath was fixed by God's decision, when the wicked would be destroyed and all evil disappear, only the Sons of Light surviving, endowed with supreme divine bliss. But the desired victory still did not come. This meant for the sect that by the mysterious will of God the evil powers which rule this world prevail for the time being and that it would therefore be a sin for the Sons of Light to oppose them. "[There shall be] eternal hatred against the man of perdition, in a spirit of concealment, so as to leave to them property and the labor of hands, as a slave does to his master, subdued before him who lords it over him. So he [the member of the sect] shall be a man zealous for the ordinance and its [relation to the proper knowledge of God's] time, toward the Day of Vengeance so as to do what is [God's good] pleasure in all activities and in all his ruling as He (God) has commanded. And all that is done to him he accepts willingly" *(Manual of Discipline* IX, 21 ff.).

This is both the fateful and fruitful Essene concept of "peaceful coexistence", originally based upon an eschatological doctrine of predestination and an ideology of hatred. The positive possibilities of this attitude became manifest in another passage from the same Essene document: "I will not return evil to anybody, with good will I pursue man, for with God rests the judgment of every living being, and he is the one to repay man for his deeds... And the trial of a man of perdition I will not handle until the Day of Vengeance. But my anger I will not turn away from the men of deceit, and will not be content until he has established judgment" *(Manual of Discipline* X, 17-20).

We find similar ideas, but of course without the Essene precept of hatred, in Paul's Epistle to the Romans, in a passage (12, 8b-13, 7) which is so imbued with Essene ideas and phraseology that it is probable that Paul here made use of an Essene document, which he read in Greek translation. Paul says, *inter alia:* "Bless those who persecute you; bless and do not curse them. Repay no one evil for evil. If possible, so far as it depends upon you, live peaceably with all. Beloved, never avenge yourselves, but let the Wrath of God have its way; for it is written: Vengeance is mine, I will repay, says the Lord. No, if your enemy is hungry, feed him; if he is thirsty, give him drink; for by so doing you will heap burning coals upon his head. Do not be overcome by evil but overcome evil with good."

As in the Essene ideology, here too non-retaliation is linked with the eschatological outlook of divine vengeance upon the evil-doers. Non-resistance to the evil powers led the Essenes to a submission to all governments, because even wickedness exists according to divine predestination. The Essene swears "that he will for ever keep faith with all men, especially with the powers that be, since no ruler attains his office save by the will of God" (Josephus, Jewish War II, 140). Thus, it is logical that the above-cited passage in the Epistle to the Romans ends with the following words: "Let every person be subject to the government authorities. For there is no authority except from God; the existing authorities have been constituted by God. Therefore he who resists the authorities resists what God has appointed, and those who resist will incur judgement" (Rom. 13, 1-2). Paul's following implication (13, 3-7) mitigates the previous statement.

Paul's words: "Do not be overcome by evil but overcome evil with good" have an almost exact parallel in the above-quoted passage from the Essene Manual of Discipline: "I will not return evil to anybody, with good will I pursue man". Through the channels of Christianity, this way of reacting rooted in the Essene *Weltanschauung*, had a very deep influence upon European civilization. In another ideological context, when this concept is freed from its context of preordained eschatology and from the ideology of hatred against the sinners, the precept of non-violence can be understood as a means of overwhelming the wicked by beneficence and of making him better. This idea is developed in a Jewish apocryphal work, "The Testaments of the Patriarchs", especially in "The Testament of Benjamin". Many scholars have rightly recognized the strong ties between this work and the Essenes. "The Testaments of the Patriarchs" were composed in a Jewish group which on the one hand was imbued with Essenism, but on the other accepted from the Pharisees the idea of mutual love. The great commandment to love one's neighbor as well as the commandment to love God is often stressed in this book, as well as in the so-called "Two-Ways", the Jewish source of the Christian "Didache" (Teaching of Apostles), which also shows strong links with the Qumran literature. A similar fusion of the Essene social approach and the Pharisaic doctrine of love can be found in Jesus' social message. It is therefore very probable that the teachings of Jesus on these points were derived from semi-Essene circles, in which "The Testaments of the Patriarchs" were composed. Thus, the development of the idea of overwhelming the wicked by beneficence, into its more humanistic form in the Testaments of the Patriarchs and in Jesus' message was facilitated by the influence of the "Pharisees of love" upon these semi-Essene circles.

Thus in this new, semi-Essene context of love instead of hatred the idea of victory over the sinner receives a new meaning. "For the good man has not a dark eye; for he shows mercy to all men, even though they be sinners. And though they devise with evil intent concerning him, by doing good he overcomes evil, being shielded by God" (Test. Benj. 4, 2-3). As in Essene thinking, here too non retaliation is a weapon, but now it becomes a struggle of love. "If anyone does violence to a pious man, he repents; for the pious man is merciful to his reviler, and holds his peace. And if anyone betrays a righteous man, the righteous man prays; though for a little while he is humbled, yet not long after he appears much more glorious, as was Joseph my brother" (Test. Benj. 5, 4-5).

No one familiar with the New Testament can, after reading these passages, avoid the conclusion that Jesus was influenced on this point by the marginal ideas of Essenism. The most striking examples of this attitude of Jesus are in his Sermon on the Mount: "But I say to you: Do not resist one who is evil. But if any one strikes you on the right cheek, turn to him the other also, and if any one would sue you and take your coat, let him have your cloak as well... Love your enemies and pray for those who persecute you, so that you may be sons of your Father who is in Heaven..." (Matthew 5, 39-48).

Although Jesus proclaimed this doctrine, nowhere in his words do we find the idea that by acting beneficently towards the wicked, they will be overwhelmed and change their ways. If the absence of this motivation in the Gospels was not an accident, then there are several possible explanations for Jesus' refusal to accept this rationale. But even if Jesus dit not argue as the Essenes (and Paul) did, that by behaving well towards the evil persecutor, one opens the door to Divine wrath and that non-resistance to the authorities is a weapon, and even if he did not, like the semi-Essene "Testaments of the Patriarchs", stress that by one's good deeds one reforms the wicked man and leads him to repentance, all the movements which accepted this teaching of Jesus did so without knowing its sources in the Essene, and certainly not in the semi-Essene, form. This has been true of many Christian sects and denominations until our own times, and non-retaliation as a weapon was taken over from these Christian circles by many modern thinkers, of whom Tolstoy is only one example. In its secular form, this attitude which originated in the Sect of Essenes, provided often the ideological background for modern pacifism. The survival of the Essene social message in the

Middle Ages and in modern times would be well worth studying. It is interesting that, although these ideas were transmitted by the New Testament writings only partially rather than as a complete system, these motifs tend to attract one the other and to revert to their earlier, pre-Christian form. The Christian ideal of poverty was often combined with contempt and even hatred for the wealthy and sometimes with economic communism. Frequently these ideas once again became eschatological and apocalyptic. Groups which practiced poverty or even economic communism often adopted the attitude of non-retaliation and passive resistance as a weapon for peace. Sometimes this idea was combined with the aim of pleading the wicked to repent, and it did not always exclude a precept of hatred towards the authorities.

The Essene heritage with all its implications and ramifications came into its own after the great crisis of the Church in the late Middle Ages and during the Reformation. When Christians were disturbed by awkward questions, they sought the answers in the documents of primitive Christianity. Often, when they expected to find in the New Testament genuine Christian doctrines, the pre-Christian Jewish, Essene, or semi-Essene doctrines they actually discovered attracted them because of their ideological vigor and social appeal. It was then that the Essene heritage revived, its latent forces becoming active. At first, Wycliffe discovered both the doctrine of predestination and the ideal of poverty of the Mother Church. The doctrine of predestination, according to which election is a gift of divine grace, became important for the Great Churches of Reformation, the Lutherans and Calvinists, who found in it a firm foundation for their separation from the Catholic Church. The ideal of poverty and the eschatological hopes became important for groups and sects which recruted their members from poor and simple folk. In these denominations, the idea of non-resistance to the evil powers very often became a weapon in their social struggle and a way of life. Thus, with the Reformation, the old Essene motifs not only were revived in their more or less original meaning, but they also fulfilled a new function in the various branches of the new Churches. In modern secular society, the Essene heritage often assumed a secular function in seeking for solutions to social and political problems.

The Essene social message is not dead: it lives on both in Christian and in secular movements. The modern world with its social and political problems and its large masses offers it, in its different forms and varieties, a field of activity. We cannot say whether this Essene heritage will prove a blessing or a curse, whether it will solve our problems or complicate them, but the long history and the efficacy of this message through the ages shows that a small ancient Jewish sect, through its ability to understand the problems of human society, could ask questions and propose solutions which are fruitful even today.

E. E. URBACH

THE TALMUDIC SAGE — CHARACTER AND AUTHORITY

I

THE period of Jewish history associated with the first temple in Jerusalem is aptly characterized by the acts of the prophets. Not so the era of the Second Hebrew Commonwealth. Here we encounter a new category of spiritual leadership—the Hakhamim—who exercised paramount influence in the guidance of Eretz-Israel and Babylonian Jewry. Indeed, this situation continued, *mutatis mutandis*, throughout the entire Jewish diaspora of mediaeval times up to the very dawn of the modern era. However, though the prophets left an unmistakable imprint upon the historical scene of the kingdoms of Israel and Judah after the division of the kingdom, theirs was not an exclusive ascendancy. Nor were their opinions at all times decisive. There were kings and princes, temple priests and "they that handle the Law" as well as false prophets. Against these and their associates did the great Hebrew prophets direct their fiery messages. The fact, however, remains that only the latter's orations and visions, condemnations and consolations have survived and been committed to writing. In association with the Law of Moses and other inspired writings these assumed the status of holy scripture, being the canonical writings of the Bible. It was as a result of the deliberations of the Hakhamim that this corpus came into being. With its threefold division into Torah, Prophets and Hagiographa, the Bible constituted the chief object of study and contemplation for the Hakhamim. It was the Bible as a discipline that determined their character in a gradual process which was to culminate towards the end of the Second Hebrew Commonwealth. By this time, which coincided with the definitive stage in the canonization of the scriptures, the image of the Hakham presented itself in full maturity. It was a complex image, comprising the outlines of several functionaries in the Jewish community, who did not always see eye to eye. The typological diversity of the Hakhamim could hardly be accounted for only by differences in individual character. Rather did it reflect residual elements of several types of authority that varied in function as well as outlook.

II

The keepers of the holy writ (sefarim) assumed the title of Scribes (soferim). Originally their function was to write down or copy the sacred literature and ensure the faithful transmission to posterity of this body of writings. Later authorities have defined their duty thus: "The early scholars were called soferim because they used to count all the letters of the Torah" (Kiddushin 30a). This rendering of "sofer" from the original sense of its root 'safar'—to count, though hardly of etymological significance, is yet substantially correct. The scrutinizers of the texts, who possessed specific authority, derived their livelihood from the temple funds and appear to have been of priestly stock.[1] They doubtless did not belong to the upper hierarchy. Whether belonging to the temple or working beyond its confines, these scribes were by no means wealthy.

Ben Sira who wrote during the years 190–170 B.C.E., shortly after Eretz-Israel had passed from Ptolemaic to Seleucid rule, regarded the skill of the scribes as an asset which, whilst enhancing their wisdom, did not contribute to their social standing and general esteem. For those employed in this art, like artisans in general, "shall not be enquired of for public counsel and in the assembly they enjoy no precedence".

The Hakham, on the other hand, lacked a definite vocation. Occupying the seat of justice, his mind was directed to the contemplation of law and righteousness "who serveth among great men and appeareth before princes". In their role as exponents of the Torah, the scribes interpreted and disseminated the scripture. All these connotations of the term "sofer" can indeed be found in the sources. Both in the scope of their activity as well as method of procedure, the scribes bear comparison with the Alexandrian school of Greek grammarians and interpreters of Homer, who flourished during the third century B.C.E. The Hakhamim, cn the other hand, as depicted by Ben Sira, were wealthy men who regarded their activity as chosen to fulfil a mission. They served at the courts of law and were members of the supreme council. This was the γερουσία mentioned in the dispatch of Antiochus III in 190 B.C.E. beside "the priests and scribes of the temple".[2]

As their forerunners, the men of the "Great Assembly" or their descendants, the officers of the Sanhedrin, so the members of the "Gerousia" exercised their judicial and other public functions without remuneration. The contrast in the respective positions of scribes and

[1] Jer. Shekalim, Ch. 4, Hal. 3, p. 48a.
[2] Josephus Antiquities, Ch. 12:3,8.

Hakhamim was not unlike that known to us from the annals of Roman Law during the classical period. On the one hand there were the jurists, arbiters and makers of law, and on the other men who interpreted the ancient body of laws. Judicial matters did not however claim the exclusive interest of the Hakhamim. In the words of Ben Sira (38:20–30) they would ponder the will of the Almighty, meditate upon the writings of the prophets and delve into the wisdom of the ancients. Their minds dwelled upon the discourse of eminent authorities, their parables and esoteric utterances. This intellectual activity was, moreover, imbued by a fear of God, expressing itself in prayer, thanksgiving and a keen sense of moral purpose. The Hakham portrayed by Ben Sira, no less than the one depicted in the book of Proverbs, was no doubt expected to be imbued with fear of the Lord, and be zealous in the performance of His commandments (1:23; 19:20; 25:14–15). He was to eschew the company of men of violence and iniquity and to seek that of men of virtue. In no instance, however, does the Hakham appear to mingle with broader sections of society. Though his bearing and wisdom may be extolled by the public at large, he always retains his distance. Nor do we hear of the Hakham acting within the community for the weal of the many. The exclusive character and status of the Hakham in the Hellenistic period preceding the Hasmonean revolt comes to evidence in the following dictum of the contemporary Jose b. Joezer: "Let thy house be a meeting-house to the Sages and sit amid the dust of their feet and drink in their words with thirst" (Aboth 1:4). True, another contemporary—the Jerusalemite Jose b. Johanan—has put forth an entirely different plea: "Let thy house be opened wide and let needy be members of they household" (Ib., 1:5). However, although the latter pronouncement stresses the call for charity and relief rather than wisdom, it is no less aristocratic and philanthropic in character. Both appeals are significantly directed towards the householder.

III

At the turn of the second century B.C.E. Palestine was rocked by upheavals with far-reaching consequences. There were the repressive measures of Antiochus Epiphanes against the Jewish religion in the year 167, to be followed by countless deeds of martyrdom. Then came the raising of the banner of revolt under the leadership of the Hasmonean family of priests at Modi'in. They were joined by "many who were seeking righteousness and justice" as also by "a company of Hassidim, mighty men of Israel who willingly offered themselves for the Law".[3] The military victories of the Maccabees and attendant enhancement of

[3] I Maccabees 2:29 and ib. 41.

Judean power were of decisive significance to the subsequent course of Jewish history.

This was the first uprising in history directed against religious repression. The struggle of the bands of Hassidim, faithful adherents to the Torah, was waged both against the hostile power from without, as well as against the Hellenizers from within, who had absorbed a foreign way of life.

A new national leadership emerged in the wake of the Maccabean military triumph and resulting increase in the power of the Judean state. The solemn proclamation in the year 140 B.C.E. by the "Great assembly of priests, the people, leaders of the nation and elders of the land" appointing Simeon as high priest and ethnarch, heralded the rise of the Hasmonean era with all its expectations and disappointments and bitter social political and spiritual conflicts. Less evident are the changes wrought in the sphere of institutional authority. Hasmonean ascendancy no doubt resulted in the displacement of privileged families of extremist Hellenizers and the raising to positions of influence of faithful warriors in the Hasmonean cause.

The replacement of the Zadokite family of high priests by priests of Hasmonean descent, though politically significant, did not denote the essence of the transformation that had occurred. Of greater consequence was the fact that the hitherto existing distribution of orders and functions had disintegrated. True, there were still priests, scribes and the judiciary dealing with tort, but their positions were now taken over by the Hakhamim. From now on there were Hakhamim-priests, Hakhamim-scribes, Hakhamim-judges and Hakhamim-saints.

According to the earliest data in our possession, the Hakhamim's appearance upon the historical scene is not unlike that of such early prophets as Nathan, Gad, Ahia and Elijah, who remonstrated with kings and princes. But whereas prophetic leadership was of a charismatic nature and its appeal stemmed from the divine call, the Hakhamim derived their authority from their intellectual standing. This in turn entailed an intimate knowledge of the Torah and Halakhah whose discipline and provisions elicited their unqualified loyalty.

The source material at our command draws our attention to the first Hakham of the Hasmonean era—to Simeon b. Shetah. We meet him seated at the court of law in order to pronounce judgement upon a servant of King Alexander Jannaeus, charged with homicide. In accordance with the Halakhic stipulation that the master must appear in court, the king was summoned by Simeon b. Shetah: "The king accordingly came and sat down, then Simeon b. Shetah said: 'stand on thy feet, King Yannai, and let the witnesses testify against thee...' 'I shall not act in accordance with what thou sayest, but in accordance with what thy colleagues say' he answered. Simeon then turned first to the right and then to the left, but they all looked down at the ground. Then said Simeon b. Shetah unto them: 'Are ye wrapped up in thoughts? Let the Master of thoughts come and call you to account!' ".[4]

The other members of the Sanhedrin, though sharing Simeon's functions at court, do not appear also to have shared his views and his courage.

Simeon's measures were aimed at improving existing legal procedure. Evidence of this is found in his Halakhic pronouncements on the examination of witnesses, the rejection of verdicts based upon circumstantial evidence and the punishment of false witnesses.[5] The judges were enjoined to adhere to the following general principle: "Examine the witnesses diligently and be cautious in thy words lest from them they learn to swear falsely" (Aboth 1:9). His ordinance requiring the husband to include in the marriage deed a provision rendering all his property liable to his wife as a security, was intended as a barrier to rash divorce. The clause also acted as a safeguard of the woman's economic plight upon separation.[6] According to one source it was Simeon b. Shetah who ordered "that children be sent to school".[7] The precise nature of this provision and its relation to other traditions regarding the instituting of an educational system are not sufficiently clear. The report of this Hakham's exertions in the sphere of popular education is in itself of telling significance for the purpose of this survey. Likewise we meet Simeon b. Shetah bent upon enabling indigent Nazirites to release themselves from their vow and providing the required sacrifices.[8] Like the prophet Elijah, he too is reported to have acted zealously for the Lord when, as an emergency measure, he ordered the execution of eighty women found guilty of sorcery and indulgence in licentious orgies at Ascalon.[9] In the Talmud we also find traditional accounts of friendly relations between Simeon b. Shetah and King Yannai.[10] Thus the Hakham is seated by the side of the king at a reception accorded to the envoys of the king of Persia who remembered Simeon's words of wisdom from previous visits. The general atmosphere depicted in these accounts may be convivial, nevertheless they also point to the Hakham's unyielding spirit. His conversation, though cordial, does not lack an unmistakable note of reproach. It may well be assumed that several of Simeon's measures originated during this period of close relations with the royalty. The exalted position and reverence he was accorded, the Hakham

[4] B. Sanhedrin, p. 19a.
[5] Jer. Sanhedrin, Ch. 6, Hal. 5, p. 23a; B. Hagigah, p. 16b.
[6] B. Shabbath, p. 14b; B. Ketuboth, p. 82b.
[7] Jer. Ketuboth, Ch. 8, Hal. 11, p. 32c.
[8] Jer. Berakoth, Ch. 7, Hal. 2, p. 11b; Jer. Nazir, Ch. 5, Hal. 2, p. 54b.
[9] Mishnah Sanhedrin 6:6; Jer. Hagigah, Ch. 2, Hal. 2, p. 77d; Jer. Sanhedrin, Ch. 6, Hal. 9, p. 23c.
[10] B. Berakoth, p. 48a, also cf. above note 8.

characteristically attributed to his Torah learning. To eke out a livelihood
he worked as a flax-dresser. In his dealings with fellow men he was forever mindful of a need to act in such manner as would lead to the
sanctification of the Lord; that men might say: "Blessed be the God of
the Jews".[11]

IV

Though fragmentary, our sources about this early Hakham contain
valuable information as to the basic attributes which were to shape the
Hakhamim of future generations. It was Simeon b. Shetah's norms of
conduct that posterity was to regard as ideals to be cherished and
emulated.

The activities of the Hakham and his leading influence within the
community were not necessarily related to the assumption of public
office. Whether or not occupying a position of power, the Hakham felt
obliged to instruct the public and guide their actions. The force of his
authority derived first and foremost from his knowledge of the Torah. Thus
also was his attitude to the powers that be or to the rich, at all times determined solely by their morals. He neither sought nor shunned their company but was intent upon retaining his position of independence, gaining
a livelihood by means of manual occupation. The guiding principle contained in the dictum of Simeon's disciple Shemaiah: "Love labour and
hate mastery and seek not acquaintance with the ruling power" (Aboth
1:10), may well reflect the lessons drawn from the personal history of
his master, whose conduct set the standard for the Hakhamim's attitude
to work, authority and the ruling power. The Hakhamim strove for a
reform in the conduct of communal affairs, in the dispensation of law
and justice, family status and popular education. All was to be impreg-
nated with the spirit of the Torah and fear of God.

The outlines of Simeon b. Shetah discernible in our scanty source
material are instructive in their positive implications. But we learn no
less from the elements and qualities omitted in the accounts of his deeds,
such as the contemplative and mystical, or supernatural and miraculous.
This is not to imply that Simeon b. Shetah must have necessarily rejected
such manifestations; it does however indicate that these were not the
dominant traits of his personality. In his company were also found
miracle workers. Such a one was Onias the Circle-maker, who, as Elijah
before him, invoked prayer in order to relieve his people from the terrors
of a severe drought. His entreaty to God: "I swear by thy great name
that I will not stir hence until thou have pity on thy children" and the
stress laid upon his own person in the words: "Thy children have turned
their faces to me" were foreign to the spirit of Simeon b. Shetah. True,

[11] Jer. Baba Metzia, Ch. 2, Hal. 5, p. 8c.

Onias' prayer had proved effective, but this did not deter Simeon from addressing Onias with a message wherein recognition was mingled with reproof: "Hadst thou not been Onias I had pronounced a ban against thee! But what shall I do to thee?—thou importunest God and he performeth thy will like a son that importunest his father and he performeth his will". [12] A measure of disapproval of Onias' action is evident in these words. At the same time, however, Simeon could not but recognize the singular status enjoyed by Onias in the presence of God. He may likewise have been impressed by the reverence in which Onias was held by large sections of the population.

Simeon b. Shetah was the legitimate heir to one important aspect of the prophetic tradition in assuming the prerogative of intervening in matters of state, admonishing kings and rulers and waging a relentless struggle against all corruption. But Onias the Circle-maker—the first of a long line of saints and men of virtue known to us by name—inherited a no less authentic element of early prophecy, viz., the ability to invoke the supernatural and perform miraculous deeds. True, the early prophets combined both aspects, whereas in our case these had become separated. Yet the two elements continued to function under one and the same roof. The common people appear to have viewed Onias as an image of Elijah and when the rains came in answer to Onias' prayer, this merely enhanced his popularity. As for Simeon, he was satisfied by clarifying the situation with a definition of his own. God had granted Onias' wish as a father might accede to the plea of his son. Simeon b. Shetah's treatment of Onias displayed a typical strain of the Hakhamim when dealing with groups and currents whose trends and principles did not wholly agree with their own. Rather than challenging such factions, the Hakhamim would impress their attitudes from within, thus modifying such views until they met their own. Being so disposed, the Hakhamim did not hasten to banish groups and eliminate manifestations which they could not sanction, even when they were in a position to do so. Evidence of this may be found in the record of relations between the Hakhamim and the Sadducees. When the latter constituted the dominant party, they sought to turn their adversaries into a sect of schismatics (Porshim), hence the designation 'Pharisees' (Perushim). Not so the Hakhamim, who, when the tables had turned in their favour, did not proceed to ostracize the Sadducees. At any rate no such tendency is discernible in the general tenor of their disputations or in the recorded accounts of these.[13] If, none the less, we do find a growing severity towards heretics, this was the result of dissidence on the part of individuals and sects, e.g., the

---

[12] Mishnah Taanith 3:8; Tosefta ib., Ch. 3, Hal. 1; Jer. ib., Ch. 3, Hal. 11, p. 66d; B. ib., p. 23a.
[13] Mishnah Makkoth 1:6; Mishnah Yadaim 1:6–8; Mishnah Erubin 6:2; Tosefta Yoma, Ch. 1, Hal. 8.

Judaeo-Christians of the second century C.E.[14] This sect, whilst pleading for the abolition of Israel as a separate congregation, yet demanded recognition as the legitimate heirs of Jewry.

The Hakhamim aspired to the leadership and instruction of the broadest strata of the population, whose manner of living they wished to share. A not inconsiderable reason for the success of their bid was the fact that the Hakhamim actually did come from all classes and walks of life. There were aristocratic priests, men of wealth, the sons of great landowners, as well as destitute craftsmen, serfs, farmers, hired hands and the sons of proselytes. In their endeavour to fashion the character of the people and guide the destiny of the nation, the Hakhamim would encompass the entire gamut of classes and estates. Hillel's maxim "Keep not aloof from the congregation" (Aboth 2:5) had already served his mentors Shemaiah and Avtalyon who refused an oath of allegiance to Herod. Shemaiah's dictum "seek not acquaintance with the ruling power" was, however, complemented by that of Avtalyon: "Ye Sages, give heed to your words lest ye incur the penalty of exile" (Aboth 1:11).

Those lacking circumspection in their choice of words were always liable to be condemned to exile or to the mines by despotic rulers of Herod's brand. It was wrong to supply a tyrant with a ready subterfuge for ridding himself of men who recognized the true nature of his motives and thus deprive the people of their natural leaders. A measure of the popularity of the two sages and their relation to the high priest—possibly the Hasmonean Aristobulus, or someone appointed by Herod—may be gained from the following story: "It happened with a high-priest that as he came from the sanctuary, all the people followed him, but when they saw Shemaiah and Avtalyon, they forsook him, and went after Shemaiah and Avtalyon. Eventually Shemaiah and Avtalyon visited him, to take their leave of the high priest. He said to them: 'May the descendants of the heathen come in peace!' They answered him: 'May the descendants of the heathen who do the work of Aaron arrive in peace, but the descendant of Aaron, who does not do the work of Aaron, he shall not come in peace!' "[15].

Both sages were willing to pay due homage to the high priest. But when the latter reacts angrily to the preference displayed by the people towards the Hakhamim, insultingly pointing to their alien descent, their reply is ready at hand. What mattered was not a person's ancestry, whether or not he was of Aaronic descent. The real question was whether his deeds conformed to Aaronic standards. This same spirit informed the plea made by the discipline of Hillel: "Be of the disciples of Aaron, loving peace and pursuing peace, loving mankind and bringing them nigh to

---

[14] Tosefta Berakhot, Ch. 3, Hal. 24; Jer. ib., Ch. 2, Hal. 4, p. 5a; Tosefta Shabbat, Ch. 13, Hal. 5; Jer. ib., Ch. 16, Hal. 1, p. 15c; B. ib., p. 115b.
[15] B. Yoma, p. 71b.

the Law" (Aboth 1:12). Those imbued with such virtues are reckoned disciples of Aaron and are nobler than his physical descendants who do not follow in the footsteps of the ancestor.

Encompassing the temple precincts were the abodes of families of the high priests, who occupied leading positions as treasurers and senior officers. With the passage of time there arose households who for generations held a monopoly of such appointments. They likewise possessed a lore of their own in regard to certain forms of temple worship, the secrets of which would be transmitted from one generation to the next. Close to the destruction of the Second Temple there lived in Jerusalem a Hakham by name of Saul b. Batnith, a shopkeeper, who assailed these priestly families for their exclusive hold upon the senior positions and for their violent habits. These were his words: "Woe unto me from the House of Elisha, woe unto me from their fists, woe unto me from the House of Ishmael b. Piabi, who are high priests and their sons are treasurers and their sons-in-law temple officers and their servants come over us and beat us up with sticks." [16]

A similar accusation is found in another source about the "powerful among the priests" who entered the temple and forcibly removed the skins from the sacrifices, thus preventing a just allocation of the perquisites to the officiating priests. [17] The families of initiates who refused to teach their skills to others elicited the censure of the Hakhamim as persons dedicated to the cultivation of their own glory rather than that of Heaven. [18] Moreover, the priests' excessive regard for the rules of ritual purity too was condemned by the Hakhamim, there being priests for whom "the ritual uncleanness of a knife was graver than the shedding of blood". [19] However, the Hakhamim did not rest satisfied in merely voicing their disapproval of certain acts. They actively strove to propagate their views within the temple precincts and impress their notions upon the temple service that it might conform to their own customs and traditions.

V

Hillel, who came to Palestine from Babylonia, was able to prevail upon the B'nai Bethera, probably also Babylonian immigrants, who had been appointed by Herod to a leading position in the temple, subsequent to the king's ejection of the Hasmoneans from the high priesthood. In his disputation with the B'nai Bethera, Hillel resorted to the seven hermeneutic principles applied to the interpretation of the Torah, in order to prove that the paschal sacrifice superseded the Sabbath if the 14th of Nissan fell on the seventh day. Such was the ruling he had

[16] Tosefta Menahoth, Ch. 13, Hal. 20.
[17] Tosefta Zebahim, Ch. 11, Hal. 16.
[18] Mishnah Yoma 3:11; Jer. ib., Ch. 3, Hal. 9, p. 41a.
[19] Tosefta Yoma, Ch. 1, Hal. 12.

received from his mentors, Shemaiah and Avtalyon. This Halakhah had receded into the background, leaving the matter open to differences of opinion, inasmuch as it was only rarely that the eve of Passover ever happened to coincide with the Sabbath. Hillel's view gained ascendancy, not only having traditional authority in its favour, but also because the multitudes of pilgrims to Jerusalem appear to have shared his opinion. Thus, when the B'nai Bethera pleaded: "What shall become of the people who have not brought to the temple their knives and paschal offerings?", Hillel was able to counter: "Leave them alone, the holy spirit is upon them and if they are not prophets, they are the sons of prophets." To be sure, the people solved the problem by taking along their paschal lambs and slaughtering knives in their ascent to the temple, as did their ancestors before.[20]

Hillel's singular combination of scriptural evidence with Rabbinic tradition and popular usage was a significant factor in the general acceptance of his views. Ultimately his patriarchal authority was also recognized by the B'nai Bethera in the Halakhic regulation of the temple service. Evidence of Hillel's predominance is likewise to be gained from an enactment directed at the temple treasury. The latter served i.a. as a centre of financial transactions having no direct bearing upon the temple as such. It was controlled by the temple officers and treasurers. In order to circumvent the Biblical injunction which enables the seller of a house in a walled city to redeem it every twelve months, some buyers would go into hiding on the last day, thus rendering their acquisition irrevocable. Thereupon: "Hillel the Elder ordained that he that sold it could deposit his money in the Temple Chamber."[21]

In order to implement the enactment, several banking practices had to be carried out by the temple officers in charge of the treasury, e.g., registering the name of the depositor and that of the buyer to whose credit the sum would accrue. A person reduced to selling his house was no doubt in dire straits and it was in order to prevent the rise of conditions under which he could never regain possession of his property, that Hillel's ordinance was conceived. Similary the enacting of the Prosbul by Hillel was rooted in the Hakham's solicitude for the interests of the impecunious artisan, shopkeeper and petty trader, forever in need of credit "in order that prospective borrowers should not find the door of their benefactors locked before them".[22] This provision, though virtually abrogating sabbatical provisions in regard to the remission of debts, was nevertheless truly mindful of the underlying idea and spirit of the sabbatical institution.

As pointed out above, the acts of the priests and their customs

[20] Tosefta Pesahim, Ch. 4, Hal. 1–2; Jer. ib., Ch. 6, Hal. 1, p. 33a; B. ib., p. 66a.
[21] Mishnah Arakhin 9:4.
[22] Mishnah Shebiith 9:3; B. Gittin, p. 36b.

relating to the temple service did not always accord with the notions and standards of the Hakhamim. There is little doubt of the historical relevance to the period of Hillel in the Mishnaic account of the elders of the Beth Din who adjured the high priest not to deviate from their instructions concerning the order of the temple worship.[23]

In his public and judicial capacity, Hillel revealed himself as a capable man of action, whose keen and far-sighted mental faculties inevitably gained him a position of influence. All the more remarkable are the traditional accounts of the more intimate aspects of his personality with its proverbial qualities of the rarest patience and humility. These no doubt greatly facilitated his endeavour to attract men to the Torah. Proof of his achievements were the many disciples who flocked to him as well as the proselytes to whom Hillel's wisdom was the gateway to the God of Israel.

It is in the traditional accounts of Hillel that we first encounter two fundamental notions which informed the spiritual world of the Hakhamim. First of these was the concept of "Oral Torah" applied to all the rabbinic traditions, scriptural interpretations and homiletic insights, in contradistinction to the "Written Torah". It is to Hillel that tradition imputes the view that the "Written Torah" is not to be conceived of without the elaborations and amplifications of the "Oral Torah".[24] In itself, the need for exegesis and supplementary enactments did not constitute a novel departure on the part of the Pharisaic Hakhamim. The Sadducees too possessed their methods of interpretation and homiletics, as did the Essenes and other sects. Proof of this is readily found in the Apocryphal literature as well as in the Dead Sea Scrolls. The contrast between the Hakhamim and sectarian doctrine expressed itself both in the substance of the Halakhot, as well as in the very concept that underlay them. In sectarian writings, such as the Book of Jubilees, Halakhah emerges as law hailing from the patriarchal era. A different method was employed in the recently discovered scroll entitled "The Torah of God". Here the Halakhot are made to appear as an integral part of Biblical scripture, thus obscuring the distinction between text and exposition. Both are presented as the word of God. The Pharisaic Hakhamim, on the other hand, considered their traditions and homiletical interpretations as oral lore, not to be equated with the written Torah. Only the latter was definitive and thus could not suffer change. The framing of decrees and provisions was, no doubt, within the jurisdiction of the Hakhamim, as was the interpretation and elucidation of the Biblical text. At no time, however, were their pronouncements regarded as definitive Biblical law—"Divrei Torah". A distinction was maintained

[23] Mishnah Yoma 1:2; Tosefta ib., Ch. 1, Hal. 8.
[24] B. Shabbath, p. 31a; Aboth de R. Nathan, vers. A, Ch. 15, vers. B, Ch. 29; Ed. Shechter, pp. 61-62.

throughout between the latter and "Divrei Sofrim", or "Divrei Hakha-mim". The principle of keeping the scriptures free from the interpolation of oral traditions was meticulously observed. Again it is in the pro-nouncements of Hillel that we first meet the notion of life in a world to come as a reward for the deeds of man upon earth. Ben Sira's observation (41:18), "Vanity is man concerning his body, but the name of the pious shall not be cut off. Be in fear for thy name, for that abideth longer for thee than thousands of precious treasures," is paralleled by that of Hillel: "If one acquires for himself a good name he acquires something for himself." But he adds: "If one acquires for himself knowledge of the Torah he acquires for himself life in the world to come" (Aboth 2:7). With Hillel no dichotomy of body and soul, flesh and spirit was implied by the notion of heaven any more than by that of the resurrection of the dead. Nor did he subscribe to the ascetic concept of liberating the soul from the body. This certainly did not imply any tendency on the part of Hillel to condone unbridled pursuit of pleasure or uncontrolled indul-gence in luxury. A fair indication of his attitude to materialism is found in the utterance: "The more flesh, the more worms, the more possession, the more worry, the more wives, the more witchcraft..." (Aboth 2:7). On the other hand the gratification of one's physical requirements rather than being a mere necessity, was to be regarded as an actual Mitzvah. This view comes to the fore in the following story which is also indicative of the didactic methods of Hillel: "For once when he left his disciples, they said to him, 'Whither are you going?' He replied 'To execute a pious deed.' They asked, 'What may that be?' He said, 'To take a bath.' They said, 'Is that a pious deed?' He said, 'Yes, for if the man who is appointed to polish and wash the images of kings which are set up in the theatres and circuses receives his rations for doing so, and is even raised up to be regarded as among the great ones of the kingdom, how much more is it obligatory on me to polish and wash my body, since I have been created in the divine image and likeness.' ".[25] Having been created in the image of God, man was likewise obliged to take due care of the cleanliness of his body and its general wellbeing.

It has been reported of Hillel that all his actions were performed "for the sake of Heaven"[26] and such indeed was his unlimited trust in God that it banished in him all fear and anxiety.

His tolerance, love of mankind and quest for peace did not diminish the force of his moral and religious principles. Man was to be regarded as a fully responsible being, who must strive for personal perfection as well as for the common weal. It was necessary for man to act because: "If not I for myself, who then?" At the same time little could be achieved in solitary seclusion. Man was to bear in mind: "And being for myself,

[25] Leviticus Rabbah 34:3.
[26] B. Betzah, p. 16a; B. Berakoth, p. 60a.

what am I?" Nor must he forget that his sojourn upon earth was limited, leaving no time for procrastination, thus: "And if not now, when?" (Aboth 1:14). Inter-human relations were to be guided by the sublime precept: "What is hateful to thee do not do to thy fellow." Moreover, man was to refrain from hasty judgement upon his fellow-man and from the unwarranted justification of his own person, thus: "Put no trust in thyself until the day of thy death" and "Do not judge thy comrade until thou hast stood in his place" (Aboth 2:4). At the same time man's humility and awareness of his limitations must not serve as a pretext for shunning the burdens of the many: "Do not withdraw from the community" (ib.:ib.), Hillel warns, adding: "And where there are no men, strive to be a man" (ib.: 5). In his quest for religion man must be imbued with fear of sin and with saintliness. These qualities cannot, however, be achieved without the acquisition of the substance of the Torah, inasmuch as "The boor is no fearer of sin, the Am Ha'arez cannot be a saint." Hillel's disciple, Rabbi Yohanan b. Zakkai, expressed the relation between wisdom and fear of sin by the following simile: "A wise man pervaded by fear of sin... he is like a craftsman with the tools of his craft in hand; a wise man devoid of the fear of sin... he is like a craftsman who does not wield the tools of his craft; the sin-fearing who is not wise... he is not a craftsman but the tools of his craft are with him." [27]

VI

The total impression gained from the traditional accounts of Hillel, his pronouncements and deeds, is that of an ideal Hakham, in whom saintliness and humility are the outstanding features. The keynotes in this type of saintliness are simplicity and frugality as distinct from the extravagant practices of the ascetic and hermit. Moreover, though humility is a constant theme, it is never allowed to imply the extinction of human individuality. Nor is the abrogation of private property called for. A saint is he who declares: "What is mine is thine and what is thine is thine" (Aboth 5:13), whereas he who affirms the common possession of things by saying: "What is mine is thine and what is thine is mine" is but a boor.

Study and instruction were the principal functions of the Hakham, charity and loving-kindness his chief characteristics. Being part of the community, he aspired to a decisive role in shaping the character of the supreme national institutions such as the Temple, Sanhedrin and Priesthood. His was to be the authoritative voice in all matters of Halakhah. The source of his influence lay however in his spiritual powers alone. It was the qualities and deeds of the Hakham which determined his standing among the people. A similar light upon the

[27] Aboth de R. Nathan, Ch. 22, p. 74.

character of the Hakham is shed by Josephus, a near contemporary of Hillel, in the closing part of his "Antiquities": "For our people do not favour those persons who have mastered the speech of many nations, or who adorn their style with smoothness of diction... But they give credit for wisdom to those alone who have an exact knowledge of the law and who are capable of interpreting the Holy Scriptures." In yet another reference to the Hakhamim, Josephus makes the claim that "Even if they say ought against the king or high priest, their words gain immediate acceptance". [28]

A characteristic feature in the realm of the Hakhamim during the Second Commonwealth until the days of Hillel is the absence of any bureaucratic organization. There was no set procedure of appointment, no grades of advancement and, in fact, no salary. Moreover, there was no apparatus for training a Hakham, nor even a definition of his functions. It was with the rise of Hillel that the status of the Hakhamim was to undergo a profound change. This was in no small measure due to the impressive results achieved by Hillel in his labours. It is actually during this period that we first encounter the designation "Beth Hillel", with its dynastic connotation. This is not lessened by the fact that Hillel's son, Simeon, grandson Gamaliel and great grandson Simeon did not rule as patriarchs in the sense in which the Hasmonean Simeon had done. Nor even did they compare with the Hillelite patriarchs in the period following the destruction of the Second Temple. Nevertheless it is beyond doubt that they enjoyed a special status in the Sanhedrin and that in certain fields theirs was a central role. Both the growth in the number of disciples belonging to Beth Hillel as well as the hegemonic character which it assumed, intensified the contrast between this school and Beth Shammai. As the Second Commonwealth drew to its tragic end, political sectarianism and internecine strife began to intrude into the realm of the Hakhamim as well. However, when the temple finally lay in ruins and central authority had broken down leaving the nation leaderless, the redeeming element appeared in the person of Rabbi Yohanan b. Zakkai. The changed circumstances called for the recreation of a supreme governing body charged with the rehabilitation of the religious life of the nation and to this end Rabbi Yohanan devoted all his energy and skill. The historical record leaves us in the dark on the question of his status as well as on the nature of the academic Sanhedrin which he brought into being. The fact remains that in his immediate succession we meet at Yavneh the Hillelite Rabban Gamaliel assuming the role of Patriarch beside being Av Beth Din. His having taken sanction from the Roman proconsul of Syria demonstrates the nature of his external standing. Within, too, he appears as a dominant national figure, not only as Hakham and Av Beth Din, but also by virtue of his Hillelite lineage.

[28] Antiquities 13, p. 288.

Such indeed was the pre-eminence of the Hillelite dynasty of patriarchs
—subsequently established as of Davidic descent—that its reign endured
for over three hundred years until the last Rabban Gamaliel (the fifth or
sixth), who died heirless during the reign of Theodosius II, at about
425 C.E. That this supreme institution remained for so long in the face
of the countless vicissitudes of this period, in the hands of a single family,
is in itself an eloquent testimony of the distinction and resilience of the
patriarchate.

The status of the patriarchate no doubt varied considerably with the
character and personality of the particular incumbent, his erudition and
administrative skill. A great deal also depended on relations with the
foreign power, i.e., Roman authorities. The very diversity in the stature
and accomplishments of individual patriarchs and the not infrequent
changes in the attitude of the foreign rulers towards the Jews and their
authorities, is further proof of the constancy of this institution. A closer
inspection of the patriarchate through the sources at our disposal,
however, reveals that it is only from a bird's eye view that we can speak
of stability. In actual fact it was beset by many a crisis during the long
course of its history. Indeed, the very factors which made for its greatness
as a symbol of remaining freedom and independence, were the ones to
militate in its disfavour. For inasmuch as the leadership was drawn from
among the ranks of the Hakhamim, they risked being generally identified
with power and the perversities and defects which it connotes. This
danger was averted largely due to the circumstance that in every generation there were found individuals among the Hakhamim who were
prepared to continue the struggle against the excesses of high priests,
kings and potentates. At this juncture, however, the confrontation was
with the power and authority of leaders who, rising from the ranks of
Hakhamim, were now endeavouring to assert their ascendancy over
them. Changed political circumstances had conferred upon the patriarchs
functions hitherto exercised by other bodies. The supervision of Halakhic
pronouncements in the judicial and religious spheres was maintained by
centralizing appointments and scrutinizing the choice of disciples. In
the view of Rabban Gamaliel II of Yavneh, it was the task of the patriarchs to set up a centrally controlled judicial system which would
operate in the towns and villages. The maintenance of ties with diaspora
Jewry was likewise to be taken care of by the patriarchs. This meant
more than the journeys to Rome undertaken by the patriarch in the
company of his elders. Emissaries were to be sent to overseas centres in
Arabia, Cilicia, Africa, Galatia, Cappadocia and Gazaka in Media. All
this required the appointment of functionaries and the placing of communal affairs in the hands of public officials. The control of Halakhic
decision introduced by Rabban Gamaliel II led to a head-on collision
between the patriarch and those among the Hakhamim who insisted on

the right of unrestrained Halakhic exposition. When Gamaliel II resorted to punitive measures to assert his authority, a rebellion ensued, resulting in the deposition of the patriarch. Subsequently a compromise was reached in the setting up of an oligarchal leadership, as it were, but this too did not succeed in eliciting the unqualified concurrence of individual Hakhamim who would brook no interference in what they considered as their unquestionable right of defining Halakhah in the light of their own reason. As is evident from this confrontation as well as from the crises that were yet to arise, majority opinion would in no case allow antagonism to develop to the point of severing the bond between the House of Hillel and the patriarchate. Opposition expressed itself merely in strongly worded condemnations of patriarchs whose actions and deportment called for censure.

VII

The problem of the sustenance of Hakhamim holding public office was to effect a profound transformation in the social and economic standing of many Hakhamim. It even threatened to affect the moral image of the Hakham, whose salary could not be assigned from public funds. Inasmuch as he was not well-to-do, his livelihood depended upon the people's foremost patron—the patriarch, whose resources were to provide for an ever-increasing number of Hakhamim. This condition was a decisive factor in fostering in the Hakhamim a social class-consciousness. As Torah learning became synonymous with their avocation, the Hakhamim came to be regarded as one among other classes of professionals. This novel association of Torah with a man's calling likewise led to the notion that like other crafts, it could be transmitted as an heritage from father to son. In the light of these developments must be seen the proclamations deprecating the tendency among certain families to regard the Torah and the dignity and privilege which it bestowed, as a substance that could be passed on·by inheritance. The very establishment on a national scale of a spiritual leadership in whom dissemination of Torah and exposition of Halakhah combined with the assumption of public office and authority, constituted a novel departure from traditional practice. The recently risen hierarchy produced a new type of Hakham who in addition to his spiritual functions, also controlled the affairs of the community and whose authority passed on to his offspring. Nor were all the trappings of power, its pomp and circumstance, wanting in the deportment of the new ruling class. It was due to developments such as these that the Hakhamim at the close of the Tannaitic period and throughout that of the Amoraim became distinguished as a class apart. The individual Hakham was recognized even in his "way of walking, manner of speech and outdoor dress"[29]. It is noteworthy that evidence of disaffection should be found at the very period when the incumbent to the patriarchate was none other than Rabbi Judah the Prince, known as 'Rabbi' or teacher par excellence. Carrying his office with rare dignity he had succeeded in re-establishing the badly shaken position of his people. His religious stature and Halakhic authority likewise gained universal recognition. Attacking "Rabbi" for his "veneration of the rich", style of living, ruling habits and the regal aspect assumed by his court, his opponents proceeded to direct their strictures at the Eretz-Israel patriarchate and Babylonian exilarchate as such.[30] 'Rabbi' himself was not unaware of the contradictory nature of the elements the present leadership was endeavouring to combine. On the one hand was the Talmid Hakham whose life of Torah learning and good deeds tended towards the Kingdom of Heaven and world of the spirit. On the other were power and wealth—the palpable emblems of political ascendancy. Thus, in his message to posterity, the great patriarch ruled in favour of severing the functions of the patriarch from that of the Head of the Academy. The separation of the supreme national-political authority, i.e., the patriarchate, from the presidency of the academies was actually retained even when the patriarch was a man of great Torah learning. It was to endure after 'Rabbi' throughout the remaining period of the patriarchate. A similar division of authority obtained in the great Babylonian Jewish centre, where the heads of the academies retained their prerogatives vis-à-vis the exilarch, whose influence began to be felt only at the close of Rabbi Judah's rule.

Increasing evidence of the tensions and conflicts marking relations between the Exilarchs and heads of Academies has come to the fore with the mounting information now available on Jewish life in the Babylonian diaspora. Differences centred on the question of relative powers as well as on the style of life and discharge of authority on the part of those in power. The division of powers did not banish strife from the Hakhamim in their own realm inasmuch as many of them maintained family bonds with the dynasties of the Eretz-Israel patriarchs or Babylonian exilarchs. Several Hakhamim, moreover, received public appointments from these rulers and held office in the vicinity of the central authorities. Naturally enough, such Hakhamim would largely refrain from assuming a critical attitude, identifying themselves increasingly with those in power. Conflict thus became inevitable with those Hakhamim who displayed extreme disapproval of the powers that be, whose refusal to countenance detrimental manifestations led to their shunning of all contact with authority.

---

[29] Sifre Deuteronomy, par. 343, and cf. Jer. Bikkurim, Ch. 3, Hal. 3, p. 65c; Jer. Nedarim, Ch. 11, p. 42b.
[30] B. Sanhedrin, p. 38b. 1. J. NEUSNER, A History of the Jews in Babylonia, III, Leiden, 1968, p. 41-94.

However, there was also a positive aspect to the mutual recriminations and strictures that issued from the two foci of dominion. They prevented a decline in the moral and religious fervour of the Hakhamim, safeguarding the distinct character of their ascendancy. For theirs was no arbitrary rule of institutional authority. It was the triumph of personality and single-minded devotion to the study and dissemination of Torah. Herein lay the source from which the entire nation was to draw its sustenance, regardless of rank or class.

VIII

The veneration of the Hakham was first and foremost a result of his mastery of Torah—both written and oral. The traditional lore transmitted by the Hakhamim from one generation to the next comprised Halakhot, legal decisions, directives, enactments, preventive measures and usages. But it also contained expositions and homiletic interpretations relating to Biblical stories, prophetic utterances and the wisdom of ancients. The study of both Halakhah and Aggadah was at all times attuned to prevailing social, economic and political conditions. Developments in these spheres were reflected in the language, style and method employed by the Hakhamim. New realities thus impressed themselves upon the very substance of both Halakhah and Aggadah whether positively, by assimilation into the corpus of Judaism, or negatively, in their outright rejection.

Jewish lore had come to embody the six orders of the Mishnah, divided into sixty-three tractates. These were edited by 'Rabbi' around the year 200 C.E. This was followed by the redaction of the Baraithot, or extra-Mishnaic dicta of the Tannaim, i.e., Hakhamim of the period from Hillel to Judah. Beside the Palestinian and Babylonian Talmuds, there arose a series of Aggadic compendia relating to the Biblical text. By the side of Tannaitic statements these contained the deliberations and exegetic endeavours of Eretz-Israel and Babylonian Amoraim until the beginning of the sixth century. This vast body of literature embraces much more than religious and legal matter, and does, indeed, cover the most variegated aspects of living reality. This abundant source material has provided invaluable data for the investigation of such important spheres as the state of agriculture and methods of cultivation, or the flora and fauna of Palestine and neighbouring countries. In it we find accounts of housing conditions, style of building and various household goods. There are significant revelations about the pottery and metal implement industries, about eating habits, meals and ways of preparing food. The numerous pages of this literature likewise harbour a wealth of information on dress, the weaving and dyeing industries, jewellery and other items of decoration and the spice and cosmetics industries. We learn about writing instruments and methods of preparing parchment, weights, measures and coins, as also about means of transport and communication. Moreover, these records of the deliberations of the Hakhamim reveal the extent of their knowledge and grasp in such fields as medicine and anatomy; mythology, astrology and magic; astronomy, mathematics, geography and ethnology. It must at the same time be borne in mind that all these fields of investigation were but ancillary to the discussion of Halakhic topics such as the Sabbath and appointed seasons; benedictions and prayers; the regulation of temple service and sacrifices; personal status and family life; laws of property, torts and the hiring of slaves and labourers. Of similar historical significance are the Halakhic considerations of court procedure and the penal code; laws of ritual cleanness and uncleanness; the heave offerings and tithes; allocations for the poor; alms giving and deeds of loving kindness. Lastly, our insight into the spiritual world of the Hakhamim is illuminated by a wealth of homiletic reflections interspersed in the Oral Torah. They cover such themes as the nature and attributes of the godhead; God's concern with the world and regard for his creatures; man's character and role in life; the fate of the righteous and the evil-minded; reward and punishment; the nature of Israel's election, its past fortunes and future destiny; the messianic age and world to come. The Hakham was generally expected to concern himself with and gain a thorough grounding in all the provinces of the written and oral Torah, even though at times his proficiency in a particular field may have gained special emphasis. In fact we find the noted Tannaim and Amoraim concerning themselves with all manner of "Derekh Eretz"—ways of the world. The latter concept, it should be noted, signified the entire span of human endeavour and individual conduct: as husband in his conjugal relations, as father and as a responsible person shouldering the burdens entailed in being a member of the congregation. Several Hakhamim at the same time devoted themselves to preaching and homiletic exposition of scriptures and to Aggadah. Some displayed a contemplative and mystical turn of mind. The scope of the intellectual accomplishments required of the Jewish sage was indeed catholic. He was even expected to familiarize himself with strange gods and their modes of worship and gain an insight into various mystery cults. He had to acquaint himself with the customs practised during gentile feasts as also with the formulae and methods of magic and witchcraft. Not least, the Hakham had to probe into the ways of the impostor and defrauder of customs and tolls: "That the deceivers might not say 'the scholars are unacquainted with our practices' ".[31]

Ben Zoma defines the Hakham as "He that learns from all men" (Aboth 4:1). Indeed we observe that during Tannaitic times "the

[31] Mishnah Kelim 17:16; Tosefta ib. Baba Metzia, Ch. 7, Hal. 9.

Hakhamim consulted the physicians"[32] and doubtless learnt a great deal from them. In his consideration of a controversy between Jewish and gentile men of learning on the course of the sun, 'Rabbi' concludes with characteristic urbanity: "And their view is preferable to ours". [33] Neither were the Hakhamim averse to learning the meaning of difficult words in the Bible and Mishnah from a maidservant in the household of 'Rabbi'. [34] An outstanding scholar like Rabbi Joshuah b. Hananiah, who had contended with the leading citizens of Athens, Alexandria and Rome and had met the verbal challenge of the emperor and his daughter[35], is reported to have stated: "No one has ever had the better of me except a woman, a little boy and a little girl". [36] An Amora named R. Yohanan ruled: "Whoever says a wise thing even if he is a non-Jew is called wise". [37] Significant though these direct quotations may be in establishing the extent of the intellectual intercourse of the Hakhamim with the surrounding and more distant cultures, they are outweighed by the linguistical evidence of the texts themselves. These abound in Greek, Roman and Persian terms current among the Hakhamim,[38] who likewise made free use of aphorisms prevalent in these languages. Some of the parables with which the Hakhamim would grace their utterances belonged to the realm of popular sayings and folklore and were international in character. [39] Yet others, e.g., the "kingship parables", arose from the social and political scene. They enable us to reconstruct several noteworthy aspects in the lives of the Roman emperors: the manner in which they imposed their authority; the hegemony exercised by the legions and their commanders; the habits of the court ladies and royal mistresses and the practices of their slaves and servants. [40] Common ground between the Hakhamim and the Greek grammarians and "Rhetors" can be detected in the kindred methods of exegesis employed by both. When it suited their purpose, the former would also avail themselves of the idiom current among interpreters of dreams or score their point with the aid of wit and humour. [41] In order to dramatize and give a topical bent to a particular message of the scriptures, they would conjure up dialogues between the

---

[32] B. Niddah, p. 60b.
[33] B. Pesahim, p. 94b.
[34] Jer. Shebiith, Ch. 9, Hal. 1, p. 38c; B. Rosh Hashanah, p. 26b.
[35] B. Bekhoroth, p. 8b; B. Niddah, p. 69b; B. Shabbath, p. 119a; B. Hullin, p. 53b.
[36] B. Erubin, p. 53b.
[37] B. Megillah, p. 16a.
[38] S. Krauss, *Griechische und lateinische Lehnwörter im Talmud, Midrash etc.* (Berlin, 1899); S. Lieberman, *Greek in Jewish Palestine* (New York, 1942); S. Telegdi, "Essai sur la Phonétique des Emprunts iraniens en Araméen talmudique", *Journal asiatique* (1935), pp. 177–256.
[39] L. Ginzberg, *The Legends of the Jews*, Vol. V (1925), Preface p. vii.
[40] I. Ziegler, *Die Königsgleichnisse des Midrasch beleuchtet durch die römische Kaiserzeit* (Breslau, 1903).
[41] S. Lieberman, *Hellenism in Jewish Palestine* (1950), pp. 46–82.

Biblical heroes and colloquies between personified Biblical concepts. In their educational endeavours the Hakhamim saw no harm in putting to their own use the intellectual equipment employed by the adherents of popular stoicism in their διατρῐβή. Neither did they shrink from adopting any of the artistic forms prevalent at the time, even indulging in hyperbole and sport, when a particular message of the Aggadah seemed to call for these. The deeper connotation of Aggadah yet remained eminently serious and could hardly be overrated, thus: "If thou wishest to know the one whose word brought forth the universe, learn Aggadah, for in this manner thou comest to know the Holy One blessed be He and adhere to his ways." [42] In this supreme aim of the Aggadah also lay the criterion for acceptance or rejection of extraneous substance. In matters of Halakha too the Hakhamim followed a similar course. The Biblical laws and commandments, it will be noted, did not always specify the exact manner of their implementation. Then, there were also problems thrown up by the ever changing conditions of a living and dynamic society, which the Bible had not had occasion to consider. Furthermore, there was a growth of oral traditions, enactments and stipulations of the Beth Din, specified wording of bonds and other legal documents, the decisions of famed courts of law serving as legal precedents, and lastly a wealth of local traditions and customs practised by particular groups. At the academies of the Tannaim scholars applied themselves to drawing conclusions from scripture as well as associating prevalent Halakhot with relevant Biblical passages. This was achieved by means of exegesis, subtle textual inference, analogy and the reconciliation of discrepant passages. To this end they readily availed themselves of the insights provided by philology, as well as making free use of current principles of logical reasoning.

Such was the mental discipline employed in the interpretation of the views held by antecedent Tannaim, as recorded in the Mishnah or compilations of Baraithot. Obscure Halakhot enunciated in a lapidary style were open to several interpretations. There were also many contradictions between sources dating to different periods and differences of opinion between Hakhamim of the same generation. These contrasts called for reconciliation and judgement as to the view that was to be declared normative. By raising points of disagreement, variant renderings and by posing problems of a casuistic nature, novel Halakhot actually came into being. These were related to the Biblical text on the tenuous grounds of a "hint" or "suggestion". The careful scrutiny of minutiae and collation of dissimilar elements resulted in the formulation of general rules and abstract principles that underlay Halakhot in such disparate spheres as divorce, the allocation of tithes and the sacrifice of the paschal lamb.

[42] Sifre Deuteronomy 10:49.

IX

The scholarly deliberations at the academies of the Hakhamim were conducted in an unrestrained spirit. In spite of the authoritative status of the written Torah and obligatory character of the traditions and Halakhot of antecedent authorities upon subsequent scholars, the latter enjoyed a large degree of autonomy. This manifested itself in the very act of interpretation which they claimed as their prerogative. A forceful if paradoxical expression of scholarly independence is found in the dictum: "Read not 'Haruth' (graven upon the tables) (Exod. 32:16) but 'Heruth' (freedom)" (Aboth 6:2). It likewise vividly emerges from that remarkable Aggadah, wherein Moses is led into the Academy of Rabbi Akiba. Listening to the learned discourse of the great master, Moses the Lawgiver is utterly bewildered as he fails to comprehend utterances which the Tanna traced to the Torah of Moses. [43] This story of Rabbi Akiba, told by none other than Rab—the dean of Babylonian Amoraim —constitutes a culminating point in the long drawn out contest between two opposing lines of approach. On the one hand were the traditionalists who largely confined themselves to the time-honoured precepts of the oral heritage, whilst on the other were the protagonists of the right to a free exposition of both written and oral Torah. Whereas Rabbi Akiba's masters—Rabbi Eliezer b. Hyrkanos and Rabbi Yehoshua— based themselves principally on orally delivered tradition, [44] the former decided in favour of an exegetic method, wherein innovation and spontaneous insight were the chief elements. The rabbinic interpretations and enactments based on the niceties of the biblical text were regarded by him to be an integral part of the Torah revealed to Moses at Sinai. [45] Rab's Aggadah on Moses' visit to Rabbi Akiba expresses the triumph of the latter school in that its innovating view is vindicated by God himself.

The scholarly research and discussions at the academies of the Tannaim and Amoraim were conducted in an atmosphere marked by lack of inhibition. Such also was the quality characterizing relations between master and disciple. Halakhah was decided on the merits of the reasoned case adduced, [46] with no consideration of age. Indeed, there were disciples whose scholarship exceeded that of their masters. At no time was decisive authority a concomitant of office or class. It devolved upon men who displayed a thorough mastery of the sources due to an excellent memory and upon scholars possessing unusually keen minds and great dialectical skill. Both intellectual qualities were seldom found

[43] B. Menahot, p. 29 b.
[44] Mishnah Parah 1:1; Mishnah Nazir 4:4; Mishnah Niddah 3:1, B. Sukkah, p. 27 b.
[45] Sifra Leviticus, Behukotai 8:12.
[46] B. Baba Bathra, p. 146 b.

in one and the same person. The resultant differences in approach often led to tensions, as is evident from diverse utterances evaluating the relative merits of the proficient Sinai (the erudite likened to the Mount of Sinai) and keen-minded "uprooter of mountains". Both are found earning alternate praise or disparagement. Intense disputations sometimes led to the slighting of a disciple or colleague. Invective too did not fail to make its appearance in the heat of argument. This could even result in the banishment of an opponent or other forms of punishment. [47] A further cause of strained relations was the rivalry in attracting gifted students who used to wander from one academy to another. These were familiar manifestations of a society placing a high premium on intellectual attainment, a prevailing phenomenon in the academic world. At the same time, however, it must be pointed out that the clashes and rivalries between the Hakhamim were at no time actuated by considerations of material advancement. There was none, as they taught without receiving a salary. Neither did their academic activities depend on the holding of an official position. Moreover, the admittance of a disciple into the ranks of the Hakhamim by ordination, whilst conferring the right to teach and enunciate Halakhah, also placed upon him the manifold cares and burdens of the community.

The dissemination of knowledge was not limited to the strict confines of the academy. The small talk of the Hakhamim was thus also considered as Torah. Even the extremist Rabbi Simeon bar Yohai who lived at a time when "Men dispaired of the Torah", for whom the study of Torah took precedence over aught else, who spurned all worldly avocation and, contrary to his master Rabbi Akiba, even regarded visiting the sick as a trifling occupation [48]—he too concluded:"... To wait upon a master of Torah is more important than the study thereof." [49] The intense preoccupation of the Hakhamim with legal matter, their searching analysis of cases and problems arising in the realm of torts and other civil claims, did not overshadow the deeper aspects of their vocation. These remained uppermost in their minds. Extraneous influence upon the framing of Halakhic law can hardly be denied. Investigations of the latter reveal elements from the legal approach of the ancient East and legal concepts of Greek and to a lesser extent Roman provenance. This is borne out by the prevalence of borrowed terms, e.g., "apotheke" (pledge), "diatheke" (disposition of property), "apotropos" (guardian), "omologia" (receipt) and the like. Further, indication of this trend may be gathered from the wording of legal documents, declarations and rules, as also

---

[47] Jer. Berakhot, Ch. 7, p. 10c; Jer. Shekalim, Ch. 3, Hal. 2, p. 47c; Jer. Moed Katan, Ch. 1, Hal. 1, p. 81 b–c; B. ib., pp. 16a–17a.
[48] Sifre Deuteronomy 10:42; Jer. Berakhot, Ch. 9, p. 13d; B. ib., p. 35b; Aboth de R. Nathan, vers. A, Ch. 41, p. 130, and cf. B. Nedarim, p. 40a.
[49] B. Berakoth, p. 7b.

from reference to institutions, all of which were unheard of hitherto.[50] It was by process of integration and adaptation to the existing system that these alien notions could play their part in answering new requirements as well as filling the breaches suffered by the original framework. The Hakhamim understood, however, that no matter how broadminded and astute the administrators of the law, the principle of strict legality in itself could not fully comprise the notion of justice. For this reason man was left with ample scope to prove his worth by doing "that which is right and good" in accordance with Biblical precept (Deut. 6:18). Though coached in general terms, this moral exhortation led to the formulation of several Halakhot.[51] In their own case the Hakhamim would renounce title even to that which they could legally claim as their own. Thus actuated by the principle of superrogation[52] they expected others to follow suit. This is illustrated by the following story: "Some porters negligently broke a barrel of wine belonging to Rabbah son of R. Huna. Thereupon he seized their garments; so they went and complained to Rab. 'Return them their garments' he ordered. 'Is that the law?' he enquired. 'Even so,' he rejoined. 'That thou mayest walk in the way of good men' " (Prov. 2:20). Their garments having been returned, they observed: " 'We are poor men, have worked all day, and are in need. Are we to get nothing?'. 'Go and pay them' he ordered. 'Is that the law?' he asked. 'Even so' was his reply 'and keep the path of the righteous' ".[53]

Of Rab himself it is told that he was guided by the principle of Hassiduth (saintliness) rather than strict justice. Thus Rabbi Hisda, a disciple of Rab, also referred to certain Halakhot of the Mishnah, saying: "They spoke here of pious conduct"[54] viz., ruling beyond the strict letter of the law. In the Mishnah itself it has already been stated that whoever chose this path "The sages are well pleased with him".[55] Nevertheless in addition to the ordinary Mishnah, scholars were expected to act in accordance with Mishnat Hassidim, the undefined code of the pious and saintly.[56] In the Amoraic deliberations mention is made of the Mishnah of Hassidim Rishonim (early saints) and their pronouncements concerning torts. The Amora Rab Judah declared: "He who wishes to be pious

---

[50] A. GULAK, *Das Urkundenwesen im Talmud und Midrasch im Lichte der griechisch-ägyptischen Papyri und des griechischen und römischen Rechts* (Jerusalem, 1935); R. YARON, *Gifts in Contemplation of Death* (Oxford, 1960); B. COHEN, *Jewish and Roman Law, A Comparative Study*, Vol. I and II (New York, 1966).

[51] B. Baba Metzia, p. 35a, p. 108a.

[52] B. Baba Kamma, p. 99b; B. Baba Metzia, p. 24a, p. 30b; B. Ketuboth, p. 97a.

[53] B. Baba Metzia, p. 83a. The word translated by 'even so' is lacking in some manuscripts of the Talmud: cf. Jer Baba Metzia, ch. 6, Hal. 8.

[54] Jer. Shabuoth, Ch. 10, Hal. 9, p. 39d; B. Shabbath, p. 150a; B. Baba Metzia, p. 52b; B. Hullin, p. 130b.

[55] Mishnah Shebiith 10:9; Mishnah Baba Bathra 8:5.

[56] Jer. Terumoth, Ch. 8, Hal. 10.

must fulfil the laws of Nezikin". [57] The saintly ideal was cherished as the *summum bonum* even by such Amoraim whose name in the Talmud appears solely in connexion with problems of a decidedly legal character, men whose principal qualities lay in keen differentiation and subtle analysis. As their forerunners, so the Amoraim too did not consider the principles of law and justice as an exclusive basis for realizing the ideal of the saintly Hakham. In the view of the Eretz-Israel Amora Rabbi Alexandri (end of the 3rd century), "A man who remains silent even when hearing himself reviled is called 'saintly' " [58] and according to an anonymous source the quality of saintliness expressed itself in constant fear of sin even when there was no apparent cause for such anxiety. [59] Some Amoraim drew extreme conclusions from Rabbi Akiba's doctrine which maintained that the loving acceptance of chastisement was the supreme goal of the devoted worshipper of God. [60] Evidence from the Amoraic period points to the prevalence of acts of renunciation and fasting. But these ascetic practices or "exercises" as it were, were never carried to the extreme point of a total rejection of this world. Generally acts of mortification were evoked by the dread of sin. There is no indication that they were ever allowed to assume unnatural proportions. No one ever challenged the view held by Rabbi Akiba that man was not allowed to inflict bodily harm upon his own person, not even when sanctifying the name of God during martyrdom [61]. On the other hand many scholars rejected asceticism even in moderate form. Referring to vows of self chastisement, Rabbi Dimi (4th century) declared: "Is it not enough for thee to abstain from what is forbidden in the Torah, that thou seekest to abstain from other things." [62] Resh Lakish moreover two generations before explicitly points to the Hakhamim in his ruling: "A scholar may not afflict himself by fasting because he lessens thereby his heavenly work." [63]

The lives of the Hakhamim were marked by constant preoccupation with the Bible. Its affirmation of a creative life, vivid human narrative and poetic account of natural phenomena penetrated their innermost being. Moreover, they were forever called upon to grapple with the real-life problems of the Halakhah. All this had the natural effect of a safeguard against extravagant asceticism. Among most Hakhamim, indeed, the resultant attitude was one of delight in life and blithe enjoyment of its fruits. A pertinent example of this is Rab's dictum: "Men shall be called to account for whatever his eyes have beheld and he did not

[57] B. Baba Kamma 30a.
[58] Midrash Psalms 16:11.
[59] Midr. Tanhuma Hukkath 25, and cf. B. Nedarim, p. 10a.
[60] B. Berakoth, p. 61b; Tr. Semahoth, Ch. 8.
[61] Mishnah Baba Kama 8:6; B. Abodah Zarah, p. 18a.
[62] Jer. Nedarim, Ch. 9, Hal. 1, p. 41a.
[63] B. Taanith, p. 11b.

partake thereof." [64] His disciple Rab Judah similarly declared that anyone seeing the trees in full bloom during the month of Nissan, must utter the blessing: "Blessed be He who hath not left His world lacking in anything and has created in it goodly creatures and goodly trees for the enjoyment of mankind." [65]

Two basic elements of extreme asceticism, i.e., total abstinence from sex and a life of solitude, were entirely absent from the world of the Hakhamim. The latter lived all their lives among the people and did not part from their families. In this sphere they endeavoured to implement the high standards they had set for an ideal moral and religious life. The Hakhamim were fully aware of the power of man's evil inclinations and sway of his passions. At no time did they underestimate these forces. They realized that "Even the most pious among the pious is not to be appointed a guardian against inchastity." [66]

The acknowledged hero was he who conquered his evil impulse, said the Tanna Ben Zoma (Aboth 4:1). This principle was corroborated by the Amoraim on the strength of their own life experience, which demonstrated that "The greater the man the greater his Evil Inclinations". [67] The Hakhamim spoke up openly on problems of sex, never exhibiting a false sense of modesty when discussing the subject. They proffered sympathetic advice, to man in his moral predicament against the evil impulse. In order to restrain the inner assailant the Hakhamim recommended the method of "repelling with the left hand and beckoning with the right". [68] The strongest weapon in this moral conflict was, however, the study of Torah. Herein lay the most potent means of keeping the passions at bay. It was through their sublimation that victory would come.

X

In their role as spiritual leaders and moral shepherds, the Hakhamim were faced by a dilemma. How were they to treat their flock and the people at large? On the one hand they strove for a close relationship with the people and tried to gain their confidence and affection by being accommodating. On the other they had to ascertain that good relations were not attained at the expense of surrendering principles. An extreme view of this situation was taken by the fourth century Babylonian Amora Abbaye, who declared that if a disciple of the Hakhamim was regarded with affection by his townsfolk it was no indication of the former's excellence, but rather of his refusal to denounce their mal-

[64] Jer. Kiddushin, Ch. 4, Hal. 12, p. 66b.
[65] B. Berakoth, p. 43b.
[66] Jer. Ketuboth, Ch. 1, Hal. 1, p. 25d.
[67] B. Sukkah, p. 52a.
[68] B. Sukkah ib.; B. Berakhot, p. 5a.

practices. [69] But exhortation was not the sole cause of friction between the Hakhamim and various sections of the population. To be sure there was a pronounced tendency towards egalitarianism and the abolition of social barriers, both in the domain of Halakhah and in general usage. It was Rabbi Akiba who made the pronouncements: "All Israelites are the sons of Kings" and "All Israel are worthy of that robe (rank)". [70] At the same time, however, he demanded utmost reverence for the Hakhamim. This requirement he daringly expressed in the homily " 'The Lord thy God shalt thou fear' (Deut. 6:13)—this is meant to extend to the disciples of the Sages". [71] Yet he issued no less severe an admonition to his fellow scholars on the need to avoid indulgence in self exalting pride. His own experiences whilst still unlettered taught him the pitfalls of an overbearing demeanour. This produced aversion for the Hakhamim among the simple folk. Thus he declared: "Whowever exalts himself through words of Torah, to what is he likened? To a cadaver thrown by the wayside; everyone who passes by puts his hand to his nose and goes away seeking its distance." [72]

The search of the Hakham for a balance between the desire to command respect for his own person and thus indeed for the Torah, and the avoidance of pride [73] had its ups and downs. The continued existence for hundreds of years of an intellectual elite in itself raised a number of problems. The custom had grown among broad sections of the community to accord outstanding Hakhamim a variety of grants and concessions. In the course of time these came to be regarded as a class privilege and were even incorporated in the Halakhah. Any attempt to discontinue these practices was deemed by the Hakhamim tantamount to contempt and degradation. [74] On the other hand the Hakhamim never wearied in pointing out and stressing the extent of the responsibility devolving upon the Hakham. His actions and way of life in general, and more particularly the discharge of his public functions were under constant scrutiny. In the opinion of Rabbi Judah b. Ilai, a disciple of Rabbi Akiba, the unintentional sins of a disciple of the Hakhamim are counted as wilful acts, whereas the wantom deeds of common folk are regarded as having been committed inadvertently. [75]

Throughout the Tannaitic period the disciples of the Hakhamim are called upon to cultivate a distinct language, gait and garb. This eventually developed into a very code of manners to be followed by the Hakham in his public appearance. Rabbi Yohanan thus warned that

[69] B. Ketuboth, p. 105b.
[70] B. Baba Bathra, p. 155a; B. Baba Metzia, p. 113b.
[71] B. Pesahim, p. 22b.
[72] Aboth de R. Nathan, vers. A, Ch. 11.
[73] Jer. Yebamoth, Ch. 13, p. 13a.
[74] B. Kiddushin, p. 70a; B. Baba Bathra, p. 8a; B. Sanhedrin, p. 99b, and cf. B. Shabbath, p. 119b.
[75] B. Baba Metzia, p. 33b.

"any scholar upon whose garment a grease stain is found, is worthy of death".[76] There was ultimately but one criterion by which the deportment of a Hakham was to be judged: did his deeds and behaviour lead to the sanctification or desecration of the name of Heaven. This principle whose origin is attributed to Simeon b. Shetah was to remain in force throughout the period under consideration. It elicited an almost endless variety of interpretations and specifications. It is suitably summed up in the following Baraitha delivered by the Amora Abbaye: "As it was taught: 'And thou shalt love the Lord thy God' (Deut. 6:5) i.e., that the Name of Heaven be beloved because of you. If someone studies Scripture and Mishnah and attends on the disciples of the Sages, is honest in business and speaks pleasantly to persons, what do people then say concerning him? 'Happy the father who taught him Torah, happy the teacher who taught him Torah; woe unto the people who have not studied the Torah, for this man has studied the Torah—look how fine his ways are, how righteous his deeds!' Of him does scripture say: 'And He said unto me: Thou art my servant, Israel, in whom I will be glorified'. But if someone studies Scripture and Mishnah, attends on the disciples of the Sages, but is dishonest in business and discourteous in his relations with people, what do people say about him? 'Woe unto him who studied the Torah, woe unto his father who taught him Torah; woe unto his teacher who taught him Torah! This man studied the Torah look how corrupt are his deeds, how ugly his ways'..."[77]

Whenever it was feared that a situation might result in the desecration of the name of God it was necessary to set aside all considerations of personal standing and prestige. It was to be kept in mind that "whenever a profanation of God's name is involved no respect is paid to a teacher".[78]

The meticulous regard for the conduct of the individual Hakham[79] was prompted by a concern for the status and honour of the entire body of the Hakhamim and their institutions, and ultimately for the glory of the Torah itself. Being distinctive in character as well as outward appearance, the Hakhamim as a group were for ever exposed to public scrutiny. The tendency was to impute the sins, short-comings and pretences of the individual to the institution as a whole. Manifestations of such disregard for the Hakhamim among certain sections of the community are reported by Abbaye's companion Rava in the words: "Of what use are the Rabbis to us?"[80]

The national standing and influence of the Hakhamim throughout the Talmudic period derived from two fundamental features in their

[76] B. Shabbath, p. 114 a.
[77] B. Yoma, p. 86 a, and cf. B. Pesahim, p. 113 b.
[78] B. Berakoth, p. 19 b; Baba Bathra, p. 57 b, and cf. above No. 29.
[79] B. Taanith, p. 7 a; B. Moed Katan, p. 7 a.
[80] B. Sanhedrin, p. 99 b.

work and character. One of these was the democratic constitution of the Talmudical academy whose doors remained open to rich and poor alike. As we pointed out before no account was taken of any privileges of ancestry. In this spirit must be understood the words of the Tanna R. Jose: "Make thyself fit for the study of the Torah, for it will not be thine by inheritance" (Aboth 2:12). They were meant as a warning to Hakhamim not to place undue value on lineage. Indeed, it is noteworthy that throughout the entire Talmudic era this tendency prevailed and we do not encounter "households" of Hakhamim, as was the case with the Soferim of old. Moreover, in several instances, when both fathers and sons were Hakhamim, the latter outstripped the former in scholarship and it was the fame of the son which redounded to the honour of the father. Considering it a paradox, the Amoraim of the fourth and fifth centuries posed the question: "And why is it not usual for scholars to give birth to sons who are scholars?" The solutions proffered: "That it might not be maintained—the Torah is their legacy" and "That they should not be arrogant towards the community" ,[81] actually rather pointed to the effect than cause of this manifestation. The very accessibility of the Talmudic academies and the free competition between them prevented the intrusion of class and family privilege into the realm of Torah. It likewise ensured the supply of a steady stream of vigorous and unconventional intellects.

The other factor of decisive significance in forming the character of the Hakhamim is to be found in the profound words of the Psalmist: "The fear of the Lord is the beginning of wisdom" (Ps. 111:10). The burden of this all important message of the inadequacy of Torah learning unfortified by the fear of Heaven, was driven home at all times with ceaseless application. The famed Amora Rava thus declared: "The object of wisdom is repentance and good deeds." [82] Accordingly we find in the Talmud Hakhamim who are not credited with any Halakhic or Aggadic pronouncement, but are noted for the saintly character of their deeds. Moreover the Talmud is not averse to citing manifestations of goodness, righteousness and loving kindness; of innocent faith and fear of God, when these came from the simplest folk or even the humblest elements on the periphery of the Jewish congregation [83].

In their admiration for such popular traits and practices, certain Amoraim addressed themselves to the congregation of Israel with the words: "The transgressors in Israel are as full of good deeds as a pomegranate." [84] Throughout their extended spiritual career the Hakhamim regarded themselves — and were regarded by their audience—not only

[81] B. Nedarim, p. 81a, cf. B. Baba Metzia, p. 85a, and Baba Bathra, p. 59a.
[82] B. Berakoth, p. 17b, and cf. B. Shabbath, p. 31b; B. Yoma, p. 72b.
[83] Jer. Taanith, Ch. 1, Hal. 4, p. 64a; Leviticus Rabbah 9:3, B. Taanith, p. 24a.
[84] B. Erubin, p. 19a; B. Hagigah, p. 27b; Canticles Rabbah 4:3.

as teachers and instructors of individual members of the community, but as mentors and spiritual guides of the congregation of Israel as a whole.

XI

The Jewish people, although composed of various elements, was considered by the Hakhamim as a single entity. As such it qualified for the title of a nation chosen by God and as such it carried throughout all the vicissitudes of history the responsibilities and hardships conferred by this rank. Inspired by the words of the Torah "as a man chasteneth his son, so doth the Lord thy God chasten thee" (Deut. 8:5) and by those of the prophet Amos (3:2) "You only have I known of all the families of the earth; therefore I will punish you for all your iniquities", the Hakhamim understood the idea of election essentially in terms of added responsibility. Evidence of Israel's chosen state was seen by Rabbi Akiba not only in their Biblical designation as "children of God" but also in their having received a "precious implement" i.e., the Torah (Aboth 3:18). The national responsibility for the upkeep of the Torah gave rise to the idea of a mutual pledge. Rabbi Simeon b. Yohai explained the rule "All Israelites are accountable for one another" [85] in the following manner: "It may be likened to a company of men who were in a boat when one of them took a drill and began to bore a hole next to his feet. Said his companions to him: 'Why do you act thus?' Answered he: 'What care you, is it not beneath my own place that I am boring?' Said they: 'But you are inundating the boat for all of us'." [86] This idea of a common pledge had a particular significance for the Hakham. The Tanna Rabbi Nehemia held that "My son, if thou be surety for thy friend, if thou hast stricken thy hand with a stranger" (Prov. 6:1) referred to the Hakhamim: "This was said of ordinary scholars (Haverim); as long as one is but an ordinary scholar, he has no concern with the congregation and is not punished for its lapses, but as soon as he is appointed head and dons the cloak of leadership, he must no longer say: 'I live for my own benefit, I care not about the congregation' but the whole burden of the community is on his shoulders. If he sees a man causing suffering to another, or transgressing, and does not prevent him, then he is held punishable. The Holy Spirit then exclaims, 'My son, if thou art become surety for thy neighbour'. Thou art responsible for him, because 'Thou hast struck thy hands for a stranger'—le-zar (ib.). The Holy One, blessed be He, says to him: 'Thou, by assuming office, hast placed thyself in the arena (lezirah), and he who places himself in the arena stands either to fail or win'." [87]

[85] Sifra Leviticus Behukotai, Ch. 4.
[86] Leviticus Rabbah 4:2.
[87] Exodus Rabbah 27:9, and cf. Midrash Psalms 8:3.

The ordinary Jew too, however, was bidden to consider his actions as of decisive importance, not only in settling his own fate for weal or woe, but also that of his people and, indeed, that of the whole world .[88] Mutual responsibility meant readiness to sacrifice oneself for the physical and spiritual wellbeing of one's fellow-man, a mutual willingness "to pledge one's own person for the benefit of another". [89] Such principles could only be implemented where people regarded themselves as part of a united body—"when they are joined in a single band and not into several bands" [90]. National unity would be an effective instrument for obliterating differences in the moral and religious standards of various sections of the population, as also for alleviating the lot of the weak and backward. An homiletic expression of this notion is found in the observations of an anonymous preacher upon the Biblical injunction of the "four species" required on the feast of Tabernacles (Lev. 23:40): " 'Fruit of goodly trees'—this is a symbol of Israel: just as the citron has taste and pleasant fragrance, so there are in Israel men who are at once learned and strictly observant. 'A branch of the palm-tree'—this is a symbol of Israel: just as the lulav whose fruit is palatable but without fragrance, so there are those who are learned, but are not fully practising. 'Myrtle-branches'—this is a symbol of Israel: as the myrtle has a pleasant odour but is tasteless, so there are men of good deeds, who possess no scholarship. 'Branches of the willow'—this is a symbol of Israel: as the willow is neither edible nor of agreeable fragrance, so there are those who are neither learned nor possessed of good deeds. And what does the Holy-One-blessed-be-He do to them? To destroy them is not feasible. Therefore said the Lord: 'let them be bound into one bundle and they shall atone for one another'." [91]

Observing the long and tortuous course of Jewish history, the Hakhamim—both Tannaim and Amoraim—gained a thorough insight into the character of the Jewish people .[92] They did not shrink from revealing some of the more damaging or puzzling traits of the Jews but rejected outright denunciation. On this point they even took issue with the prophets, criticizing some of their generalizations as amounting to a "defamation of Israel" .[93] Whilst reprimanding individual Jews whenever the occasion called for it, the Hakhamim were staunch defenders of the nation as a whole.

In the eyes of the Hakhamim Jewish national existence was an

[88] Tosefta Kiddushin, Ch. 1, Hal. 14; B. ib., p. 40 b.
[89] Mekilta de R. Ishmael, Ed. Horovits-Rabin, Tractate Bahodesh, Ch. 1, p. 206; ib., Ch. 5, p. 219.
[90] Sifre Deuteronomy par 346.
[91] Leviticus Rabbah 30:13.
[92] Jer. Shekalim, Ch. 1, Hal. 1, p. 45 d, and cf. B. Betzah, p. 25 b; B. Megillah, p. 16 a.
[93] B. Yebamoth, p. 49 b; Pesikta de R. Kahana 14, Ed. Mandelbaum, p. 246, and Canticles Rabbah 1:6.

essential prerequisite, not only for the immediate fulfilment of Jewish law and faith, but also of the prophetic visions of an ideal future. It was a precondition for the realization of the prophetic notions of human perfection and universal harmony in a world imbued with the spirit of God: "And the Lord shall be king over all the earth: in that day shall there be one Lord, and his name one" (Zachariah 14:9).

The Hakhamim cherished these ideals and perpetuated them in the sublime language of their liturgy. They applied to the prophetic utterances all their exegetic talents and rich homiletic imagery. They were at one with the prophet Ezekiel (20:32–34) in affirming the indisputable duty of each individual Jew to act for the preservation of the Jewish nation with its obligations under the divine covenant. A fourth century preacher who lived in Palestine expressed it thus: "Said the Holy-One-blessed-be-He to Israel: 'If you will not proclaim my Godhead among the nations of the world I shall call you to account'." [94]

It was essentially a regenerative type of messianism that the Hakhamim believed in and propagated. Hope was to be fostered in the revival of erstwhile glory. The Hakhamim thus envisioned the re-establishment of the Israelite monarchy, redemption from foreign servitude, the ingathering of exiles and finally the rebuilding of the Temple in Jerusalem. The aspirations of the Hakhamim were not altogether free from utopian and apocalyptic trends cultivated in certain circles. Some of these ideas could hardly be absolved of an antinomian or anarchistic bias. Nevertheless, the soteriological notions of the Hakhamim fundamentally retained their realistic orientation towards a religious-national-political restoration.[95] Jewish national revival was a *conditio sine qua non* for realizing the universal principles that were to unite hitherto hostile nations and pave the way to a new era where goodness reigned supreme. It was an historical development culminating in the ideal world to come.

The Hakhamim considered themselves as champions of the national integrity and faith of a people pledged to God by a unique covenant. Upon the maintenance of this singular bond depended the future existence and mission of this people. The discharge of their principal function remained uppermost in the minds of the Hakhamim, overshadowing any considerations of their personal standing in the community. The great, the constant and devoted among them were, however, duly recognized by the people, who accorded them the highest distinction, being the "crown of a good name" (Aboth 4:17). Of all emblems, this one was considered the noblest, which even the crowns of priesthood and royalty could not excel.

---

[94] Leviticus Rabbah 7:6.

[95] G. SCHOLEM, "Zum Verständnis der messianischen Idee im Judentum", *Judaica* (1963), pp. 1–75; "Toward an Understanding of the Messianic Idea in Judaism," in *The Messianic Idea in Judaism* (New York, 1971), pp. 1–36.

SHMUEL SAFRAI

ELEMENTARY EDUCATION, ITS RELIGIOUS AND SOCIAL SIGNIFICANCE IN THE TALMUDIC PERIOD

T HERE is general agreement among scholars that the Talmudic Period came to an end in all its aspects with the final redaction of the Palestinian and Babylonian Talmuds, at the end of the fourth century in Palestine and about a century later in Babylonia. The beginning of the period is less precise; its definition depends not only upon one's viewpoint and attitude but also upon the particular problem dealt with. With regard to the subject of education, it seems best to begin with the last generations of the Second Commonwealth, or even slightly earlier, from the time that the rule concerning the obligation to educate the children became widespread, and with the founding of schools in the cities and villages of Palestine and later in Babylonia.

In this period, the Jewish culture developed within the broad framework of Hellenistic-Roman culture. In most of the Greek cities spread along the coast, in Transjordan, and here and there in central Palestine, cultural life was formed after the Hellenistic model with its educational institutions for young people and children. Certainly one might find points of contact and similarity, as in other areas of life, between the educational institutions of the Greek cities and the educational institutions of the Jews; however, in order that we may perceive the place of Jewish education in the life of the people, as well as its position with regard to the culture which surrounded it, we must indicate beforehand the distinctive traits of the Jewish school. The schools of Hellenistic cities, as their other cultural institutions, were essentially urban and discriminating, intended to serve a narrow or broader stratum of their population, and were never intended to encompass all of the residents of the Greek cities. Certainly the overwhelming majority of the rural community, born in Egypt or in some other Hellenized land, never attained any educational framework at all.[1] In contrast, the Jewish school, as will become clear to us, was intended for all the children as Jewish law obliged every father and every settlement to attend to the education of the children.

[1] See: A. H. M. JONES, *The Greek City* (1940), 220–226; M. P. NILSSON, *Hellenistiche Schule* (1955), 85–92.

The Hellenistic school, at all levels, taught reading, writing and, generally, some other subjects which prepared the student for civic life,[2] while the Jewish school, as will be seen, was intended to instruct the pupil in the reading and understanding of Scripture, in the knowledge of the traditions of the Oral Law so as to prepare him for the study of Torah and for Divine Worship. The importance and significance of this elementary education in various areas of life, will be understood best by analyzing the principal sources in their historical context.

The earliest notice concerning the obligation to provide elementary education, that is, the general organization of elementary education, is contained in a tradition preserved in the Palestinian Talmud which states concisely: "It was Shimon ben Shetah who initiated three things... and that the children should go to school."[3] One must not simply conclude that in the days of Shimon ben Shetah (in the beginning of the first century B.C.E.), obligatory education was established and from then on, all the children used "to go to school". The process of the expansion of education and the establishment of obligatory education did not begin in the days of Shimon ben Shetah and, as we shall note later, neither was it completed in his day. Yet, one must not reject out of hand this explicit tradition; surely during his time a concrete step was taken in the expansion of obligatory elementary education even though we are unable to ascertain what was the particular innovation of Shimon ben Shetah in this matter. In the Babylonian Talmud, we find a more clearly stated tradition, which pertains to the last days of the Second Commonwealth:

"Rabbi Judah said in the name of Rav: Verily the name of that man is to be blessed, to wit Joshua ben Gamala, for but for him the Torah would have been forgotten from Israel. For at first if a child had a father, his father taught him, and if he had no father he did not learn at all... they then made an ordinance that teachers of children should be appointed in Jerusalem... Even so, however, if a child had a father, the father would take him up to Jerusalem and have him taught there, and if not, he would not go up to learn there. They therefore ordained that teachers should be appointed in each prefecture, and that boys should enter school at the age of sixteen or seventeen, (They did so) and if the teacher punished them they used to rebel and leave school. Finally Joshua ben Gamala came and ordained that teachers of young children should be appointed in each district and each town and that children should enter school at the age of six or seven."[4]

The tradition as it is before us has undergone a literary stylization; therefore one should not regard as historical fact each detail or stage which it describes; however, its core is certainly historical. It was related by Rav, a Babylonian Amora who dwelt many years in Palestine and brought back with him many reliable traditions. It is not often that Talmudic tradition attributes creditable achievements to the high priests of the last days of the Second Commonwealth. Therefore one

[2] See: ARISTOTLE, *Pol* VIII 1338a, 15–17, 36–40; H. I. MARROU, *A History of Education in Antiquity* (1956), 155 ff.; 172 ff.
[3] P Ket, end of VIII.
[4] B BB 21a.

may accept as historical fact that in the time of the priesthood of Joshua ben Gamala, in the last years of the Second Commonwealth (63–65 C.E.), an important step was taken in extending the obligation to establish schools in each city. Tannaitic sources of the years following the destruction of the Temple, 70–135, count school among the essential institutions which each city is obliged to establish.[5] Various Halakhoth of this and later periods assume as a fact the existence in the cities of schools for children and the payment of "wages to the scribes and repetitors."[6] Rabbi Shimon ben Yohai, who lived in the middle of the second century, blames the destruction of the villages during the rebellion of Bar Kochba on their not "keeping up payments to scribes and repetitors."[7] In one source from the end of the third century, we hear of three of the leading sages of that generation, who were sent by the Patriarch Rabbi Judah "to go through the cities of Palestine and appoint scribes and repetitors." In one place where they found "neither a scribe nor a repetitor", they blamed the inhabitants for their negligence.[8]

When Talmudic sources seek to describe the preeminence or increase in population of a city, they mention the number of schools and the great number of pupils which are to be found there. Concerning the last days of Jerusalem before its destruction at the hands of Vespasian, a legend relates, with some exaggeration, that there were there four hundred and eighty synagogues; each one had a school for the study of Scripture and an academy for the study of Mishnah.[9] Such a description occurs in the case of Beitar too which expanded in the sixty odd years between the destruction of the Temple and the Bar Kochba rebellion.[10]

The Talmudic sources speak, in general, of the establishment and existence of schools in the 'cities'; however one must not conclude that the villages were outside the net of schools. The distinction between 'cities' and 'villages' does not make a division between large urban settlements, as we visualize them today, and small settlements engaged in agriculture. Actually this distinction is drawn between organized settlements, whether of medium size or small, which are engaged in various crafts or agriculture on the one hand, and tiny settlements on the other hand, which do not support organized public institutions because their population is too small and poor. Not only does the distinction between village and city not fit our conception of 'village' and

[5] In B Sanh 17b, the baraitha counts ten institutions which each city is obliged to provide. The list dates from before the generation of Rabbi Akiva (who died approximately 135 C. E.) since he adds a detail to this list which had been crystallized before his time.

[6] P Hag I, 76c and elsewhere.

[7] P *ibid*.

[8] *Ibid*. and parallels. Compare B Shab 119b where the tradition determines that a city which does not establish schools is to be banned.

[9] P Meg IV, 73d and parallels.

[10] P Ta IV, 69a and compare B Git 58a.

'city', it also does not fit the Greek concept. Schools did exist in all the 'villages' (according to the Greco-Roman administrative concepts), and we also know of tens of scholars throughout the period of the Talmud who rose up and worked in these villages. This phenomenon is certainly inexplicable unless one assumes the existence of educational institutions in all those settlements from which men of Torah could arise and before whose populace such scholars might teach as they grew up. In all its manifestations Jewish culture and literature in the Talmudic period is not "urban" in the Hellenistic-Roman sense, either in its carriers, or in its forms or contents.

With regard to the teaching of Torah to adults, we note different attitudes; there were those who thought that one should not teach Torah or raise up disciples except among the fit and proper and the 'pure of heart' and there were those who taught any man and did not openly examine those who came to study Torah.[11] However, with regard to the teaching of Torah to young children, it was clear to all, that one should include each child—the son of a pauper or a rich man, the son of a *Haver* (fellow) or a notable of the city together with the sons of ignorant men and people of low descent or even the sons of various evil doers and wicked men. Education was not given for nothing and parents had to pay the wages of the teacher, but the city participated in one way or another, defraying the cost of the scribes and repetitors and thus made possible the education of the sons of the very poor as well as of the orphans who were unable to pay any of the expense. In any case we hear of no rebuke or complaint from sages that children of the poor were unable to go to school or that they were expelled from school because of their poverty.[12]

Education and teaching which were considered obligatory for everyone included two main stages: reading substantial sections of Scripture, and secondly the Oral Law which meant principally the study of Mishnah. Our sources clearly distinguish between the 'scribe' and the repetitor (of the Mishnah which was originally transmitted orally) and there were even separate institutions—a school for Torah and an 'academy' for the Mishnah.[13] Study began between the age of five and seven and at the age of twelve or thirteen the pupil finished his studies. According to the Mishnah, the period of study is divided into two stages. At five years one begins the study of Torah, at ten years the study of Mishnah.[14] The tradition about the founding of schools by Joshua ben Gamala also states that "One brings them to school at the age of six or seven years." The Amora Rav commands one of the well known teachers

---

[11] See Avoth deRabi Natan, version II, Ch. 4 and B Ber 28a.
[12] See B Bez 17a and B Ta 24a.
[13] P Ma'as III, 50d and others.
[14] Ab, end V.

of children in his generation (the first part of the third century), Rabbi Shmuel bar Shilath, as follows: "Less than six don't accept them; at six years old, accept and stuff them (with Torah) like oxen."[15] The law requires the father to concern himself with the education of his son up to the completion of the first stage of studies;[16] in the middle of the second century, however, the rabbis of Usha ordained "that a father should bear with his son until the age of twelve" and only after that should he begin to make him participate in his (the father's) work or the study of a trade.[17] In the period of the Amoraim (from the third century until the end of the fifth), this became the prevailing custom: to send the child to school until the age of twelve or thirteen.[18]

In the main, this was the framework of the obligatory education. A youngster who yearned to continue his studies and had proved his capacity in the previous years would begin by sitting at the feet of the teachers of Torah in his city or nearby, much as did adults who studied Torah after work on weekday evenings and especially on Sabbath and holidays. Talent and persistence in study during these years would enable such a young man, either before or even after his marriage, to go and study Torah with one of the well-known sages or he might go to live for a number of years in one of the centers for the study of Torah.[19] A formal educational framework, similar to the secondary school of our days, did not exist in Israel in this period, as far as we know. Most of the youths were educated in the schools for scriptural study and to a lesser degree in the schools for the study of Oral Law.[20] These two institutions formed the backbone of the system of elementary education which shaped the culture of the majority of Jewish society.

Education and instruction in these schools were wholly intended to inculcate a knowledge of Torah and to bring up the boy to good acts and towards a dutiful civic and filial attitude. The leaders of Israel believed that knowledge of Torah leads to correct religious and social behavior. Hillel the Elder, one of the great teachers of Talmudic Judaism, used to say: "An uncultured person is not sin-fearing, nor is an Am-Haaretz pious."[21] Circa 130 C.E. (around the time of the Bar

[15] B BB 21a; B Ket 50a.
[16] B Kid 30a.
[17] B Ket 50a.
[18] Gen. Rabbah Ch. 63 and others.
[19] In Tannaitic sources we find opinion divided concerning the preferred situation for a young man; is he to marry first and then study Torah or should he study Torah initially? In the Amoraic period, the rabbis in Babylonia ordained that the man might marry first—here the economic situation was better. But in Palestine one of the leading authorities during the period of anarchy in the third century, Rabbi Yohanan, ordained "that one ought not to marry first" since the "millstone (of providing for wife and family) would be around his neck" when he ought to be studying Torah. See: T Bek VI, 10 and B Kid 29b.
[20] In Lev Rabbah ch. II and parallels: In reality a thousand men begin the study of Scripture and one hundred remain, a hundred study Mishnah, etc.
[21] Ab II, 5.

Kochba rebellion) the question was raised and disputed amongst the sages whether 'study' was more important than 'deeds' or the 'deeds' were to be preferred to 'study'; "all agreed that study was preeminent, since study led to deeds." [22]

Instruction in all its stages was intended, all of a piece, to inculcate Torah in its various branches and only this. Other sciences, such as mathematics (Gemetriot, as they called it) or astronomy were not in the syllabus; and these seemed to them as 'non-essential to wisdom', that is, the wisdom of Torah. [23] This attitude did not preclude the study of these sciences privately later on.

There has arisen recently some difference of opinion amongst students of Jewish history and culture as to the impact of Hellenistic culture on Jewish culture, spiritual as well as material. Scholars disagree as to the degree of similarity, evidence of contact and transmission of thought patterns and philosophical ideas to be found between the above mentioned culture and Jewish life and thought in the period and area under consideration. There is also lack of agreement as to the extent of knowledge and actual use of Greek in Palestine. One set of facts stands out clear: Greek language and culture were studied in Palestine only by the narrow aristocratic circles close to the Patriarchal court or to other leadership centers; they considered this culture part of their education for leadership, a task involving the needs and problems of the Hellenistic-Roman Jewish Diaspora and contact with Gentile rulers and authorities. The general Jewish school system dealt neither with Greek culture nor with their language. [24]

Education and instruction in the schools during this period had a specific character both in their aims and in their methods. Education

[22] Sifrei, Eikev, paragraph 41 and parallels in the two Talmuds. Historians tend to assume that this discussion took place in the days of the religious persecutions which followed the Bar Kochba rebellion when the authorities forbade the study of Torah, the observance of the commandments and all the Jewish way of life. At that time the sages gathered to discuss the matters to which a Jew ought to devote himself; they decided that priority must be given to the study of Torah over the observance of the other commandments. However, almost all the Tannaim who are mentioned in that controversy (Rabbi Tarfon and Rabbi Yosi Hagalili, for example) did not remain alive in the days of the harsh decrees following the rebellion and therefore one ought not to assume that this meeting of the sages could have taken place in the days of these decrees in Aris' house in the city of Lud in Judea, which served as a place of meeting for the sages before the rebellion. This decision, that study preceded the act, and that study leads to an act, was part of the crystallization of a world-view of Tannaitic Judaism which came into being during the Yavneh period, the period between the destruction of the Temple and the rebellion of Bar Kochba (70–132). The sages taught along these lines and later generations followed their lead.

[23] Ab end Ch. III.

[24] P Shab VII, 7d; B Sot 49b and see especially the books of S. LIEBERMANN, *Hellenism in Jewish Palestine* and *Greek in Jewish Palestine* and his article, "How Much Greek in Jewish Palestine", *Biblical and other Studies*, I (1963), 123–141. See also the rejoinder of G. ALON to Liebermann's view in the *Collection of Researches in the History of Israel*, II, 248–277 (soon to appear in English translation).

was on the whole intended to enable the child to read the books of the
Torah and the Prophets and to bring him to an understanding of them
so that his knowledge of the Torah would be sufficient to serve as a basis
for his absorbing the tradition of the Oral Law. As we shall see in the
sequel, the basic intention was to make the boy participate in public
study of Torah and to encourage him to take part in the development
and broadening of the oral tradition. Reading was not taught by means
of writing or with the help of writing, but rather through learning to
know the shape of the letters, by the repetition of the sounds they
represented and following this, the repetition of words and whole chapters. Needless to say, the traditions of the Oral Law were acquired by
listening to the words of the teacher, and by repetition and memory
drill. Writing was not studied in the schools. The copying of the letters,
and at a later stage, the copying of whole sentences and chapters from
Scripture, was done by the teacher and not by the pupil. Writing was
taught separately not as part of the school syllabus; yet it was fairly
widespread and knowledge of reading certainly made it easier. Men
copied books for themselves or prepared books for the use of their sons,
but the knowledge of writing did not reach the extent of the knowledge
of reading which was the common possession of all. There were scholars,
even the most notable of their generation, who did not know this craft
and one of the sages of the first half of the third century held the opinion
that a scholar ought to acquire the knowledge of writing for use on
behalf of the community.[25]

The area of diffusion of education and its formal and material
achievements comes out clearly in some of the principal sources; we
shall choose for our purpose sources emanating from several social circles
in Palestine and Babylonia. Josephus emphasizes in several passages the
great social and national role of education; the devotion of the people
to Torah and its commandments is formed by it. He speaks of the cultural gains of these studies: "Amongst us, there is not even one man for
whom it is not as easy to recite all the laws by heart as it is to pronounce
his name, since we learn them from the time that we reach the age of
understanding until they are engraved on our hearts." [26]

Three hundred years after him, the Church Father Jerome who came
to live in Palestine, wrote about the knowledge of the Jews in general
and their knowledge of history from the times of the first man to the
period of Zerubavel; that is to say, from the Book of Genesis to the last
books of the Bible.[27] A passage from the Babylonian Talmud which
discusses the laws of impurity, tells that they were totally forgotten by
some men and were transgressed out of ignorance. The passage wonders

25 B Hul 9a.
26 Contra Apion I, 12; ibid. II, 18.
27 Letter to Titus III, 9.

at the ignorance of men: "Is there a man who is devoid of school teaching?" The passage goes on to explain that such a situation could arise "in the case of a child who was held captive among the gentiles."[28] Varied literary sources indicate that books were found in many private houses in Palestine throughout the period under discussion.[29]

The history and character of Jewish education is woven into the history of the culture and the faith in the period of the Second Commonwealth at the time that the Torah assumes greater importance in the life of the people and in the development of society and social relations. With the prevalence of pure monotheism, with the strict adherence to the Law from the times of the Babylonian Exile, and the beginning of the Return to Zion, there emerges predominantly one of the distinctive traits of this period: the importance of the Torah in the life of the people. Beginning with the first generations of the Second Commonwealth, the Torah not only forms the foundation of civil law and the individual's way of life, but it is also the book of study and meditation for all the people. Scripture and the Oral Tradition which was based on it, merged as a united force that shaped and formed not only civil and religious law but also the individual's code and pattern of behavior from birth to death, in his family life and in his surroundings. Each problem, whether practical or theoretical, was referred to the holy text for authoritative solution. Sometimes the text was used just for formal confirmation, and at other times because they were seeking a direct answer from the text. Thus the Spirit of the Lord spoke to them, as it were, through the scripture and the hermeneutic tradition. The question was raised in the Tannaitic schools, one which we find in Greek literature and other literatures as well, about two men, "who walked in the wilderness with water in their jug sufficient for only one of them; should only the one drink so that he might reach a place of settlement for if both were to drink, then both would die? They decided it, or at least they based the answer to it on the Torah verse 'and let thy brother live with you'" (Leviticus 22:35).[30] In Scripture they sought to know the nation's future and the fate of its hopes, searching for good tidings for Israel and all mankind. Moreover, Scripture, in their eyes was a Divine book of life written for each and every generation reflecting all experience and its recurring problems and solutions, in short the path that all generations ought to follow. The sons of each generation have to know how to read, interpret and expound the written text in order to discover in it their circumstances of life and if they delve in it they will bring forth the words of the Lord spoken and prophesied for that same generation.

---

[28] B Shav 5a.
[29] See: BLAU, "Studien zum althebräischen Buchwesen", *Jahresbericht der Landesrabbinerschule in Budapest* (1902), 84–97.
[30] Sifra Behar Ch. VI and parallels.

This conception of sacredness, eternity and actuality combined in the Word of God and adumbrated in the Oral Law brought as its corrolary the tendency to include as wide a sector of the population as possible in the knowledge of its Law and fate, past, present and future, and hence, a continuous spread of education. In the tractate *Avoth*, we find a list of the leading sages of previous generations and some of their sayings which they taught and transmitted. At the head of this 'chain of sages' stands not an individual name but that of a collegium, whose members were called "Anshei Knesset Hagdola" (the men of the great synagogue).[31] They are said to have enjoined: "Raise up many pupils." This injunction of theirs was honoured in the unremitting efforts of Academies and teachers throughout the period to multiply students. About one of the most striking and significant personalities in the history of the Oral Tradition, Rabbi Akiva, it was said that he had twelve thousand pairs of pupils who came from Gvat to Antipatras, that is, from the Land of Judah, an exaggeration pointing to the importance attached to the number of pupils. According to tradition, all his pupils died or were killed in the Bar Kochba rebellion, as many scholars assume, yet Rabbi Akiva tried in his old age to raise new pupils.[32]

The Sages taught not only in the seats of learning. They taught wherever people gathered and were willing to listen to their words. Sages went from place to place, alone or accompanied by a group of their outstanding pupils; they taught in the courtyards of the Temple in Jerusalem, in private houses, in the market place and the gates of the city, in the fields, 'under the olive tree,' and 'under the fig tree.' In the early sayings of the tractate *Avoth* we read: "Let your house be a meeting place for the sages."[33] Rabbi Judah I the Patriarch who lived at the end of the second century, tried to limit teaching in the market place; nevertheless, after his time the rabbis continued to teach in the market place and in other public areas, although there were scholars who considered it improper to teach Torah except in the place devoted to it, in the Beth-Midrash.[34] The same picture emerges from the gospel account concerning Jesus who travels with his disciples and teaches in the cities of Palestine and in other places till he comes to teach in the court yards of the Temple in Jerusalem; this is no different in form or outward framework from what the sages did before and after his time.

The accepted occasion for public teaching of Torah was the sermon

[31] There are different opinions as to the character of this body or institution and the definition of its era. See: ENGLANDER, "The Men of the Great Synagogue", Hebrew Union College *Jubilee Volume* (1925), 145–169.

[32] B Yeb 62b.

[33] Ab I, 4.

[34] Most of the sources have been collected in BÜCHLER, "Learning and Teaching in the Open Air in Palestine", *J. Q. R.*, IV (N. S.), 1914, 485–491 and see Tanhuma Behukotai, Ch. X, 3.

delivered by a sage to a wide audience on the Sabbaths and the holidays or any other time of public gathering such as at the proclamation of a public fast for any distress which might occur. The sermon on the Sabbaths was based on the portion from the Torah or the chapter from the prophet which was read that day during the prayers. There were sermons which included only Aggadic material: an expanded interpretation of the words of Scripture pointing out the moral and historical lesson derived from Scripture, a lesson which is related to the actual problems of the community and the nation; that is, problems of a moral, social, and political nature, the relationship of Israel and the nations and their hopes. In these sermons, the rabbis both raised problems and pointed out solutions to the problems of man as an individual or as a member of a social group with the help of their hermeneutical rules and homiletical means, stretching sometimes quite far the text they based themselves on. Some sermons began with or connected with legal matters (Halakha) furnishing moral or ideational explanations for these legal matters. The sermon broadened the formal halachic problem to its widest religious and human dimension. In the main, the sermons have reached us not complete but rather in fragments. These are traditions or partial notes which were transmitted from generation to generation, and only later, often after as much as two or three hundred years, were these written down. In the Babylonian Talmud in the tractate Shabath (Fol. 31), one finds a sermon preserved almost in its entirety; we have an opportunity to see from this example the usual structure of a sermon from beginning to end. The sermon starts with a question asked of Rabbi Tanhum of Naveh: "Is it permissible on the Sabbath to put out a candle for the sake of a sick person?" The preacher sets forth a wide canvas of ideas while using verses from all parts of the Bible concerning the value of the living man as compared with the dead body, the merit of the fathers (which benefits the progeny), the case of David who sought to build the Temple even though this was permitted only to his son Solomon, the problem of sin and repentence, Aggadic material on the death of David, concluding after this profusion of quotations and allusions with the matter in hand: "As to the question which was asked: a candle is a candle, the soul of man is also called a candle; better that the candle made by man be extinguished rather than that created by the Holy One, Blessed be He." Thus the sermon is not to be regarded solely as preaching but rather as an hermeneutical lecture on the words of Torah, delivered in public: the preacher had recourse to various effects in order to emphasize his words, such as parables and sometimes hyperbole and various images, since he was speaking to a wide audience which included women and children. Nevertheless the sermon retained its basic element of scholarly teaching as well as its didactic and ideational essence.

Torah learning, which was thus widespread and variegated, always

sought to activate pupils and listeners and was not content to have a
mere passive audience. The tradition in the tractate *Avoth* relates that
Rabbi Yohanan ben Zakai told five of his most important pupils "to go
forth and ascertain what is the straight path that a man must adhere
to" and then: "He told them to go forth and ascertain what is the path
of evil that a man must avoid."[35] The preacher, too, used to suggest
questions to his listeners; one finds such a category of sermonic literature
in remnants which are quite frequent in the *Yelamdenu* Midrashim which
begins with the formula *Yelamdeinu Rabeinu* (Let our Master teach us).
The sermon is in its structure no more than an expanded answer to the
question which is initially raised. One may learn more about the active
participation of the public in the sermon from the fact that occasionally
the preacher suggests an idea while interpreting the text and the public
does not accept his words.[36]

Talmudic literature has much to say with regard to the great interest
which the scholar takes in the questions of his pupil and the degree of
progress in the study of Torah which is evidenced by these questions.
Rabbi Hanina, one of the great Amoraim in the first generation after
the codification of the Mishna, after 220, once said: "From my masters,
I have learned much, and from my friends I learned more than from
my masters, but I learned most from my pupils."[37] Before Rabbi
Yohanan ben Zakai moved to Jerusalem during the last decades of the
Temple's existence, he dwelt eighteen years in *Arav* which is in the
Galilee. At one point he strongly denounced the people of the Galilee
who too infrequently used to ask him questions about the Torah: "Oh
Galileans, you who loath the Torah, you play into the hands of the
(Roman) tax collectors."[38]

Public Torah study and the raising of large numbers of pupils was
certainly dependent on elementary education which embraced the vast
majority of male youth and gave them at least a basic knowledge of the
books of the Bible. Many times the sermon was based on the text in the
Bible or the Biblical narrative, not only because they sought Scripture's
authority or because it was used as an authority for innovation, but also
because of the fact that the words of the Torah and the Prophets were
familiar to the great majority of the listeners in their content and language, narrative and laws. The Sages interpreted Scripture, enlarged
upon its words, and continued, so to speak, the narrative in the Bible
from the point where the text ceased to be explicit; their words were
well received by their listeners and were enscribed in their memory.

However, we have not yet said all about the place of Torah in the

---

[35] Aboth II, 9.
[36] Gen Rabbah 28:2; Tanhuma Breishit, ed. Buber, 10a.
[37] B Ta 7a.
[38] P Shab end 17.

life of the people nor have we explained the importance of elementary education in this context.

From the time of the Second Temple, stress is placed on study of Torah as a means of relating the individual and the community to their God. One studies of course to acquire knowledge but it is a religious experience at the same time, a commandment unto itself, a part of public worship of God. Psalm 119, which we may attribute to the beginning of the Second Commonwealth, describes this concept of Torah study: "Thy statutes were songs to me in the house where I sojourn" (54); "Oh how I love Thy law! All the day it is my meditation" (97); "Make Thy face shine upon Thy servant, and teach me Thy statutes" (135). Many hundreds of sayings expressing this concept of the study of Torah are found throughout the Jewish literature of the Second Commonwealth and through to the end of the period under discussion. This concept is expressed in a variety of literary forms. The obligation to study Torah is the same for rich or poor, humble or great, scholars or simple men; as there is no special hour or prescribed pattern, it follows that a man is obliged to study any time that he is able to free himself for this; furthermore, any place is proper for study, either in the house of learning or when a man walks by the way: "These are matters for which there is no measure, the *peah* (the corner of the field left for the poor), the first fruits, the pilgrimage to the Temple, charitable acts, and the study of Torah." [39] From the time that the child learns to speak, "his father teaches him the *Shema* and the Torah—"Moses has commanded us (to study) Torah, the inheritance of the congregation of Jacob" (Deuteronomy 33:4). [40] And from that time on, a man saw himself as obliged to study Torah all his life. This attitude served to make the study of Torah a concrete reality for the widest circles, as countless numbers of the people practised this whether as students or as teachers, each according to his intellectual ability, his degree of adherence to the *Mitzvah* (commandment) and his persistence. A characteristic expression of this reality was the call that went out in the first public gathering in Usha which followed the slight relaxation of the harsh and devastating decrees which came after the Bar Kochba rebellion: "Anyone who teaches, let him come and teach, anyone that does not teach, let him come and learn." Anyone able to teach who fails to do so, scorns the word of the Lord and steals, as it were, from his friend: "Rabbi Judah said in the name of Rav (in the beginning of the third century), anyone who keeps the Law from a pupil, it is as if he has stolen from the inheritance of his fathers, as it is said: 'Moses has commanded us (to study) Torah, the inheritance of the congregation of Jacob' (Deut. 33:4); it is an inheritance to all Israel from the six days of Creation." And before

[39] Pe in the beginning.
[40] T Hag beginning Ch. 1; B Suk 42a.

him, Rabbi Meir said (in the middle of the second century): "He who studies Torah and does not teach it, has scorned the word of the Lord" (Numbers 15:31).[41]

The same picture emerges from the regular patterns for the study of Torah amongst the Essenes, who studied "a third of all the nights of the year"; the evidence for this comes from descriptions as well as from the writings of the sect itself. There is no essential difference from the general rule in Israel except that the Essenes, as was their manner in other matters, gave a hard and fast form to this law.[42]

The clearest expression of the reality of the public study of Torah is the literary form of Talmudic literature in its totality. Almost no work of a single author has survived. Almost all the remaining works of Oral Law are collective creations. Nor is the editing of the principal collections of Talmudic literature the work of one man but of an academy led by either one man or a small group of scholars. The very act of formation of a new collection consisted not so much in the collating of the words of scholars of many generations but rather in the questions and accretions added by students and non-students, and even by *Amei Haaretz* (common people) whose words were accepted in the academies. In these houses of learning the words were transmitted through study from generation to generation and included collections of the Law or the sermons. Sayings, as well as controversies among scholars of previous generations, were somewhat worked over and changed in the processes of addition and crystallization through study in the academies throughout the period. A single story out of many will serve to illustrate this pattern of a mosaic of Talmudic literature: "An *Am Haaretz* once said to Rabbi Hoshiya (in the beginning of the third century): If I were to tell you something good, would you relate it in my name in public?—What is it? asked the rabbi. He explained that all the gifts which our father Jacob gave to Esau will be returned in the future by the Gentiles to the King Messiah who is yet to come. What is the reason? (The proof is contained in the verse:) 'The kings of Tarsus and the islands will return the tribute' (Psalms 73:10). 'Return' is written in the text, rather than 'bring'.—I swear that this is a good thing, and I will relate it in your name."[43] Rabbi Hoshiya hears an idea based on an implication attributed to the choice of wording of a Biblical text and accepts this tradition from a common man and even agrees to preach it in his name.

It was only natural to a society having such an attitude toward learning that the school for children possessed a moral and religious value in its own right, above and beyond its institutional and practical standing. Torah study by children is wholly pure for they have never

---

[41] Song of Songs Rabbah Ch. II, 5; B Sanh 91b; ibid. 99a.
[42] Philo, *Every Good Man is Free*, par. 80–82; *The Scroll of Conduct*, VI, 7.
[43] Gen Rabbah Ch. 78, 12.

tasted sin. "The world endures only for the sake of the breath (of the mouth) of school children... breath in which there is no sin." [44] The sages considered the orderly maintenance of the schools the secret of the survival and strength of the people. When the enemies of Israel came to take counsel with the wicked Balaam whether they might fall upon Israel to destroy it, he said to them: "Go and observe the synagogues and the houses of learning, and if the children are chirruping there then you will not overcome them; for their father has promised them, saying: 'The voice is the voice of Jacob, but the hands are the hands of Esau.' (Genesis 27:22). As long as the voice of Jacob is found in the synagogues and the houses of learning, the hands of Esau have no effect upon you; but if (the voice) is not there—the hands of Esau may prevail." [45] The pressures in Israel's circumstances in those days to suspend the study in the schools were not at all slight—whether for a shorter or a longer period; however the teachers of the people vigorously withstood these kinds of pressure. In the name of Rabbi Judah Hanasi, Patriarch in the middle of the third century, it is said: "One does not suspend the studies of the school children even for the building of the Temple." [46]

Elementary education had overwhelming importance for the religious arrangements of this society's daily life. These arrangements were based on prayer and Torah reading with the participation of the entire congregation, and thus a member of the congregation led the prayer or reading, and not necessarily a priest or a sage. [47] This 'lay' structure of the synagogue went far beyond its walls.

The synagogue was one of the socio-religious institutions most influential in public life both in Palestine and the Diaspora. One ought not to imagine a Jewish settlement of any importance in Palestine or the Diaspora, at least in the last two or three hundred years of the Second Commonwealth, without its own synagogue; there were several of them in the large cities. We have no evidence as to the synagogue's existence in the First Commonwealth, neither have we any justification for the supposition, which was quite prevalent among historians beginning with the last century, that the synagogue was founded as a replacement for the destroyed Temple; therefore its beginning is to be assigned to the times of the Babylonian Exile. This supposition is based on the notion that the synagogue is to be regarded primarily as a place of prayer, it suggests that following the destruction of the Temple when they could no longer offer sacrifices, Jewish exiles in Babylonia founded the synagogue as a place for the worship of God after a new fashion. However, the primary purpose of the synagogue was to serve as a place for the

[44] B Shab 119b.
[45] Gen Rabbah Ch. 65, 20 and parallels.
[46] B Shab 119b.
[47] See J. ELBOGEN, *Der jüdische Gottesdienst*, 155-205.

public reading of Torah; and only in a later period was prayer attached
to it. Hence it could not be a replacement for the sacrificial cult in the
Temple. Moreover, we have no valid allusion to the existence of a synagogue in the Babylonian Exile or at the beginning of the Second Commonwealth. The beginnings of the synagogue are to be seen in the
gatherings of the people in the courtyards of the Temple in the days of
Ezra and Nehemiah, where the people listened to the words of Torah.
In Ezra's activity we find for the first time reading of Torah as a means
of worshipping the Lord and from this the practice appears to have
spread to the rest of the cities of Palestine and became widespread later
on in the Diaspora. Thus the synagogue was, in fact, the result of the
deepening of public religious experience. In the later days of the
Second Commonwealth we find many synagogues built in Jerusalem
and some even in the courtyards of the Temple.[48]

Two elements of the synagogue constitute a turning point in the
history of religion and society in Israel. 1) The entire Divine Worship
is done by meditation on Torah or by public prayer, not by sacrifices.
2) Laymen teach and conduct the worship, unlike in the Temple where
priests and other consecrated persons performed the service. The status
and the holiness of the synagogue were determined only by the gathering
of the worshipping congregation, for which at least ten men were needed.
Even the Torah scroll which was to be found in the synagogue was not
essential to it; from early days until approximately the end of the third
century, the scroll had no established place in the synagogue; it was
kept in a courtyard and brought into the synagogue only when it was
to be read from, that is, on Monday and Thursday each week and on the
first day of the month; three or four men were called up to the scroll on
this occasion. On the Sabbath, at least seven men were called to read
from the scroll, and on this day readings from the Prophets were added.
Until the end of the period which we are discussing, there was no special
Torah reader in the synagogue; each man called up to the Torah scroll
read his portion aloud, while another stood by him and translated his
words, usually into Aramaic, so that all the people, including the women
and children, might understand the words of the Lord. The men called
up to read were mostly laymen. In Halakhic discussions we read of a
synagogue which had only one or two men who were qualified to read
from the Torah and we read as well of instances when a man was invited
to read and had not prepared himself for the reading or where a man
came to a synagogue in which the practice of the lectional cycle was
different from the custom of his synagogue and thus was not prepared
to read the portion read there; generally, however, the men called to

---

[48] See S. KRAUSE, *Synagogale Altertümer*, 52 ff. and 66 ff.; SAFRAI, *The Pilgrimage
in the Days of the Second Commonwealth* (Hebrew), 8.

read from the Torah and the Prophets were prepared and came up and read the selections before the congregation.[49]

A similar practice obtained with regard to prayer. Here, too, there was no fixed *Hazan* (cantor) in the synagogue of this period. The *Hazan* mentioned many times in Talmudic literature and in Greco-Jewish inscriptions was not an official leading the worship as in later periods but was rather an overseer of the synagogue. The man who led in prayer was then called the *Shaliah Tzibur* and was a layman invited to lead the entire service or a part of it on week days, Sabbaths, and holidays; laymen were also invited to offer special prayers during days of distress when a fast was proclaimed and special prayers were ordained. In the period under discussion, the final form of the prayers was not as yet crystallized. Later on in the Talmudic period the prayers became increasingly more fixed. It was already set that the prayer of the eighteen benedictions, for example, begins with three benedictions of praise, must have after them twelve of petition and must end with three of thanks. However there was not yet a binding text of the individual benedictions so that there were some who shortened them and others who recited a longer formula. Prayer was subject to change especially at the hands of the *Shaliah Tzibur* on services for special occasions; he would be free to add many verses from Scripture and to formulate prayers fitting the specific occasion and day of gathering.[50] Not everyone was actually able to officiate under these circumstances as *Shaliah Tzibur;* in fact, with regard to the public fast, it is explicitly stated that the people sent down before the ark a man who was "wise (or: old) and well-versed (in prayers)". Even this demand does not indicate the monopoly of sages or scholars on the office of *Shaliah Tzibur;* indeed it was a layman who officiated on most occasions. Furthermore, there are many traditions about men who were not learned and about others who seemed to be hardened sinners, yet these people went before the ark and their prayers were accepted.[51]

The gathering in the synagogue was then the most important framework for community and social activity; participation in Torah reading and in public prayer ought to be seen from this communal aspect too, and not only from the aspect of participation in religious ritual. The people gathered in the synagogue for other needs as well. The public administrative bodies, especially those of a wider character, also assembled in the synagogue. It would seem that the *Musaf* service on the first day of the month—which later became a part of the general prayer which the entire community as well as the individual used to recite—

[49] In the third and fourth chapters of Meg are set forth the main regulations concerning the reading from the Torah and compare Luke 4:17 and Acts 13:15.

[50] B Meg 17b; B Ber 34a.

[51] Ta II, 2 and in P Ta I, 64b a group of tales are related about simple peo who went before the ark in the days of public fasts and whose prayers were receiv

was said in the earlier period only when the notables gathered—the *Hever Hair*.[52]

The nexus Torah-prayer-learning is well illustrated by the institution of the *Maa'madot*. According to the tradition and views of the Pharisees, the obligatory sacrifices which were offered on weekdays and appointed festivals were to be bought from public money coming only from the half-shekel donation that all Israel was obliged to pay. To emphasize that the daily offerings belonged to the entire community, it was conceived that each priestly watch going up to work in the Temple during its week of duty, should be accompanied by a delegation from its district, and this delegation remained that same week in the Temple; this watch and its district were called *Maamad* (=the presence). The priests were divided for service in the Temple into twenty-four watches and all of Palestine was divided into twenty-four *Maamadot*. The men of the *Maamad*, besides standing by during the sacrifice offering, were principally engaged during their week at the Temple, in Torah reading and prayer together several times each day. Parallel to the delegation's occupation in Jerusalem, the men of its region gathered in their cities for reading Torah.[53] It is not to be assumed, however, that every one participated nor that all who participated in the *Maa'mad* activities were able to read the Torah. It is clear, however, that all these public and religious arrangements were based on a wide stratum of men from the villages and cities who had achieved at least the ability to read Torah without vocalization which required substantial training and thorough acquaintance with the text. (Torah reading began before the tradition of vocalization was established, moreover the text of the scrolls is not vocalized to this day.) In other words, it is suggested that for a man to take part in certain public and religious activities and to a certain extent in civic leadership too, a thorough acquaintance with text, fluency in Scripture and some knowledge of the Oral tradition was a prerequisite.

In the Second Commonwealth Judaism crystallized its social and spiritual substance through continuous struggles which were already evidenced in the first generations of the Return to Zion. The remnants of the Jewish settlement in Judea, Transjordan, and Samaria, which included leading and influential people, joined by various aristocratic circles from the gentile and half Jewish population—e.g. the Samaritans —sought to prevent the establishment of those who returned from Exile. The reason for this antagonism was that these people had remained in Palestine and did not take part in the spiritual and religious evolution which set apart the Jews who had experienced the Babylonian Exile and had remained faithful to the Torah, its teaching and its legacy to the people. It is not our purpose to blur or minimize the significance of

52 Ber IV, 7.
53 Ta IV, 2, 3 and T *ibid* and the two Talmuds.

other political and social elements which stand revealed in these struggles. We seek, however, to indicate and emphasize the social and cultural element in the conflicts which continued even after the period described in the books of Ezra and Nehemiah and which emerge, although in disconnected narrative, in Josephus' presentation. These struggles, in their various manifestations and aspects, continued throughout most of the period in the midst of the Jewish society and mainly evolved around Jerusalem and the Temple, which served as a center of Jewish spiritual and social life and formative activity. They continued not only as open conflicts, accompanied by violence in times of strife, but these tensions can also be discerned in normal, peaceful days. Just before the Hasmonean war for freedom and during the war itself, these socio-religious antagonisms took the form of a struggle between the scribes and the Pious (Hassidim) against the Hellenizers.

During the last two hundred years of the Temple, we frequently hear of struggles between the Sadducees and the Pharisees, which are to be seen as the struggle between a small but powerful group centered around the priestly aristocracy and the plutocracy and a wider social stratum, on the other hand, whose leaders were scribes and teachers of Torah. Interwoven in this struggle of the popular party were other aims involving conflicting religious concepts and traditions about many aspects of civic life, religion, and law. In contrast to ancient times in Israel, the battle was not waged between those faithful to the God of Israel and His Torah and those who diverged from them completely in one aspect or another; for the scribes and Pharisees in their struggle with the Sadducees, and to a large extent, even the pietists vis à vis the Hellenizers, were not in opposition to groups who refused to recognize the Torah and the words of the Prophets, or regarded themselves as removed from them. During the Second Commonwealth, all currents in the Jewish community, or at least all those which are discussed in the historical sources, proclaimed their devotion to the Torah and recognized it as the supreme authority. The struggle between Pharisees and Sadducees was rather about the interpretation of the Torah and how it was to be taught to the people. The Pharisees upheld oral tradition in their opinions, beliefs, and commentaries on the Torah and their sages saw themselves as authorized to interpret Torah, just as they pressed the spreading of Torah among wide strata of the people. The Sadducees who held aloof in their own circles, regarded the Torah "as sealed and set upon a pedestal" and adhered closely to the literal interpretation of the written Torah and refused to participate in any of the formative process of the Oral Law nor in teaching it to the public. The Sadducees denied the beliefs of the Pharisees with regard to resurrection and other elements of Pharisaic creed which are not explicitly and clearly mentioned in the Bible; they further denied all those practical regulations which the

Pharisees derived from their commentaries on and amplification of the
words of Torah.

In the last decades of the Second Commonwealth and to a large
extent even before this time, we witness the widening influence of the
Pharisees among the people; so that even though the high priesthood
was mostly Sadducean, it was forced in the Temple and other public
matters to follow the practice of the Pharisees, for they were "most
trusted by the people so that all matters of religion pertaining to prayers
or the offering of sacrifices was done according to their interpretation".[54]
After the destruction of the Temple, the Sadducees disappear completely
as a social movement or group which aspires to influence and leadership
in the life of the people, though here and there, in the sources, a Sadducee
or a Sadducean woman does appear. The Pharisaic movement which
was already during the Second Commonwealth one of the decisive
forces in the shaping of Jewish culture and society, became, with the
destruction of the Temple, the only movement to shape Judaism in
succeeding generations. Without doubt, many factors combined to bring
about the strengthening and the triumph of Pharasaic Judaism. At this
point we may note among these factors the existence of schools everywhere as well as the obligation to study which became increasingly
widespread during the last generations of the Second Commonwealth
and following the destruction of the Temple. The very idea of disseminating the Torah and teaching it in public is basic to the world-view
of the Pharisees. No doubt the founding of the school system and the
formulation and inculcation of the obligation to study, as mentioned
above, were due to the influence and prodding of the Pharisaic sages,
whether or not we attribute the specific regulation to Shimon ben
Shetah or to the high priest who was not numbered among the Pharisees.
Although we possess no direct proof of this, it seems most likely that the
great majority of the teachers of Scripture and certainly the teachers of
the Oral Law, came from the circles of the Pharisees and their pupils.
Furthermore, the great influence of these teachers of Scripture and Oral
Law was felt in the character and manner of their teaching. The laws
of the Torah and the words of the Prophets were given a Pharisaic
interpretation in the schools and this no doubt contributed to the
triumph of Pharisaic Judaism.[55]

In the last generations of the Second Commonwealth, there emerges
a phenomenon, a kind of social current of *Amei Haaretz* (common people),
whose organizational framework is loosely defined. An *Am Haaretz*
neither denies nor contradicts the Written or Oral Law, nor is he usually

[54] *Antiquities*, XVIII, 1, 3.
[55] There is much written about the character of the Pharisees. A summary may be
found in the essay by LEO BAECK, "Die Pharisäer", in the collection *Aus drei Jahrtau-
senden* (1938); *The Pharisees and Other Essays* (New York, 1947).

suspected of committing sins or being careless in the performance of the commandments of the Torah. From the many laws which deal with the relationship between the *Haverim* (members of the fellowship) and the *Amei Haaretz*, and from the various definitions which had been set forth in different generations with regard to this phenomenon, this current seems to have had two principal features: 1) Carelessness in the laws of purity and impurity (the strict observance of which was also a hallmark of the Essenes) and in part of the laws connected with the different tithes of the produce of the land and the cattle. 2) Withdrawal from Torah education and knowledge: "Who is an *Am Haaretz?* Whoever is unable to read the chapter of *Shma* in the evening and morning prayers... and whoever has sons and does not raise them in the study of Torah."[56] In some generations the element of ignorance is more stressed in the description of the *Am Aratzuth* phenomenon, while in other generations the element of carelessness in the performance of certain of the commandments is more prominent. The social and spiritual phenomenon of the *Am Haaretz* was despised by its learned opponents and by others who took on themselves the laws of *Haveruth* (fellowship). This mutual enmity was aggravated by those who asserted their *Am Aratzut*, turning their conduct into a matter of principle. This is singularly true of the Yavneh period (70–135 C.E.), a generation or two after the destruction of the Temple. Those days were marked by the increasing crystallization of the people's life and the disappearence of the various sects so that the remaining tension between the scholars and the common people increased, as it were, in scale. Only in the Amoraic period (after 220 C.E.) does the tension between the two factions subside and in fact, later in this period, our sources bear witness to a rapprochement and an identification between the men of Torah and the common people.[57] In the Midrash of Leviticus Rabbah, we read: "Just as the leaves of the vine cover the clusters of grapes, so too, in Israel; the Amei Haaretz cover the scholars"; elsewhere in the same Midrash: "'Thou shalt bring home the lowly poor' (Isaiah 58:7)—these are the scholars who enter the homes of the common people and quench their thirst for words of Torah."[58]

Those who had only slight knowledge of the Torah never entirely disappeared from Israel but the phenomenon of a social stratum with a separate *Am Aratzuth* consciousness, which intentionally withdrew from the men of Torah, despised them, and sought to usurp their place did disappear during the period of the Amoraim.

With regard to the *Am Haaretz*, it is. possible to suggest various explanations for the diminution of this phenomenon and its final elimi-

[56] B Ber 47b.
[57] Most of the sources that are relevant to this problem are discussed in A. BUCHLER, *Der galiläische Am-ha-Arez* (1906); but our views differ from his conclusions.
[58] Ch. 36b; *ibid.* 34, 13.

nation. To a large extent, the gradual ceasing of the practices of purity and impurity in the later Amoraic period brings this about. The observance of purification rites involved the possibility of cleansing oneself from severe impurity, such as follows touching a dead body, by sprinkling waters of purification, that is, pure waters from the spring, together with scattering a small amount of the ashes of the red heifer on the water. Following the destruction of the Temple, a small quantity of these ashes was preserved for a few generations, but since the Temple was not standing, they were unable to prepare new ashes and so the supply dwindled and with it, the purification practices disappeared as well. Strictness in the laws of purity was one of the causes of the tension between the *Haverim* and the *Amei Haaretz*, and thus the discontinuance of these laws in practice naturally led to the end of the conflict. The disappearance of the division between the Amei Haaretz and the sages was also brought about by the efforts of those sages who frequently spoke to and guided the common people. Yet there can be no doubt that for the duration of the Tannaitic and Amoraic period, the spread of education served as one of the important causes for the disappearance of the *Am Haaretz* as a distinctive group, and created a feeling of social and spiritual equality among all sectors of the people.

LISTE OF ABBREVIATIONS

SELECTED BIBLIOGRAPHY

BACHER, W., "Das alt-jüdische Schulwesen", *Jahrbuch für Jüdische Geschichte und Literatur*, VI (1903), 48-82.

DRASIN, W., *History of Jewish Education from 515 B.C.E. to 220 C.E.* (1940).

EBNER, E., *Elementary Education in Ancient Israel* (1956).

MORRIS, W., *The Jewish School from the Earliest Times to the Year 500* (1937).

PERLOW, J., *L'Education et l'Enseignement chez les Juifs à l'époque Talmudique* (1931).

SWIFT, F. H., *Education in Ancient Israel from Earliest Times to 70 C.E.* (1919).

WISSEN, J., *Geschichte und Methode des Schulwesens im Talmudischen Altertum* (1892).

S. D. GOITEIN

JEWISH SOCIETY AND INSTITUTIONS UNDER ISLAM

ISLAM, whose appearance and expansion changed the course of world history, affected also the destinies of the Jewish people in each and every respect. Less than a hundred years after the death of the founder of the new religion, the majority of the Jews found themselves living within the empire of the caliphs. And about three hundred years after the rise of Islam the Hebrew Bible had been translated into Arabic more than once, the tenets of the Jewish faith had been set forth in the language of Islamic theology, and rabbinical law had been formulated with the aid of Muslim legal terms. By the end of the same period the Jewish community had made progress in many directions: a certain economic and social rise was accompanied by spiritual efflorescence and an increase in the authority of the central religious institutions. How, then, should we explain this seeming contrast : a high degree of assimilation to the new Arabic Muslim environment on the one hand, and rejuvenation and vigorous self-assertion on the other.

Trying to answer this question with the means at our disposal at present would be a hazardous undertaking. The two hundred or so years before and after the advent of Islam are the most obscure post-biblical Jewish history. Next to no datable Jewish sources have been preserved from this period. Islamic sources, beginning with the Koran itself, contain quite a number of references to Jews, some of which are detailed and comparatively objective. But it is natural that they speak about Jews only when Muslim issues are involved—such as the help extended by Jews to the Arab conquerors—and only as far as Muslim observers were interested in noticing and able to understand a population foreign to them. Moreover, the Koran excepted, the Muslim sources have come down to us in the form in which they were fixed during the third Islamic century, when they were already intermingled with much tendentious legendary material. A comparison of present day historical research with that of the previous generation gives the impression that the work of critical disentanglement of the historical core from later accretions has regressed rather than advanced.

The specific difficulties of the Jewish historian are compounded by another deficiency of modern historiography: the lack of adequate research into the fate, during the first centuries of Islam, of the subject population in general. The old legend of the diffusion of Islam by fire and sword has long ago been discarded. But there can be no doubt that the wars of conquest must have been a traumatic experience for the peoples concerned, and the subsequent years of rule by a warrior caste who regarded the masses governed by it as a booty bestowed by God must have been equally hard. We read about fabulous treasures amassed by the conquerors; these represented, of course, the property taken away from countless people. Most of the Muslim scholars and litterateurs of the second century of the Hijra were the grandsons of persons who had been reduced to slavery during the wars of conquest and dragged from one corner of the caliphal empire to another. To quote just two outstanding examples: Ibn Isḥāq, the author of the classical biography of the prophet Muhammad, was the grandson of a man (of which religion we do not know), who was captured in Iraq and carried off to Medina in Arabia. The grandfather of Abū Ḥanīfa, the founder of the most famous Muslim school of law, was brought by his Arab proprietor from distant Kabul in Afghanistan to Kufa in Iraq. His name was Zūṭā (Mr. Small), a common Jewish name, but the sources did not care of course to note the religion of a slave. The unlimited supply of slavegirls and concubines apparent in Arabic literature during the first two centuries of Islam can also be explained only through the assumption that the males connected with these hapless women had been either killed or reduced to slavery or had been robbed of their children. The most tangible illustration of the impact of the Islamic conquest is provided by the total blackout effected by it on Persian literature. The great people of Iran, which had ruled for centuries from the Euphrates to the Indus, was so stunned by the Arab onslaught that not a single account in the Persian language is known for at least three hundred years after that crucial event. Since the majority of the Jewish people had lived at the time of the Arab conquest in the territory held by Persia, we are not surprised to find a similar dearth of information in contemporary Hebrew literature.

We forgo, then, the description of the *immediate* effects of the advent of Islam on Jewish society and institutions. We have to make another, and even more far-reaching, restriction. Islam does not represent a unified civilization. After the turbulent periods of conquest, colonization, and multifaceted attempts at consolidation, a certain degree of uniformity prevailed in Islam during what could be called its classical period, approximately between 900 and 1200 of the Christian era. Later on, regional cultures developed, owing their origin to specific geographic, linguistic, political and other factors.[1] The Jewish communities partici-

[1] S. D. GOITEIN, "A Plea for the Periodization of Islamic History", *Journal of the American Oriental Society* 87 (1967).

pating in these regional cultures differed from each other considerably and partook also in the change of times as much, if not more than their Muslim neighbors. Think of the Jewish society of Istanbul around 1500, as compared with that of Yemen at the same period, or contrast the Jews of Egypt during the eleventh century with those of the same country, as they appeared in the fifteenth. An attempt to draw a general picture of the Jews under Islam would be futile and would result in a schematic image which nowhere was a reality. Here, we confine ourselves to Jewish society during the classical period of Islam and shall comment on developments during the preceding era of conquest and consolidation, the subsequent period of regional cultures, and modern times, only when called for by specific reasons.

By the year 900, Islam had come of age as a distinctive civilization, which the three subsequent centuries carried to full maturity. During the same period Judaism developed and crystallized in every respect. Jewish law, ritual and liturgy were systematized into a well organized body of regulations and texts, an activity culminating in the code of Moses Maimonides. Sectarian schisms kindled religious thought, which was condensed in theological treatises of lasting authority. The Hebrew language was scientifically studied and its proper usage was established, providing a firm base for an exact understanding of the biblical text. Neo-Hebraic poetry, a by-product of this activity, fulfilled important functions both in social life and in the synagogue, and in some of its creations reached the greatness of the Psalms. Jews also took part in secular studies, such as mathematics, astronomy and philosophy, and, above all medicine and pharmacology.

Naturally, such spiritual activities had to be supported by a society of good standing, enjoying a certain degree of economic prosperity and civic liberties. Fortunately, we possess for this period a historical source depicting this society in great detail: the documents of the Cairo Geniza. These are manuscripts mostly in Hebrew characters, but predominantly in Arabic language. They were originally preserved in a synagogue, partly also a cemetery, of Fustat (Old Cairo), the ancient capital of Islamic Egypt, and later dispersed in many libraries all over the world. This material originated not only in Egypt, but also in other Islamic countries of the Mediterranean area, inclusive of the sea-route to India, and comprises official, business and private correspondence, court records and other juridical documents, contracts, accounts, receipts and inventories, writs of marriage, divorce and manumission and the like.[2] In many respects the Geniza material is of unique value also for the

---

[2] See Shaul SHAKED, *A Tentative Bibliography of Geniza Documents* (Paris-The Hague, 1964); Norman GOLB, "Sixty Years of Genizah Research", *Judaism* 6 (1957), pp. 3-16.

history of Islamic society, since it provides information about the life of the middle and lower classes not obtainable from other sources.[3] The present writer has attempted to convey an idea of the rich content of the Cairo Geniza documents in a three volume book, of which the first was due to appear by the end of 1967. For the manuscript sources of statements made in the following the reader is referred to this book.[4]

The first question occupying the student of a minority group is its demographic aspect, its size in comparison with the main population. E. Ashtor has paid particular attention to this problem,[5] and although his data occasionally need revision,[6] I am inclined to accept his general results, in which, as may be remarked in passing, he is in agreement with a former study on the Jewish population of Fatimid Egypt made by D. Neustadt (now: Ayalon).[7] The number of Jewish settlements in Egypt was considerably higher than registered by Ashtor.[8] The Geniza seems also to indicate that the average size of a family was larger than assumed by him.[9] Great uncertainty prevails as to the size of the Muslim population of Egypt or other Islamic countries, such as Syria or Spain. It can be assumed, however, with a certain degree of likelihood, that the Jewish community of Egypt or Spain during the High Middle Ages did not amount to more than one percent of the total population—with the important qualification that in the cities and towns, where the Jews lived, they formed a far higher percentage of the inhabitants.

[3] See *Encyclopaedia of Islam*, second edition, s.v. "Geniza". Also S. D. GOITEIN, "The Documents of the Cairo Geniza as a Source for Islamic Social History", in *Studies in Islamic History and Institutions* (Leiden, 1966), pp. 279-294.

[4] *A Mediterranean Society: The Jewish Communities of the Arab World as Portrayed in the Documents of the Cairo Geniza* (University of California Press, Berkeley and Los Angeles, 1967).

[5] E. ASHTOR, "Prolegomena to the Medieval History of Oriental Jewry", *Jewish Quarterly Review* 50 (1959), pp. 55-68, pp. 147-166. Also E. ASHTOR, "The Number of Jews in Moslem Spain" (Hebrew), *Zion* 28 (1963), pp. 34-56.

[6] The assumption of Jacob MANN, *The Jews in Egypt etc.*, I, p. 88, n. 1, accepted by ASHTOR, *JQR* 50, p. 58 (see preceding note) to the effect that there were 300 heads of Jewish families in Alexandria, is based on a misunderstanding of the text which says: "You have sent us (for the ransoming of captives) 200 dinars, which was as helpful as if you had sent 300".

It is not correct that besides Benjamin of Tudela there is no evidence for the existence of a Jewish community at Palmyra, see ASHTOR, *JQR* 50, p. 63. There are quite a number of references: R. GOTTHEIL and W. H. WORRELL, *Fragments from the Cairo Genizah in the Freer Collection* (New York, 1927), No. XIII, p. 66, line 11; TS (Taylor-Schechter Collection of the University Library, Cambridge) 13 J 20, f. 2; S. SCHECHTER, *Abraham Berliner Jubilee Volume* (1903), 110-112, where Tadmor is to be read despite the remark in J. MANN, *Jews in Egypt*, II, p. 341. Palmyra was one of the communities addressed by the Gaon Samuel ben Eli (1164-1193), see S. ASSAF, *Letters of Samuel b. Eli* (Jerusalem), 1930, 50.

[7] *Zion* 2 (1937), p. 221.

[8] ASHTOR, *JQR* 50, p. 60. See now N. GOLB, "The Topography of the Jews of Medieval Egypt", *Journal of Near Eastern Studies* 24 (1965), pp. 251-270 (to be continued).

[9] This subject is dealt with in volume III of *A Mediterranean Society*, see note 4.

As to the composition of the Jewish communities reflected in the Geniza documents, a large part, if not the majority of the Jews of Egypt, were immigrants or the descendants of such. In the eleventh century, when our information is particularly detailed, an older layer of arrivals from Iraq and Iran, even Central Asia as far as Nīshāpūr and Samar-qand, can be discerned, alongside a younger and most vigorous one from Tunisia and Sicily. There was a permanent influx from Palestine and Syria and a sprinkling of newcomers from all parts of the Jewish dia-spora, including France, Italy and Byzantium.

One wonders what accounted for the comparatively limited number of Jews in the area considered. One would particularly like to know whether much substance was lost in this early period by conversion to Islam. In the case of the Christian population, which in the course of two to three centuries was reduced to a minority, this loss is both self-evident and testified by historical sources. Conversely, the steadfast attachment of Jews to their faith is attested both for the time of Muham-mad and for that of the conquest of Egypt. It is also noteworthy that in such widely separated areas as Yemen, Morocco and Bukhara, all of which contained important Christian communities prior to the rise of Islam, only Jewish enclaves have survived. For this fact, to which I had drawn attention previously,[10] I wish now to adduce an explanation with special reference to Yemen. The Muslim sources deal at great length with the expulsion of the Christians from Najrān in South Arabia, but make no mention of similar measures against the South-Arabian Jews. As a matter of fact, we learn from letters of a head of a Jewish academy in Iraq that Jewish communities were scattered all over Yemen and Yamāma (Central Arabia) in the fourth century of Islam.[11] As is well-known, this situation prevailed until the mass exodus of the Jews from Yemen in 1949/50.[12] I am inclined to ascribe the preferential treatment of the Jews in this case to the very fact that they were widely dispersed in the country and, as artisans and craftsmen, both inconspicuous and indispensable, while the Christians belonged to the more comfortable merchant class and were concentrated in the city (which was the seat of a bishop). Thus, their expulsion presented no administrative problem, while there were enough Arab traders to take their place.[13] The small size of the Jewish population in most Islamic countries was either pre-

[10] S. D. GOITEIN, *Jews and Arabs: Their Contacts through the Ages* (second edition, New York, 1964) (also paperback), p. 65.

[11] "The Contribution of the Jews of Yemen to the Maintenance of the Babylonian and Palestinian Yeshivot and of Maimonides' School", *Tarbiz* 31 (1962), pp. 357-370.

[12] Investigations carried out by me among the immigrants from Yemen to Israel in and after 1949 showed that they hailed from over one thousand and fifty different localities.

[13] The Muslim reports about the expulsion of the Christians from Najrān are much confused, see the literature discussed by A. MOBERG in the article "Nadjrān" in the *Enc. of Islam*.

Islamic or was caused by the upheaval accompanying and following the Arab conquest, or both.

The ecology of the Jews under Islam, i.e. their topographical distribution with reference to their sources of sustenance, is particularly well illustrated in the Geniza. No ghettoes existed in Fustat, Alexandria, Jerusalem or Kairouan (then the capital of the country now known as Tunisia), or in provincial towns. Contracts and other documents prove that houses belonging to Jews bordered everywhere on Muslim and/or Christian properties. Muslims lived together with Jewish tenants in houses belonging to Jews, and viceversa. On the other hand, predominantly Jewish neighborhoods centering around a synagogue are found everywhere. Thus, there was enough physical contact with gentiles to prevent seclusion, but also sufficient concentration for the healthy growth of intensive communal life.

Nor was there an occupational ghetto. In this field, that of Jewish occupations and their role within the economic life of Islamic society in general, the study of the Geniza is made to revolutionize our traditional concepts. Israel Abrahams, in his charming book *Jewish Life in the Middle Ages*[14], enumerates thirty-three "occupations of the Jews of the Levant, Persia, Syria and the East generally (chiefly up to the twelfth century)." Of these, only ten were manual. Against this, the Geniza makes mention of about 250 manual occupations exercised by Jews and of another 170 types of activities in commerce, the professions, education and administration. On the other hand, Abrahams' statement: "agricultural laborers (many)", might have been true for Iraq in early Islamic times. In Egypt, in the period considered here (900-1200), Jews possessed agricultural land and sometimes supervised in person the harvest and of course such operations as grape pressing and cheese making which involved religious taboos, but the soil was tilled by non-Jewish fellahin exclusively. Even orchards belonging to the Jewish community were leased to Muslims against a yearly payment. Jews had an important part in the processing of flax, the staple export of Egypt, but only after the peasants had cut, soaked, and dried it. The manual occupations of Jews where those of artisans and craftsmen.

In this respect it is necessary to dispel certain notions that appear again and again in our historical writings, namely that the Jews were concentrated mainly in occupations despised by Muslims. This misconception has its origin in another one, already censured by us, namely that which regards the long history of Islam as one single unit and does not pay proper attention to the differences of time and general level of culture. In periods of decline and oppression Islamic peoples found

---

[14] Ed. Meridian Books, 1958, pp. 245-246, based mainly on the Responsa of the Gaons and Benjamin of Tudela.

an outlet for their own humiliation and misery in the even greater degradation of the helpless minorities living in their midst. At a time in recent centuries, when Bukhara, Morocco and Yemen were in a very backward state, the Jews of those countries were forced to collect the contents of cesspools and to dry them for use as fuel for bathhouses (other fuel being scarce in those countries). It was incumbent on the local communities to provide persons for this odious task. Even then and there, however, the situation was by no means simple. Again taking Yemen as an example, the Jew was utterly humiliated as the member of another religion, but was honored in his capacity of artisan, who fulfilled an indispensable role in the primitive economy of the country. A Jew used to be addressed as Uṣṭa, or "master", the supposition being that he was competent in his craft and also possessed manifold additional skills. It is noteworthy that the despised professions of cleaners of cesspools or of bathhouse attendants never appear in the Geniza as performed by Jews. Had the Jewish community of Fustat comprised such persons, some of them would have had to appear in the many lists of indigent people assisted by the communal chest.

With regard to early Islamic times much has been made of a passage by the Iraqi Muslim writer al-Jāḥiẓ (around 850), who states that the Jews follow only lowly professions, those of tanners, dyers, cuppers, butchers and cobblers, as opposed to Christians who were government officials, physicians and accountants.[15] Similarly, the Jews of Isfahan in Iran were described as being engaged in unclean professions, such as those of tanners and butchers.[16] Tanning and dyeing are mentioned as Jewish professions—together with others and without the taint of lowliness—with regard to Syria and Palestine (end of tenth century).[17]

These often quoted passages should be seen in their proper perspectives. Tanning and dyeing are very conspicuous occupations, because the hides and textiles treated are spread out for drying in open spaces in or outside a city.[17a] Muslims normally did not pay much attention to Jews, but the Jewish tanners and dyers could not escape them because of the very conspicuousness of their trade. Thus Muslims were prone to assume that most Jews were engaged in these occupations.

---

[15] Al-Jāḥiẓ, Thalāth Rasā'il, ed. J. Finkel (Cairo, 1344 A.H.), 17. Trans. Journal of the American Oriental Society 47 (1927), pp. 327-328, see Salo W. Baron, Social and Religious History of the Jews, IV, p. 318, n. 17.

[16] Quoted by A. Mez, Die Renaissance des Islams (Heildelberg, 1922), p. 35, n. 3, according to a Leiden manuscript of a history of the city of Isfahan. This manuscript has meanwhile been edited by S. Dedering (Leiden, 1931), but the edition is not available to me at present.

[17] Al-Muqaddasī, ed. de Goeje (Leiden, 1906), p. 183.

[17a] The present writer vividly remembers this sight during his visit to the Aden Protectorate in 1949: the first thing to attract the attention of a visitor to a traditional Muslim town were these widely stretched materials and the persons attending to them.

The Geniza enables us to check these data and to arrive at some kind of statistics. For a period of 300 years (965-1265) I have noted so far only six persons described as tanners and the family name Tanner has been ascertained in this period only for a Muslim shipowner and for Muslim scholars. The references quoted above should by no means be taken as a proof that in classical Islam this was a specifically Jewish occupation.

The situation was different with regard to dyeing. Colors (and not the cut) were the pride of the medieval attire. Dyeing was one of the greatest and most central industries of the period, and there is no doubt that Jews were very prominent in this field in Islamic as well as in Christian countries. Next to the preparation of drugs, dyeing was the most common Jewish occupation, but it was by no means confined to them. The family name Dyer was as common among Muslims as among Jews. Because of the size of the profession, it comprised both poor and well-to-do families. Characterizing dyeing as despised or low is an unjustified generalization.

It may well be that the majority of Jews known to al-Jāḥiẓ held a lowly position in society. Presumably these were the descendants of peasants who formed a part of the new urban proletariat like many other members of the agricultural population who were forced to forsake their homesteads because of an oppressive taxation. It is also likely that Jews in certain quarters of Isfahan may have lived in wretched conditions in the eleventh century, as they still (or again) did in 1966. But just as the existence of some great Jewish merchants in tenth century Baghdad, who were able to grant large loans to the government, should not induce us to believe that the Jews were the Rothschilds of the Islamic world, thus we should not assume that all were paupers at the time of al-Jāḥiẓ. It is true that the great Muslim theologian Ghazzālī (d. 1111) describes the Jews as being rich, in a sweeping way reminiscent of modern anti-semitic literature. But he was impressed by the conspicuous, just as al-Jāḥiẓ was 250 years before him, only in the opposite direction.

In short, as far as the classical period of Islam is concerned, wherever we have detailed and trustworthy information and not only casual and often tendentious observations, we find that the Jews were more prominent in some arts and crafts than in others, but that they were not confined to specific occupations shunned by Muslims. About a subject on which Israel Abrahams was able to provide a few lines, it is now possible to write a comprehensive book. Once this will be done, Jewish arts and crafts during the heyday of Islam will be revealed in their proper social setting and in all their rich variety. The enforcement of professional humiliation is the product of a later period of decay and bigotry.

A similar revision is necessary with regard to our notions about Jewish commerce and banking under Islam. Since L. Massignon published his article on Jewish bankers,[18] exaggerated ideas of the economic importance of the Jews in Islamic society—fashioned after certain developments in both medieval and modern Europe—have become widely diffused. Both well-meaning[19] and less amicable Islamic scholars have taken the same stand. In a previous paper, I tried to describe the rise of Middle Eastern bourgeoisie as an inner-Islamic development, the merchant-class becoming the real bearer of Islamic religious culture. The subsequent economic and social transformation of the Jews into an urban element was understood as a by-product of this development.[20] That study must be complemented in two respects. The archeological soundings of Robert C. Adams in the lower Diyala plains east of Baghdad have uncovered a mass of urban construction from the Sasanid period (preceding the Arab conquest) "far in excess of anything before or after."[21] Such a degree of urbanization is unthinkable without a strong merchant class. Thus we must assume that in this respect, as in many others, Islam continued pre-Islamic conditions, although our sources, because of the blackout described above, leave us in the dark as to the details of this development.

As to the Jewish aspect of the problem. I should like to mention that some of the most ancient and most prominent scholars of the Babylonian Talmud, Abba, the father of Samuel (the founder of Babylonian spiritual leadership) and Ḥiyya Rabba were wholesale silk merchants, the latter commuting to Palestine and Tyre in this business.[22] The fact that Babylonian Jews should have engaged in commerce is not surprising, since already some of the Judaeans exiled by Nebuchadnezar took to this profession. The salient point is that such merchants were bearers of Jewish scholarship, a fact corroborated by a passage from the Syriac life of Adday: "Even Jews skilled in the Law and the Prophets, who traded in silk, they too were convinced and became disciples (i.e. Christians)."[23] Thus it appears that Islam did further rather than initiate the development of that remarkable type of merchant-scholar who was economically independent and therefore able to create a religious law independent of the state.

[18] L. MASSIGNON, "L'influence de l'Islam... sur la fondation et l'essor des banques juives", *Bulletin de l'Institut Français de Damas* (1932), pp. 4 ff.

[19] E.g., Dr. Shaikh INAYATULLAH, *Islamic Culture, its Growth and Character* (Lahore, 1957), 13.

[20] *Journal of World History,* III (1957), pp. 583-604, also in *Studies in Islamic History and Institutions,* pp. 217-241.

[21] Robert C. ADAMS, *Land behind Baghdad* (Chicago, 1965), p. 69. The two last words in the quotation were italicized by me.

[22] Midrash Samuel 10.3, ed. S. BUBER, p. 35. Genesis Rabba 79.9, ed. THEODOR-ALBECK, p. 946. These often quoted passages are discussed in their true historical perspective in Jacob NEUSNER, *A History of the Jews in Babylonia,* I (Leiden, 1965), pp. 88-89.

[23] W. CURETON, *Ancient Syriac Documents* (London, 1864), p. 14, quoted by J. NEUSNER, *op. cit.* (see preceding note), p. 89.

As in the arts and crafts, the Jews were prominent in some branches of commerce more than in others, but did not monopolize any. They excelled in textiles, particularly in flax and silk (see above), also in hides and leathergoods ; in many types of Oriental products, such as spices, perfumes, dyeing and varnishing materials; in pharmaceutical products of both Oriental and Mediterranean origin; in metals of all kinds, including raw material for the mints; in foodstuffs such as oil, honey and dried fruits; finally, in a great variety of specific goods, such as corals, exported from the western Mediterranean, and cowryshells, coming from the countries of the Indian Ocean. They had little share in the trade of wheat and barley and none in that of horses, mules, cows and other animals, or of arms. In many respects there is a direct correlation between the branches of commerce and the arts and crafts favored by Jews in classical Islamic times (dyers, pharmacists, gold- and silversmiths, workers in the mints and in the food industry, in particular in the production of sugar). Many Jews were glass makers. In accordance with this we find great quantities of glass vessels exported by a Jewish firm from Tyre to Egypt shortly before 1011,[24] or red Beirut glass and local Egyptian glass ordered from Cairo by a Jewish merchant in Aden around 1140.[25]

In the fields of money and finance Jews were active as government accountants, high and low (*jahbadh*, later *naqqād*), and also as money changers and bankers (*sayrafi*). The accounts of a Jewish banker from the eleventh century show that the number of his Muslim fellow bankers with whom he had dealings far exceeded the Jewish.[26] Both professions are frequently mentioned in Arabic literature as being exercised by Muslims. Jews occasionally took loans on interest from Muslims when they were in need, and the same happened in the other direction. Loans on interest for commercial purposes were uncommon until the middle of the twelfth century, and even later they were of little importance, for business was financed through partnerships. Some great Jewish merchant bankers who were able to issue suftajas, or bills of exchange, are known to us from the eleventh century, but we also see Jews taking suftajas from Muslims. [27]

Since the question of Jewish participation in the international trade of the classical period of Islam is one of considerable interest for world history in general, and since the Geniza provides particularly detailed

[24] S. ASSAF, *Tarbiz* 9 (1938), p. 196, 1. 15: 37 baskets of glass. (In the text, the Hebrew word for "glass" is overlined as if of uncertain reading. I have checked the manuscript and can confirm that the reading is above doubt.)

[25] *India Book* (a collection of Geniza papers related to the India trade, prepared by the present writer for publication), No. 50.

[26] S. D. GOITEIN, "Bankers Accounts from the Eleventh Century", *Journal of the Economic and Social History of the Orient* 9 (1966), pp. 28-66.

[27] "The Business Correspondence of Ibn 'Awkal", *Tarbiz* 36 (1967), No. 1, line 32.

information on this point, a summary of our present state of knowledge is appropriate.

The well-known passage from the Muslim geographer Khurrādādbeh (ninth century) about the Jewish Rahdanite merchants who travelled from France through Muslim territory to India and China and exchanged the goods of the countries traversed by them has given rise to the notion that the Jews served as middlemen between the Christian and the Muslim worlds. To a certain extent, this might have been the case, but probably at a time preceding the date when Khurrādādbeh wrote his book.[28] By the end of the tenth century, when detailed information is first available in the Geniza, a totally different picture emerges. Close and continuous commercial exchange took place between the northern and the southern shores of the Mediterranean, but the Jews had little share in it. The Jewish trade evolved mainly within the realms of Islam. The Rūm, the Europeans with whom Jews dealt, were exclusively Christians. There were close cultural and social connections between the Jews of Europe and those of the Islamic countries, but no commercial relations. Not a single business letter from a European Jew of this period has been preserved in the Geniza.

As to Jewish trade within Islam, mutual cooperation between Muslims and Jews existed even to the degree of the conclusion of formal partnerships. But the bulk of interterritorial business reflected in the Geniza was effected by a large but closely knit group of Jewish merchants who, in the first part of the eleventh century, had their base in Kairouan. From there they extended over all the Muslim countries of the Mediterranean. This Jewish "Hanse" succeeded not by its great capital, but by its mobility and close cooperation. The Jewish merchant could trade in a great variety of goods because he had business friends who assisted him with their expert knowledge in both buying and selling. He, or one of his partners, supervised in person the processing of the goods destined for export (such as Egyptian flax), accompanied the finished products on their hazardous voyage over the seas, and, again, was able to sell in the port of arrival to business acquaintances known to him personally or recommended to him by his friends (or relatives). Despite limited means he prospered because he was able to offer good services.

It is difficult to assess the share of the Jews in this inner-Islamic overseas trade, although it is certain that it exceeded by far their percentage in the total population. In three cases, Jews formed about ten

---

[28] The latest summary of this often treated subject is found in *The World History of the Jewish People, The Dark Ages*, ed. Cecil ROTH (Tel Aviv, 1966), pp. 23 and 386, notes 11 and 12, which failed, however, to notice the challenging article by Claude CAHEN, "Y a-t-il eu des Rahdānites?", *Revue des Etudes Juives* 3 (123) (1964), pp. 499-505. Cahen surmises that the Rahdānites belonged to an earlier period.

percent of the merchants travelling in a ship or convoy. Comparatively few great houses, both Karaite and Rabbanite, stood out on the Jewish side. With rare and doubtful exceptions, the Jews did not own ships in the Mediterranean during the eleventh century, at a time when we know most about their economic activities.[29] The ships, and with them the riches, were owned by persons belonging to, or affiliated with, the government—such as sultans, governors, generals, qadis—or by affluent merchants and industrialists of the Muslim faith.

The correspondences of the great Jewish houses, such as the Ben 'Awkals and Tustaris in Old Cairo or the Tahertis in Kairouan, or the references to them in the letters of others, show us that the volume of their business was far beyond the reach of the average Jewish merchant. There are also indications that their economic power was used by them at times in a highhanded way. Their riches conveyed social status which occasionally finds expression in the utmost deferential tone of letters addressed to them. But many other letters are not particularly respectful; the great by no means disdained to participate in commercial ventures of limited scope or to attend to small personal matters of their less illustrious business friends. All in all, the Geniza letters convey the impression that, in the Jewish society, the great merchant was *primus inter pares*, and not a member of a secluded oligarchy.

This socio-economic situation reflected in the Geniza documents is discernible also in the organization of the Jewish community, as it appears to us in the classical Islamic period. It stands to reason that with regard to communal organization, as in other respects, the Islamic environment could not have been without influence. In a recent paper, E. Ashtor has stressed this point with great emphasis.[30] Against this entirely justified consideration, others, equally if not more important, should be made. The Jews (and Christians) living within Islam during the High Middle Ages formed communities of a very specific character. They were a state not only within the state, but also beyond the state because they owed loyalty to the heads and central bodies of their respective denominations, even if these were in far away countries. They were concerned with the upkeep of their houses of worship, seats of religious learning and their courts of justice. The social services, which in our time are provided by local and state authorities, were in those days the responsibility of the Synagogue: education of poor children, care for the old, the indigent, the orphans and widows, the provision of shelter for the needy traveler and ransome for captives, as well as help in many special cases. To meet these needs, the Jewish community had its local,

[29] During the twelfth century we find Jews as shipowners on the India route (Aden-India-Ceylon). Cairene Jews bearing the title *nākhudā* (shipowner) acquired it in the India trade, not in the Mediterranean.

[30] E. ASHTOR, "Some Features of the Jewish Communities in Medieval Egypt", *Zion* 30 (1965), pp. 61-78, pp. 128-157 (in Hebrew).

territorial and ecumenical institutions and organizations, which were
pre-Islamic, while Islam had nothing comparable to the Jewish Kehilla.
Muslim society was an amorphous mass, autocratically ruled, the mosque
being a meeting place rather than an organizational unit. Thus, both by
its history and its very character, the Jewish community differed essentially from its Islamic environment. With the economic, social and numerical decline of the Jews, which coincided with the ascendance of
military feudalism and Muslim clericalism and bigotry (thirteenth century), the Kehilla lost its vitality, the Jewish dayyān, like the Muslim
qadi, began to unite in his hands functions which had been fulfilled previously by elected members of the laity. In the following, we will try
to outline Jewish communal life during the period preceding this decline.[31]

When the curtain rises over the Jewish scene illuminated by the
Geniza documents, it is dominated by the Yeshivoth, the Jewish "academies", and their heads, the Gaons. The allegiance of a local community
to the Palestinian or one of the two Babylonian academies did not indicate solely that it followed the rite and the liturgy adopted by that body.
It meant far more. The Head of the Yeshiva[32] was the highest religious,
communal and juridicial authority. The local dāyyanīm, or rabbis, and
lay leaders were appointed or confirmed by him in their offices and were
regarded as representatives of the Yeshiva. The local spiritual leaders
often were ḥavērīm, i.e. either had actually been members of the Yeshiva
for some time or received honorary membership. The title ḥāvēr at that
early period was reserved for scholars, while otherwise the Yeshivoth
were most inventive in creating and granting honorary titles as an award
for liberal donators and sponsors.

The Yeshivoth insisted that in each country they should have one
leading representative to whom all funds collected should be remitted,
who would screen and pass on the queries submitted by local scholars,
and who should make on-the-spot decisions in matters which suffered
no delay. Whether this diocesan organization was influenced by the
model of the Church, or is of pre-Christian origin, lies outside the scope
of this article. It certainly influenced subsequent developments under
Islam, where we find territorial authorities of the Jewish communities,
known in certain countries and times, under the title Nagid (pronounce:
Nagheed).

[31] This subject is treated in Vol. II of *A Mediterranean Society*. For the time being
cf. S. D. GOITEIN, "Jewish Community Life in the Light of the Cairo Geniza Documents", *Zion* 26, pp. 170-179; "The Local Jewish Community, etc.", *Journal of Jewish
Studies* 12, pp. 133-158; "The Social Services of the Jewish Community as reflected in
the Cairo Geniza Records", *Jewish Social Studies* 16 (1964), pp. 3-22, pp. 67-86; "The
Title and Office of Nagid", *Jewish Quarterly Review* 53 (1962), pp. 93-119; "The
Qayrawan United Appeal etc.", *Zion* 27 (1962), pp. 156-165.

[32] This (and not: Gaon) was his official title in both Hebrew and Arabic (*Ra's al-
Mathība*).

Nagid was a title originally granted by a Babylonian Yeshiva to a particularly meritorious sponsor belonging to a Gaonic family. The first communal leader outside Iraq to receive this title was Abraham ben 'Aṭā', a court physician of the ruler of Tunisia, on whom it was bestowed, it seems, in summer 1015. He was followed in 1027 by the famous Samuel ha-Nagid of Spain, and subsequently by the latter's son. In Egypt the title does not appear at the beginning of the Fatimid period (969, as was often asserted), but a hundred years later. The first official head of the Jewish community of the Fatimid empire of whom we have detailed knowledge as bearer of the title Nagid was Mevōrākh ben Saadya (around 1100). In the subsequent century, several official heads of the Jewish community including Maimonides, were not entitled Nagid. Only beginning with Abraham, Maimonides' son, was the title Nagid permanently connected with that of the Ra'īs al-Yahūd, or Head of the Jews.

It is not known at what time exactly the Fatimid government started to appoint a Ra'īs al-Yahūd. The abundant testimony of the Geniza documents proves that during the first half of the eleventh century the Jewish community of Egypt, Palestine and Syria was under the jurisdiction of the Head of the Yeshiva of Jerusalem and that the latter was confirmed by the Fatimid government. A still unpublished Geniza document in Arabic characters which was aimed at securing government approval for a Gaon, shows that he was supposed to have all the prerogatives which, according to later Islamic sources, were granted to the Ra'īs al-Yahūd. Thus, it stands to reason that the office of the Ra'īs al-Yahūd was created, or, at least, received its full import when the Jerusalem Yeshiva, owing to the conquest of Jerusalem by the Seljuks (1071) and other calamities, gradually lost its status. But when the Head of the Palestinian Yeshiva Maṣlīaḥ moved to Cairo in 1127, he served as Ra'īs al-Yahūd, as is proved by many documents issued under his authority, as well as by the titles given to him by the government (as reported in another still unpublished Arabic Geniza paper).

Unlike the Yeshivot, the Rōsh ha-Gōlā, or Head of the Diaspora, was of limited ecumenical significance. His claim to be a scion of the house of David (which was acknowledged also by the gentiles) gave the Jews satisfaction, comparable to the role played by the caliph in Islam, but his actual influence, like that of the latter, was confined to Baghdad and its environs. Various members of the house of the Rōsh ha-Gōlā, the so-called Nesī'īm, comparable to the Alids in Islamic society, occasionally became influential in various parts of the Jewish diaspora.[33]

[33] "The Nesī'īm of Mosul etc.", *Braslavy Jubilee Volume* (Tel Aviv, 1968), where further literature on the subject is provided.

The local Jewish communities centered around the synagogues, but mostly shared their rabbinical courts, the social services and representation before the government and similar public issues. There were ups and downs in this respect. Congregational separatism and factionalism alternated with the spirit of cooperation and with common sense.[34] All in all, the Geniza papers convey the impression of an extremely intensive communal life. The small size of the communities made it possible for everyone to take part in the deliberations, and often also in the decisions made for the common good. The Jewish plutocrats were either not wealthy or not interested enough to impose their exclusive leadership on the congregations. The leaders whom we actually see at the head of the communities for decades were mostly scholars and not persons who owed their position to their wealth or the rank occupied by them in the gentile society. This reverence for scholarship is indeed the most distinctive (and most pleasant) aspect of Jewish public life apparent during the Geniza period. The Islamic environment, which then was in its most creative stage, certainly furthered this tendency.

In the preceding pages, repeated reference has been made to the periods of decay that befell Islam and, to an even greater degree, the Jewish communities within its orbit. The appalling conditions in which Jews lived in some Islamic countries even in the twentieth century have often been described. In each case, the specific causes of such situations have to be investigated. One wonders, however, whether the religion of Islam as such has a share in this lamentable state of affairs. The question must be answered in the affirmative. According to Islam, the members of another faith must be held in degradation. Many laws to this effect are found in the Islamic religious codes. Islam shares this attitude with all groups, religious and others, that regard themselves as righteous and everyone else as failing. Necessarily, under such legislation, albeit incompletely applied, life could not be good for a non-Muslim at any time. It was indeed, as we learn from the utterings of the great representatives of "the Golden Age" in Spain or the humble writers of the Geniza letters, at most a second best.

[34] "Congregation versus Local Community", *Schirmann Jubilee Volume* (Jerusalem, 1968).

Bibliography

Article "Dhimma" by Claude CAHEN in the *Encyclopaedia of Islam*, II (Leiden, 1965), pp. 227-231, lists the literature on the legal and actual position of Jews (and Christians) under Islam.

Salo W. BARON, *A Social and Religious History of the Jews*, III-VIII (New York, 1957-1960).

S. D. GOITEIN, *Jews and Arabs: Their Contacts through the Ages* (New York, 1964) (also paperback).

S. D. GOITEIN, *Studies in Islamic History and Institutions* (Leiden, 1966).

For E. ASHTOR's recent articles which are not listed in Cahen and Baron, see above, notes 5 and 30.

I. TWERSKY

ASPECTS OF THE SOCIAL AND CULTURAL HISTORY OF PROVENÇAL JEWRY

I.

T HE following remarks—facts and generalizations, conclusions and hypotheses—should be read as prolegomena to a comprehensive study of the social and especially the cultural history of the Jews in southern France (Provence)[1] during the High Middle Ages (C. 1100-1400). Scholarship has only recently begun to explore and illumine various aspects of this rich and fecund period and we shall probably have to wait for some time until we have a work of synthesis which will integrate the heterogeneous, polyglot literary output of the period while analyzing its institutions and socio-political conditions.[2]

Jewish history in southern France, often seen merely as an epicycle of the Spanish or northern French spheres of influence, invites scholarly attention both because of its intrinsic, substantive value as well as its

---

[1] The area under consideration may be designated as Provence *(Provincia Narbonensis)* only if understood as covering the widest territorial limits to which this term is applied, including lower Languedoc, Roussillon, Comtat Venaissin, Cerdagne and other countries. See H. GROSS, *Gallia Judaica* (Paris, 1897), pp. 489 ff; see the brief, mostly archaeological survey by M. LOWENTHAL, "The Southlands of France", *A World Passed by* (New York, 1933), pp. 101-119; and the literary-historical survey by A. M. HABERMAN, "Mi-shut be-Erez Provence", *Ozar Yehude Sefarad,* VI (1963), pp. 17-31. On Avignon, Carpentras, Cavaillon and L'Isle-sur-Sorgue, see A. TEMKO, "Four Holy Communities", *Commentary* (March, 1959), pp. 223-242. Some of the major centers are: Aix, Argentière, Avignon, Bagnols, Beaucaire, Béziers, Bordeaux, Carcassonne, Carpentras, Cavaillon, Lunel, Marseille, Montpellier, Narbonne, Nîmes, Orange, Perpignan, Posquières, Salon, Tarascon, Toulouse, Trinquetaille.

[2] See the observation of L. Zunz, referred to by A. Z. ESHKOLY in *Zion,* X (1945), p. 107. Examples of significant scholarly advances on various fronts will be cited below. The importance of Provence has always been appreciated; see H. MALTER, *JQR* I (1910), p. 153. "As center for this widespread learning of the age, Provence stood second only to Spain. Its geographical situation made it the meeting point for the scientific culture developed under Arabic influence in Spain and the Talmudic learning of the French Jews. In Provence the last of the compilers of the Haggadah lived. There, since the time of Tibbon, numerous translators were busied with Arabic works, and there in the thirteenth century secular learning continued to be cultivated with zeal and enthusiasm. There also appeared many famous scholars, who united a comprehensive knowledge of the Talmud with broad general learning, and who exerted a lasting influence upon later ages."

self-transcending methodological relevance. On one hand, the chronological span of the period is rather clearly delimited and therefore sustains one's hopes for a meaningful overview of or synoptic approach to the entire period and, on the other, the cultural productivity is sufficiently impressive and comprehensive so as to present a colorful microcosm of medieval Jewish intellectual history. Independent literary and intellectual activity makes its appearance toward the middle of the eleventh century—with the works of R. Moses ha-Darshan of Narbonne[3]—and continues uninterruptedly, with vigor and intensity, until the beginning of the fourteenth century—with the works of R. Menaḥem ha-Me'iri of Perpignan.[4] In the intervening centuries, there is a remarkable efflorescence of Jewish culture in Provence: rabbinics, philosophy, mysticism, ethics, exegesis, grammar and lexicography, poetry and belles-lettres are cultivated. Certain clearly defined indigenous trends reach maturation while there is an appropriation of new intellectual motifs and tendencies. There is hardly a facet of the total Jewish religious and intellectual experience that is not reflected—and all in a compact period of time. There are legists who enriched all the major genres of halakic literature and accelerated the development of a new, critico-comparative method of Talmudic study which was to become a mainstay of halakic thinking and writing.[5] There are students of philosophy and philosophers and devotees of philosophy, as well as patrons and protagonists, who are responsible for preserving and transmitting the accumulated

---

[3] See A. Epstein, *R. Moses ha-Darshan* (Vienna, 1891); *Midrash Bereshit Rabbati*, ed. Ch. Albeck (Jerusalem, 1940) and French translation by Jean Joseph Brierre-Narbonne (Paris, 1939). It is noteworthy that this preoccupation with midrash, operating on different levels and with different methods of interpretation, persists in southern France as indicated, e.g., by the works of Moses ibn Tibbon and Yedaya ha-Penini Bedersi at the end of the thirteenth and beginning of the fourteenth century. See also Kaspi in *Hebrew Ethical Wills*, ed. I. Abrahams, p. 155.

[4] See the extensive introduction of S. K. Mirsky to the edition of ha-Me' iri's *Ḥibbur ha-Teshubah* (New York, 1950). I have chosen R. Menaḥem ha-Me' iri as the terminal figure because of his undisputed importance, the centrality and versatility of his activity, and because the date of his death (c. 1315; see M. N. Zobel in *Eder ha-Yekar: S.A. Horodezky Jubilee Volume* (1947), pp. 93-96) can easily be synchronized with the expulsion of the Jews from France (1306). To be sure, Jews continue to live and create after 1306 in the Papal states (around Avignon) and other southern areas (e.g. Arles, Marseille) not yet incorporated into the royal domain, but with diminished vigor, restricted scope, and magnified malaise. On the expulsion of 1306, see I. Loeb, "Les Expulsions des Juifs de France au XIVᵉ siecle", *Jubelschrift H. Graetz* (Berlin, 1887), pp. 39-56; S. Schwarzfuchs, "The Expulsion of the Jews from France (1306)", *JQR Seventy-fifth Anniversary Volume* (1967), pp. 482-490.

[5] See B. Z. Benedict, "Le-Toledotaw shel Merkaz ha-Torah be-Provence", *Tarbiz* XXII (1951), pp. 85-109; I. Twersky, *Rabad of Posquieres* (Cambridge, 1962). Manuscript sources of rabbinic literature—commentaries, codes, and responsa—are being published in rapid, almost dizzying, succession thanks to the industrious editorial work of S. Atlas, J. Blau, M. Hershler, J. Kapah, A. Sofer, and others. Such figures as R. Meshullam b. Moses *(Sefer ha-Hashlamah)*, R. Meir ha-Kohen *(Sefer ha-Me' orot)* and R. David b. Levi *(Sefer ha-Miktam)* are just now emerging into the full light of history.

philosophic and scientific learning of Arabic-speaking Jewry as well
as for interpreting it, disseminating it, and extending its frontiers.[6]
There are kabbalists who—at first haltingly and reservedly, then boldly
and confidently—move mystical speculation and experience to the center of the stage: some of the oldest known kabbalistic texts were re-
dacted or first circulated here and the earliest devotees of the new doctrines organized themselves in Provence at this time.[7] Poets energetically
ply their humanistic trade and enthusiastically vindicate it—producing
rationales of the poetic art, articulating the consciousness of the artist,
and defining his place in society.[8] Exegetes make durable contributions
to the field of Scriptural commentary and enlarge its scope by combining midrashic interpretation with philosophical allegory and philological insight.[9] Polemicists and apologists marshall erudition and ingenuity in their defense of Judaism against persistent theological arraign-
ments and social-economic attacks.[9a]

All in all, one can observe here many dynamic features of Jewish
history such as the confrontation of conventional cultural preoccupations
with new secular learning, the relationship or integration of apparently
disparate cultural disciplines, the role of charismatic and rationalistic
forces within the framework of traditional communal institutions, personality clashes and polemics. Furthermore, the interaction of Jewish and
general cultural developments—e.g. troubadour poetry and belletristic

[6] See, in general, S. MUNK, *Mélanges de Philosophie juive et arabe* (Paris, 1859);
S. STEINSCHNEIDER, *Die hebräischen Übersetzungen des Mittelalters* (Berlin, 1893);
E. RENAN and A. NEUBAUER, *Les Ecrivains juifs français du XIVe siècle* (Paris, 1893);
E. MYERS, *Arabic Thought and the Western World* (New York, 1964), ch. 7, pro-
vides a check-list of translators from which one gets a good idea as to the role of
Jewish translators.

[7] See G. SCHOLEM, *Reshit ha-Kabbalah* (Jerusalem, 1948) and the revised German
edition, *Ursprung und Anfänge der Kabbala* (1962); S. BARON, *Social and Religious
History*, VI, pp. 29-42; *Rabad of Posquieres*, pp. 286-300.

[8] See L. ZUNZ, "Die jüdischen Dichter der Provence", *Zur Geschichte und Literatur* (Berlin, 1845), pp. 450-483; H. SCHIRMAN, *Ha-Shirah Ha-Ibrit Bisefarad ube-
Provence*, 2 v. (Jerusalem, 1956); I. DAVIDSON, *Parody in Jewish Literature*, esp. pp.
15-29; J. CHOTZNER, *Hebrew Humour and Other Essays* (London, 1905), ch. 8 (on Y.
Bedersi), ch. 11 (on Kalonymus b. Kalonymus). At the beginning of the thirteenth
century Judah al-Harizi *(Taḥkemoni*, ch. 18) is able to praise the poetry of Provence while at the beginning of the fourteenth century Immanuel of Rome *(Maḥberot*,
p. 43) echoes and intensifies this paean. See Y. PENINI, *Sefer ha-Pardes* in *Ozar ha-
Sifrut*, III (1890), section 6, pp. 1-17.

[9] A study of the commentaries of David Kimḥi, Samuel and Moses ibn Tibbon,
R. Menaḥem ha-Me'iri, Joseph ibn Kaspi, Levi b. Gerson, and others would sustain
this generalization. See, e.g., M. BAROL, *Menachem ben Simon aus Posquieres und
sein Kommentar zu Jeremia und Ezechiel* (Berlin, 1907); W. BACHER, "Joseph ibn Kaspi
als Bibelerklärer", *Judaica :* Festschrift zu Hermann Cohen (Berlin, 1912), pp. 119-
135.

[9a] See, e.g., F. TALMAGE, "R. David Kimḥi as Polemicist", *HUCA*, XXXVIII
(1967), pp. 213-235 ; M. STEIN, "Me'ir b. Simeon's Milḥemeth Misvah", *JJS*, X (1959),
pp. 45-63.

writing[10]—is significant and, finally, the measured influence of relatively favorable social, political and economic circumstances upon cultural creativity is noteworthy. Provence in this period thus provides a case study for the analysis of the rise and fall of Jewish culture in a foreign environment.[11]

2.

Jewish cultural history unfolds against a checkered, shifting political background in which a situation of relative comfort and tolerance, the Jews enjoying definite economic and political privileges and opportunities, is replaced by a "decline in political status and economic prosperity, growing insecurity in face of widespread massacres and unpredictable fits of governmental intolerance".[12] The political fate of Provence and its Jewish inhabitants is tied up with diverse and conflicting forces: the ever-increasing centralization of the royal domain of France, the expansionist tendencies of the rulers of Catalonia and Aragon,[13] the sacerdotal and imperial vicissitudes of the papacy, and the stubborn independence of powerful suzerainties and ancient municipalities. Expulsions (national and local, reaching successive stages of finality in 1306, 1394 and 1500), popular uprisings and social revolutionary movements (e.g. the Pastoureaux of 1320), libels and accusations, personal humiliation and discrimination, chronic fiscal exploitation and harassment—these punctuate the history of the Jews even in the comparatively hospitable milieu of the Midi. On the whole, at the risk of some oversimplifying schematization, the graph of the socio-political destiny of Provence Jewry may be plotted in bold downward strokes. It should be remembered, however, that at all periods in Provence Jews suffered humiliation and discrimination, their position was precarious, social indignities were common, the process of compulsory restriction of

[10] See the studies of H. SCHIRMANN, "Isaac Gorni, poète hébreu de Provence", *Lettres Romanes* III (Louvain, 1949), pp. 175-200; "Iyyunim be-Kovez ha-Shirim weha-Melizot shel Abraham Bedersi", *Sefer Yovel le-Yizhak Baer* (Jerusalem, 1951), pp. 154-173. S. DURAN, *Magen Abot* (Leipzig, 1855), p. 55b, refers to the fact that French Jews borrowed melodies from troubadours.

[11] Cf. F. BAER, *History of the Jews in Christian Spain* (English tr.; Philadelphia, 1961), v. I, p. 2.

[12] S. BARON, *Social and Religious History of the Jews*, X, p. 117. The facts and vicissitudes of the socio-political life of the Jews have been carefully reviewed by BARON, *op. cit.*, pp. 82-91 (see especially pp. 82-83 and 87 for working generalizations) and XI, pp. 212-225. There is a brief summary of the twelfth-century situation in *Rabad of Posquieres*, pp. 20 ff.

[13] The political interrelatedness of northern Spain and southern France had cultural repercussions as well; see below, p. 193. Hebrew writers of Catalonia and Provence often call attention to their geographic unity and separateness from the rest of Spain; see e.g. the references of R. Zerahya ha-Levi, *Sefer ha-Ma'or*, and Naḥmanides, *Milḥamot* on *Berakot*, 11a. The close contacts between the two regions during the controversy over philosophy should also be seen in light of these facts. The Jewries of southern France and northern Spain were thus tied by personal, economic, political (sometimes), and intellectual connections.

spheres of economic activity was having its effects, and the consciousness of exile was never dulled or de-sensitized.[14]

While this situation at first allowed substantial Jewish involvement and prominence in commerce, medicine, communal affairs and many Jews, because of their great wealth, and concomitantly high social position, rose in the political hierarchy, there does not seem to be a Provençal counterpart to the Spanish-Jewish "aristocracy". The phenomenon of court Jews is not prominent in southern France—especially after the Albigensian crusade when northern princes acquired suzerainty over Languedoc and Provence and Jews were officially excluded from administrative posts. This needs to be underscored in light of the importance which has been attached to the Spanish-Jewish aristocratic intelligentsia in the history of ideas and evolution of a corrosive, anti-traditional rationalism in the Jewish communities of Spain. Provence had no entrenched courtier class and yet became the seat of rationalism.[15]

The socio-communal fact, however, that appears to have had most

[14] See *Rabad of Posquieres*, p. 21; J. Katz, *Exclusiveness and Tolerance* (Oxford, 1961), p. 128. A poem by Shem Tob b. Joseph Palaquera provides an eloquent description of the mood and the reality:

> "Can the lorn Jew be joyous, when
> Accursed is his lot among men?
> For, thou' to-day his wealth be more
> Than sand upon the ocean's shore,
> To-morrow goes he stripped and sore.
> What justice can there be for Jew,
> His foe being judge and jury, too?
> Or how should Israel raise his head,
> Wallowing in blood and sore-bestead?
> O God, redeem Thy people's state,
> And glorify and vindicate
> Thy name, which foes now desecrate!"

See Malter, *JQR*, I (1910), p. 156. The archival materials analyzed by R. Emery, *The Jews of Perpignan in the Thirteenth Century* (New York, 1959), suggest a revised view of the economic realities of the period.

[15] See Baer, *op.cit.*, pp. 189, 237, 241 and *passim*. He notes, in passing (p. 241), that Provence was different—but draws no conclusions from this concerning his major thesis about the relationship of social-economic interests and cultural-ideological positions; see the critique of I. Sonne in *JSS*, IX (1947), pp. 61-80. Indeed, one might well use Provence to illustrate a more idealistic approach, for from the very beginning—when R. Meshullam b. Jacob (see below, p. 197) provided tranquillity and sustenance for translators and other scholars—there is no persuasive social-economic explanation for the enthusiastic reception and energetic diffusion of philosophic literature in Provence. Some of its patrons and devotees were, to be sure, wealthy but others—notably Levi b. Ḥayyim, about whom see L. Baeck in *MGWJ*, XLIV (1900), pp. 24-41—were pitiably poor. Some—e.g. Jacob Anatoli or Kalonymus —accepted invitations of Frederick II or Robert of Anjou to spend time at the royal court as "visiting scholars"—see M. Steinschneider, "Robert von Anjou und sein Verhältnis zu einigen gelehrten Juden", *MGWJ*, XLVII, pp. 713-717, and Willy Cohn, "Jüdische Übersetzer am Hofe Karls I. von Anjou... (1266-1285)", *MGWJ*, LXXIX 246-60; others never left their communities. On the whole, Prof. Baer's thesis needs modification. The differentiation that he suggests (p. 304) parenthetically between the interests of members of the liberal professions—physicians, translators, litterateurs—and of the social aristocracy is valid and, indeed, significantly modifies his general thesis.

significant cultural repercussions was the relative openness of the society, the grassroots contacts between Jews and Christians, the ease of
social intercourse, and the cultural liaison entered into by Jewish and
Christian intellectuals. One writer is unabashedly proud of the presence
of Christian notables and clergymen at his son's wedding.[16] A prominent
Talmudist records his discussions with a Christian and notes the resultant stimulus which he received for the composition of a comprehensive
work on the theory and practice of "repentance".[17] We know of ardent
Jewish students of Averroes living for two days—on bread and water—
in the house of a Christian philosopher in order to copy part of a manuscript which was not available elsewhere.[18] This intellectual rapport will
help account for and contribute to an outer-directedness in the philoso-
phical-scientific activity of Provençal Jews—an awareness of the profile
of the Jews "in the eyes of the nations" and a need to project continuously the image of a "wise and understanding people"—and will, indeed, provide a persuasive motive for much of this activity.[19] People
engaged in philosophy and science, their profound particularistic commitments notwithstanding, must have a sense of universality, a community of interests that supplement historic-religious interests without supplanting them, a conviction that "all nations share in the sciences and
they are not restricted to one specific nation".[20] The desire to be "wise
in the eyes of the nations", especially in areas cultivated jointly by the
nations, can be a powerful catalyst for cultural activity.

3.

Probably the most remarkable fact about the development of Jewish
culture in Provence is the manner in which a Torah-centered community,

[16] Judah ibn Tibbon in *Hebrew Ethical Wills*, ed. I. ABRAHAMS (Philadelphia),
p. 67. See J. KATZ, "Sublanut Datit be-Shitato shel R. Menaḥem ha-Me'iri", *Zion*,
XVIII (1953), p. 29.

[17] R. MENAḤEM HA-ME'IRI, *Ḥibbur ha-Teshubah*, p. 2.

[18] See L. BERMAN, "Samuel b. Judah of Marseille", *Jewish Medieval and Renaissance Studies*, ed. A. ALTMANN (Cambridge, 1967), p. 297.

[19] See below, pp. 204-205.

[20] This is the statement of Shem Tob Palaquera; see MALTER, *op. cit.*, p. 169.
Note the analogous statement of ibn Khaldun cited by M. MAHDI, *Ibn Khaldun's
Philosophy of History* (Chicago, 1957), p. 76. This idea, of course, underlines the
apothegm "Accept the truth from whoever expresses it" which is found in Maimo-
nides, *Eight Chapters*, introduction (ed. Gorfinkle, New York, 1912), p. 36 and p. 6
(Hebrew section), as in R. ZERAHYAH HA-LEVI, *Sefer ha-Ma'or*, introduction, and
becomes practically the motto of subsequent writers—e.g. Jacob ANATOLI (*Malmad ha-
Talmidim*, introduction, end), Shem Tob Palaquera (MALTER, p. 168, n. 31), Joseph
Kaspi (ABRAHAMS, *Ethical Wills*, I, p. 155), Profiat DURAN (*Ma'ase Efod*, p. 25)
and many others. The idea of the universality of philosophic learning is forcefully
articulated by R. Eliyahu Mizraḥa, She'elot u-Teshubot, n. 57, p. 176. Of course, the
enlightenment of the eighteenth century— one may search for medieval antecedents as
well—led to a situation in which the universality of philosophic interests did indeed
supplant particularistic religious commitments.

widely respected throughout Jewish Europe for its wide-ranging rabbinic scholarship and deep-rooted piety, whose sages were constantly beseeched for scholarly advice and learned guidance, turned with remarkable zest and gusto to the cultivation of philosophy and other extra-Talmudic disciplines. This cultural dynamism and interaction in the spheres of religious and secular learning pervades the period, produces tensions and frictions as well as substantive achievements in many areas. Given the limitations of space in this article, it seems best to focus on this dynamic characteristic which is woven into the very fabric of Jewish history in Provence: its multi-faceted contributions to rabbinic learning, its serving first as a receptive, then a creative center for philosophic learning and broad humanistic culture, and its turbulent attempts to preserve both harmoniously and fruitfully. Its attainments and triumphs —indeed, even its frustrations and failures—its controversies and compromises left their imprint on the evolution of Jewish culture.

Provence is inarticulate, almost mute in the early centuries.[20a] We have documents and traditions about the establishment of the academy at Narbonne, we are scantily informed about certain individual Provençal scholars—but there are no literary remnants or scholarly monuments.[21] It is a period of oral study, appropriation and dissemination. Provence is marking time, preparing to make its literary debut at the end of the eleventh, beginning of the twelfth century. This is accomplished with great intensity and originality, and the twelfth century (continuing into the early decades of the thirteenth) is marked by dynamic study of Talmudic literature and midrash and innovation in halakic ideas, methods, and literary genres. A sturdy succession of Talmudists is forged.[22] They compose codes and commentaries, studies of existing codes or abridgements of the Talmud and treatises of the Talmud itself, custumals, and, of course, voluminous responsa. Their literary activity thus encompassed all the usual genres or rabbinic literature and most of

[20a] During this period rabbinic literature bursts forth in Spain under the aegis of Hasdai ibn Shaprut (d. 975) and in the pioneering achievements of R. Moses (the Captive), his son R. Ḥanoch, and R. Joseph ibn Abitur and reaches its first peak in the codes and commentaries of R. Samuel ha-Nagid (d. 1056), to be followed by R. Isaac ibn Giat, R. Isaac Alfasi, and R. Judah b. Barzilai, and Franco-German Jewry basks in the luminous achievements of R. Gershom the "light of the Exile" (d. 1040), his Lotharingian disciples and Rashi (d. 1105).

[21] See BENEDICT, op. cit., pp. 97 ff.

[22] R. Abraham b. Isaac (Eshkol), R. Meshullam b. Jacob, R. Moses b. Joseph, R. Zeraḥyah ha-Levi (Sefer ha-Ma'or), R. Abraham b. David (Hassagot), R. Isaac b. Abba Mari (Ittur), R. Jonathan ha-Kohen (Alfasi Commentary), R. Isaac ha-Kohen, R. Moshe ha-Kohen (Hagahot), R. Abraham b. Nathan ha-Yarḥi (ha-Manhig), R. Meshullam b. Moses (Hashlamah), and Meir ha-Kohen (Me'orot). In addition some Provençal Talmudists assumed positions of leadership elsewhere—e.g. R. Meshullam b. Nathan, who settled in Melun and becomes the uncompromising antagonist of R. Tam; R. Phinehas b. Meshullam and R. Anatoli b. Joseph, who become judges in Alexandria and are highly esteemed by Maimonides; and before them, R. Joseph Tov 'Elem (Bonfils) who came to Anjou from Narbonne.

these sages secured for themselves honorific positions in the gallery of immortal Talmudic celebrities. Their works are not merely of antiquarian interest; they are still studied and debated. Even their corporate character is recognized and their collective influence is reverently acknowledged in such designations, found in later chronicles and rabbinic texts, as "sages of Provence", "elders of Narbonne", and "wise men of Lunel".

Given a large measure of uniformity (formal and conceptual), often repetition, in medieval rabbinic literature, how does one evaluate the individual works of this genre and what significant features does one seek to identify in them? I would suggest the following: (1) halakic novelties in theory or practice; (2) methodological advances; (3) reflection of social and historical realities; (4) sometimes, material from cognate areas of nonhalakic learning (e.g. philosophy, philology, exegesis). In all these respects, the rabbinic literature of southern France, much of which has just recently been published and has yet to be analyzed properly, is suggestive and significant.

A few special observations about this literary output are in order at this point. The chronological facts concerning the emergence of this literature mean that Provençal writing confronts initially a respectable and weighty Spanish literature, which it must master and assimilate but against which it must sustain its own accumulated oral traditions, tendencies and customs.[23] One of the dialectical results of this is the evolution of a distinct Provençal "school" and native halakic literature. From R. Moses b. Joseph[24] to R. Menahem ha-Me'iri,[25] rabbinic scholars thwarted the attempts of the Spanish school, represented first by the monumental works of R. Isaac Alfasi and R. Judah b. Barzilai, and later by the aggressive disciples of Naḥmanides, to dominate southern France and were assiduous in preserving Provençal traditions in the face of foreign imports and innovations. The attitude was one of reverence, tempered by independence; many interpretations and practices were adopted but local color was not erased and native custom not obliterated.

This situation is reflected in another way in the special relationship of Provençal commentators and critics to the two greatest rabbinic works

[23] There are, of course, influences from northern France—the emergent Tosafistic school represented by R. Samuel b. Meier and R. Jacob Tam—as well (see *Rabad of Posquieres*, pp. 232 ff.) but the cumulative impact is different. Rabad, for example, chides R. Zerahyah ha-Levi for being a satellite of the French writers, especially Rashi; see *Rabad of Posquieres*, p. 233. R. Tam (*Sefer ha-Yashar*, p. 89), on the other hand, accuses R. Meshullam of aggressiveness in propagating Provençal views and customs—an aggressiveness that is abetted by the modesty and weakness of French scholars.

[24] Benedict, "R. Moses b. Joseph", *Tarbiz*, XIX (1948), pp. 19-34.

[25] Ha-Me'iri, *Magen Abot*, ed. I. Last (London, 1909). See *Rabad of Posquieres*, pp. 11, 236 ff., and my article in the *Harry Wolfson Jubilee Volume* (Jerusalem, 1965), Hebrew section, pp. 179-180.

of Sefardic Jewry—the *Halakot* of R. Isaac Alfasi and the *Mishneh Torah* of Maimonides. One may say that both of these works were "launched" on their careers in Provence. As a matter of fact, the most sustained and fruitful activity in the realm of rabbinic literature is the study of the *Halakot* and the *Mishneh Torah*. The *Halakot* spread rapidly, in some respects superseded the Talmud as the basic text of study —it quickly earned the epithet "miniature Talmud"; it is in this context that we should understand the fact that Provence produced a rash of expository works of all kinds, criticism, defense, commentary and supplement, while it expounded initial methodological rules and insights for study of the *Halakot*. These works gradually became the standard companions of the *Halakot*.[26] It is noteworthy that all the works on Alfasi, regardless of point of departure, are partly approbatory, partly critical. One finds neither blanket criticism nor blanket endorsement, total dependence nor absolute independence; instead, stricture and supplement co-exist.

The same is true for the reception and spread of the *Mishneh Torah*. From the moment it arrives in southern France, an area on which Maimonides pinned his hopes for the survival of rabbinic scholarship,[27] the main contours of its future influence and study are fixed. Its strengths and deficiencies were noted almost instantaneously. Its value as a commentary as well as a code was promptly appreciated. Critics and commentators—e.g. R. Abraham b. David, R. Moses ha-Koken, R. Jonathan ha-Kohen of Lunel, R. Meshullam b. Moses, R. Manoah—work side by side in the exhaustive study, searching analysis, and honest appraisal of the *Mishneh Torah* which thus became a highly charged "instrument of legal progress".[28]

As a concomitant—and partial consequence—of this fruitful activity, Provençal sages contributed to the development of a critico-conceptual approach to Talmud study. I have previously described this method of halakic criticism as follows:[29] The Provençal scholars probe into the

---

[26] S. BARON, *Social and Religious History*, VI, pp. 86-89; *Rabad of Posquieres*, pp. 230, 248. The epithet "miniature Talmud" (*Talmud katan* and later *Gemara ze'ira*) is first used by Abraham ibn Daud in the *Sefer ha-Kabbalah*. R. Menahem b. Zerah (*Zedah le-Derek*, 6) notes that at the time of R. Meir ha-Levi Abulafia only the *Halakot* of Alfasi were being studied. See also the testimony of R. Joseph Rosh ha-Seder, cited by GOITEIN, *Sidre Hinnuk* (Jerusalem, 1963), p. 148. Profiat DURAN, *Ma'ase Efod* (Vienna, 1865), p. 19, undoubtedly has all these works in mind when he speaks of the "Halakot of Alfasi and the commentaries by the rabbis of Catalonia".

[27] *Kobez Teshubot ha-Rambam*, II, p. 44. On the chronology of Maimonides' correspondence with the sages of Provence, see S. M. STERN, "Halifat ha-Miktabim ben ha-Rambam we-Hakme Provence", *Zion*, XVI (1951), pp. 18-29.

[28] S. BARON, VI, p. 107; see my article on "The Beginnings of Mishneh Torah Criticism", *Biblical and Other Studies*, ed. A. ALTMANN (Cambridge, 1962), pp. 161-183. HA-ME'IRI, *Bet ha-Behirah*, introduction, refers to the use of the *Mishneh Torah* for purposes of commentary.

[29] *Rabad of Posquieres*, pp. 62-64.

inner strata of Talmudic logic, define fundamental Talmudic concepts, and formulate the disparities as well as similarities between various passages in the light of conceptual analysis... They performed for halakic study something similar to what Aristotle accomplished for philosophic thought by the method of abstraction. They were not only expositors of the text but also investigators. They were "constantly looking for new problems, discovering difficulties, raising objections, setting up alternative hypotheses and solutions, testing them, and pitting them against each other."[30] This method attunes one to whispers of contradictions but also persuades one that all contradictions are resolvable.[31]

In casting a hurried glance at the thirteenth century we may single out the fact that there was much tension concerning the proper study of Talmud. On the one hand, many Talmudists continued or duplicated or seemingly perfected the major tendencies of the twelfth century: critical commentary on the *Halakot* and *Mishneh Torah,* independent study and explication of the Talmud in depth, composition of new up-to-date codes.[32] Just as, to a great extent, later, post-Maimonidean Hebrew philosophic literature is a sort of dialogue between philosophers—by virtue of quotations, discussions, endorsement or refutation of classic views— rabbinic literature also has this characteristic: most of the writing revolves around the views of R. Zeraḥyah, R. Abraham b. David (Rabad), R. Jonathan ha-Kohen, and, of course, Alfasi and Maimonides—and sometimes R. Jacob Tam and his fellow Tosafists. Although rabbinic literature in the thirteenth century moves more or less on a plateau— whose elevation was fixed by the giants of the preceding century—it retained sufficient vitality and originality to command the respect of R. Solomon ibn Adret in Barcelona.[33]

On the other hand, many Provençal intellectuals questioned the prudence of this conventional, all-embracing and therefore time-consuming study in view of the ready availability of classic abridgements and codes —especially that of Maimonides—which, to their mind, satisfied all the basic needs and demands of Talmudic study.[34] Scholars are chided in

[30] H. A. WOLFSON, *Crescas,* p. 26.
[31] This last sentence is more or less the formulation of my brother-in-law Haym Soloveitchik in an unpublished paper.
[32] E.g. R. David b. Levi *(Sefer ha-Miktam),* R. Judah Lattes *(Ba'ale Asufot),* R. Menahem ha-Me'iri *(Bet ha-Beḥirah),* R. David b. Samuel d'Estella *(Sefer ha-Batim),* R. Aaron ha-Kohen *(Orḥot Ḥayyim),* R. Jeruḥam b. Meshullam *(Toledot Adam we-Hawah).*
[33] *Teshubot* I, 624. The volume of responsa *(Teshubot Ḥakme Provence)* published by A. SOFER (Jerusalem, 1967) just as this article was being completed provides much important information concerning the relations between ibn Adret and the Provençal scholars of his time. I hope to analyze this material elsewhere. On the notion of dialogue in post-Maimonidean literature, see S. PINES' article on "Jewish Philosophy" in the new *Philosophical Dictionary* (1967).
[34] For example, Joseph EZOBI, *Ka'arat Kesef;* Jacob ANATOLI, *Malmad ha-Talmidim;* Shem Tob PALAQUERA, *Sefer ha-Mebakesh* and others; see S. ASSAF, *Mekorot le-Toledot ha-Hinnuk,* II, pp. 30, 43 and *passim.*

contemporary sources for repeatedly delving into the subtleties and dialectics of Talmudic discussion, for seeking elaborate proofs and explanations of laws, instead of accepting the codified traditions of Maimonides which were perfectly reliable and most convenient.[35] This restrictive, pragmatically oriented emphasis is most poignantly delineated by Joseph ibn Kaspi who does not even shrink from the rather radical suggestion that great Talmudic scholarship need not be the highest ideal, the ultimate consummation devoutly to be desired and pursued by all students of Jewish lore.[36] A measure of philosophic knowledge is more universally indispensable.

4.

Provençal Jews were initially immersed head and shoulders in traditional learning—Biblical exegesis, midrash, Talmudic study, pietistic thought, liturgical poetry—and devoted themselves exclusively to its development. Unlike their coreligionists in Moslem Spain, where, in addition to rabbinic learning, Jewish scholars welcomed and absorbed the culture of the Moslems and emulated them in the cultivation of non-liturgical poetry, comparative linguistics, philosophy and natural science, the rabbis of Provence were scarcely exposed to secular literature and their culture was rather monolithic—with all the strengths and short-comings inherent in such a situation.[37] A passage from the works of one of those who introduced Spanish Jewish culture into France accurately describes the condition of Jewish learning in Provence as he found it as an exile from Spain in the middle of the twelfth century. Coming from the land of the Moslems which is usually described in Hebrew as the "land of Ishmael" and referring to the Jews living under Christian rule by the conventional medieval phrase "the Jews of Edom", he says concerning the Jews of southern France:

> Also in the lands of the Christians there was a remnant for our people. From the earliest days (of their settlement) there were among them scholars proficient in the knowledge of Torah and Talmud, but they did not occupy themselves with other sciences because their Torah-study was their (sole) profession and because books about other sciences were not available in their regions.[38]

[35] See "Beginnings of Mishneh Torah Criticism", p. 172, n. 51.

[36] *Hebrew Ethical Wills*, ed. I. ABRAHAMS, p. 138. YAVETZ, *Or ha-Ḥayyim*, ch. 9, realized the full implications of this and denounced Kaspi for denigrating the study of the Talmud.

[37] Cf. the characterization of German Jewry by G. SCHOLEM, *Major Trends in Jewish Mysticism* (New York, 1941), p. 80; 3rd rev. ed., New York, 1961.

[38] Judah ibn Tibbon, Introduction to *Ḥobot ha-Lebabot*, ed. A. ZIFRONI (Jerusalem, 1928), p. 2. In the testament addressed to his son Samuel, he implies that there were no tutors for secular studies available in Provence and he had to import at great expense a special instructor from abroad; see *Hebrew Ethical Wills*, ed. I. ABRAHAMS, p. 57. Note also Abraham ibn Daud, *Sefer ha-Kabbalah*, ed. A. NEUBAUER, I, 78.

Abraham ibn Ezra, who visited Béziers and Narbonne, also had reason to contrast "Edom" and "Ishmael".[39] Similarly, another Spanish Jewish writer, an astronomer and philosopher who lived in Provence for a while, records with patent disapproval the ignorance of French scholars with regard to mathematical and geometrical problems.[40]

The rather clear-cut terminus provided by these observations—the sudden, rather intensive exposure at mid-century—makes it possible to chart the course of this extra-rabbinic culture in Provence from its beginning through its periods of ascendancy and conflict to the age of decline and exhaustion.

The transmission of the Judeo-Arabic achievements in philosophy and philology from Spain to Provence resulted from the confluence of two factors: the arrival in Narbonne and Lunel, of Judah ibn Tibbon and Joseph Kimhi, émigrés from the Almohade invasion of Spain who carried with them their secular learning and Arabic scholarship, and the remarkable zest of Provençal Jews for philosophic learning and Hebrew writings on non-Talmudic subjects. For while Abraham bar Hiyya, who sojourned in southern France,[41] condemns the indifference and ignorance of French scholars with regard to very practical aspects of geometry and algebra, in the same breath he mitigatingly notes that there were absolutely no Hebrew books available on these subjects and that the Provençal sages repeatedly urged him to provide them with Hebrew texts, either translated or original.[42] The same discrepancy

[39] See the quatrain in D. Rosin, *Reime und Gedichte des Abraham ibn Ezra* (Breslau, 1885), p. 87; and, in general, the important study by J. L. Fleisher, "R. Abraham ibn Ezra be-Żarfat", *Mizrah u-Ma'arab* IV (1930), pp. 352-360, V (1931), pp. 38-46, 217-224, 289-300. Ibn Ezra in fact helped trigger those developments which were to change the cultural complexion of Provence Jewry. Already Judah ibn Tibbon calls attention to ibn Ezra's significant role in the transmission of learning, especially grammatical knowledge, to Provence; see his Introduction to *Sefer ha-Riḳma*, pp. 4-5. Jedaya ha-Penini Bedersi reports a family tradition describing the joy with which the "pious and the rabbis" of Provence received ibn Ezra who "began to open [people's] eyes in our regions"; see his *Iggeret ha-Hitnazlut, Teshubot ha-Rashbah*, 418. Thus it is not only that ibn Ezra—as did Bar Hiyya—wrote in Hebrew and thereby made his scientific works available to the non-Arabic-speaking West but he augmented and vivified his literary influence by direct personal contact.

[40] Abraham bar Hiyya, *Hibbur ha-Meshihah weha-Tishboret*, ed. J. Guttmann (Berlin, 1913), p. 2. On the influence of this work on the development of scientific learning in Provence, see Guttmann's introduction and S. Gandz, "Studies in Hebrew Mathematics and Astronomy", *Proceedings of the American Academy for Jewish Research*, IX (1939), pp. 5-55.

[41] Zunz (*Zur Geschichte und Literatur* [Berlin, 1845], p. 483), Graetz (IV, p. 128), and Renan (*L'Histoire Littéraire de la France*, XXVIII [1877], p. 523) maintain that Abraham bar Hiyya was in Provence. Gross (*GJ*, p. 369) doubts it. Cf. Guttmann, introduction, *op. cit.*, IX, nn. 2-3. It seems certain that he had direct contact with Provençal scholars and in all probability lived there for a while.

[42] Cf. his revealing introductions to *Żurat ha'Arez* (Offenbach, 1720) and *Sefer ha-'Ibbur* (London, 1851). These were composed at the request and for the sake of the Provençal sages. Also the introduction to his encyclopedia *Yesode ha-Tebunah*, published in German by Steinschneider, *ZfHB*, VII, p. 336, n. 12.

between their restricted knowledge and their intense desire for philo-sophic works is indicated later by Samuel ibn Tibbon in his introduction to the Hebrew translation of *Moreh Nebukim*. On one hand, he observes, they do not occupy themselves with secular sciences, while on the other, the yearning of these wise men for more wisdom leads them to plead with Maimonides for a copy of his philosophic opus.[43] Judah al-Harizi's characterization of the scholars of Marseilles[44] as well as R. Jonathan of Lunel's letter to Maimonides on the translation of the *Moreh Nebu-kim*[45] both underscore this stimulating tension between the available and the desirable. The zeal and eagerness of the Lunel circle, of which R. Meshullam b. Jacob is representative, for learning which they did not possess has also been depicted by Judah ibn Tibbon in a statement which we shall presently quote.

It was then at such a juncture, when Provençal Jewry's intellectual ambition was great and the receptivity quotient high, that Judah ibn Tibbon and Joseph Kimhi, two enthusiasts of Judeo-Arabic culture who would spare no efforts to preserve it, made their appearance. A decisive change, for which the time was ripe, was to take place under the aegis of R. Meshullam b. Jacob of Lunel whose home served as a sort of clear-ing house and center for translations from the Arabic to the Hebrew. His house and school were, generally, dynamos of religious and secular learning. Judah ibn Tibbon settled in Lunel about the middle of the twelfth century and became very friendly with R. Meshullam and his family, especially his two sons Aaron and Asher. In glowing metaphors he describes R. Meshullam as "the pure candelabra, lamp of the com-mandment and the Torah, the great rabbi, a saintly pious person, Rabbi Meshullam... The oil of his understanding is pure and beaten (for the light) to cause the lamp of wisdom to burn continually. He craved for books of wisdom and according to his ability assembled, disseminated and had them translated..." [46]

The new knowledge which ibn Tibbon and other *émigrés* carried must have been, as we have observed, enthusiastically received. The Hebrew poetry of Gabirol and ha-Levi, as well as the philosophic poem

[43] Samuel ibn TIBBON, introduction to *Moreh Nebukim*.

[44] Introduction to Hebrew translation of Maimonides' Mishnah Commentary. See also n. 56 below.

[45] A. FREIMANN, *Teshubot ha-Rambam* (Jerusalem, 1934), LII-LXI. See also Jonathan's praise of Samuel ibn Tibbon in *Ginze Jerusalem*, ed. S. WERTHEIMER (Jerusalem, 1899), p. 33; introduction to *Sefer ha-Rikma*.

[46] Judah ibn Tibbon, introduction to *Hobot ha-Lebabot*. See also Benjamin of Tudela, *Itinerary*, p. 3, and Berechiah ha-Nakdan, *Ethical Treatises*, ed. H. GOL-LANCZ (London, 1902), Hebrew text, p. l. At a later date, protagonists of philosophy made much of the fact that the great R. Meshullam, respected scholar and munificent maecenas of Jewish culture, encouraged the methodical transmission of the philosophic and scientific learning of Spanish Jewry to French Jewry; see the letter of Jacob b. Makir to R. Solomon ibn Adret, *Minhat Kena'ot* (Pressburg, 1838), p. 85.

of Baḥya, was presumably known in Provence, even though it does not seem to have been incorporated into their liturgy; Berechiah ha-Naḳdan, for instance, uses the poetry of Gabirol.[47] The commentaries of Abraham ibn Ezra supplemented what they knew about Saadia Gaon from the current Hebrew excerpts of his writings. Now, in his discussions with interested Provençal scholars, Judah ibn Tibbon probably informed them that these same authors had also written theological and ethical works in Arabic. He transmitted to them the contents of these works. It is very symbolic that before Judah ibn Tibbon produced a written version of Baḥya's *Ḥobot ha-Lebabot*, R. Meshullam had ordered him to translate the first chapter orally.[48] The same was true for Gabirol's *Tiḳḳun Middot ha-Nefesh*. Judah first discussed the contents of this little book with Asher b. Meshullam, one of his cherished tutees. Later, at the request of Asher, whose pious soul was fascinated by the moral maxims contained in this work, Judah produced a complete written translation.[49] Somewhat later, adhering apparently to a similar procedure, Samuel ibn Tibbon translated random selections of the *Moreh Nebukim* for Jonathan ha-Kohen and his avid, intellectually curious colleagues. After they had sampled the high quality of Maimonides' philosophic writings and personally experienced the maturity and profundity of his speculative faculties, they entreated Samuel to produce an unabridged translation.[50] These illustrations suggest a companion means of transmission which supplemented and also prepared the ground for literary works. Spanish *émigrés* carried oral traditions with them and circulated the scientific news which they brought by word of mouth. Many views and theories on science, ethics, and philosophy must have been disseminated in such a fashion. Such an atmosphere, moreover, increased the appetite of many for more accurate and direct information, for reliable Hebrew translations.

Consequently, stimulated and encouraged by R. Meshullam, Judah ibn Tibbon embarked upon a 25-year program of planned translations. He selected his works methodically and prudently, for he was writing for popular consumption. His translations reveal a progression—too marked to be inadvertent—from the light to the difficult. The same is also true of Joseph Kimḥi, who likewise sought easy works for translation, thus

[47] J. GUTTMANN, "Zwei Jungst edirte Schriften des Berachja ha-Naḳdan", *MGWJ*, XLVI (1902), p. 545.

[48] Judah ibn Tibbon, Introduction.

[49] See ibn Tibbon's dedicatory letter to Asher, in *The Improvement of the Moral Qualities*, ed. S. WISE (New York, 1902). A lengthy excerpt is available in A. GEIGER, *Nachgelassene Schriften*, I, p. 16.

[50] Samuel ibn Tibbon, Introduction. At a later date, Kalonymus b. Kalonymus describes the circumstances of his translation of the *Iggeret Ba'ale Ḥayyim* (translated from the twenty-first treatise of the Encyclopedia of the Brethren of Purity) in a similar manner; see *Iggeret Ba'ale Ḥayyim*, ed. M. HABERMAN (Jerusalem, 1949), p. 1.

duplicating many of Judah ibn Tibbon's works.[51] In 1161 Judah ibn
Tibbon translated the first chapter of R. Baḥya ibn Paḳuda's *Ḥobot
ha-Lebabot (Al Hidayah ila Faraid al-Ḳulub)* at the request of Meshullam. Only the first chapter on the "Unity of God" was actually of a
philosophic nature and introduced new terms and concepts, while the
remaining nine chapters of this popular work dealt with conventional
moral teachings, occasionally using new terminology perhaps. That
Judah considered Baḥya primarily a moralist rather than a philosopher
—an issue still debated by modern scholars—is clear from the brief history of that literary genre to which the translated book belongs, which
he sketches in his introduction.[52] His first impulse was not to translate
the last nine chapters, for he believed that their contents were succinctly
presented in a simple straightforward ethical work by Solomon ibn
Gabirol: the *Tiḳḳun Middot ha-Nefesh.* Choosing the path of least
resistance and simultaneously desiring to fulfill the requests of Asher
b. Meshullam, he proceeded to translate Solomon ibn Gabirol's moral
composition into Hebrew. Meanwhile, Joseph Kimḥi took advantage of
this omission on the part of Judah ibn Tibbon. Finding that only the
philosophical chapter of Baḥya's treatise had been translated, Kimḥi
hastened to complete the remaining chapters and then to retranslate the
first chapter as well. The translation of Kimḥi was obviously defective
and those few competent scholars, *émigrés* from Spain most likely, who
knew Arabic and could detect the deficiencies, were not slow to criticize
this work, publicize its deficiencies, and convince the people of its short-
comings. As a result of this, we find Rabad urging Judah to resume his
task so that the readers in southern France should not have to rely upon
Kimḥi's unsatisfactory production. Judah prefaced the second install-
ment of his translation of the *Ḥobot ha-Lebabot* with a long discourse
on intelligence and fools who undertake tasks incommensurate with their
ability—a reference to Joseph Kimḥi, as is clear from the immediately
following paragraphs.[53]

Meanwhile, Judah turned to Halevi's *Cuzari (Kitab al-Khazari),*
which was ready in Hebrew by 1166. To this early period of translations

---

[51] They both translated the *Ḥobot ha-Lebabot* and the *Mibḥar ha-Peninim;* see
A. MARX, "Gabirol's Authorship of the Choice of Pearls and the Two Versions of
J. Kimḥi's Shekel ha-Kodesh", *HUCA,* IV (1927), pp. 438-448. On the "duplicate
translations" from Arabic to Hebrew, see I. SONNE in *MGWJ,* LXXII, p. 67 and J. I.
TEICHER, "The Latin Hebrew School of Translators in Spain", *Homenaje à Millas-
Vallicrosa* (Barcelona, 1946), II, pp. 440-443. On the creative role of translators—
"ministers armed with unlimited discretionary powers"—see the beautiful statement
in P. HAZARD, *The European Mind* (New York, 1963), p. 72. It should be added, however, that translators have discretionary powers not only in the art of translation but
in the very selection of texts which determines what will be accessible to the average
reader.

[52] He discusses briefly various works on ethics, thereby indicating the great need
for Baḥya's work.

[53] Judah ibn Tibbon, introduction to chapter II of *Ḥobot ha-Lebabot* (p. 55).

also belongs most likely the translation of Solomon ibn Gabirol's *Mibḥar ha-Peninim,* a sort of ethical anthology which Gabirol intended to uti-lize as the basis of his larger ethical treatise.[54] Compilations of proverbial sayings enjoyed immense popularity among the Jews from Biblical times onwards and contact with Arabic writings merely provided a special impetus for this type of gnomic literature. Ibn Tibbon's translation of the *Mibḥar ha-Peninim,* along with the metrical paraphrase-translation of Kimḥi entitled *Sheḳel ha-Ḳodesh*[55], is thus representative of a vene-rable literary genre which was achieving renewed prominence. Alḥarizi's Hebrew translation of Honein b. Isḥak's *Musre ha-Pilosofim,* prepared at the request of the sages of Lunel, also enjoyed considerable vogue as one of the famous Arabic collections of ethical apothegms.[56]

A lengthy interlude in the translation of philosophic literature en-sued, during which Judah ibn Tibbon produced Hebrew translations of ibn Janaḥ's grammatical-lexicographical treatises (1171)—and Kimḥi was probably teaching and writing original works, for it should be pointed out parenthetically that, while we are here primarily concerned with his work as a translator, Kimḥi's essential activity as a Hebrew popularizer and transmitter manifested itself in his teachings and in original Hebrew works based upon Arabic writings, in contradistinction to Judah ibn Tibbon who earned his reputation through professional translations, his original compositions being few and of ephemeral value. Ibn Tibbon finally brought forth a translation of Saadia's *Emunot we-De'ot* (1186).[57] This was after the Provençal reading audience had been exposed to lighter philosophic works and was now presumably prepared to grapple with a full-fledged technical work of philosophy represent-ing the quintessence of Kalam speculation.

It should be recalled that prior to this exact, literal translation, an-other translator and popularizer, Berechiah ha-Naḳdan, who was also a member of Meshullam's illustrious circle had epitomized the *Emunot we-De'ot* on the basis of earlier translations. Berechiah, commissioned by R. Meshullam—who in this respect anticipates a Renaissance patron who would assemble various writers and commission them to translate clas-

---

[54] For a review of the historical scepticism and excessive textual agnosticism that surrounded both the author and translator of this work, cf. A. MARX, "Gabirol's Authorship of the Choice of Pearls", *HUCA,* IV (1927), pp. 438-448. STERN (*Zion,* XVI, pp. 19-28) had adduced important new evidence both for Gabirol's authorship and ibn Tibbon's translation.

[55] Ed. Herman GOLLANCZ (Oxford, 1919). J. DAVIDSON, *JQR,* XI (1922-1923), pp. 507-512. Cf. J. WEILL, *REJ,* LXX (1920), pp. 216-223. MARX, *op. cit.,* conjectures very plausibly that we possess two entirely different versions of this translation and not merely two divergent manuscripts.

[56] Ed. A. LOEWENTHAL (Frankfurt a. M., 1896); STEINSCHNEIDER, *Die Hebräischen Übersetzungen des Mittelalters,* p. 350.

[57] 1186 is the date found in a colophon to the Constantinople edition of 1562: MALTER, *Saadia Gaon,* p. 370.

sical works—to write and translate, also produced a Hebrew paraphrase of Adelard of Bath's *Quaestiones Naturales*.

Moreover, just as Judah ibn Tibbon was the main but not sole translator, similarly R. Meshullam was the most important but not exclusive director and initiator of translations. We have seen, for example, how Rabad urged ibn Tibbon to disregard Joseph Kimhi and produce a literal, exact translation of the last nine chapters of the *Ḥobot ha-Lebabot*. David Kimhi (son of Joseph), an important author and popularizer in his own right, also encouraged the translating activity of his time. In the introduction to his translation of Isaac Israeli's *Sefer ha-Yesodot*, Abraham b. Ḥisdai, Hebrew translator of the famous *Ben ha-Melek weha-Nazir*, informs us that he consented to this undertaking as a result of the persistent request of "that great scholar", David Kimhi. Besides desiring to fulfill the commandment of the latter, whose lofty intention and aspiration was to disseminate philosophic knowledge, our author indicates an additional motive for his translation: to save the book from perdition. The contemporary linguistic milieu was not favorable to the preservation of unintelligible Arabic texts; their sole chance for survival lay in translation.[58] This Abraham also translated Algazali's ethical work *Mozene Ẓedek (Mizan al-'Amal)*.

To sum up, of the important Spanish Jewish thinkers, Abraham ibn Ezra and Abraham bar Ḥiyya wrote in Hebrew and their works were immediately available for monolinguists in southern France. Solomon ibn Gabirol's *Mibḥar ha-Peninim* and *Tiḳḳun Middot ha-Nefesh* were translated into Hebrew. The *Ḥobot ha-Lebabot* and the *Cuzari*, ambivalent works capable of stimulating both philosophical and mystical speculation, were definitively translated in the sixties. In addition to these Spanish productions, the first major philosophic work of medieval Judaism, oriental in origin but of inestimable importance in the West—the *Emunot we-De'ot* of Saadia—was also made available in a complete translation. This activity was crowned by the Hebrew translation of the *Moreh Nebukim*. Moreover, several commentaries on the *Sefer Yezirah* by Shabbetai Donnolo, Saadia Gaon, and Judah ben Barzilai were in circulation. On the basis of this, we conclude that in the last decades of the twelfth century a Provençal Jew, who was an earnest and dedicated Hebrew student, could already begin to amass a definite measure of knowledge concerning philosophy even though he was igno-

---

[58] *Sefer ha-Yesodot*, ed. S. FRIED (Frankfurt a. M., 1900), p. 3. At a later date, the celebrated Talmudist R. Nissim Gerondi—in a letter written for the benefit of a certain Isaac, descendant of the famous Tibbonide family—underscores the same motive of preventing a "work of truth from being defiled in stammering lips and a strange tongue" and of "giving it an everlasting redemption" via translation into Hebrew; see S. ASSAF, *Meḳorot u-Meḥkarim* (Jerusalem, 1946), p. 181. This ongoing process of linguistic change also resulted in the Hebrew translation of rabbinic works— e.g. Maimonides' *Sefer ha-Miẓvot*.

rant of Arabic, something which, all its lingering limitations notwithstanding, was radically novel and previously totally inconceivable. In
the course of the thirteenth century many of the original works of Aristotle together with the writings of the greatest of his commentators Averroes were translated into Hebrew so that "Hebrew literature became
also the repository of the whole Aristotelian heritage of Greek philosophy".[59] It should be added, furthermore, that by striving for fidelity
of rendition rather than felicity of expression, the translators on the
whole achieved exactness in literary transmission which enabled others
to achieve exactness in philosophical comprehension.[60]

5.

The next steps—sometimes taken concurrently by many of the same
people involved in the process of translation and transmission—
entailed the production of commentaries on philosophic classics and
composition of independent philosophic works. Translators and commentators, philosophers and scientists, encyclopedists and popularizers[61]
are representative of this multi-dimensional development in which southern France passes hurriedly from the receptive to the creative stage,
from the preservative to the innovating, and emerges in the thirteenth
century as the main center of philosophic activity.[61a] Not only Saadia
Gaon and Maimonides, but Al-Ghazali and Averroes, and needless to
say Plato and Aristotle, became household names for Hebrew writers
as a result of the translating, paraphrasing, commentatorial and critical
work of these people.[62]

---

[59] WOLFSON, Crescas' Critique of Aristotle (Cambridge, 1929), IX.
[60] Cf. ibid., p. 7.
[61] Figures such as Jacob Anatoli, Samuel ibn Tibbon, Levi b. Ḥayyim, Jacob
b. Makir (ibn Tibbon), Abraham Bedersi, Isaac Albalag, Moses Narboni, Shem Tob
Palaquera, Yedaya ha-Penini Bedersi, Gershom b. Solomon of Arles, Joseph Kaspi,
Kalonymus b. Kalonymus, Moses b. Samuel ibn Tibbon, Moses b. Solomon of Salon,
Samuel b. Judah of Marseille, Levi b. Gerson (Gersonides), Abba Mari b. Eligdor.
[61a] Truth to say, it is difficult to draw rigid lines between Catalonia and Provence which, sometimes united politically, regularly appear as one cultural sphere. The
locale of some of these people—e.g. Isaac Albalag—cannot be precisely determined;
see G. VAJDA, Isaac Albalag: Averroiste Juif (Paris, 1960).
[62] See H. A. WOLFSON, "Revised Plan for the Publication of a Corpus Comment-
atorium Averrois in Aristotelem", Speculum, XXXVII (1963), pp. 88-89. Most of the
Averroian commentaries, for example, were translated by Moses ibn Tibbon and
Kalonymus b. Kalonymus. On the importance of Palaquera for the history of philosophy see M. PLESSNER in Homenaje, II, pp. 161-186. A. MARX, "The Scientific Work
of Some Outstanding Medieval Jewish Scholars", Linda Miller Essays and Studies
New York, 1928), pp. 117-171, has information on many of these people. For examples
of recent studies, see G. VAJDA, "An Analysis of the Ma'amar Yiqqawu ha-Mayim by
Samuel b. Judah ibn Tibbon", JJS, X (1959), 137-151 ; S. PINES, "Ha-Zurot ha-
Ishiyot be-Mishnato shel Yedaya Bedersi", Harry Wolfson Judilee Volume, Hebrew
section, pp. 187-203; A. IVRY, "Moses of Narbonne's 'Treatise on the Perfection of the
Soul': A Methodological and Conceptual Analysis", JQR, LVII (1967), 271-97; L.
BERMAN, referred to above in n. 18.

Especially noteworthy is the extent to which philosophic material permeates other, more conventional literary genres. Bible commentaries, Talmud studies, homilies, codes, poetry—all are saturated in various degrees with philosophic motifs, terminology and trends of thought. Aside from their substantive importance—and no history of Jewish philosophic thought can be complete without incorporating the abundant material embedded in these disparate sources—these references, quotations, critical analyses, and digressions contributed significantly to the process of popularization. These writers fulfill the function of intellectual brokers and middlemen who help keep alive, and in the fulness of its vigor, the spirit of rationalism while they familiarize average readers with provocative philosophic theories.[63] Some are reminiscent of later pamphleteers and gazeteers. Sometimes it is just the nonchalant exposure—and gradual habituation—of the audience to intellectualistic patterns of thought and exegetical methods which is the far-reaching determinant.[64] This permeation is so extensive that even the opponents of the philosophic movement—e.g. Abba Mari of Lunel and R. Solomon ibn Adret[65]—are rather well versed in philosophic literature, and their own writings contain material for the history of ideas. They use phrases from the vocabulary of rationalism and introduce concepts from the realm of philosophy. There are few who do not reflect awareness of and acquaintance with philosophy. Even the kabbalists, many of whom are vituperative in their condemnation of philosophy and its detrimental consequences, are, in any event, not innocent of it.[66] One may conclude that, allowing for varying degrees of profundity or shallowness, rationalism and rationalistic habits were entrenched in the Provençal communities and inextricably woven into the fabric of its religious culture.[67]

The general impression is that there are few truly seminal figures or intellectual heroes in Provence—Gersonides, e.g., is an obvious and weighty exception—but many sensitive, remarkably industrious, versatile, deeply committed writers eager to disseminate and vindicate philosophy, to prove that it was not an upstart discipline alien to religious

---

[63] E.g. R. David Kimḥi, *Judges* IX : 13 (on theory of attributes) or *Jeremiah*, VII : 22 (explanation of sacrifices). Scriptural exegesis is perhaps the major vehicle for popular philosophic expression.

[64] *Sefer ha-Miktam on Pesaḥim*, ed. A. Sofₑr (Jerusalem, 1959), p. 433, or *Orḥot Ḥayyim*, I, p. 102a. Ha-Me'iri's long introduction to the *Bet ha-Beḥirah* is of this nature.

[65] *Minḥat Kenáot*, n. 96; see *Teshubot ha-Rashbah*, I, pp. 9, 60, 94.

[66] I. Zinberg, *Toledot Sifrut Yisrael*, Vol. II, gives many examples. See also G. Scholem, *Major Trends*, pp. 203, 398.

[67] Apparent inconsistencies and equivocations in the later controversy are more intelligible in light of this fact. It is clear, for example, that attempts were made to involve ibn Adret in the rationalistic debate and make him commit himself on certain issues : see e.g. *Teshubot ha-Rashbah* I, pp. 395, 413.

concerns.[68] They defended the cause of philosophy with elegance and persuasiveness, sometimes with a touch of lyricism, always with passion. What is more, there is not only strength of conviction but even agressiveness in their temper. As Joseph ibn Kaspi put it, "neither timidity nor diffidence is in place where truth is concerned."[69] Its adherents should possess intellectual integrity and courage. Philosophic believers could be as fanatical as naive believers. In their *apologia pro scientiae*, they sought to disabuse their co-religionists of any possible error concerning the legitimacy and religious respectability of philosophy. Indeed, they unequivocally asserted the primacy of the intellectual experience and cognitive attainment in Judaism and, consequently, the indispensability of philosophy. Philosophic knowledge as a duty was the nuclear notion of their program.[70] They did not conceal the fact that they found perfunctory piety or unexamined traditionalism uncongenial and that routine Talmudism divorced from spiritual animation was not at the top of their scale of values. Rationalism is here in an upright posture and a militant, confident mood. They taught (e.g. Levi b. Ḥayyim), preached (e.g. Jacob Anatoli), propagated (e.g. Joseph Kaspi and Kalonymus b. Kalonymus), interpreted (e.g. Moses Narboni) and explored new areas (e.g. Levi b. Gerson) with verve and gusto.

A prominent component of the philosophic apologia is the desire, indeed the compulsion, to show the world (i.e. fellow intellectuals) that Judaism has not forfeited its claims to, or skills in, philosophy and science. The vision of contemporary Judaism that writers such as Samuel ibn Tibbon, Jacob b. Makir, Joseph Kaspi or R. Menaḥem ha-Me'iri evoke—with good polemical advantage—is one of diminution of philosophic expertise, of intellectual backsliding, and resultant loss of prestige.[71] Judaism, the source of so much of mankind's religious inspiration and philosophic wisdom, suffers from atrophy, indifference, and misguided hostility to philosophy. This accounts, in their opinion, for a pejorative, condescending attitude of non-Jews to Jews, who are portrayed as lacking in sophistication and skill. This attitude must be corrected. It is one of the lasting achievements of Maimonides that he helped restore lustre and dignity to Judaism by commanding the respectful attention of Christians and Moslems. The fact that they regularly quote and rely on Maimonidean writings enhances the importance of Jews in the eyes of non-Jews and triumphantly refurbishes the label "a wise and under-

---

[68] It has been said that history—or historiography—likes to upgrade mediocrities. Actually, there is no need to upgrade them; it is enough to recognize their importance for intellectual history, in which they may surpass great « classical » thinkers.

[69] *Hebrew Ethical Wills*, I, p. 152.

[70] Cf. in this context, H. A. WOLFSON, *The Philosophy of the Church Fathers* (Cambridge, 1956), pp. 99-100.

[71] *Yikkawu ha-Mayyim*, p. 173 ; *Minḥot Kena'ot*, n. 39, and introduction to Hebrew translation of Euclid (*Sefer ha-Yesodot*); '*Ammude Kesef*, introduction; *Ḥoshen Mishpat* in Zunz Jubelschrift (*Tif'eret Sevah*), p. 192.

standing people" (Deuteronomy 4: 7) which should remain the appropriate designation of the Jewish people.[72] The relative openness of the intellectual society and the rather frequent contacts between Jews and Christians add weight to this matter.[73]

These devotees of philosophy genuinely believed—or satisfactorily convinced themselves—that they harmoniously combined piety and devotion to the study of Torah with the cultivation of philosophic-scientific disciplines. They passionately repudiated the charge that they were lax in religious observance or deficient in traditional knowledge because of their allegiance to philosophy. Torah and ḥokmah went hand in glove in Provence, where scholars had diversified interests and proficiency.[74] The articulate proponents of rationalism, e.g. Yedaya Penini, ha-Me'iri, Kaspi, Kalonymus—even Moses Narboni—usually described themselves as the center party, waging war on two fronts: against the extreme allegorists or really untrained philosophers who seem to be, willy-nilly, paving the way for the destruction of the religious tradition —those who consider themselves philosophers but are not—and against the unswerving literalists who seriously complicate religious commitment and do violence to the requirements and essentials of faith—those who consider themselves sages but are not. Those with a true conception of the role of philosophy and its relation to faith consistently disavow the fringe groups and intrepidly affirm the centrality of their own position. This spirited affirmation is a recurrent theme in Hebrew literature from R. David Kimḥi to R. Menaḥem ha-Me'iri.[75] Anyone who contended differently was malicious or had been duped by flagrant misrepresentation of the Provençal reality.[76]

---

[72] Ha-Me'iri in *Hoshen Mishpat, loc. cit.*; Yedaya Bedersi, *Iggeret ha-Hitnazlut, Teshubot ha-Rashbah*, n. 418, end; Kaspi, *Hebrew Ethical Wills*, p. 154. See, in general, J. GUTTMANN, "Der Einfluss der maimonidischen Philosophie auf das christliche Abendland", in *Moses b. Maimon* (Leipzig, 1908) and D. KAUFMANN, "Der 'Führer' Maimunis in der Weltliteratur", *Gesammelte Schriften*, Vol. II (1898).

[73] Samuel ibn Tibbon's assertion *(Yikkawu ha-Mayyim,* p. 175) that philosophy was more widespread among Christians than Moslems would be good reason to intensify and extend philosophic learning among Jews in southern France. Professor S. Pines has recently been trying to document the extent of the influence of Christian scholasticism on such philosophers as Y. Bedersi, J. Kaspi, and Levi p. Gerson.

[74] See, e.g. ha-Me'iri, *op. cit.*, pp. 162-163. There are two parts to his statement: (1) Provençal scholars combined Talmud and philosophy—and one could easily cite many examples of this intellectual type; (2) even those who did not devote much time to Talmud and were very proficient in philosophy were men of piety and religious integrity. One of the crucial issues here was the method and extent of rationalization of the religious commandments; see e.g. ha-Me'iri, *Commentary on Abot,* pp. 129-130.

[75] E.g. Kimḥi, *Kobez Teshubot ha-Rambam,* III, 3d; Y. Bedersi, *Iggeret ha-Hitnazlut,* beginning; Kaspi, *Mishne Kesef,* ch. 5; Me'iri, *loc. cit.; Minḥat Kena'ot,* p. 48. See the suggestive statements of Moses Narboni (concerning Abner of Burgos) cited by F. BAER, *op. cit.,* I, p. 332, and I. ZINBERG, *op. cit.,* II, p. 116.

[76] This was the thrust of Bedersi's answer to ibn Adret. See now A. HALKIN, "Yedaiah Bedershi's Apology", *Jewish Medieval and Renaissance Studies*, pp. 165-184.

The fact of the matter was, however, that they had no unified or monolithic interpretation of their own position and they criticized each other for inconsistencies and extremism—witness the differences between Kalonymus b. Kalonymus and Joseph Kaspi.[77] There is actually a wide spectrum with positions shading off one into another. Their opponents—e.g. R. Solomon ibn Adret, R. Asher b. Yeḥiel, Abba Mari of Lunel—were also not cut from the same cloth and they represent diverse, sometimes incongruent tendencies. Adherents of philosophy shared many convictions with the opponents of philosophy. The former proposed more or less the same restrictions and called for the same safeguards as the latter. Their common attitude to Maimonides was one of almost undiluted awe and reverence—and criticism of Maimonides was usually couched in apologetic terms. The fact that the lines were not clearly drawn had conflicting results: attitudes on both sides could be conciliatory in order to avoid exacerbating wounds, rivalries, and antagonisms or else emotions could be aroused, tempers quickened and tolerance diminished, in order to protect one's position.

It is out of such a matrix that the well-known controversy concerning philosophy flares. The facts have often been reviewed in modern scholarly literature.[78] Opponents of philosophy repeat the charge that the bounds had been transgressed. Basic beliefs and mores seem to be disintegrating. Philosophers are censured for their destructive views, rampant allegorism and indiscriminate publication of the same. All sides agreed that the unqualifiedly exoteric nature of philosophic activity was at fault: loose preaching and teaching which engulfed an unqualified audience which did not need and therefore could not appreciate the philosophic approach.[79] The adherents of philosophy conceded that there were exceptional instances of unjustified extremism and that the involvement of the masses was especially regrettable, but a few lapses should not be allowed to disqualify the rationalistic enterprise. Their opponents contended that these negative facts were quite widespread, terribly objectionable, and potentially disruptive of the Jewish tradition. The

[77] See the letter of Kalonymus, ed. F. PERLES (Munich, 1879). Contemporary medieval literature, to be sure, does portray absolute types. The great spiritual tension between them is accurately reflected in the apparently sterotyped debates presented in such works as Palaquera's *Sefer ha-Mebakesh* and Kalonymus' *Eben Boḥan;* also I. Polqar, *'Ezer ha-Dat,* part II, and Meir Aldabi, *Shebile Emunah,* section eight. See also Profiat Duran, *Ma'ase Efod,* introduction. Later opponents of philosophy similarly lump their antagonists—e.g. I. Albalag, M. Narboni, J. Kaspi, Gersonides—together. See J. Yabetz, *Or ha-Ḥayyim;* Shem Tob b. Shem Tob, *Sefer ha-Emunot,* and others.

[78] J. SARACHEK, *Faith and Reason* (Williamsport, 1935); F. BAER, *op. cit.,* I, pp. 289 ff. (and bibliography); A. NEUMAN, *The Jews in Spain* (Philadelphia, 1948), II, pp. 97-146.

[79] See, e.g. *Minḥat Kena'ot,* pp. 48, 94, 134, 175; Y. Bedersi, *Iggeret ha-Hitnazlut,* passim; Kaspi, *Ḥazozrot Kesef,* p. 104; *Ḥoshen Mishpat, op. cit.,* p. 167; *Malmad ha-Talmidim,* introduction, p. 92.

reduction of the law to pragmatic-utilitarian categories was considered to be the prelude to antinomism. They feared the victory of the "God of Aristotle" (as defined by Judah Halevi) who is removed from and unconcerned with human affairs, who is not accessible in prayer, who would not and could not intervene miraculously in the natural course of events. The postulates as well as the objectives of the philosophical movement were thus unnerving. In a word, the reasons for opposition to religious rationalization as articulated in the introduction to Saadia's *Emunot we-De'ot* were still applicable: "There are people who disapprove of such an occupation, being of the opinion that speculation leads to unbelief and is conducive to heresy".[80] The arguments and counter-arguments, incriminations and recriminations, bans and counter-bans spent themselves over the years and were abruptly interrupted by Philip the Fair's edict of expulsion in 1306.[81] As for the fate of rationalism in Provence, Y. Penini seems to have struck the most characteristic note: the movement of philosophy was irreversible and, indeed, any regression would be lamentable.[82] The achievements of Gersonides— to cite only one—show in fact that the ban was not much of a deterrent. Philosophy, astronomy, mathematics, medicine remained popular. Y. Penini's predictive declaration was initially substantiated and finally contradicted only because of external developments. The debate was left in abeyance.

Code

JQR	Jewish Quarterly Review
JSS	Jewish Social Studies
MGWJ	Monatsschrift für Geschichte und Wissenschaft des Judentums
ZfHB	Zeitschrift für hebräische Bibliographie
HUCA	Hebrew Union College Annual
REJ	Revue des Etudes Juives

[80] Tr. S. ROSENBLATT (New Haven, 1948), p. 26. Cf. H. A. WOLFSON, "The Jewish Kalam", *JQR Seventy-Fifty Anniversary Volume*, pp. 554-555. Such an argument is also cited by Jacob ANATOLI, *op. cit.*

[81] See, e.g., D. KAUFMANN, "Deux Lettres de Simeon b. Joseph", *REJ*, 29 (1894), esp. pp. 225-228.

[82] "It is certain that if Joshua the son of Nun arose to forbid the Provençal Jews to study the works of Maimonides, he would scarcely succeed. For they have the firm intention to sacrifice their fortunes and even their lives in defence of the philosophical works of Maimonides." Tr. in I. ABRAHAMS, *Jewish Life of the Middle Ages*, p. 371.

H. H. BEN-SASSON

THE "NORTHERN" EUROPEAN JEWISH
COMMUNITY AND ITS IDEALS

I

I N its formative period, the Middle Ages, the "Northern" European
Jewish community lived its life entirely within the walls of the
Christian city. Its fate depended to no small extent on the good will
or hostility of the townsmen. Its institutions, jurisdiction and functions
were in many cases patterned on those of the commune. Its social life
and activity, its decisions and enactments were largely shaped by the
current civic aims. To a certain extent it can be viewed as an harassed
Jewish city, eking out its life alongside that of the Christian city, cons-
titutionally unable and unwilling to merge into it, owing to the religious character of civic life in those times. Yet the Jewish community
in these Western lands and cities had ancient roots and problems and a
specific socio-economic structuring of its own that combined to fashion
its character and ideals in a way very different from that of its "host
city".

Opinions are divided as to the beginnings of the continuous settlement of Jewish communities in the West, north of the Pyrenees; some
would like to see their uninterrupted existence from the fourth century,
starting with the Cologne community mentioned in an imperial edict
of 331, while others consider that the destruction in the wake of German invasion of these districts broke the continuity. Be that as it may,
from the sixth century there is evidence enough of the presence of a
substantial number of Jews in the towns of the Frankish kingdoms; in
the diplomata of Emperor Louis the Pious (granted before 825) not
only do individual Jews obtain considerable rights, but two Jews of
Lyons get the rights *cum pares eorum,* which sounds very much like
rights for a community of equals. As early as this first quarter of the
ninth century these Jews are exempted from the irrational examination
by ordeal of any kind—*et nullatenus volumus, ut praedictos ad nullum
iudicium examinandum, id est nec ad ignem nec ad aquam calidam seu
etiam ad flagellum*—a hallmark much later of the turning of the Christian commune to rational law and proof, suited to its way of life and

thought; one has to keep in mind of course that in the case of Jews there would be not only their well-established legal tradition but also the effect of their religious aversion and opposition to ordeals "showing" the power of the Christian ritual. The very important rider to this exemption in the Carolingian diplomata, which was to be repeated as a general and central principle in various formulations in numerous privileges granted to the Jews through the Middle Ages—*nisi liceat eis secundum illorum legem vivere vel ducere*—may be regarded as a kind of reformulation acceptable to Christian rulers (who would not admit that the Jews in the Christian era were following in the steps of their fathers) of the ancient right given by Hellenistic kings to Jewish communities in the Diaspora "to live according to the Laws of the fathers" (τοῖς πατρίοις νόμοις χρῆσθαι). Whatever the elements of tradition and innovation, of merchant mentality and Jewish law and religion, in these legal formulas requested and obtained by Jewish groups as early as the Carolingian period, they were no doubt in accord with the economic and social life and function of these pioneer Jewish communities on the soil of northwest Europe. They came and were accepted as merchants; international trade gave them their niche in society and must have shaped their organizational habits and actions.

From the aspect of Jewish institutional and constitutional history and development, on the other hand, there are grounds for regarding the local community of northwest Europe not only as a new departure, but even as a revolutionary one. The ancient hallowed Jewish past had known the leadership of charismatic and holy men—prophets, "judges", priests—or of institutionalized charisma and sacrality—royal dynasties, such as the House of David, and Temple high-priest families. The towns of Eretz Israel as well as the synagogues and communities of the Greco-Roman Diaspora had enjoyed variegated forms and degrees of local autonomy towards the end of the Second Temple era and in the centuries following its destruction. Sects and ascetic groups shaped their own patterns of self-government, in some cases very intricate ones, e.g., the Essenes, the Judean sect of Cumran and the early Christian communities. At the very same time and in the same countries there arose the functions of the Scribe and Sage, whose charisma stemmed from their learning and its holiness. Individualistic and authoritative by nature, it quite early became institutionalized in Academies and Patriarchal families, the latter claiming for themselves the royal charisma, through supposed Davidic descent. Except for the sects, the autonomous institutions and trends tended to subordinate themselves, ideally and formally at least, to the charismatic and centralistic forces and institutions. The Western Diaspora and Eretz Israel experienced relatively early the fructifying and straining effects of the tension between local autonomy and central authority.

It would seem that there was no such development of local leadership in the eastern or "Babylonian" Diaspora, among the masses of Jews living under Parthian/Persian rule, at least as far as the available documentary evidence goes. Later on, in the days of Islamic rule in these regions, we find Jewish society in the Caliphate organized in a most remarkable system of leadership, centralistic to its core in theory, and most of the time and in most places in this realm in practice too, down to the middle of the eleventh century. It was essentially an attempt, successful to a large measure for some centuries, to combine the principles and ways of scholarly charisma, hereditary succession to this charisma, and strict hierarchical structure in the shape of two sacred Academies, whose membership was generally drawn from the sons of a narrow circle of "families of Sages", the heads of which—the Gaonim—came as a rule from a much narrower circle of "Gaonic" dynasties. Exceptions to this rule, when they occurred, were noted as a breach and rarity in contemporary chronicles. There was a place for the royal principle; the system included the Exilarch, from a family claiming Davidic descent, who was much honoured, even if his share of leadership was often contested by the heads of the Academies. This system left no place for local autonomy. Appointments of local dignitaries and judges were made by the Academies, through their Gaonim, and by the Exilarch. The teachings and fame of this system, its venerated institutions and heads, were well known in northwest Europe.

To be sure, as Y. Baer has shown, there is some evidence that even in the heyday of this system there was a kind of "subterranean" existence of local autonomy. The rule of centralism was sometimes honored in the breach, especially as the central authority weakened beginning with the second half of the tenth century. All this considered, there is still an important change from this centralism to a system where *local* Jewish community leadership is the rule and centralistic trends and elements the intruders.

II

The perplexities attending the transition from centralist leadership to a local one are of course clearly expressed in the "southern" community, where appointment from high was in the ascendance up to the tenth century. In a collection of formulas of legal deeds, assembled by a native of Barcelona, Rabbi Jehuda (*fl.* end of eleventh and beginning of twelfth century), we find a deed-formula that is described by this collector as having been taken from "some ancient versions"; it stands to reason that it was formulated around the tenth century. It has to do with the election and scope of authority of a community leader. His election takes place "in the presence of all the members of our community... great and humble together". He is to deal with religious and moral matters and has the power to punish transgressors. From the aspects of institutional and ideational development, the main interest lies in the preamble of this formula. Great care is taken there to stress that the critical state of morals and affairs justifies a community in electing its own leader. People have become "like a flock without a shepherd; some of our community go around without proper dress; some speak obscenities; some mix with the Gentiles, partake of their food, have assimilated to them to a degree that only the name of Judaism differentiates them" *(Sepher Ha'Shetaroth,* ed. S. J. Halberstamm [Berlin, 1898], pp. 7-8). The correct, legal, mode is to have your leader appointed by some central authority. You have to be seen to be in dire straits to justify your daring to be sufficient unto yourself in local leadership. The trouble had to be compounded of religious, national, moral and social matters, for such is the complexion of the Jewish community.

This compound of characteristic traits and problems holds true for the "northern" community as well, the difference between north and south lying only in the circumstances surrounding the emergence of the local community to a leading role. There is an ever-present and all-pervading difference between the Christian Commune on the one hand and the Jewish Community everywhere on the other. The first is an "artificial", voluntary, association in its origins, albeit religious and often authoritarian; the other in its own view is above all a "natural" unit, a cell of an ancient body, dispersed but not broken up. This difference gave rise to basic variations in the expression and maintainance of corporate identity and belonging, about which later.

Returning to the phenomenon of the upsurge of the local community, there is north of the Pyrenees no feeling of a need to apologize for its clear-cut autonomy, at least as far as the documentary evidence goes. These groups of merchants who ventured to build their Jewish way of life without the primary background of a Jewish agricultural settlement, and who lacked direct contact with the seats of the traditional centralistic sacral leadership, certainly had no thought of establishing similar centers and traditions in their relatively young dispersion of the northwest. Not only did these not suit their economic structure and function, but conditions in these Christian countries were not favorable for such a transplantation of centralistic and sacral Jewish institutions from the East. We must consider the possibility that this spontaneous, as it were, rise of local autonomy was not so much a break with the Balylonian traditions—which it certainly was up to a certain point—as a revival and adoption of the ways of leadership and modes of organization current in late classical times in the synagogues of the Western Diaspora (which were after all closest in location and in way of life to these northwestern communities of the tenth century) and of the autonomy that the towns of Eretz Israel had enjoyed before the days of the Caliphate. (Northwestern Jewry had the origins of its culture from Eretz Israel through southern Italy, and not from Babylonia, as is well established.)

Partly through continuity with one tradition of leadership and partly through a break with another (certainly well known to them, if from afar), we learn from documents from the tenth century onwards—both Hebrew and Latin—that the individual assumes leadership by sheer force of personality, ability and knowledge, that locality is the formative and decisive mode by right of the expressed will of the commonalty of inhabitants in a given town. Learning in Israel in those days was never divorced from sacred veneration of the Sage, yet the external paraphernalia of this status and the institutionalized heredity and hierarchy had vanished in the West. In many places, the people actually deciding were the *meliores* only, yet their decision is in principle for the locality and based on a recognition of the partnership in burden, interests and responsibility binding all Jews living within the walls.

The local community gathers unto itself, as it were, various traditional types of authority. We hear in the tenth century about "the custom prevalent in most Jewish communities"; this custom and additional decisions arrived at by "the [heads of ? the] communities gathered together" at what from the context seems to be a great fair at a port, are approved by a great Talmudic scholar (Rabbi Gershom, *Responsa*, ed. S. Eidelberg, #67) by equating the authority of the community leaders to that of the father in the family and that of the law court in legal matters, irrespective of the degree of learning of those local leaders.

Local leadership is seen in the eleventh century as the carrier of national and religious Jewish authority. The theory of its plenitude of power is formulated by the famous Bible and Talmud commentator, Rabbi Shlomo, son of Yitzhak ("Rashi", *fl.* in northern France, 1039-1105). On one occasion he reproaches people who refused to submit to a disciplinary decision of local leaders for their attempt "to transgress a divine commandment *[mitzvah]* ...not to obey the laws of the Jewish code [enjoining] to fulfil the command of their Elders, the fence builders and fortifiers of the lines; they should be under excommunication because of the community ordinance they disobeyed" (*Responsa*, ed. I. Elfenbein, #70). This view of his that disobedience of the decisions of the local community is tantamount to a religions sin is buttressed by an unusual Biblical authority. Such behaviour is an attempt "to turn to nought divine commandment and to slide back from the laws of Israel; for so runs the verse: 'Incline thine ear and listen to the words of the wise'" (ib., #247). The community has become the repository of binding wisdom, absolute legally and from a religious point of view, needless to say under the supreme authority of Biblical and Talmudic law, on their basis, for the sake of their implementation and for the welfare of God's People under changing circumstances. This idealization of the local community is expressed by medieval Sages in its Midrashic definition, recurrent in their writings, as "His vault founded on the earth" (after Amos 9:6).

In the description of the martyrdom of the Rhine communities in 1096 (recorded in the first half of the twelfth century) we find the pride of a great community, i.e. Mayence, in its glorious past and its recent sacrifices for the glory of the God of Israel and his people.

III

The city phenomenon has recently been characterized as "the Crossroads within the Wall" (R. S. Lopez, in *The Historian and the City*, ed. by O. Handlin and J. Burchard [1963], p. 27). Insofar as this succinct definition does justice to the communicational security and unity for the sake of keeping peace and a rational system of law within a given perimeter circumscribed by the city walls, it also serves many of the elements of Jewish community realities, in particular in times and places where the Jews were an active colonizing element, as for example in the kingdoms of the Iberian peninsula in the early stages of the Reconquista or in the Ukraine in the sixteenth and first half of the seventeenth centuries. In its own feeling and ideals, viewed from its historical roots, social character and cohesion-building ideas and ideals, the Jewish community would probably be more accurately described as "the fragmented nation beating against the Wall". The confines and the particularism of the city of course exerted their influence, and clashed continually with the far-flung, all-embracing national conception of Jewish unity. The latter combined in its thought and activity elements reserved in Christianity to princes and Church respectively; the two conflicting principles clashed in its life and thought with civic elements and ideas, as the city often clashed with Church and ruler.

This specific ideological content and social character of the Jewish community and the tensions it gave rise to find vivid expression in the twelfth and the first half of the thirteenth centuries in a basic conflict about the openness of the community to newcomers or its closure, on the one hand, and in the crystallization of extremist ideas as to the tasks of the local community and the character of its cohesion, on the other.

The conflict concerned the acceptance of the civic trend to close the community to new settlers, as far as possible. This trend usually prevailed in cities whose economic horizons were narrow, and whose sources of income were relatively local, or of limited territorial scope. Cities ruled by artisan guilds tended to a more stringent closure, while cities dominated by patrician, great merchant circles, were inclined to keep the gates wide open. The economic horizons of twelfth and thirteenth century Jewish communities in the northwest were narrow by force of their circumstances. The Jews in these countries were increasingly shut off in the ambit of moneylending to the local population, to feudal and Church dignitaries living near their host-city, or to more distant potentates who had a say about the security of the Jews. A new moneylender in town was certainly a prospective rival. The old settlers had cemented bonds of unity and common "property" on rights and arrangements got almost certainly in the case of Jews either thanks to economic service or for hard cash. Each community had its customs and ordinances, considered as wise, good and moral: which could guarantee the attitude and behavior of strangers? The limiting tendencies of the commune had much apperceptive material in the community. Small wonder that in the first half of the twelfth century "the four Kingdoms—France, Lotharingia, Burgundy and Normandy—have introduced this ordinance" restricting the right of permanent settlement in a community, making it contingent on the newcomer's getting prior agreement of the old settlers. The Paris community formulated its rules of prohibition and permission of settlement as follows: "Lest there enter the city anyone in addition to its living members as of now and their offspring to be born, males only but not females ...they enacted, that no one may settle in the city and fifteen miles around it, unless they will agree to it, present members and their sons excepted." The economic motivation against newcomers is very much in evidence, as well as the civic sentiment that citizenship is something valuable, to be inherited or granted properly. For the claimant states: "I am a citizen of this city; whereas you are a citizen of another one. I am against you earning any more in this city. Get out... I permitted you temporarily only (literally: "I gave you on loan") my inheritance" (from the "Responsum of the Sages of Rome to the Heads of the Paris Community", *Beth Ha'Otzar*, vol. I, 1847, pp. 57-58).

Against this pronounced civic and economic particularism there arose an equally strong opposition, motivated by the national elements of Jewish social thought. The expression of this opposition comes from the second half of the twelfth century in France. The timing proves conclusively that this opposition cannot be ascribed to any widening of economic horizons. If anything, moneylending had become even more exclusively the profession of Jews in France. Civic influence also had more time to penetrate the social consciousness of the Jews. Yet the great Talmudic scholar and leader of the communities, Rabbi Jacob son of Meir Tam (the grandson of "Rashi"), came out strongly against closure. It was his pupils' tradition "that were he present, he would have opposed this prohibition of settlement". This school of thought gave another motivation of the prohibition, thereby changing its nature, to fit the broad conception of the community as a cell of the living Jewish body national. According to this interpretation "prohibition of settlement is [in force] only against violent men, delators and those that refuse to pay their share of the tax; against other people there is no such ordinance" in force (*Or Zarua*, Zhitomir [1862], Berakhoth, *Responsa* #115). What reads almost like a translation of these anti-particularistic views is found in Latin in 1266: "*Communitas Judeorum Cantaurie, qui sigillantur in hoc starro, recognoverunt per starrum suum, quod juraverunt et intraverunt in sentenciam, quod nullus alius Judeus de alia villa preter quam de Cantauria manebit in eadem villa, scilicet, homo mentitor, inidoneus et accusator*" (*Select Pleas, Starrs and Other Records from the Rolls of the Exchequer of the Jews*, ed. by J. M. Rigg, [1902], pp. 35-36). It is worth remembering, that this was a community of moneylenders, living under difficult circumstances, twenty-four years before its end through the total expulsion of the Jews from England (1290). The tension between the tendencies to open or to close the communities went on through the Middle Ages, and with certain mutations even beyond that period. It reveals in its argumentation and modifications the peculiar tensions embedded in the character and ideals of Jewish communal life.

These tensions, the impact of the ideal on reality, and the complex likely to be shaped thereby, are given expression in the theories of an outstanding group of Jews active in Germany, mainly in the second half of the twelfth and the first half of the thirteenth century. They are called "Ḥassidim ("the Pious") of Ashkenaz". The group was minute in numbers, influential far beyond its numerical strength. Its leaders used to teach through morality tales (= exempla). One describes "a locality in which pious people only settled and they had pious leaders". To preserve for eternity the exemplary community, it decided "that no one may give his daughter to one who is not of this city, if he intends him to settle with us, lest he have an influence for bad on the citizens (the same goes for a woman from another locality), unless the majority of our Sages are convinced of their decency; in that case they may settle with us" (*Sepher Hassidim*, ed. Wistinetzky [1891], #1301). Their ideal is to create and maintain a community of Pious, like in lineage and morals; it is for the sake of this ideal that the closure of the community is to be applied. The tale ends with the failure of both the legal restriction and the moral ideal; later generations did not keep their settlement in its purity, they admitted unproven settlers through marriage, and for this they were direly punished.

This real or imaginary ideal community and its safeguards were postulated out of a view that it was the destiny of the community to serve primarily moral and religious purposes. Fines imposed for transgressions on these counts are just, though their financial burden be heavy and exacting. "Yet a fine imposed not for the sake of religion must lead unto sin—such a fine is sheer robbery." The examples given in this context for sinful fines reveal a sharp edge of social opposition to tendencies of economic gain through community enactments. The examples chosen for improper use of communal rights are those of "citizens who wanted to gain and they proclaimed under the sanction of excommunication that no one may sell wine or grain cheaper than a certain price; or that these commodities should not be imported from elsewhere, in order they be able to sell at an exorbitant price—they are those about whom the Bible says, 'for the earth is filled with injustice through them'" (ib., #1293). Whether the actual social tensions in Ashkenazi communities were sharp or mild, the basis and background of those pronouncements on them was the specific "natural" character of the Jewish community.

This character shaped the uniqueness of the community and is expressed distinctly by important differences in instruments of cohesion and legal sanctions between the commune and the community. The Christian city commune is originally and self-consciously a coniuratio; in many towns it continued as a coniuratio *reiterata,* returning in yearly ceremonies to oath-taking of all the citizens, demanding always the oath from new citizens (the works of W. Ebel have described the importance of the oath in the city commune). The Jewish community has no such consciousness of having originated in a binding by oath, nor does it have ceremonies of oath-taking, neither upon the acceptance of new citizens, needless to say, nor general, yearly ones. The community of course employs the oath for many and various purposes. Its total absence as a binding and cohesive element is all the more striking in view of the religious character of the community and viewed together with the pronounced influence of civic trends and institutions in many fields of community life and thought. Jewishness is the enduring, inborn basis and hallmark of belonging to this preeminently "natural" cell of the Jewish body politic and religious, astray and shut in by accident of exile within the Christian city walls.

On the other hand, the community makes lavish use of a sanction which in Christianity is reserved to the Church: excommunication (Ḥerem). It is the most effective sanction for the community's enactments—to such a degree that many ordinances are designated by contemporary sources simply as "excommunications".

The nature of the Jewish community as part and parcel of an ideally living and united society, one in the interleaving of nationality and "Church" in its web, is expressed clearly, as if on two sides of a coin, through the lack of the civic oath and the all-pervading presence of the excommunication.

IV

This national and religious structure was accompanied by a pronounced "royal" or "imperial" inclination in Jewish community thought and practice. For practical reasons of security the Jews tried to find a strong protector—bishop, prince, king or emperor—whose hand could reach over the walls to defend them from exactions of the city council and from depredations of its mob. This "centralistic" tendency found theoretical expression in Jewish thought and writings. Rabbi Ḥayim (*fl.* second half of thirteenth century) told the Regensburg Jews that legally and morally they had no obligation to share with the city in the amount it had to pay the King; this on two counts: "The city is not under the sovereignty of the citizens (literally: "The city does not belong to the citizens"), therefore their decisions are not law; they have no right to demand that the Jews pay taxes". To this he joins an argument against the ruling merchant, wine-growing class; this social protest could be made in common by the Jews and the artisans of the city. He goes on to instruct the Regensburg Jews: "You have written that the citizens have to pay the King of Austria for their merchandise and for their wine. This (the demand that the Jews share in the burden) is no doubt plain robbery... Do the Jewish community members or other townsmen, who are neither merchants nor do they own wine, have to give their money for that purpose, for the merchants and for their wine?". He also points out that this sharing of burdens is one-sided and unjust on that count to Jews. "Would the Jews be obliged to pay the King to save their goods and wine, they [the citizens] would have given them no help; it follows that they deal with the Jews on a different footing than amongst themselves" (*Responsa*, #110).

Jewish ideas on self-government, autonomy and rights are to be sought not only in Jewish writings; they are implicit in the formulas and mutations of the privileges granted them, even if their elucidation would have to proceed very cautiously. The warning of F. Rörig is pertinent in this case too: "One should not be misled by the form of the privilegia as to the substance behind it. Certainly, some medieval dynast grants—so does the text run—out of his uninfluenced judgment and from special grace" some rights to some city or citizens. "Yet the content of these privilegia were given substantially by the cities themselves. *Their* wishes and demands were dressed up in the cloth of princely grant. The permanent financial dependence of the rulers must have made these demands not too modest" (*Wirtschaftskräfte im Mittelalter* [1959], p. 397). Viewed in this light, the privileges dealing with Jewish autonomy bear out the above conceptions of national and religious basic traits of the community and of its anti-communal tendencies. Of course, one has constantly to bear in mind that religious and social antagonism surrounding Jewish existence must have made their demands "too modest".

This ideational system used to the operation of autonomous units of the same faith combined, it would seem, with the first stirrings of nationalism in twelfth century France, to cast its projection in some wideawake minds on the shape of things to come. The quintessence of this Jewish harmony and tension of "natural" national cohesion and sublime religious striving is unconsciously expressed in the commentary of the French Rabbi Eleazar of Beaugency (*fl.* twelfth century) on Isaiah 2: 3-5: "And many peoples shall go 'finding their trust and hope on God's Temple true and not disappointing; they will say, let us go up to the Lord (the full text: "to *the mountain* of the Lord")... He will teach us of His ways, and we will walk in His paths; for out of Zion shall go forth the Law'. There is no Law and Word of God but the one going forth from Zion and Jerusalem. Out of entering into a covenant with the Lord to walk in His paths and to obey His Word will God be judge and guide between nation and nation challenging and warring against one another. They will submit to His decisions and laws, if against them or for them; each one will go back to his land in peace. Nation against nation will not have recourse anymore to the sword against the one that takes his land from him, to make war on him in order to get it back from him. Instead he will summon him to Court in Jerusalem, to get the judgment of our God's Law, [the aggressor] will not disobey [the summons]. To this degree will they have fear of Heaven in their hearts. The party adjudged guilty as the one found right will equally submit to His judgment. That is the sense of the above mentioned 'Come Ye to God... and He will teach us of His way'—if I or you are in the right or in the wrong. 'Come ye... let us go' is the summons of the litigant. As they will not have recourse to war any more they will devote themselves to the development of the Oikumene, to toil each on his soil" (e. J. W. Nutt [1879], p. 6).

The eschatological vision is of nations united in faith yet sometimes divided by their individual interests, they will need a kind of a Divine "International Court" to make possible peace and creativity on earth. Law shall be the guide of the many "natural" national units.

The "Northern" Jewish community was creative both in thought and institutionalization through the creative tension between its primary character as a limb of an encompassing and ancient society and the influence of the new conjurative city commune on it; it had in its nature what would be termed in medieval parlance "Church" and "Royal" traits. Self-interest and theoretical considerations made it an opponent of the assertive commune and an ally of the central ruling authorities. Its thought encompassed the needs of the moment as well as the End of Days.

BIBLIOGRAPHY

Y. Baer, "The Origins of the Organization of the Jewish Community in the Middle Ages" (in Hebrew with substantial English summary), *Zion*, XV, pp. 1-41.

S. W. Baron, *The Jewish Community*, Vol. I-III (Philadelphia, 1942).

L. Finkelstein, *Jewish Self-Government in the Middle Ages* (New York, 1924).

HAIM BEINART

HISPANO-JEWISH SOCIETY

I.

THE history of the Jews in Spain until their expulsion in 1492 is the history of a people settled in one place for a very long time—at least as long as Christian dating.[1] To this land of the Diaspora the Jews brought their own way of life and their own institutions. Here they evolved, both influencing and being influenced by their surroundings, and adopting what they needed for their own customs and forms of life. Historically, this long period begins in the days of Roman rule over *Provincia Hispania*. Afterwards, when Byzantines and Visigoths held sway in the Iberian Peninsula, the people underwent harsh decrees and persecution, for their rulers sought to force Christianity upon them and to eliminate them as Jews. The Visigothic regime, relying on Conciliar decrees to which it had been a party, sought to destroy their public and social framework, without suggesting any solution to the bewildering problem of how people who had accepted Christianity under duress were to exist. It was not only that Christian Visigothic society and government were incapable of offering any such solution; they were a sort of upper stratum in the state—a ruling caste. Obviously, this ruling caste had no interest in the problem of relations other than taking the steps necessary to keep itself in power in the Peninsula. The existence of a separate and distinct Jewish people and society did not suit its purposes at all. In the hundred years of Visigothic rule, the government failed to create values that might serve as a foundation for public and social evolution in the state. Its efforts at different times to mould a Christian society amounted to little more than paper decisions.[2]

In 711 the Arabs burst into the Iberian Peninsula and this government fell. The Jewish public, some of whom lived in areas where Visigothic rule had been weak, and some of whom had arrived to settle in the wake of the conquest, were faced with many public and social

[1] H. BEINART, "¿Cuando llegaron los Judíos a España?", *Estudios*, 3 (1961), pp. 1–32.
[2] J. PARKES, *The Conflict of Church and Synagogue* (2nd printing, Cleveland-New York, 1961), pp. 345 ff. (See bibliography there); J. VICENS VIVES, *Historia Economica de España* (Barcelona, 1959), pp. 81–89; J. VIVES, *Concilios Visigoticos e Hispano-Romanos* (Barcelona-Madrid, 1963), *passim*.

problems, connected with their organization as a community living as wards in "protected" congregations. Of course, the problems of existence and organisation in Moslem al-Andalus were no different from those to be found in any other territory ruled by Islam. But the independent Ommayad rulers of al-Andalus soon had need of the Jews, for internal and external reasons. The appearance of Jewish leaders like Hasdai Ibn Shaprut, who was appointed head of the Jews of al-Andalus in the tenth century, or Jacob Ben-Jo, appointed tax-collector and Head of the Jews of al-Andalus and the Maghreb, the fact that they both resided in Cordoba, the subsequent rise of R. Shmuel ha-Nagid in Granada—all these attest the close links between the government and the Jews and are a clear sign of Jewish organization. And although social relations were still rather limited between the Jews and the government and the surrounding Moslem world, it seems that as the government ramified, so did the network of relations grew more complex. As a general rule, however, the Jewish public in the communities of Moslem Spain—and here and there in the ever-advancing, ever-conquering Christian Spain— never went outside the religious-national framework. They kept to themselves, whether in matters of organization and social structure or in those outward forms of life that they had adopted in Spanish lands. This general rule goes far to explain the social and public characteristics of Spanish Jewry, despite the fact that Jewish communal organization in Christian Spain was influenced by the forms of organization of the Christian public. Another important fact is that Christian rule was divided among kingdoms and principalities and the fiefs of churchmen and nobles. This was a unique phenomenon, of whose total extent under Christian sway we shall speak in greater detail. We shall try to build up a picture of the Jewish society that existed for centuries, through many vicissitudes, in the kingdoms of Castile and Aragon.

2.

At the outset we may fairly ask: is it in fact possible to ascribe a particular social personality to the Jewish public in Spain? The characteristics of Spanish Jewry were, after all, shared by Jews in other countries. There were city-dwellers, smalltown dwellers, villagers. All social relations, public and social tension, existed in streams both above and below the surface. Spanish Jewish society contained rich men, middling men and poor men—the latter supported by the public—, scholars, students, religious dignitaries renowned for their learning, physicians, merchants, artisans in the widest variety of crafts, and peasants lease-holders and freeholders. Thus, socially, they were no more exempt from the stress of relations than any society and any community. And this, it seems, describes the network of relations in the Jewish public in Spain throughout the centuries of its existence. Yet, the social situation of the congregations of Israel in Spain was not the same at all times and places. Changing political conditions affected them. We should remember that Christian Spain existed for hundreds of years in the political stress of *Reconquista* and in the problems of resettlement of the frontier, on which there was room for the Jews as a community. These conditions of stress affected the Jewish public, laying it open to the challenge of settlement, the challenge of creating centres and new congregations. These were especially demanding tasks, since in conquered cities, townships and villages there were old communities which had now to fit into the conquering Christian state. This is not to say that the communities, wherever they were, had to undergo changes in their organization, or that the social structure of the Jewish public in the conquered areas underwent an immediate change. The Jews of the conquered places met (sometimes as ransomed captives)[3] Jewish settlers who had come from the Christian zones. The new Jewish settlers from Spanish-Christian ruled areas enjoyed settlers' privileges and were given lands, estates, vineyards, houses and workshops in the conquered areas.[4] Both sides built up the Jewish communities anew, without more friction than is normal in any community.

The condition of settlement in new places and the demand for Jewish settlement continued among the Jewish public until the last Reconquista campaign to conquer Granada, in the eighties of the fifteenth century. Yet in this final campaign of conquest, whose aim was to cast out the last stronghold of Islam in Europe, in arrangements for resettlement of the area about to be conquered, the victorious Ferdinand and Isabella had not the slightest intention of calling on the Jewish element in settlement or its power of initiative. As is well known, the Catholic kings intented to found a purely Christian state. And it must be said that this idea contained as a prior assumption, the expulsion of the Jews from Spain. It was an idea that had grown out of the religious and social evolutionary process that had been going on since 1391, through the wave of forced conversions and abandonment of the Jewish faith. This process continued throughout the fifteenth century.

In every Jewish community in Christian Spain, whether in the kingdoms of Castile-Leon, Navarre or Aragon, the style of public life was set by members of the best families, those, that is to say, whose pedigree

---

[3] The government sometimes demanded that the Jewish public should ransom its Jewish brothers in the conquered Moslem territories.

[4] On this question see, e.g., R. CARANDE, "Sevilla, Fortaleza y Mercado," *Anuario de la Historia del Derecho Español*, 2 (1925), *passim*; J. GONZALEZ Y GONZALEZ, *Repartimiento de Sevilla*, 1–2 (Madrid, 1951); J. TORRES FONTES, *Repartimiento de Murcia* (Madrid, 1960).

was good, who also possessed property in the city or its surroundings.[5] Some of these pedigrees were imaginary, amounting to no more than the fact that the family in question had been among the first settlers in the place. Such families were Abu-Alafia, Ibn-Ezra, Alfakar, Ibn Shushan and Ibn Zadok in Toledo; the families of Caballeria, Alconstantini and Golluf in Saragossa; the families of Abravalia and Berfet in Barcelona; the Portela family in Tarragona and so on. Not all had an ancient pedigree on which to base their claim to place for themselves and their descendants. Not a few families owed the success of their claims within (and sometimes without) the community to contacts with the government and connections with kings, bishops, princes and dukes.[6] But it would be utterly baseless to say that only persons whose origins are insufficiently clear to us, or persons having government connections, were the social and moral arbiters of the Jewish public. Within these very families we find rabbis and scholars. We also find great rabbis from other families who exercised much greater influence than these families on the Jewish way of life and on the leadership of the Jewish public. It is enough to recall a few of their names: Ramban (R. Moshe b. Nachman, Nachmanides), R. Shelomo ben Adret (Rashba), R. Aaron ha-Levi na Clara, R. Hasdai Crescas in Aragon, R. Joseph Orabuena in Navarre, or Rabbi Joseph ha-Nasi ben Pruziel, known as Cidellus, R. Abraham Ibn-Shushan, R. Judah Ibn Wakar, R. Meir Alguades, R. Abraham Benvenisti of Soria, R. Isaac Abrabanel in Castile. It was such personalities and many others like them, who set the pattern for public and moral life in Spanish Jewry for generations. Needless to say, there were also Jewish leaders from "good" families who were pushing and unlearned. And there were others too among the men of "lineage" who cared and worked for the Jewish community. Whether in their own native place or in the state where they lived. Only against rioters, violent men, rough attackers did the sages of Israel in Spain in every generation see it as their duty to fight—sometimes even with government aid—for the sake of the welfare of Jewry. And if, on the other hand, the sages of Israel saw danger of an outburst from within that might harm the Jewish community, they did not hesitate to take measures against those who had lost control of themselves, and would even employ local strong men in order to impose discipline on the Jewish community.[7] Throughout Spain, we may justly see in the sages of Israel the wardens of the Jewish

[5] See H. H. BEN-SASSON, "The Generation of Spanish Exiles on Itself," *Zion*, 25 (1961), pp. 23–64 (Hebrew).

[6] H. H. BEN-SASSON, *Chapters in the History of the Jews in the Middle Ages* (Tel Aviv, 1958), pp. 144 ff. (Hebrew). See H. BEINART, *The Character of the 'Court Jews' in Christian Spain: Elite Groups and Leadership Strata* (Jerusalem, 1966), pp. 55–71 (see bibliography there).

[7] Rashba's way, for example, is known. See F. BAER, *History of the Jews in Christian Spain* (Philadelphia, 1960), I, pp. 257 ff.

community, the guardians of its path towards a decent way of life based on public and social morality, as all true Jewish life must be.

Jewish communal leaders and sages were, however, only a thin stratum of Jewish society. If we turn to the more go-ahead members of the community, we find that their chief business was large-scale credit for state and private needs, tax-farming and tax-collecting—activities that spread throughout Castile and Aragon. They were the first to receive lands in border areas; they had shops and commercial enterprises in many parts of Spain. Alongside these dwelt persons of middle and lower rank: grocers and craftsmen, who did not differ much from each other. A valuable criterion for assessing social differences in Spain is the amount of the annual tax paid by individuals to the chest that existed in every congregation to meet the tax that Jewish communities were required to pay every year to the king's treasury.[8] In this respect we find that a line can be drawn between the great ones or 'great taxpayers', as they were called, and the 'medium' and 'small' men; we shall revert to this topic later. We find concentrations of small craftsmen in almost every community in Spain; the 'great ones', the rich are scarcer.

It is certainly possible to find a "rich man" in every community—be he merchant, money-lender, owner of vineyard or olive-grove—compared with whom the other members of the community live on a very modest level. But we must remember that the criterion of wealth is purely relative. Among the merchants, the cloth dealers of Saragossa enjoyed special status and filled important positions in the communal leadership.[9] There were also perfume dealers, apothecaries, goldsmiths, etc. In a community of 50 families like that of Segovia or Avila in Castile, Teruel in Aragon or Tudela in Navarre, we find a full array of skilled workers, a wide variety of crafts and services to supply every private and public need.[10] Weavers, shoemakers, tailors, butchers, furriers, smiths, saddlers, tanners, leatherworkers, potters, cloth dyers and so on very often sold their products themselves. Some of these skilled craftsmen had a plot of land next to their homes on which they grew vegetables for their own table. Some families had a few head of sheep or cattle grazing on the common pasture of the village, township or town. Only a minority actually owned land on the waste outside the town or township. This land, which grew unirrigated field crops, vines or olives, was cultivated by the owner aided in some cases by his Jewish or Christian serfs or

---

[8] See BAER, *History*, I, pp. 198 ff.

[9] Jews worked in every stage of this profession, from the spinning of the woolen thread, the weaving of the cloth and the dyeing to the selling of the cloth and the making of the garment.

[10] See BAER, *History*, I, p. 197. It is impossible here to enumerate every trade in which Jews engaged. See F. CANTERA and A. GARCÍA ABAD, *Sefarad*, 27 (1967), pp. 39-63.

non-Jewish labourers. Such was the general arrangement throughout the centuries of Jewish settlement in Spain, and lists of property sold about the time of the 1492 expulsion confirm it.[11] However, the Jews of those days cannot be called farmers in any accepted contemporary or modern sense of the word. There was a Jewish doctor in almost every settlement, who served not only the Jews but the community at large—whoever needed his help, whether in ordinary times or in time of plague. Towns expressed their thanks more than once to the Jewish physician.[12] His services were given despite the fact that the Church and civil authorities alike forbade Christians to be treated by Jewish physicians and forbade Jews to practise medicine.[13] Kings had their Jewish physicians, as did bishops, abbots and nobles in their degrees. Indeed to employ a Jewish physician was felt to lend tone by many nobles and great men of the realm. Clearly, money lending at interest was by no means the only Jewish profession,[14] though Jews engaged in it. It was a service needed by a society unable to find any other source of financial credit; it is unnecessary to repeat the reasons that drove Jews to support themselves by moneylending. Jewish society included, along with all these, widows and orphans, poor people, religious functionaries, teachers and cantors, all of whom were supported at the public charge. They were exempt from taxes: the Jewish community paid their taxes for them. Small and medium-sized communities not frequently depended in this respect on their rich and 'great' brethren, or on the one individual in the place who was rich enough to help the whole community in its need. This kind of communal support was given throughout the period of Jewish settlement in Spain, middling and large communities alike.

The majority of Jews were of the middling sort: they had little capital, and what they had was sunk in their trade or craft. When they were forced to abandon Judaism in the troubles of 1391 and during the fifteenth century, they brought with them into the Christian fold all the traditional Jewish crafts and callings handed down for generations. Thus we can sometimes tell a man's origin by his occupation, and say: that is a Jew by origin. Christian society in Spain in the fifteenth century was unable to absorb this special world, this Jewish public forced from its faith and its framework. It was not only that the Christians lacked the necessary public and social means to absorb the Jews: they lacked the socio-psychological conditions as well. The public debate that went on in Castile in the middle of the fifteenth century shows how much the

[11] See, e.g., F. BAER, *Die Juden im christlichen Spanien*, 2 (Berlin, 1936), pp. 429–435 *(JchS)*. R. del ARCO and F. BALAGUER, *Sefarad*, 9 (1949), pp. 390 ff.

[12] BAER, *History, passim.*

[13] See, e.g. the Decrees of Valladolid of 1412; BAER, *JchS*, 2, pp. 263 ff.

[14] H. BEINART, "Judíos y Conversos en España después de la Expulsión de 1492," *Hispania*, 24 (1964), pp. 293 ff.

problem of the *Conversos* and their absorption into Christian society was
a social problem. It had various aspects: there was the question of sheer
subsistence for the Conversos and there was the question of the need for
a partial change of heart by the society that was supposed to absorb
them. The difficulties were particularly prominent in professions which
had never admitted Jews, like those of public notary and judge, and
other positions of decisive weight in the Christian society of genuine,
original Christians. The educated Conversos could find no place for
themselves in this Christian community and were pushed firmly back
by legislation aiming to forbid people who 'are of the Jews' (i.e. of
Jewish origin) from taking posts involving jurisdiction over Christians.[15]
But for the majority, the mass of skilled workers, the question of sheer
subsistence was the crucial one. For hundreds of years, Christian Spain
was forced to grapple with the problem of absorbing a whole society
that had been cut off by force from the faith of its fathers. Without
entering into a discussion of the religious aspects of forced conversion,
or the deep desire of Conversos to return to their ancestral faith, or their
efforts to practise Judaism in secret, we shall see that the social problem
of their existence remained unsolved. It is still unsolved in a way in some
localities at the present day.

3.

It was organization that gave each Jewish community its character.
For in addition to the administrative side, there were social demarcation
lines and fixed relations in the representative institutions. At the outset
we must stress that the guiding light on the paths of Jewish leadership
was the *Halacha*, the Jewish law as interpreted by Sages, but one must
take into account in Spain the actual conditions of the time, which
influenced the solution of many problems within the Jewish community.
These considerations apply when we are assessing the leaders' desire for
a regular Jewish life and their approach to the daily life that the Jewish
community had to endure. In Spain, as in all the Diaspora, the community was the basic unit of organized Jewish life. The style of life of the
Jews was set within the communal bounds, as were the institutions of
which every son of Israel stood in need: synagogue, Jewish court, kasher
food supply, cemetery—all aspects of an organized life. In Spain, special
privileges for all these needs were granted by the government to the
Jewish community, whether for communal needs or private needs. Yet
by no means all the public and social aspects of the Jews were expressed
and defined in official privileges. It is enough to mention Jewish education

---

[15] See H. BEINART, *Conversos on Trial before the Inquisition* (Tel Aviv, 1965), pp. 14
ff. (Hebrew).

and welfare to show that everything that grew and expanded *in* the Jewish community was rooted in a living organism. Thus we see that if the organized Jewish community was a personal lighthouse of security for every Jew, the Jewish communal institutions were like the ship and the leaders of the community the captains of each generation, steering the community to the safe haven of Jewish existence. As to the conditions of this existence among Spanish-Jewish communities, we must recall again the differences in political conditions between one kingdom and another. Changing political conditions were a decisive factor in the life of all communities throughout the centuries of Jewish settlement in Spain. The varying attitudes of the authorities affected more than the actual relations between Jews and government; they sometimes affected the forms of Jewish organization and occasionally even the relations within the community itself. These vicissitudes did not, however, change essentially the patterns of life laid down when the people of Israel dwelt in its own land, living its own life.[16] Yet there were differences between one community and another in Spain, so that it is virtually impossible to generalize about organization. As Baer remarks of the communities of Aragon: 'No other Jewish society in all the Diaspora accepted the ideas and political trends of its time so openly as did the communities of Aragon.'[17] This is equally true of other regions of Spain. The influence from outside appeared first and foremost in external forms and in the functions of administrative office-holders in the leadership of each community. Particular local influence also had their effect on the Jewish public in different parts of Spain. We see an illustration of this in a Responsum of Rashba (R. Shelomo b. Adret) in 1264, where he writes to the community of Saragossa in answer to a question about communal leadership:[18]

Local custom in these matters is not everywhere the same, as there are places where affairs are run entirely by the advice of the elders and councillors and there are places where even the majority has no right to do anything unless they consult all the people and obtain their consent, and there are places where they set people in authority to do as they see fit in all general affairs, and they are as wardens there.

Here, perhaps was one of the factors that prevented the setting of national overhead organizations in Spain to cover all the communities. On only two occasions in the history of Spanish Jewry is it recorded that efforts were made to combine on a national basis, once in the kingdom of Aragon and once in the kingdom of Castile. In Aragon the attempt

[16] See F. BAER, *Zion*, 15 (1950), pp. 1–41. (Hebrew).
[17] BAER, *History*, I, pp. 212 ff.
[18] Responsa (Leghorn press), 1778, III, No 394.

was made in 1354 after the Black Death riots, which brought destruction upon the Jewish communities.[19] Among the initiators of the attempt were R. Nissim ben Reuben Girondi and Crescas Shelomo who sought to establish a permanent executive council to represent the Jews of the kingdom. The council was to have been composed of two representatives from Catalonia and two from Aragon, while the kingdoms of Valencia and Majorca were to have sent one each. But the Aragon communities failed to cooperate in the setting up of this overhead organization. The initiators sought to establish a council on a national scale, to represent all the Jews of the state and to negotiate with the government on matters regarding Jewry. Internally, such a body might have benefited the Jewish communities. It might have showed them one way to an organization with centralized means and centralized powers, something to combat the deep-rooted parochialism that saw little or nothing outside the community.

A second attempt to found a ceiling organization was made in 1432 in Valladolid for the Jews of Castile. This attempt was much more practical, perhaps because of the different conditions in which Spanish Jewry found itself in the fifteenth century. Rabbi Abraham Benvenisti of Soria, the court Rabbi [20] who initiated the step, set out from the assumption that self-organization on a national scale was needed to rebuild and restore the Jewish communities destroyed in Castile by the pogroms of 1391, the results of the decrees of 1412 and the Disputation of Tortosa in 1413–1414. He invited representatives of the Castilian communities to Valladolid, and the meeting drew up five heads or 'gates' of statutes, according to which the delegates would try to establish one legislation and one regulatory framework for all the communities of Castile.[21] In these statutes, which were written in a mixture of Hebrew and Spanish, there is an evident attempt to lay down the outlines of action which the delegates hoped would restore the ruined congregations of Castile and make possible the building of a stable life. Had it been possible to put into effect the ideas embodied in the five 'gates', perhaps the life of the communities might have been restored; but for this sort of effort fifteenth century Castile did not offer the conditions that had prevailed in the previous centuries.

Self-organization on a smaller scale can be seen in the *Collecta*, or tax-districts of various communities. Although the specific aim was limited—simply to form one purse for taxation purposes on behalf of

---

[19] For a detailed description see BAER, *History*, II, pp. 24 ff.; A. LOPEZ DE MENESES, "Una Consecuencia de la Peste negra en Cataluña: el Pogrom de 1348," *Sefarad*, 19 (1959), pp. 92–131; pp. 321–364.

[20] For the nature of the post see below.

[21] The 'gates' or sections are: Study of the Torah; Choosing of Judges and Other Appointments; Traditions; Taxes and Works; Dress. See BAER, *JchS*, 2, pp. 280–297.

the government—the *collecta* did create a link between the communities. As Rashba wrote to the community of Montpellier:[22]

Know that we and the community of Villafranca and the community of Tarragona and Montblanch have one chest and one pocket between us in paying the taxes and property dues and all that the kingdom imposes on us. And whenever they wish to make new agreements in fixing taxes or giving reminders or obtaining what we seek from our lord the king, we never impose anything upon them, even though we be the greater number, and the head of all matters; for if we act without their advice they will not heed our voices. Sometimes we send people to them and sometimes delegates come from them to us with their consent. And if they do not heed us, to do any of these things, we force them by the arm of the government to come to us, or to resolve and enforce in their local community, as we have done. But in other places the chief community may decree that the lesser ones must come, even against their will; for in all these matters the custom of places differ. This is and has always been the law and custom with us.

The *Collecta* acted all over Spain, and formed an important element of inter-community relations, insofar as these were based on taxes paid to the state treasury.

Another unifying force in Spanish Jewry was the Court Rabbi, Rab de la Corte,[23] who sat as a judge in appeals involving Jews. It is true that Rashba in Aragon and after him R. Hasdai Crescas had in their time been appointed supreme judges of the Jews in certain defined fields, but these appear to have been appointments for a specific purpose, quite unlike the position of court Rabbi in Castile. The Court Rabbi of Castile did not necessarily have to be ordained Rabbi to teach and judge. The holder of the post might equally well be some public figure in favour with the king, sufficiently trustworthy to be put in charge of the farming and collection of royal taxes. Rashba already noted[24] the necessity of distinguishing between such persons and real Rabbis of Israel: "But he who is no Rabbi but a royal appointee is not of this status; we only punish anyone who puts him to shame for what he is; and this only if he shames him in deed, but not in word." It is necessary to emphasize that the Court Rabbi was not the chief rabbi of the Jews in the state or head of other rabbis. The 'real' rabbi, as we have shown, led a unique part in forming the character of the Jewish community in Spain, he was a leader in his generation. And some generations were indeed blessed in their leaders—rabbis like Ramban (Nachmanides), Rashba, R. Aaron

---

[22] Responsa III, Nº 411.

[23] The post existed in Portugal too; the title was Arrabi Moor dos Judíos. See M. KAYSERLING, *Geschichte der Juden in Portugal* (Leipzig, 1867), pp. 9, 48 ff. It was also found in Navarre: the king's physician R. Joseph Ora Bona was appointed to the position in 1394, under the title of Rabi Mayor de los Judíos. See BAER, *JchS*, 1, pp. 601–603. See also I. LOEB, *REJ*, 6 (1886), p. 208, and S. W. BARON, *The Jewish Community*, I (Philadelphia, 1948), pp. 292–294, and *passim*.

[24] In the Responsa attributed to Ramban (Nachmanides), No. 248.

ha-Levi na Clara, Ritba (R. Yom Tov Asbili), Ribash (R. Yitzhak b. Sheshet), R. Hasdai Crescas in Aragon; R. Asher b. Yehiel and his son R. Yehuda, R. Abraham ibn Shoshan in Toledo, R. Meir Alguades in Segovia, and many other like them, heads of Spanish Jewry. Alongside such men and their work, the court Rabbi looks no more than an administrative functionary of the crown, whose sphere of duty happened to be the Jewish community. Thus the Court Rabbi helped·to decide how much tax the Jewish congregations of the kingdom should pay annually. Yet, he must also, it seems, be regarded as the spokesman of Jewry in his time. Not all generations had their outstanding leaders.

Let us now turn to the actual organization of the communities. The council of 'seven upright men of the town' is a fundamental institution in Jewry. But in Spain, and especially in Aragon, it was often not maintained. As far as ideas go, there seems at first to be no more to the expansion of the Council than a deviation from the number of members accepted for generations. But if we study what was done in the kingdom of Aragon we shall find that the kind of representation was altered too. Here we notice particularly the representation by 'rank': 'great ones', 'middling ones', 'small ones'. It must be said that they reached this type of representation comparatively late in the existence of the communities. The influence of the city is unmistakable in eastern Spain. 'Class differences' (if one may use the term here) which found expression in the Christian town, helped to lead to the establishment of the Council, an expanded council in the Jewish community (primarily the large community).[25] This expanded body was in addition to the existing communal institutions, lending them a more representative character, so that they should contain delegates of the public acting for it in the expanded council and forming a bridge to the people at large. However we must remember that, whether larger or smaller, no council could change the nature of the public rule that prevailed in large—and medium—sized communities alike. In the eighties of the thirteenth century there was a permanent 'Council' in Barcelona with twenty-five advisory members, but it is impossible to make clear the functions they fulfilled. From the end of the century tasks began to be more clearly defined in the communal leadership, and from the beginning of the fourteenth century we find a body of thirty members established on the lines of the *Consejo de Ciento*, the Council of Hundred in the city. This body formed an addition to the seven 'trustees' who in effect ran communal affairs, and like the city council was made up of representatives of three classes: upper, middle and low; the proceedings were according to regulations adopted in 1327.[26] We must emphasize that in the Jewish community the 'Council

[25] On the method of electing council members, see below.
[26] For the statute see BAER, *JchS*, 1, pp. 251–256. It was confirmed by King Jaime II.

of Thirty' had greater weight than the 'Council of Hundred' in the city.[27] Those who served on the former had to be men of particular distinction, for all public affairs depended upon them and they were chosen for their public and private rectitude. Although representatives of the middle and lower classes were supposed to participate in the Council of Thirty, in practice the greatest influence was exerted by these 'great men', who formed the Jewish aristocracy of the town. The regulations laid down, *inter alia*, that this council should appoint all public office holders: trustees (*secretarii*),[28] religious court judges (*dayanim*), accountants and charity treasurers. They were to arrange the levying of taxes, amend regulations and appoint committees for special purposes. To a certain extent the Council was dependent on the trustees elected by its members. It was the trustees who invited the council members to meetings, and they who fined late or absent council members. The trustees and the judges elected the Council once every three years by a majority vote. As against this, the activities of the trustees depended on the consent of the Thirty.[29] The community of Barcelona continued to be run on these lines even after the Black Death. In 1386 a new public constitution was introduced in the city and confirmed by king Pedro IV.[30] This constitution laid down that the community should be run in the same way as the city, i.e. by the establishment of a Community Council composed of representatives of three classes: notables of the congregation, merchants and craftsmen. A complicated system of electing communal leaders was laid down, a replica of the municipal system. Despite the fact that three Trustees and the Council of Thirty were chosen from representatives of the three estates, the lowest estate was naturally given the least voice and the advantages went to the other two. Five representatives from each estate, to whom the three trustees would be added, made up an Inner Council. Every year ten council members completed their term of service and were replaced by others chosen in their stead. This Council was short lived. The pogrom of 1391 put an end to the Jewish community of Barcelona, and the town never saw another.

The problem of maintaining an elected representative body to run communal affairs was less complex in middle-sized communities. The problem did not, of course, exist in small ones, which, as we have shown, belonged to various Collecta. In the city of Perpignan, then part of the kingdom of Aragon, the councillors (20–28 in number) were chosen for life. The great defect here was that the councillors were kinsmen.[31] When one councillor died, the others would appoint his

[27] See BAER, *History*, II, pp. 41 ff.
[28] On the office-holders, see below.
[29] On the powers of the trustees, see below.
[30] See BAER, *JchS*, 1, pp. 580–594.
[31] This was forbidden in Barcelona.

replacement. In 1384 this situation was officially approved by the Crown, despite the opposition of the Crown prosecutor.[32]

We know something of the workings of the Council of Gerona after the Black Death. The community appears to have been very much reduced, since two notables from Barcelona were in charge of its internal affairs. They set up two councils in Gerona, one with twenty-six members and the other with sixteen; they also amended the arrangements for the election of trustees, the accountants and the rest of the office-holders. Some time before the pogrom of 1391, the Infanta Violante confirmed the constitution of the community. A council of twenty-three was to be established, two of whom were to be from the Collecta, i.e. from the townships adjoining Gerona. Sixteen members were to be elected for life or with a possibility of exchanging every two to three years with a member of their family (son or brother), bearing their name. The other places were to be reserved for fifteen persons, each of whom was to sit on the council for three years. Council members could themselves be trustees but a body of electors was to appoint three trustees and one treasurer (*clavarius*) every year. The tax-assessor was to be chosen from among the small taxpayers, and must not be related to any of the trustees; he was to enjoy a fixed annual salary. The trustees, evidently, belonged to the other classes.[33] These conditions were fulfilled even after the pogrom of 1391, when the community of Gerona returned to its former strength.

In the community of Mallorca (today Palma de Majorca) the management of communal affairs until the middle of the fourteenth century was in the hands of the rich merchants.[34] Indeed, the members of the community were renowned for their great wealth and far-reaching overseas trade. While the kingdom of Mallorca was independent in the fourteenth century, six trustees headed the Jewish community. Occasionally an Eight-Man Council of 'upright men' is mentioned;[35] the conditions of the island community suggest that it was not a permanent institution. Possibly the public trustees did not activate the Council or make it party to their decisions. This situation existed even after the island was conquered by Pedro IV in 1343, and he in effect confirmed it. In 1348 the 'great taxpayers', who apparently made up the 'Community Council', sought to co-opt one of the small taxpayers to act as additional commissioner for the distribution of charitable funds. But one of the great taxpayers complained to the king, and Pedro IV decided that it was better that those who gave should distribute. In comparison with Spain

---

[32] See BAER, *JchS*, 1, pp. 565–568.
[33] See BAER, *ibidem*, pp. 626–633.
[34] See BAER, *History*, II, pp. 47 ff.; A. PONS, "Los judíos del Reino de Mallorca durante los Siglos XII-XIV," *Hispania*, 20 (1960), *passim*.
[35] See below.

itself, we note that there was a rule in force from 1356 stating that no physician or middleman might be elected to the post of public trustee. Baer assumed [36] that this was a sign of the islanders' estimate of these professions as in some towns of southern France, where their practitioners were held to be inferior and unfit to serve as communal leaders. It could, however, be a remnant of the independent kingdom of Mallorca: in Perpignan it was not insisted on. After the Aragonese conquest we find a Council of Thirty in the island community, and the governor of the island representing the central government, controlled appointments to it.

This council dealt with all the affairs of the small island communities. In 1374 the king commanded that those Jews 'who have dwelt in the community from ancient years, the honest and great taxpayers' should lead the community. He also forbade all association for the purpose of forming factions to cancel the decisions of the Council of Thirty. In this Council sat representatives of the two most substantial property-owning families in the island, Hakim and Najar, and there was a good deal of friction between them. Differences of opinion were not merely personal, but were carried over into public affairs. Moshe Hakim, self-appointed representative of the democratic interests in the community, appeared before Pedro IV in 1378 and obtained from him a confirmation of certain amendments: trustees to be elected for two years; members of the same family sitting in the Council to have their votes combined and counted as one. Despite this democratising movement, the small taxpayers were still not properly represented.

Jewish communal representation in Saragossa, chief city of Aragon, [37] was of a special kind. In that city the question of representation grew into a full-fledged public debate in the sixties of the thirteenth century. The debate centered around the assessment of the annual tax payable to the Crown. Should the levy be by 'decision' or 'declaration'? That is to say, should the rate of tax be decided by assessors drawn from the 'great taxpayers', or by the personal declaration of each member of the public. The whole question of methods of tax levy is worth considering on its own. But in Saragossa a special situation arose. Members of the middle and lower ranks of the community, 'the small taxpayers', organized themselves into a group to oppose the system of assessment by decision, claiming that this discriminated against them. Both sides appealed to the arbitration of the Crown, and the debate even found its way into rabbinical Responsa. [38] The 'great taxpayers', members of the aristocratic families of Alconstantini, de la Caballeria, Ibn Daud, Alazar and others, aspired to control the communal leadership. It is reasonable

[36] BAER, *ibidem*.
[37] BAER, *History*, I, pp. 205 ff., II, pp. 56 ff.
[38] RASHBA, III, (Leghorn Press), 1778, No. 394; see BAER, I, p. 222.

to suppose that their ambition to hold the reins was stronger than the will of the middling and small men, the 'small taxpayers', to reach a decision. The attempt of the 'faction group', as it is called in the written records, to change the system of tax levy should be regarded as an effort to remedy an existing communal situation rather than an attempt to seize power. Most of the community were shopkeepers and small craftsmen. The tendency to organize on the part of the craftsmen was on a parallel with organisation into groups for charity, welfare, mutual aid, prayer and good deeds. Such association is noticeable in the fourteenth century,[39] and some group regulations have come down to us. Among the merchants we have already mentioned the role of *draperos*, the cloth merchants, in communal leadership.

Compared with what we know about Aragon, our knowledge of Castile is slight. The publicly controlled 'Board of Elders' here took the form of a 'Closed Council' (*Consejo cerrado*) composed solely of members of distinguished families; it had complete control of communal affairs. This regime, oligarchical in nature, received support from the Castilian monarchs,[40] who saw in it an important force. Its force, however, was not always strong enough to withstand popular pressure in those turbulent days in Castile. There were periods when the power of the aristocratic families declined. This board of elders made itself responsible for all public appointments, including the Jewish religious court judges, the *dayanim*.[41]

The list of Jewish public office-holders in Spain is considerable, and shows unmistakably that there was efficient leadership in public affairs. The leadership was executive, but often took on the extra tasks of controlling Jewish public arrangements and supervising public and private morals. In the Catalonian communities public business was transacted and managed by trustees (*secretarii*), also called *mukadamin* (*adelantados*). With them worked 'sin magistrates' (*berurei averot*), a typically Catalonian institution which was transferred after the Expulsion from Spain to Jewish communities in the Ottoman Empire. The task of these magistrates was to punish offenders against religion and morals, especially in matters affecting the purity of the family. Alongside them worked magistrates of financial claims. Other communal officials were the charity commissioners and the scribe, whose job was to draw up documents and keep the public ledger. The trustees of the Barcelona community, together with the *dayanim*, had the important task of choosing the members of the Council by majority vote.[42] They in their turn were appointed by the Council for one or two years (not more). They were forbidden to

[39] On this, see below.
[40] BAER, *History*, I, p. 314.
[41] These were originally appointed for an unlimited time, but from the end of the thirteenth century for one year only.
[42] In Saragossa special arbitrators (a special electoral board) elected the council.

hold office without a break. And although they were the executive arm of the community they were dependent in most of their actions on the consent of the Council, as in laying out more than a certain sum of money or in sending emissaries to negotiate with the government in various matters, or in the appointment of beadles. The Rabbis attached great importance to the appointment of trustees and emphasized the necessity of selecting them with care.[43]

In comparison with what we know about Catalonia, our information on other parts of Spain is scarce. The *adelantados* in Aragon-Navarre were like the trustees of Castile.[44] Apparently, as councils were lacking in the kingdom of Castile, the *adelantados* were all-powerful in the leadership of the community. The overseers (*veedores*) seem to have had equal status with them. They apparently supervised public affairs with the *dayanim*. It is worthy of note that it was these publicly appointed overseers, who were proposed at the Valladolid meeting of 1432 as most suitable to head the Jewish public in the work of restoring the community and its institutions.[45] It is hard to define their functions precisely but conditions in the Castilian community in the fifteenth century suggest that they took the place of the *adelantados*. They were not public treasurers, whose functions are usually defined and who are mentioned in the same regulation. This regulation also mentions 'surveyors of public needs', whose functions are separate from those of the overseers and treasurers. Another holder of public office (apart from rabbis, Court Rabbis, mentioned above) was the *bedin* (*vedi, albedi, bedin, bedinus, albedin*),[46] who served as a sort of public prosecutor and supervisor of public order in the place. The idea may be connected with certain functions of the *Beth Din*, the court, that existed in Jewish Spain. By virtue of his post, he exacted fines imposed on offenders.[47] From the fourteenth century onwards the status of the *bedin* declined.

Within the leadership of the Jewish communities in Spain a special place is held by the Rabbi and the *dayanim*,[48] but they are somewhat outside the scope of the present discussion. We have, of course, devoted fitting attention already to the Rabbi, especially as a moral force and spiritual leader of the entire Jewish public. As far as Spanish-Jewish justice is concerned, we should pay particular attention to the *dayanim* who were a sort of lay judges appointed in Castile by the leading members of the community. It is reasonable to assume their existence in Aragon

[43] See BAER, *History*, II, p. 41.
[44] They are also *jurados* or *fideles*.
[45] See BAER, *JchS*, 2, pp. 280 ff.
[46] This post was found in several places in Aragon. The name may be a corruption of *Beth-Din* (court of law), in use among Jews.
[47] Cf. *Fuero of Castile*, BAER, *JchS*, 2, p. 37.
[48] See S. ASSAF, *Jewish Law-Courts and their Procedure after the Period of the Talmud* (Jerusalem, 1924) (Hebrew).

as well. In the course of time the job became an ordinary communal appointment, and fell into the hands of men not versed in Jewish Law. The Sages of Israel and those zealous for the Jewish faith came out in protest against the ignorance of the holders of the dayan's office, their lack of legal ability and their way of life.

We have scanty information about the methods of election of the office holders and about the nature of their ways. One description which is found in the Responsa literature,[49] runs as follows:

> And the berurim shall not consult with anybody, in the matter of the election of their successors; the berurim elected as from New Year can do nothing without the advice of the councillors; the councillors shall appoint others in their place from year to year; the berurim and the councillors, when their time shall come to appoint others in their stead, shall stand in hostages outside the city and shall eat their own food, until they conclude their agreement and declare by a congregational cantor in the synagogue at the hour of prayer: Such a one and such a one are appointed. The appointment of the berurim and the councillors shall not be done by majority rule; any one of the councillors and berurim who wants to appoint another in his stead—he may do so, even if his fellows do not agree with him in the appointment of that barur or councillor.

This rule, which was accepted in one community, suggests that there was a standard procedure in most of the communities of the kingdom of Aragon. But here we must notice that election is not by the will of the majority; one sees how appointed men kept the public leadership within a small circle of families.

The question arises whether we are to consider the elected-appointed men as *probi homines* of the Jewish public. As a rule the sources regard them as 'upright men', but they were not always so considered by the Sages of Israel.[50] Among them we more than once find violent men who intimidate the public to make it do their will. Against them fought the rabbis of Israel, the sages of the nation, its cabbalists and pietists. As a rule the leadership of the Jewish community was, as we have shown, a kind of social oligarchy, in which a group of 'aristocratic' families found means of keeping the direction of public affairs in its hands.

Social arrangements found detailed expression in the statutes that the Jewish communities of Spain laid down for the management of their affairs and the determining of their ways of life. This was a public that knew what it had to face and adapted a Jewish way of life to surrounding conditions. The public statutes dealt not only with problems for internal

---

[49] RASHBA, V, No. 284.
[50] See for instance the Responsa of Rashba, VII, No. 450 (Hebrew). "The seven upright men of the town who are everywhere mentioned are not seven men chosen for their wisdom, wealth and honour, but seven ordinary, solid citizens put up by the public *parnasim* as over their affairs and they are like wardens to them." See B. Z. DINUR, *Israel in the Diaspora*, II, 2 (Tel-Aviv, 1956), p. 326 (Hebrew).

jurisdiction; they also fixed bounds and limits to personal relations, to the duties of the individual to society, and stated the individual's duties within his community. These statutes were in force for generations, and Jews expelled from Spain transplanted them to their new communities in North Africa, in the Ottoman Empire, and wherever else they settled, and built a new life. In Spain these statutes gained the appreciation and approval of the civil authorities who considered them an important means of ensuring public order. We should remember that initially and most importantly each congregation fixed its own statutes and regulations, as the Ribash (R. Yitzhak b. Sheshet) says: 'Every community *in the kingdom makes by royal patent and enforces its own statutes'!* [51] These statutes aided religious and social discipline in the Jewish community. It is at all events worthy of note that the Jewish community found little occasion to use its wide powers of punishment (which at certain periods included criminal jurisdiction) to impose public discipline.[52] Judgments handed down by Jewish *dayanim* who went by the Torah and the Halacha, were their guiding light, and were recognized, confirmed and carried out by the Christian government and its officials.

In Spain we see again the voluntary element: each Jewish individual, belonging to his nation, accepted the yoke of the commandments and of public duty. All this was what gave Spanish Jewry its character.

4.

There is another aspect of public life on which we would dwell, and this too draws sustenance from the Jewish voluntary tradition. We have already noted how realistic the Jews were in adapting a Jewish way of life to surrounding conditions. Yet within this framework they could not always find satisfaction for all the needs of an organized community and of individuals. The need was filled by welfare and mutual help, the efforts of individuals or groups who combined to give charity and do works of mercy. When we contemplate the few records that have come down to us of these activities, we realize *on* what deep foundations they rested. Withal we must emphasize that nearly all the associations sprang from the lower classes of society, who felt the need for mutual aid and went on to fulfil the sacred duty of humanity reciprocally and together. It is impossible to be sure when these organizations began. First, perhaps, were the craft fellowships that joined together in charitable work. When such fellowships desired to pray together, they founded their own synagogues, thus giving added expression to the bonds that united them in

[51] See BAER, *History*, II, p. 77; Responsa, No. 272.
[52] On the problem of punishment see BAER, *History*, Reg. s.v. Law. See also B. Z. DINUR, *op. cit.* (n. 50 *supra*), pp. 331, 338.

the jointed fulfilment of the duty of charity. Thus we find in Saragossa [53] a fellowship of 'Doers of Mercy', another of 'Pursuers of Righteousness', a third of 'Nights of Vigil' for prayer, intercession and moral reform of the world. The 'Grave diggers' of Huesca left statutes which have survived [54] and teach something of this group devoted to works of mercy, mutual help and reciprocal duty. This combination into groups to do works of genuine mercy is also found in Christian society in Spain and sometimes among the Conversos too.[55] The Conversos of Spain drew from the source this Jewish tradition of mercy and charity.

It remains to mention among voluntary work the steps the public took to organise Torah study. There was a special tax system for this purpose,[56] and there was a method of individual dedication for *Talmud Torah*, by which people devoted a part of their property, their capital and their income for the support of scholars and sages. They would similarly support the poor and contribute to other public needs.[57] Of special interest are the public ransoming of captives and 'bringing in the bride'. Until the Expulsion from Spain we do not find among Spanish Jewry any organization whose specific aim is the ransoming of Jewish captives or bringing brides to the marriage canopy by helping to provide their dowries.[58] Every individual in Israel helped according to his means to fulfil these sacred duties, these *mitzvoth*. The needs of Spanish Jewry were answered from within.

* * *

The story of the Jews in Spain, how they organized their society and how they lived together within it, is embroidered on a background of Jewish life—the rich and full life that maintained them. Their endurance of political vicissitudes, culminating in the expulsion from Spain in 1492, is a story in itself. Their inner strength, the close-woven web of their public life, the organization and social relations of their public life, the organization and social relations that prevailed among them—all these were the heritage of Spanish Jewry, which sustained and upheld them in their wanderings after the Expulsion and stood them in good stead in their exile.

---

[53] See BAER, *JchS*, 1, pp. 855 ff.; et Reg. s.v. Confratria. And see F. BAER, "Ursprung der Chewra", *Zeitschrift für jüdische Wohlwartspflege*, 1 (1929), pp. 241–247.

[54] *JchS*, 1, pp. 229 ff., pp. 641 ff.

[55] See H. BEINART, *Conversos on Trial before the Inquisition* (Tel-Aviv, 1965), pp. 49 ff., and the bibliography there (Hebrew).

[56] See, for example, the statutes of Valladolid of 1432, n. 21 *supra*.

[57] See BAER, *JchS*, 2, pp. 156 ff.

[58] See H. BEINART, "A Hebrew Formularium from Fifteenth Century Spain," *Sefunot*, 5 (1961), pp. 80 ff. (Hebrew).

CECIL ROTH

JEWISH SOCIETY IN THE RENAISSANCE ENVIRONMENT

THIS article will deal principally with the Renaissance environment in Italy. Italy was the essential home of the movement, somewhat indeterminate in period as well as in nature, known as the Renaissance: a term which is applied, as has been said, 'to describe anything vague but splendid that happened in Italy between Dante and Michelangelo'. The reasons why the movement was centered in Italy especially were varied. They include the central position of the Peninsula from the geographical viewpoint, in close contact with Greece and the Levant and Germany at the same time, and serving as the vehicle through which the ideas as well as the commodities of these areas were interchanged; the fact that it attracted so many refugee Byzantine scholars even before the Fall of Constantinople in 1453; the omnipresence throughout the land of the physical relics as well as the romantic memories of the Roman Empire and the classical world; the financial affluence which was widespread among the mercantile classes; the humanising influence of the Papacy in Rome. But one element which had a particularly great influence was the fragmentation of the Peninsula, politically deplorable though it may have been. For it seems to be an historical rule that small states and principalities of kindred blood and language living within a small area indulge in a cultural as well as political rivalry, leading sometimes to brilliant results, as was the case also with the kingdoms of the Taifas in Moslem Spain in the eleventh and twelfth centuries. Such states cannot afford to spurn the collaboration of minority elements such as the Jews, who now therefore tend to flourish and participate in the general cultural activity. This fact explains in part the cultural activity of the Jews in Renaissance Italy.

It is significant that such participation in cultural life in monarchical South Italy—the kingdoms of Naples and of Sicily—was far less marked, although the numbers of the Jewish community were in all probability far higher: for cultural activity in such circumstances tended to be centered perhaps excessively in the capital cities, where the encouragement afforded by the presence of the royal court did not suffice to compensate for the stimulus of civic rivalry. The monarchies had moreover in Jewish history a potentially fatal characteristic. It is arguable that in medieval Jewish history absolute rulers tended to be more favourable to the Jews than republican governments—which in the circumstances of the time were inevitably 'aristocratic' and mercantilistic, highly sensitive therefore to any element which might savour of competition. On the other hand, the policy of the national monarchies was all-embracing and brooked no exception. In a politically divided country, an edict of expulsion was not necessarily fatal to Jewish life. Even in Germany, whose record was particularly harsh in this respect, the exiles from one autonomous city or territory could always find another to receive them after their expulsion, though seldom indeed gratuitously; on the other hand, the successive expulsions from unified France, England and Spain were comprehensive and (partly for this same reason) 'final'. Similarly, although temporary expulsions of Jews were known now and again all over Italy, only (or nearly so) those on a major scale under Spanish influences, in the Two Sicilies, at the close of the fifteenth and the middle of the sixteenth centuries, were so to speak universal and definite: indeed, even today there is barely any Jewish settlement in the country south of Rome—precisely the area where, in the classical period and the Darks Ages, the Jewish communities were most prominent.

The nature of the Jewish community in the Renaissance environment in Italy was unique of its sort. At the time when the center of Jewish life in the country was Apulia, with its flourishing textile and dyeing industries which all but constituted a Jewish monopoly, there are few traces of Jews in the north of the country, though the community of Rome, under the tolerant aegis of the Popes, had an uninterrupted existence from classical times onwards. It was no doubt the commercial exclusiveness of the northern cities, which regarded the Jews as mercantile rivals, which was responsible for this state of affairs. In the thirteenth century however there were two simultaneous developments. On the one hand, the economic role of the Jews of the south changed, on the other, their tranquillity was disturbed. Meanwhile in the North, with its almost feverish combination of manufacturing activities at home with banking activities abroad, a shortage of capital began to make itself felt for petty domestic operations. To put it in another way, the Italians (Tuscans, Lombards and so on) who were now to become the banking magnates of the western world, decided that the sordid activities of money-lending at home were beneath their dignity and therefore contrary to their religious principles, for the Church had now set its face determinedly against the institution of usury—that is, interest, whether great or small. The result was what one may term a credit-squeeze in the North Italian cities. To remedy this, Jewish magnates, who found themselves unable to compete further with their Gentile rivals in the textile industry and trade, began to invest their money in 'loan-Banks'—in effect, pawn-broking establishments, in the cities great and small in the center and the north (and later in the south) of the country. It was not a simultaneous process: from first to last, the process continues for something like a century and a half or more. But the upshot was that in the end the North Italian cities, 'judenrein' for generations, now began to harbour Jewish communities, grouped about a nucleus of affluent loan-bankers who had entered into a contract *(condotta)* with the civic authorities for a term of years. This is, roughly, the story of the origins of almost all the Jewish communities of the Peninsula which afterwards were to attain such distinction. It must be born in mind however that none was of any great importance numerically. At their heyday, hardly any of them probably exceeded a couple of thousands in number; the majority probably no more than a couple of hundred. On the other hand, it must be born in mind that the Italian cities were what we would today consider to be of trivial size: Florence in its heyday would not have exceeded one hundred thousand souls.

The origin of these communities had one remarkable result which had far-reaching implications. These Italian Jewish groups had—what was rare in Jewish history—what may be termed an aristocratic basis. Although merchants, pedlars, craftsmen, and so on made their presence felt at a later stage, and although there was of course from the beginning a proletarian element dependent on the magnates, from whom the latter drew their employees and their servants, the characteristic feature of all these groups was their dependence on the central nucleus of necessarily affluent Jewish loan-bankers. This was the case to the same extent probably at only one other period in Jewish history, from the twelfth century onwards, when in England, France and Germany the Jews were virtually restricted to money-lending and the Jewish communities were centered on the group of moneyed usurers who in effect acted as unofficial administrators of a government money-lending monopoly, earning all the obloquy but forced to disgorge their profits at frequent intervals to the central Treasury. It is of course obvious that money-lending (by whatever name it is called) is hardly an exacting occupation, in terms of time and energy. On the whole, the client seeks out the financier, not vice versa, and once the transaction is completed the latter merely waits for the profits to accumulate. Hence in both of the areas which have been mentioned the Jewish magnates had ample leisure for their own affairs, and in both cases this had highly interesting results on their intellectual life. In Italy, a highly developed intellectual environment, Jewish interests could not be restricted to Jewish studies and texts only and inevitably became extended to a far wider area, in which secular influences were always discernible and sometimes dominant.

This was emphasised here by a further factor. In the Western world of the past few generations, the average Jew was of 'foreign' extraction: he or his immediate ancestors had more or less recently arrived from overseas, or (in most cases) from Eastern Europe, and this 'foreignness' was accentuated by the fact that his immediate origin was from a teeming Jewish quarter cut off by social life and sometimes by language from the general environment. This feature has coloured the accepted historical picture of the Jew everywhere. But it is important to note that in relation to the Italian Jews this was the case to only a very limited extent. The nucleus of Italian Jewry, centering on Rome, was descended from the Jewish communities established in the country in Roman Imperial or even Republican times; it was not far from the truth, in view of the many invaders and pilgrims and visitors from abroad who modified the general population, to say that they were the oldest recognisable element of the Italian people. There were other elements, particularly in the north of the country, who were of more recent arrival, but they tended to become assimilated with quite remarkable rapidity to the main body. Hence the Italian Jew, however Jewish, was at the same time profoundly Italian, bound with the general body of his compatriots by ties of culture and of language. There was no need for him to learn Italian before he could immerse himself in the general cultural life—he was Italian-speaking and Italian-thinking already. To this must be added the some-what curious (and in some ways inexplicable) sociological phenomenon that the Italian Jewish communities were always so restricted in size, as has been pointed out before. The presence of the Jews may have impinged itself on the notice of the visitor, but there were in fact very few of them proportionately—not enough, certainly, to set up a social or a cultural Ghetto in the days before the formal Ghetto was established in the wake of the Counter Reformation. Thus the influence on them of their environment was particularly intense: to a degree perhaps unknown again in history until the advent of emancipation in Western Europe in the nineteenth century.

Together with this must be considered the nature of Renaissance society itself. Because of the fragmentation of the Peninsula, the political units were small, and because the political units were small, there was no place for an aristocracy of feudal aloofness or for a court of Byzantine splendour. The Dukes, tyrants, signori, magnifici of the Italian Renaissance were generally speaking bourgeois who had raised themselves to the lead by dint of having somewhat greater wealth, a shade more ability, or a few less scruples. In the fullest extent they were *primi inter pares*, still busying themselves with their commercial operations and in some cases still sending their sons abroad to learn business. Their very residences displayed this free and easy relation with the city at large: 'Palazzo' in Italy did not convey at any time the same sense as Palace does in English; and it is noteworthy that the only Florentine palazzo which is reminiscent of the Transalpine palace was that of the politically unimportant Pitti—not of the Medici, who exercised their benevolent despotism from what was in fact an average Town House like other town houses, in the Via Larga, subsequently the Palazzo Riccardi. Moreover, these same wealthy families not unfrequently managed to acquire a Cardinal's Hat for junior scions of the clan, with the result that the Papal Curia at its most resplendent was largely composed of typical members of typical bourgeois houses, whose tradition they shared and perpetuated. Of course, there was another category of the local rulers—those whose position was based on the successful careers of soldiers of fortune or *condottieri*, whose function in the city was not wholly different from that of the loan-bankers operating under contracts of a somewhat different type; in social life however there was not much to chose between the two categories and their daily existence. Hence there was no insuperable social barrier between the Jewish loan-banker who led Jewish society and the Christian banker on a larger scale who had established his domination by some means or the other over the city as a whole. They inhabited homes of the same type, even though that of the Christian magnate was more magnificent, conducted lives of the same sort, had interests along the same lines, and even when those interests diverged they were conducted in much the same way and received much the same flavour. For an Anglo-French sovereign or a feudal nobleman to have relations with a Jew except *de haut en bas* would have been incredible. In Italy, on the other hand, there was nothing unnatural in members of the San Miniato family of loan-bankers sending gifts of venison to Piero de Medici, or one of the Norsa being the gaming companion of the ruler of Ferrara, or of Jews and Christians taking part together as equals in the memorable philosophical discussions in the home of Pico della Mirandola in Florence.

It is against this background that the share of the Jews in Italian life at the period of the Renaissance and the position of the Jews in Renaissance society must be considered.

For the Italian Jewish society in the age of the Renaissance was, it may be said, a Renaissance society in miniature. The latter centered upon a coterie of wealthy magnates, with a household of somewhat greater wealth or adroitness at its head. It was around this family's residence, not necessarily finer than the rest, that not only the society but also the cultural life of the town was centered. A budding artist would look to them for patronage; a visiting poet or writer would come to them in the first place in an endeavour to arouse their interest or generosity; the family Church would be embellished by them with paintings and sculptures in order to demonstrate not only their devotion to the family's patron saint but even more so, their own wealth, impor-

tance and taste. Their villas in the country, built in many cases with
ostentatious simplicity, emphasised their modest superiority even beyond
the city walls. Other members of their family or relatives by marriage
alliances, as well as their competitors in business and social life, emulated
them, each of them having his own cultural circle of the same type.

Not far off would be the *Via dei Giudei*, where the Jewish loan-bankers
were centered. There was not so much difference in fifteenth century
Italy between the wide street and the narrow street, and the houses
were of much the same general type in the one and the other. The larger
were occupied by the one or two principal loan-bankers. Their households too were ample. Ecclesiastical legislation forbade them to have
Christians in their employment, since this would make those who had
been redeemed by the Crucifixion subject to those who were reputedly
responsible for it. This was certainly not meticulously obeyed at the time,
least of all in tolerant, sceptical Italy; yet the members of the households
of the Jewish bankers would be for the most part Jews, if only for con-
venience. The interiors were luxurious, and the furnishings of much
the same type as in the great palazzi around the corner. True, there
would be no wistful images of the Madonna or paintings of the saints
to adorn the walls. Yet it would be a mistake to imagine that the houses
were bare and oblivious to aesthetic values. There were certainly
decorative paintings, frequently of Biblical scenes. That there were
portraits too is almost certain, tho' none of this period have survived;
from the early years of the sixteenth century, in any case, the outstanding
Jewish patricians indulged in the Renaissance luxury of commissioning
portrait-medals, by artists of the calibre of Pastorino dei Pastorini.
For their ornemental metal work they patronised the most eminent
masters, although the wilful Il Caparra (Miccolô Grosso) stubbornly
refused to work for the Florentine Jews however much they importuned
him. Inevitably, they maintained friendly relations with artists whom
they patronised, and when 'Il Doceno' (Cristafano Gherardi) was in
Bologna, he went about so much in the company of Jews that he was
mistaken for one himself. On the other hand, it is by no means sure that
all the artists patronised by these Jewish magnates were non-Jews.
That Jewish artists existed at this period is attested by documentary
evidence. In Spain certainly they did not abstain even from Christian
ecclesiastical art, and without doubt the same was sometimes the case
in Italy as well, though in such circumstances anonimity, with resultant
irrecognisability, was hardly to be avoided.

One branch of art in which the Jewish magnates were able to indulge
themselves freely was the art of the illuminated manuscript. In the same
way as the Renaissance humanist in Italy desired to have his volumes
written by the most skilful scribe on the finest parchment and adorned
by the most consummate artist, so the Jewish magnate—certainly no

less fond of literature than his neighbour— followed his example. Such Latin books as he might have possessed were of the same type—indistinguishable then, and indistinguishable today, from those in general use, though it may be mentioned parenthetically that many bear tokens of Jewish ownership in the form of inscriptions in Hebrew, not necessarily inserted by loan-bankers who obtained them in pledge. The Hebrew books were however in a different category. The materials and bindings of these were similar to those of the books which circulated in the environment: externally indeed an Italian Jewish prayer-book in Hebrew and a Latin missal of the late fifeteenth century are all but identical.

For the writing an Italian school of Hebrew scribes came into being, who developed a Hebrew script of much the same general type as the humanistic characters now in vogue for Latin and Italian Mss., and to some extent showing its influence. Now the illuminator was called in, sometimes Jew and sometimes Gentile—in the latter case, a person who would be fairly carefully trained in Jewish usages and religious law so as to ensure that he should not be guilty of some gaffe. The resultant work would sometimes be of the same high quality and standard from the aesthetic point of view as the finest of the period: one may instance the Rothschild miscellany in the Jerusalem Museum, the De 'Rossi Arbáa Turim in the Vatican Library in Rome, and the great Avicenna of the University of Bologna—a work of such magnificence that it demonstrates the remarkably high social standing and economic resources of Jewish physicians of the period, for only a physician would have used a volume of this nature. Sometimes, the initial pages of these manuscripts would exhibit the family badges (it is too much to say coats-of-arms) of the families for whom they were executed, in precisely the same way as the non-Jewish manuscripts of the period. On the other hand, all such works were not necessarily executed for Jewish use. For, in the same way as Jews were interested in non-Hebraic literature, so Christian humanists went to great pains and expense to enrich their libraries with Hebrew classics. Coats of arms are significant sometimes here as well, for a number of magnificently illuminated Hebrew manuscripts bear the heraldic emblemes which were certainly not Jewish. But most convincing is the Hebrew Bible in the Laurenzian Library in Florence, finely illuminated by Francesco d'Antonio del Cherico, and depicting on the first page God the Father, the Son, and the Holy Ghost, with apposite Hebrew wording. Here is a striking exemplification of the generous Judaeo-Christian symbiosis at this period.

There was one respect in which the aristocratic structure of the microcosm of the Jewish communities of the Renaissance period was in sharp contrast with the macrocosm of their environment. This was due in part to their relative size, in part was inherent in what may be termed the Jewish ethos. In the greater society, there was possible a separation between spiritual and intellectual functions. Humanistic scholars and scribes could flourish independently of Church and chapel and the maecenas could at the same time support his household humanist on the one side and the parish priest or his private confessor on the other; the two parallel aspects of life were carried on disjointly and even contradictorily, what the householder was told by his spiritual advisers not necessarily bearing any great relation to what he was taught by his domestic tutor or scholastic mentor. In the case of the Jewish community, however, circumstances were different. The synagogue, essentially a place of study as well as prayer, was not the same in nature as the Church, essentially a place of spiritual indoctrination; the rabbi, basically an instructor or teacher, was very different from the priest, the custodian of divine mysteries and source of spiritual guidance. Moreover, the Jewish magnate was not so wealthy as to be able to support both teacher and preacher. Hence the two functions had to be combined. His household would include no doubt a single scholarly employee engaged mainly as a teacher for the children, but qualified also to guide the adults, who no doubt would at the same time eke out his livelihood by acting as a scribe, and fulfil by dint of his superior learning rabbinical functions in such matters as deciding a law-suit or presiding over the complicated details of a divorce. The Italian 'Rabbis' of the Renaissance period were on the whole persons of this type: talmudic scholars, accomplished Hebraists, with a reading knowledge also of Latin and conceivably even a smattering of Greek, able to compose Hebrew verses (for the teaching of this art was regarded as one of the basic duties of the instructor at this period) as well as to give their pupils lessons in the sober art of dancing, and knowing enough of the fashionable philosophies to be able to enter into intelligent discussion on the subject with their patrons' non-Jewish clients or guests. Their personal characters were not necessarily of the highest, but their versatility could have been remarkable in any setting. The result was that there now emerged in Italian Jewry a sequence of Rabbis, of wide external learning and therefore wide external views, whose Rabbinical writings and Talmudical decisions were imbued with the spirit of the Renaissance, unlike the great scholars beyond the Alps, whose Talmudic learning was unquestionably greater but whose outlook was on the whole restricted to this. At the same time, the many Italian Jewish physicians, educated 'in medicine and philosophy' at the local university (generally that of Padua) after studying Latin for this purpose, and accustomed to discuss matters cultural and philosophical with their numerous aristocratic patients, were at the same time Talmudically educated and served as Rabbis of their communities. Thus the circumstances of Renaissance Jewish society in Italy helped to evolve erudite and cultured Rabbis, almost of the 'modern' type, whose decisions (which they expressed in impeccable literary style) were sometimes conspicuously affected by the legal customs and outlooks of their environments.

On the other hand, there was sometimes a less desirable outcome. The domestic Rabbis to whom reference has been made were naturally expected to give decisions in support of their patrons (who themselves were generally sufficiently erudite to collaborate or to direct) or their patrons' interests, and not unfrequently showed remarkable ingenuity and persistence in doing so. The collections of Responsa produced in connexion with the business quarrels or domestic disputes of some of the Italian Jewish financial magnates of the time, neither side ever acknowledging that it was worsted and both continuing to wring the last particle of evidence or scholastic support, are among the more significant productions of the Italian Jewry of the Renaissance period. It is significant— for this could never have happened in any other environment— that in some instances in the mid-sixteenth century, the same case might engage the attention not only of the Jewish rabbinical authorities but also of the Christian jurists, to whom the party which found itself worsted in the preliminary encounter might in due course appeal.

The modest size of the states of Renaissance Italy had the inevitable result, that their rulers and aristocratic classes sought intellectual as well as physical diversion wherever they could—even within the neighbouring Jewish community, almost on the doorsteps of their palazzi, with whom their confessors told them to have no contact. Henry VIII of England could inform the Florentine Republic, when it implored him for help at the time of their heroic struggle against Pope and Emperor in 1529/30, that the Florentines with their wealth were better able to help him than he them. That may have been so. But the English or French monarchs ruled over relatively vast territories, even to progress through which took a great deal of time, and they could find social contacts and diversion in a very numerous nobility however limited their interests were. In Renaissance Italy on the other hand the geographical radius of the state and the numerical potentialities of social contact were limited. Hence the upper and ruling classes sought for diversion as well as information wherever they might find it; and the sceptical Italian mind was not seriously or at all events permanently perturbed by the comminations of spiritual advisers if they deprecated such procedure. On the other hand, the unbelievers found under such circumstances an outlet for their abilities—even such abilities as would elsewhere have been suppressed, and did not manifest themselves in Europe as a whole for another four centuries, in the period of Emancipation. Jewish musicians for instance make their appearance now throughout Italy, some of them not merely instrumentalists but also composers. This was the case especially in Mantua under the Gonzaga,

who were so devoted to pageantry of all sorts that they inevitably had
to exploit for the purpose all possible sources. Some of the composers
even had their compositions published, on the whole no better and no
worse than the productions of their unimportant contemporaries. An
exception was Salamone de' Rossi, whose work is now beginning to
receive more and more recognition. Similarly the then allied art of
dancing: Jewish dancing masters were known almost universally in the
Peninsula, however much the Church officially disapproved and one
of them, Guglielmo Ebreo of Pesaro, highly esteemed at the courts of
Ferrara, Florence, Milan and Naples, wrote a memorable treatise on
the dancing art. Whereas Salamone de' Rossi endeavoured to extend
his genius to the embellishment of synagogal chant, necessarily there
was nothing Jewish about Guglielmo Ebreo other than his name. Most
remarkable was the manner in which the Court theatre in Mantua, in
which the Gonzaga took particular pride, had recourse to Jewish
collaboration—first presumably for performances of the Jewish Purim-
Plays for the diversion of the Gentile spectators (as was known elsewhere
as well), and later, when their histrionic ability was proved, as a sort of
standing theatrical company whose services were drawn upon on important occasions, to celebrate a Ducal wedding or for the entertainment
of a distinguished visitor. And it was inevitable that, in the genius of
Leone de' Sommi at least, they should have gone on from this to writing
plays, in the vapid style of the period it is true, and to the more difficult
art of stage-direction, of which we have the monument in his *Dialoghi
dell'Arte Rappresentativa*. Let it be added here, as a further instance of the
symbiosis possible at this period in Renaissance Italy (and surely
nowhere else), that he was at the same time a Hebrew poet, founder
of a synagogue, a skilled Torah-scribe, and attempted to introduce
contemporary dramatic fashions (if not the drama as such) into Hebrew,
in the first Hebrew play in the modern sense that has been preserved.

The art of printing, which made it possible for the intellectual
process of the Renaissance to establish itself the more firmly, illustrates
more than anything else the reciprocal influence. There is vague record
of a Hebrew printer (learning his craft it is true from a Gentile) in
Avignon as early as 1444. When printing in the Hebrew language
actually began is uncertain: the fact that the earliest volumes preserved
are of 1475 is not conclusive evidence, in view of the vast degree of
destruction of Hebrew literature in the sixteenth century, as a result
of the Catholic Reaction. But here too we find a constant interplay
and interchange. It was a Jewish printer who produced the fine Naples
edition of the *Divina Comedia* in 1477.

In Spain, the Hebrew printer Solomon Zalmati, a silversmith by
trade, was associated with the printing of the Saragossan Manual of
1486 as well as of the theological works of the Bishop of Cristopoli.

The art of printing was first introduced into Portugal by Jews, who besides Hebrew books were responsible for the publication in Latin and in Spanish of the invaluable (and complicated) astronomical tables of Abraham Zacuto, used even by Columbus. The Soncino family, the most significant in the history of early Hebrew printing, published also works in Italian and Latin in half a dozen places in the Marches of Ancona—sometimes under the patronage of and with the collaboration of the City Fathers. Similarly, the Usque family of Ferrara published not only Hebrew books and books in Spanish for the use of their correligionists, but even the earliest known edition of the Portuguese classic *Menina y Moca* by Bernadim Ribeiro—whom some scholars conjecture to have been himself a Jew, or at least a Marrano of Jewish birth. Yet on the other hand the most prolific printer of Hebrew works in the sixteenth century, to whom is due the publication of the editions which set the standard for many of the greatest Hebrew classics, was the Christian from Antwerp Daniel Bomberg, who had settled in Venice. Dr. Jacob Narcaria of Riva di Trento, besides working happily at Hebrew printing under the patronage of the Cardinal Madrucci, seems to have been the 'official' publisher for certain of the literature associated with the Church Council of Trent. The fact is that in a society such as that of Italy in the fifteenth and sixteenth century genius had to be used and potentialities explored wherever they were available. It was a question of *la carrière ouverte aux talents*—even the talents of the Synagogue.

There is no need to trace here in any detail the stages whereby this symbiosis was brought to a close, but the general lines of the process are highly significant. Very briefly, the Church, scared by the process of the Reformation, in which it wrongly suspected Jewish collaboration and even incitement, decided in the middle of the sixteenth century that the old ecclesiastical legislation which attempted to break off all social contact between Jew and Christian should be rigorously implemented. The result was Paul IV's Bull *cum nimis absurdum* of 1555, which continued to guide Papal policy and to determine the fate of the Italian Jews until the French Revolution, and in some areas even after. The new legislation was not put into force everywhere immediately, nor were its results immediately apparent. But in due course the reaction triumphed, and the nature of Italian Jewry changed. Up to this time, the characteristic of Italian Jewish history had been the rich interplay of the Renaissance life; henceforth, the place of this was to be taken by the Ghetto system and the degradation which accompanied it. Italian Jewish society at the close of the Middle Ages began to show something of the spirit of the rich collaboration, results of the infusion of Jewish ability into the life of their environment, which was to be renewed in the nineteenth century. As in 1933 the reaction against the Jews as a group was artificial, and the environment as a whole suffered as well as they themselves. It is a classical instance of the power of ill-considered legislation to create a problem and to inflict not only an injustice on a minority but also at the same time irreparable loss on the generality.

BIBLIOGRAPHICAL NOTE

The material for this article has been largely derived from the following works:

CECIL ROTH, *The Jews in the Renaissance* (Philadelphia, 1959; paper-back edition, New York, 1965).
— *History of the Jews in Italy* (Philadelphia, 1946; also available in Hebrew).
A. MILANO, *Storia degli ebrei in Italia* (Turin, 1963).
— *Bibliotheca Storica Italo Judaica* (Florence, 1954; and supplement, Florence, 1964), which contains in a readily accessible arrangement most of the subsidiary studies bearing on the subject.

A bibliography by O.K. RABINOWICZ of my own writings, which touch on various aspects of it, is to be found at the close of the volume *Remember the Days* presented to me in 1966.

S. ETTINGER

THE HASSIDIC MOVEMENT — REALITY AND IDEALS

T HE Hassidic movement appeared among the Jewish people in
Europe on the brink of a decisive change in their history, at a
time when the Jews were beginning to take part in the social and
cultural world that surrounded them. The Jewish community as a
religious-social corporation, the thousand-year old corporate framework
to which individual Jews had a duty to belong, was beginning to collapse
under pressures from within and from without. Outside, jurists were
claiming in the name of absolutist principles that all corporations injured
the authority of the ruler, and that the extensive autonomy of the Jewish
community was making it a "state within the state". While inside,
'enlightened' Jews were complaining that the strict communal corporate
regime gave the upper hand to an oligarchy, which exploited the ordinary
members of the community and deliberately kept them from closer ties
with the Christian environment.

The difference in general political trends between the countries of
Central and Western Europe and those of Eastern Europe, especially the
difference in the situation of the Jewish populations of these two regions,
led to a contrast in development between eastern and western Jewry, a
contrast which grew so sharp that by the middle of the 19th century
their ways seemed to have parted completely.

In the west the Jewish community was undermined. One reason was
that the authorities withdrew their support. A more important reason
was that the socially and politically active Jews, who were able to achieve
some standing and influence in the society around them, began to
despise the 'narrow' Jewish society with its struggles and its honours and
titles and at most were prepared to regard it as a voluntary association
for the organisation of religious life. The centre of gravity of these Jews'
lives was outside and beyond the community. Their language, their culture, their ambitions were those of their Christian environment. Whereas
in Eastern Europe the authorities continued substantially to support the
Jewish corporation. The few 'educated' Jews there who called for a
merger with the life outside were regarded as rebels, or even traitors to
their people, and the formal cohesion of Jewish society grew.

The Hassidic movement that was to be the chief cause and main bearer of these trends peculiar to Eastern Europe, appeared in Podolia, a distant province of south-east Poland, at a period of decline and disintegration in that country. Jewish society there was split from within, and in the grip of violent ferments. In Polish society the upper hand was gained by those opposed to the status of the central institutions of the autonomous Jewish organisation. They claimed that continuation of the recognition of those Jewish institutions is a further proof of weakness of the central government. The result of this criticism was that government recognition of the autonomous institutions was cancelled and in 1764 they were dispersed. There is not the slightest doubt that the Hassidic movement helped to unify Jewish society in Eastern Europe from the organisational point of view and that in religion and ideas it was a revival.

Hassidism means devout piety, communion with God, special devotion by man to the service of his Creator. Even before the 18th century several movements or circles had been named Hassidic. The best-known were the groups of Hassidim faithful to Judaism in the days of persecution by Antiochus Epiphanes in the 2nd century B.C., and the Ashkenazi Hassidim of the 12th-13th centuries. The new Hassidism we are considering here is known as the Besthian Hassidism, after its originator. Rabbi Israel Baal-Shem-Tov (the Besht for short) was born in Podolia in or about 1700, apparently of humble origins and in early life worked at a variety of unskilled trades. He then became locally famous as a faith-healer, who knew how to heal the sick with magic formulae and amulets (hence the appellation Baal-Shem-Tov— Master of the good name). He gave up seclusion and took on the mantle of leader at the end of the 1730s, and in the 1740s gathered around him a group of supporters and admirors who took up his way of serving God. His personality is veiled from us by a haze of legends; one of the few surviving authentic documents on him is the letter he wrote to his brother-in-law in Eretz Israel in 1750 describing his mystical experience—how his soul rose up to Heaven, and how he met the Messiah there. On that occasion the Besht asked the Messiah when he would come and received the famous answer: "When your streams spread out", that is to say when the Hassidic teachings of the Besht spread among the people.

When the Besht died in 1760 he left behind him a genuine movement, although it is hard to estimate its size at that time. At its head was placed not the Besht's chief disciple, who preserved the Besht's words and wrote down his teaching, Rabbi Jacob Joseph of Polnoy, the man who had been closer to the late leader for many years, but a relatively new man, Rabbi Dov-Ber of Meseritz (the 'Great Magid'[1] of the

---

[1] "Magid"—preacher to the public at large, a permanent and honoured post in communities; the Magid was considered part of the recognised religious hierarchy.

Hassidim). During the Great Magid's leadership (1760–1772), Hassidism spread over wide areas of Eastern Europe, became a real public force and came to its first big clash with the existing Jewish leadership in Poland-Lithuania.

There is something novel in the rapid spread of the Hassidic movement and especially in the fact that it remained a legitimate part of a society so tradition-bound and conservative as the Jewish, whose leaders at those time waged war against it. No wonder so many scholars have tried to explain the phenomenon. The first serious student of Hassidism, Simon Dubnow[2], suggested that "by an immense psychic influence, Hassidism created a type of believer to whom feeling was more important than external observance"—as opposed to what had hitherto been the order of importance in Jewish communities. In addition, "Hassidism was the answer to the stress and sorrow of Jewish public life, for although it could not change the objective conditions of hardship in which the Jews lived, it created an ideal world for them, a world in which the despised Jew was master". In Dubnow's view Hassidism also answered the spiritual needs of the individual believer and the aspirations of the generation by transferring the solution of its problems to the world of the imagination.

Ben-Zion Dinur[3] opposes this view which tries to explain the success of Hassidism by saying that "history answered the needs of the generation", and he regards it as a simplification. His method is to study the historic circumstances in which Hassidism was created, and to examine the moralistic literature and its social criticism in 18th century Poland. His main emphasis, however, is laid upon a question: "What were the social forces in Jewish 18th century society that bore up the Hassidic movement, that gave shape to its public essence and set up its organisation?"[4]. He also investigates "the contribution of Hassidism to the solution of social crises", and stresses that the Hassidic movement belonged organically to the social opposition in the communities[5]. And he comes to the conclusion that its torchbearers were religious functionaries of lower rank, "teachers, cantors" and the like who formed "the social opposition" of Jewish society.

Using Dinur's studies as a point of departure, developing them to an extreme degree and comparing the Hassidim to members of the Sabbatean sects, Joseph Weiss tries[6] to portray the nature of the Hassidic leadership at the outset of the movement. His hard-hitting descriptions bring before us the personality of the wandering preacher—a "miserable

[2] Simon DUBNOW, *History of Hassidism* (Heb.) (Tel-Aviv, 1930), pp. 35–36.
[3] Ben-Zion DINUR, "The Beginning of Hassidism and its Social and Messianic Foundations" (Heb.), in *Bemifne Hadoroth* (Jerusalem, 1955), pp. 83–227.
[4] *Ibid.*, p. 86.
[5] *Ibid.*, p. 140.
[6] Joseph WEISS, "The Dawn of Hassidism" (Heb.), *Zion*, 16, No. 3–4, pp. 46–105.

type", according to Weiss, who "sells his teaching for alms" and "a smell of money-grubbing rises from the grubbing of these poor wretches for a living—even a smell of Sabbatean heresy"[7]. Despite this pungent description, there is, however, no evidence that the Besht's immediate circle were mainly "wandering preachers"; we know definitely that some of them were not, nor were they other representatives of 'secondary intelligentsia' (to use a currently fashionable phrase for religious functionaries other than rabbis). The outstanding example of R. Jacob Joseph of Polnoy, author of the Hassidic classic "Toldoth Yaakov Yosef" (*Toldoth*), teaches us that in the Besht's circle there were people of relatively stable social position, who were ready to endanger their position for their ideas. On the other hand, some wandering preachers known to us by name from that time were not members of the movement at its outset; or even against it. What is more, a look at the histories of some of them, the author of "Zera Beyrech Shlishi"[8], for example, shows how doubtful it is that there was any such fixed social category as 'wandering preacher': the demarcation line proposed to distinguish between the itinerant preacher and the one set up in a fixed community position was very often crossed over in reality. But it is certainly true that preachers, fixed or wandering, played an important part in the introduction and spread of new ideas, thanks to their close contacts with the people; it is also true that they sometimes took to the road out of devotion to their ideas. This may explain the decisive part played in the crystallization of Hassidic ideas and the organization of the movement by such Magidim (preachers) as the "Mokhiah" ('rebuker') of Polnoy, the 'Great Magid' of Meseritz, R. Yehiel-Michal of Zloczow or R. Haim, the Magid of Vilna. But the chief fighters against Hassidic ideas were also Magidim—R. Israel Leibl, the Magid of Nowogrodek; R. Jacob Israel of Kremenetz; R. David of Makow. And as Gershom Scholem has shown in his study of R. Israel Leibl[9], even in the sphere of ideas there were no clearly defined 'fronts'. The sharp social dividing line between the 'upper echelon intelligentsia', i.e. the rabbis, and the 'secondary intelligentsia' in 18th century Poland is completely without basis in fact. Many rabbis were dependent on the community leaders while among the rabbis and the ritual slaughterers and the wandering preachers, some are connected with the ruling group and some are against it. In all, it is hard, even at the dawn of Hassidism, to define the movement socially.

[7] *Ibid.*, p. 40, p. 56.

[8] Berachya Berakh ben R. Eliakim Getz, preacher and moralist, fierce critic of the leaders of the time; despite this he received permission from the heads of the 'Council of Lands' in Poland "to mend the breaks in the generation... to preach in every town without having recourse to permission from the rabbi and leader". See on him I. HEILPERN, *Pinkas of the Council of Four Lands*, pp. 477–479; Y. KLEINMANN, *Yevreiskaya Starina*, XII (1928) (Russian), pp. 179–198.

[9] G. SCHOLEM, "On R. Israel Leibl and his Polemic against Hassidism," *Zion*, 20, pp. 153–162.

It is far harder, as scholars have shown, to find grounds for the popular assumption that the radical social teaching of Hassidism conquered the hearts of the masses and answered their deepest needs. In fact, social matters had very little weight in Hassidic teaching: in all questions of livelihood and economy, the Lord would provide. In the words of R. Jacob Joseph: "Let not the poor man envy the rich, for man does not touch what is prepared for his fellow, and let not the craftsman hate his fellow-craftsman, nor the shopkeeper the shopkeeper, nor the publican the publican, nor the scholar the scholar" (*Toldoth*, Bo). Even where we find some sort of "social rules for the benefit of the poor and humble" like those R. Aharon of Karlin added to the communal ordinances of taxation in Nieswiez, Israel Heilpern [10] has proved that the rules are essentially the same in spirit as those commonly accepted in the communities of the time. Nor is this all. Dinur in his comprehensive study has collected a wide range of violent social criticism from the moral literature of Poland before the rise of Hassidism, and from the days when the movement was taking shape. A painstaking comparison between parts of that literature and the first Hassidic sermons [11] shows that compared with the extent and acuteness of non-Hassidic social criticism, the Hassidic literature has very little to say on these subjects and that little is moderate in tone. The very fact that there were so many moralistic books in 18th century Poland shows that the public was receptive, and the paleness and scantiness of the social morality preached by the Hassidim tells us that the source of their strength was not here.

The success of Hassidism sprang from the fact that it brought mysticism to the 'intelligentsia' of the time in a form they could accept. It particularly appealed to young students and religious functionaries. On the other hand it found an echo among the masses, for instead of the ideal personality of the pre-Hassidic generation, the remote, self-mortifying mystic, Hassidism idealised the mystic who leads the people and lives among them.

The seeds of this change lay in a religious ferment that had not subsided in Polish Jewry since the failure of the Sabbatean movement [12], and from the unceasing activities of diverse religious groups. Some of these groups were extremely radical in religious matters, and when they left the strict path of orthodoxy there is no doubt at all that they aroused opposition among the people. We seem to find an echo of this in 'Shivkhei Habesht' (Praises of the Besht), a collection of traditions and legends on the Besht that was partially written down in his lifetime and printed at

---

[10] I. HEILPERN, "The Attitude of R. Aharon of Karlin to Communal Rule," *Zion*, 22, pp. 86–92.

[11] J. SHACHAR, "Social Criticism in Moralistic Literature in Poland in the 18th Century"; manuscript (Hebrew).

[12] G. SCHOLEM, "The Sabbatean Movement in Poland," *The House of Israel in Poland*, ed. I. Heilpern (Hebrew), Vol. 2 (Jerusalem, 1954), pp. 36–76.

the beginning of the 19th century. In this work the story is told of R. Nakhman of Kossow, one of the Besht's inner circle, who came by chance to a place and prayed in a changed form of prayer: "When he finished his prayers all the people of the Beth Hamidrash (prayer house) pounced on him and asked him how he could stand before the Ark without leave and change the prayers into a version prayed neither by our fathers nor by our forefathers who were great in their generation. He answered: 'And who shall say that they are in Paradise?'"—that is to say, he cast doubt upon all the accepted religious tradition. Or there is the saying of R. Pinkhas of Koretz: "In this generation people do not occupy themselves with the [study of] Torah as in early days, for now there has spread a great fear [of God] throughout the world, and in the early days there was not such fear, wherefore they used to occupy themselves with Torah. There are few places [now] where they study; there there is no fear"[13]. This saying emphasizes the essential antagonism between the way of the Hassid and the way of the non-Hassid, for in Jewish society at that period the scholar, the man devoted wholly to study, was the ideal, and study of the Torah the commandment that outweighed all others. We note the behaviour of the followers of R. Abraham of Kolisk, a disciple of the Great Magid, "joking and mocking at the scholars"—a practice severely rebuked by the Magid of Meseritz[14]. But this was not the way of the movement as a whole, which usually shunned controversy and emphasized its faithfulness to tradition in every field of life. It was, in fact, this moderation—even in times of persecution—that enabled the movement to hold out within the Jewish communities, and not to be pushed into the position of a seceding sect.

In his article on communion with God (d'vekut), Gershom Scholem[15] noted that at the beginning of the Hassidic way of life the extreme demand for maximum communion with God was put forward as a general ideal, for every person equally. But as the movement took shape this ideal was set before the Zaddikim, the leaders, alone. And even of them it was not demanded in its pristine form. For the ordinary Hassid a broad formula was found of "adhere to your sage", i.e. the Hassid should attach himself to a Rabbi, his Zaddik. The leaders of the movement also softened the rigorous demands that many preachers made of the public; as R. Jacob Joseph tells us, from so many the threats, the public had begun to lose faith in them: "In the words of the masses: it is impossible that things can ever be as bad as they make out in moralistic books just to threaten people" (Toldoth, Nitzavim). This approach was not mere opportunism on the part of a growing movement; it seems to have

---

[13] "Light of Israel," Gleanings from R. Pinchas of Koretz, 53.

[14] H. B. HEILMANN, "Beth Rabi" (Hebrew), 2nd ed., Berditchew, 1903, p. 43.

[15] G. SCHOLEM, "Devekuth, or Communion with God," Review of Religion, XIV (1950), pp. 115–139; included in The Messianic Idea in Judaism (New York, 1971), pp. 203–226.

been part of the Besht's own fundamental approach. In "Praises of the Besht" we are told of "a sermon by a visiting preacher", whom the Besht defined as an "informer", "speaking ill of the people of Israel", i.e. the Besht considered preaching morals and religion to the public after the manner of the Magidim an evil thing. "The Besht jumped up from his place and tears splashed from his eyes and he said: 'Know that a son of Israel goes all day in the market; at evening when he is sad he grows anxious and says 'woe to me if I let pass the hour of evening prayer', and he goes into a house and prays the evening prayer and does not know what he is saying, and even so seraphim and angels are very moved at this'". And R. Nakhman of Horodenka interpreted the Besht's meaning thus: "That by fasting and mortification and persistence in study sadness grows and his way casts blame on his fellow man that none does as he did for they forsake eternal life for the temptation of transitory matters" (*Toldoth*, "Things I heard from my Teacher"). And this is how the author of *Toldoth* interpreted it in the name of his teacher "of whom is said: and the Lord sent fiery serpents among the people—preachers who awaken judgment on the world" (*Toldoth*, Kedoshim). That is to say, extreme demands from the public, or even severe self-mortification by the righteous themselves, would not only fail to help the people but would awaken judgment (i.e. would emphasize the distance between the ideal of communion with God and the behaviour of man in the market place) and thus put off redemption.

The reservations about severe self-mortifying piety, in order not 'to awaken judgment in the world', spring from another basic part of the same circle's outlook, namely seeing the organic bond between all sections of the people, seeing the people as one body. This motif recurs again and again in the sayings of R. Jacob Joseph: "For all the world together is called one figure and the masses of the people are the legs of the figure and the righteous are the eyes of the community etc., and this is the meaning of the saying that the whole world is like a ladder, that the masses of the people are arrayed on the ground, that may be called the feet of the world, and the scholars are the head, and this means 'its top reaches to Heaven'; that if the generation acts rightly, the heads of the generation rise up a degree more... and when the converse is true, they go down, as our sages said of Samuel ha-kattan (one of the early Tannaim)—he was worthy the Holy spirit should shine on him, but his generation was not worthy of it... for when the legs of man descend into the pit, the head too is brought low" (*Toldoth*, Vayetze). From this organic bond, from mutual dependence, springs the responsability of the righteous man or leader, the Zaddik, towards the whole community, and this attitude is based on a particular mystical principle. There is obviously nothing 'democratic' or egalitarian in it. The crowd is not regarded as equal in value to the Zaddik. The difference between them is a difference in kind: the righteous man, 'the man of form', is the active element, while the masses, 'the people of matter', are passive. But from this springs the demand the righteous man should take responsibility for the public. And as the movement establishes itself, we find the idea recurring and being re-emphasized that the righteous man must not justify himself by the decline of the generation. The essence of the bond is that the existence of one has no meaning without the other; in the words put into the mouth of Moses when he spoke to the Lord: "If Thou hast killed them (i.e. Israel in the desert) all at once, what need has the world for me? and what am I without them?" (*Toldoth*, Hookath).

In order to lead the crowd, the righteous man must step down from his rank, his high degree, to the material world. This is the celebrated principle of the 'descent of the righteous' in Hassidism. Whatever may be the mystic roots of the theory, it is the *raison d'être* of the Zaddik as a leader. As R. Levi Itzhak of Berdiczew put it: "Why did the Holy Name set up that the Zaddik should step down from his rank? For it would seem better that the Zaddik should always stand on his place, to serve the Holy Name with great sense and love Him with perfect love. This is the saying of the Besht and my righteous teacher Dov-Ber: that in the fall of the Zaddik and his strengthening himself to return to his place, from this souls were created, and he is like one who would raise up his fellow from slime and rubbish—he too must go down near the slime and rubbish to raise him up" (Kedushat Levi, on the Song of Songs). A doctrine like this not only does not deny "any justification" from "the masses" so long as they "remained without a leader"[16], but it puts the masses in the centre of the righteous man's interests and activity—and no doubt accounts for the immense following of the Hassidic leaders. The real test of both theory and movement came in the generation of the Magid's disciples, the period when the movement took shape and spread; and it stood the test of time. The more the Zaddik stressed his responsibility to the public and his willingness to care for them, the more his popularity grew.

It should not be concluded from this that the Hassidic leaders were not aware of the gap between the two sides of their doctrine; they were torn between two duties—that of the mystic, owing perpetual allegiance to the world above, and as it were sinning if he left off communion with God; and the duty of a leader to care for his people, one and all in body and soul. It seems that a certain amount of mystical contemplation had to be sacrificed for the sake of spreading the movement. R. Elimelekh of Lisansk, according to Dubnow, was the founder of 'practical Zaddikism', and the historian regarded it as a basic condition of his work "that they

[16] According to Jacob KATZ, *Tradition and Crisis* (New York, 1961, 1971), p. 235.

should support him lavishly and supply all his material needs"[17]. Yet it
is R. Elimelekh who brings out the peculiar tragedy of the torn soul of
the Zaddik: "It is hard to know why Moses our Teacher, peace be upon
him, was punished at the waters of Meribah when he smote the rock;
after all the Holy One Blessed Be He agreed with him, for it is written:
'and water came forth abundantly'. Now since he did what was not
right, the rock should not have given forth water abundantly... but it
appears—(of course a man of God is forbidden not to do the will of the
Creator, Blessed Be He)—that the way of the righteous man is always
to pursue the good of Israel, and even if in following this duty he has to
do something with an element of sin to it, he will do it for the good of
Israel; he will even take hell upon himself for them, for all his desire is
to do them good" (Noam Elimelekh, Balak). R. Levi-Itzhak too knows
that the secluded mystic has greater personal righteousness because of
his perpetual communion with the Divine; nonetheless, it is better to be
a righteous man who breaks off his communion and looks after the needs
of the people: "Let it be clear that we see that there are Zaddikim who
achieve through their prayers as they want, and there are righteous men
who do not achieve. The matter is thus, that the great Zaddik is he who
comes to the garden courtyard of the king's palace, the king of the
world, and recognizes that he is in the presence of the king—he forgets
what he had to ask in matters of this world and asks only that he should
always cleave to the king; for what is pleasant to him but to be a servant
of the Creator and to be a servant of the king? and he forgets all his
business. Not thus are the Zaddikim who are not of this degree, even
though they stand before the king, he remembers his petition, that he
wishes to ask; and most of all the Zaddik (i.e. the great one)—when he
comes before the king he does not remember the petition about the matter
of this world that he wishes to ask, so he does not achieve; and the lesser
Zaddik then is he who remembers his petition as he stands before the
king and makes the request of him: he therefore achieves" (Kedushat
Levi, on the Song of Songs).

In actual fact, it was not these late Zaddikim who laid down the
doctrine of the Zaddik through whom plenty comes to the world; the
Besht had already preached "Hanina my son (i.e. the Zaddik) is a path
and a pipe to continue plenty in the world" (Ben Porath, Vayehi),
intending both the spiritual and the material plenty that the Zaddik
rains on the world by his influence. But gradually the material side of
plenty became more important, until by the time we come to the disciples of the disciples of the Great Magid, the ability to provide for material
needs in practice is the recognized evidence of qualification for leadership: "The Rabbi of Lublin prided himself that he had been ordained
by the Magid of Rovno (the Great Magid) to be a Zaddik for a Hassidic

[17] S. Dubnow, ibid., p. 182.

group. For a rustic came to complain that someone had trespassed on him to take away his 'arenda'[18], and the Magid lay in bed and told him to go to the Beth Hamidrash (prayer house) and call someone to issue summons [to the trespasser]. And the Rabbi of Lublin was walking up and down in the Beth Hamidrash, and the rustic called him and he wrote an invitation and offered it to the Magid to sign. And he (the Magid) answered him: You sign it, and they will obey you as they obey me. You have no greater authority than this" (Niflaot Harabbi, 187). The grandson of the Besht, R. Moses Haim Ephraim of Sodilkow, even signed an explicit treaty in 1798 with "the chiefs of the holders of arenda in the neighbouring villages": they would "submit to his authority in all that he might say" and he would "help them with his teaching [Torah] and his prayer which effectively aids all who cleave to him", in return for 6 guildens of every thousand of their income[19].

Despite the moderation of the new movement as a whole, sooner or later it was bound to clash with the leadership of the communities over wider areas. The movement was saved from the fate of other religious sects in similar circumstances by the fact that it refused to declare war on the whole from which it sprang. It did not regard itself as a band of saints and the rest of Israel as a 'kingdom of evil'; thus it did not turn into what its opponents wanted to make it: a seceding sect cut off by both choice and necessity. Elements of religious radicalism appear in Hassidism as extraneous adjuncts. Scholars see radical elements in some of the central figures of the movement, but these tendencies found no public expression because of the view accepted in those circles that there were two separate moral systems—that of the Zaddik and that of the public as a whole. Insofar as radical elements existed, they were veiled in the clouds of the first system, in which much was mysterious and obscure. As a public movement, Hassidism proclaimed and emphasized its adherence to tradition; it rejected all radical tendencies in religion, stressing chiefly the basic teachings of unity and mutual responsibility between all parts of the nation, even including the wickedest of the wicked. As R. Arieh-Leib the "rebuker of Polnoy" used to say: "A little Zaddik likes little sinners and a great Zaddik likes and stands up for even hardened sinners". Such teachings prevented separatism.

The description of the struggle against Hassidism needs also careful examination. As is well known, relations became very strained indeed in Lithuania and White Russia, but in the Ukraine, in the sixties and seventies of the 18th century, i.e. before and even after the Ban of

[18] "Arenda"—is a lease of an inn or an income from agricultural activity connected with a manor. An important function of the community was to prevent competition between Jewish leaseholders. In the second half of the 18th century, when the authority of the communal heads weakened, the Hassidic Zaddikim took this task on themselves.

[19] A. KAHANA, *Book of Hassidism* (Hebrew) (Warsaw, 1922), p. 304.

Brody[20], there was cooperation between the heads of communities and the leaders of Hassidism.[21] In 1767 a religious court judge (Av-Beth-Din) of Rovno and his court rely on a ban in the matter of usufruct that had been proclaimed by the Magid of Meseritz, and the signed verdict of this court is validated by the famous Hassidic leader R. Yehiel-Michal of Zloczow. In 1778 the heads of the important community of Dubno make an agreement with "the honoured rabbi, head of the religious court of the holy community of Polnoy and his adherents", this being R. Jacob Joseph, the disciple of the Besht, for joint action in "the ransoming of prisoners", i.e. the freeing of a leaseholder seized by his overlord. These communal leaders seem to cooperate with the heads of Hassidism in order to get their help in matters beyond the reach of communal organization; while the authority and the ban of the Zaddik had great force in that section of the public.

The main principle at issue in the clash between Hassidim and Mithnagdim ('opponents') was the problem of authority which is to say, that in most disputes the Hassidim would be asked—: where did they get the authority 'to change the coin that the sages had minted?'[22] But such objections did not rest mainly on the assumption that it was forbidden to alter what heads of communities had uttered. These heads, even in Vilna, did not themselves tend to be extreme in persecuting the Hassidim. The authority and validity for heads of communities to persecute and oppress the Hassidim came from a man who held no official position at all and had not been chosen by 'rational choice', the Gaon of Vilna "Man of God... Rabbi Elijah Hassid, may his light shine". This was the man who "sent for the dignitaries (heads of the community in Vilna) and asked them angrily why they had dealt lightly with them (the Hassidim). Were it in my power I would do to them what Elijah the prophet did to the prophets of Baal".[23]

It is an error to suppose that the struggle between the Hassidim and the Mithnagdim, their opponents, was a clash between establishment and charism. The Gaon certainly had the authority belonging to a great scholar, but despite this (or rather because of it) his main influence was charismatic. None other than his own pupil, R. Haim of Volozhin, attested that the Gaon had had a 'revelation of Elijah' (i.e. prophetic visions). There are no doubt degrees of charism, but the clash here was between two forms and two sources of charismatic leadership[24]. An

[20] This is the first known ban on the Hassidim proclaimed in the community of Brody in 1772.

[21] Material on this has been collected by H. Shmeruk in a paper still in manuscript.

[22] See for example the dispute between R. Abraham Katzenelbogen the rabbi of Brisk and R. Levi-Itzchak of Berditchew in 1781, S. DUBNOW, *Chassidiana* (Hebrew), *Dvir*, Part I (Berlin, 1923), pp. 293–297.

[23] *Ibid.*, "Heavar" (Petrograd, 1918), p. 26.

[24] On the charismatic leadership of the Gaon of Vilna see R. J. Z. WERBLOWSKY, *Joseph Karo* (Oxford, 1962), App. F.

added proof is that R. Haim, the faithful disciple, had an approach to Hassidim completely different from that of his teacher. It cannot be merely assumed that the difference in time was responsible for the change, i.e. that Hassidism was well established by R. Haim's time. It seems more likely that Elijah the Gaon's personality, with its charismatic power, shaped the struggle he headed.

The main authority of the Hassidic leader came from his direct connection with supernatural powers—powers that he brought to the aid of the individual and the public. But the way the Hassidim were organized also played its part, in the Hassidic group ('Eda'), that clustered around the Zaddik. The open nature of this group did not bridge the gap between Hassidim and their opponents, but it did serve to exorcize the suspicion that the Hassidim have downright heretical tendencies, for these groups were open to all and exposed to the eyes of all.

The transformation from the small group to the wide movement, as is well known, was the work of the Magid of Meseritz. He transferred the centre from out-of-the-way Podolia to Volhynia, which was much more in the centre of the Polish kingdom, and sent emissaries to spread his doctrine far and wide to White Russia, to Lithuania and to central Poland. His disciples, who have no specific social distinguishing marks, came from various social strata, and were learned in equally differing degrees.

We now encounter a paradoxical element in the formation of the movement: Rabbi Dov-Ber of Meseritz, the Great Magid, the well-known figure called by his disciples the "Rabbi of all the sons of the Diaspora", who was a leader of authoritarian views, and yet directed the movement into ways of decentralization. He set up group after group with a pupil of his at the head of almost every one, with the result that after his death there was no single agreed leader of the movement. The tradition of autonomous activity in the local Jewish communities must have assisted the decentralizing tendency in the movement. But this certainly does not imply identity between any Hassidic group and a particular community. On the contrary, the Zaddik, the righteous man, had followers (Hassidim) in various places, and his influence was sometimes spread over wide areas and large communities, while he himself lived in some small remote township. But it should be emphasized that the decentralizing tradition of communal organisation was able to assist the splitting of the Hassidic leadership, in which every Zaddik and group had a great and growing degree of independence.

This process by which the Hassidic leadership grew did not lack internal stress and struggle. Few of the Besht's disciples were among the disciples of the Magid. Even in the Magid's lifetime there was no general agreement with his ways. Some disagreed with his ideas; others, apparently, with his new methods of organization in the movement. We seem to hear an echo of the latter criticism in the severe words of the author of "Toldoth": "Now we have to interpret the rest of the plagues [of Egypt] up to the plague of locusts... a multiplication of locusts.... The matter is the multiplication of leaders, that there is no [single] spokesman for the generation; just the opposite, they are all heads and spokesmen; as I heard, that was the blessing (i.e. curse) of Elijah on a town that they should all be leaders etc. And then spokesman (dabar) becomes murrain (dever) or hail, and by its force 'he covered the eye of the land'. He who is the eye of the land, like the eyes of the flock, who was worthy to keep watch over the land, has become many leaders 'has covered the eye of the land' so that they cannot see the land, to keep watch over them. And this is the significance of 'and he consumed the remnant that was left ye from the hail': when there was one spokesman for the generation it was a blessing, and when it was changed and became many leaders it was like hail and that causes destruction to the remnant of the community" (Toldoth, Bo).

Perhaps the author of "Toldoth" had hoped that the descendants of the Besht would produce 'one spokesman for the generation'. At all events R. Barukh, the Besht's grandson through his daughter, who grew up in the house of R. Pinkhas of Koretz, an opponent of the Magid's way, based his pretension to be the single leader of Hassidism on his illustrious descent. "The Holy Rabbi of Polnoy", he says, "loved me very much and out of respect (for I was tender in years and he was well aged), I did not wish to sit in his presence and he likewise did not wish to sit in mine. I was forced to be seated that he might sit. And I took my box to sniff snuff before him, and he said to me: Boruchl, I heard from your grandfather the Besht that you will be his successor; can you take snuff like the Besht? For the Besht when he wanted to go to the worlds above would take snuff..." (Botzina d'nahora ha-shalem, p. 5). Whatever the truth of the words attributed to the author of "Toldoth" in this story, it is clear that R. Barukh had claims to become 'the spokesman of the generation' by virtue of his pedigree. There is therefore a certain interest in his conversation with R. Shneour Zalman of Ladi, one of the chief disciples of the Magid of Meseritz and the founder of Habad Hassidism. After a very sharp conversation, reported by R. Shneour Zalman, R. Barukh proclaimed: "I am the grandson of the Besht and I must be respected". To which Rabbi Shneour Zalman replied: "I too am the Besht's grandson in spirit, for the Great Magid was the chief disciple of the Besht and I am the disciple of the Magid" (ibid).

This controversy touched the roots of a problem of great importance to Hassidism—and to all movements with a charismatic leadership—namely, how to transfer authority. Should it be from father to son, or from teacher to disciple? Among the disciples of the Magid, unlike the descendants of the Besht, the latter version appears to have been the

accepted one. As R. Elimelekh of Lizansk stated: "There are here two
types of Zaddikim. There are Zaddikim sanctified by their fathers who
were holy and perfect and godfearing and 'the Torah returns to its
lodgings', and there are Zaddikim called 'nazirites' because they set
themselves apart, although they are sons of common people. And these
Zaddikim (i.e. the ones who are not the sons of Zaddikim) cannot quickly
fall from their sacred rank, for they have nothing to rely on, and they
stay humble and watch themselves with open eyes perpetually. But the
Zaddikim sons of saints, even be they full of Torah and commandments,
by virtue of their fathers helping them sometimes—there can arise from
that divergence on the one hand and loftiness on the other (i.e. they will
become full of pride) and they will fall quickly from their rank. And
this is 'say to the priests the sons of Aaron' here he hinted at the Zaddikim
who are sons of Zaddikim, and are called 'priests sons of Aaron', warning
them strictly that they should not presume to think at all of the lineage
of their fathers... and choose the best way for themselves (Noam
Elimelekh, Emor). Indeed, he himself acted on the principle of transferring authority to a disciple: there is a tradition that "the rabbi Rabbi
Melekh in his old age ordered all who were sick or embittered to come
to his disciple R. Itzikel of Lanzut (the 'seer' of Lublin). Until he
accustomed everyone to come to Lanzut. And they ceased to come to
him. Then he waxed very wroth" (Ohel Elimelekh, 165). If our hypothesis of the clash between two systems of inheriting authority is correct,
there is a certain historic irony in the fact that it was from the descendants
of the Magid himself and his best disciples that the great Hassidic
dynasties arose. Departing from this tendency—possibly in reaction
against it—a Hassidic group grew up around the great-grandson of the
Besht, R. Nakhman of Bratzlaw. To this day it is the only Hassidic
group that has no living leader: it remains faithful to the memory of
R. Nakhman 'the dead Rabbi'. And there is no doubt that R. Nakhman
believed himself to be the leading zaddik of his generation, and perhaps
had claims to be 'the spokesman of the generation' according to his
family's tradition.

Many writers on Hassidism have dwelt on the difference between
'theoretical Hassidism' in its pure and pristine form, and 'practical
Zaddikism' which came later. Dubnow writes on R. Elimelekh of
Lisansk: "While R. Elimelekh did not innovate at all in the theoretical
teachings of the Besht and the Magid, he added much to the system of
practical Zaddikism, by making it a system founded in the essence of
Hassidism" [25]. In his opinion, that is to say, this evil in Hassidism stemmed
from R. Elimelekh. It is doubtful if there is any ground for the distinction
between late 'practical Zaddikism' and the earlier 'purer' kind. Why
does not Dubnow complain that the Besht took payment for writing

25 S. DUBNOW, ibid., p. 180.

amulets—which is a kind of payment for service—whereas he condemns as corruption and exploitation the money paid to the latter-day Zaddik for leading his flock? From a historical standpoint, the main problem is not the payment and its justification but the task of leadership and the way it was carried out: Did the Hassidic leadership have an influence that was destructive and corrupting on Jewish society, as many have claimed, especially those swayed by the attitude of the Haskalah writers?

It seems that the reverse is true. Where Hassidism ruled, Jewish society was less torn by conflicts and more stable than in the period before the movement took over. It is important to remember that in earlier days much of internal stability of Jewish society and the authority of its leaders came from the support of the government. Whereas from the beginning of the 19th century the governments both of Austria and Russia developed hostility to Jewish autonomy, and the unifying of Jewish society had to be achieved without the support of the government —in fact actually against it.

It is, however, true that the Hassidic group was a framework separate from the community (though not against it and certainly not a substitute for it), and the very existence of such a framework, the fact that the authority of its head, the Zaddik, was higher in the eyes of its members than the authority of the communal heads, meant that the comprehensiveness of communal leadership was weakened in Jewish life. Yet this development did not break down Jewish society, and after a bitter struggle between the two kinds of authority a *modus vivendi* began to appear. Gradually it became clear that the Hassidic leadership was capable of contributing to the strengthening of the unity of Jewish society as a whole. This was largely due to the way the Hassidic leadership was regarded by the people. The leaders of Hassidism did not make claims of principle against the authority of the community, and did not deny it; sometimes they controlled communities and sometimes they gave additional validity to community regulations and deeds, a validity that was weakened when the central autonomous institutions were abolished. The study of Shmeruk[26] has shown how the needs of communal life brought about compromise and even cooperation between Hassidim and non-Hassidim, even in regions where they had previously been at each other's throats. The way of reconciliation between the two rival camps was paved with a common effort to defend the interests, social and spiritual, of the Jewish public against the intervention of the government and against the undermining of foundations from within, by new factors such as Enlightenment.

[26] H. SHMERUK, "The Social Significance of Hassidic Shechita", *Zion*, 20, pp. 47–74.

Selected Bibliography

1. S. SCHECHTER, "The Chassidim", in *Studies in Judaism*, v. 1, Philadelphia, 1896, pp. 1-46.
2. A.Z. AECHCOLI, *Le Hassidisme*, Paris, 1928.
3. M. BUBER, *Die chassidischen Bücher*, Hellerau, 1928.
4. S. DUBNOW, *Geschichte des Chassidismus*, Berlin, 1931.
5. G. SCHOLEM, *Major Trends in Jewish Mysticism*, New York, 1961, Lecture IX.
6. M. BUBER, *The Tales of the Hasidim*, New York, 1947.
7. G. SCHOLEM, "Devekuth, or Communion with God", *Review of Religion*, XIV, 1950, pp. 115-139; *The Messianic Idea in Judaism*, New York, 1971, pp. 203-226.
8. S. H. DRESNER, *The Zaddik*, London-New York, 1960
9. J. KATZ, *Tradition and Crisis*, New York, 1961, 1971.

JACOB KATZ

THE JEWISH NATIONAL MOVEMENT

A Sociological Analysis

I<small>T</small> is safe to say that all the modern national movements emerged from the existence of a "Nation", that is to say a group which had inhabited a certain territory exclusively, even while other groups of the same ethnic origin might have existed dispersed among other nations. This ethnic group could be recognized by its language and by the attachment to certain traditional ways of life. Moreover, the keeping up of a tradition—even if only in the field of folklore— presupposes a certain degree of historical consciousness. Indeed, every ethnic group usually has an image of its historical past even if only expressed in some semi-mythological saga or popular heroic poem.[1]

This experience was common to all the generations which preceded Nationalism proper. What did not happen in those prior stages and what can be considered as the real turning point in the development of Nationalism is that the attributes of any ethnic group, its association with its homeland, practice of certain customs and use of native language, became incumbent on its members, obliging them to uphold and further these national peculiarities without regard for their usefulness or even at the cost of great losses in other fields. This consideration is apt to provide us with the best definition of modern Nationalism: it is the transforming of ethnical facts into ultimate values. While national attributes, such as attachment to one's birthplace, clinging to the mother tongue and a certain preference for one's ethnic group members are universal phenomena, it is the elevation of these traits to supreme, perhaps even sole, values that may be regarded as the distinctive characteristic of modern Nationalism.

The origin and nature of the historical factors which brought about this turning point in human history cannot be fully discussed here. It

---

[1] The literature on nationalism is extensive. See C. HAYES, *The Historical Evolution of Modern Nationalism* (New York, 1931); FR. O. HERTZ, *Nationality in History and Politics* (London, 1945); H. KOHN, *The Idea of Nationalism* (New York, 1946); E. KEDOURIE, *Nationalism* (London, 1960). Most stimulating is the classic essay of LORD ACTON, "Nationality", included in his *Essays on Freedom and Power* (New York, 1955).

has certainly something to do with the eclipse of other sets of values, primarily religious, and with the enervation of political forces in the age of the dynasties and the disintegration of the old Estates.[2] Our aim is here to give an account of one of these national movements which seems to be at variance with the normal attern of Nationalism but which nevertheless any comprehensive sociological theory of Nationalism must take into account.

* * *

The deviation of Jewish Nationalism from the normal is apparent in its pre-nationalistic foundations.[3] Jewish society lacked two of the traits which characterized the pre-nationalistic phase of ethnic groups. Scattered across four continents, Jews had no territory of their own, nor did they possess a common language. Indeed while many nationalist movements strove and succeeded in raising a particular dialect to the level of a literary language and from this dominant position it exercized a unifying function, eighteenth century Jewry was a Babel of tongues. Half spoke Jewish, others Ladino and yet others the language of their native countries.

In spite of these deficiencies nobody would have doubted at the end of the eighteenth century that the Jews were an ethnic unit, separate from the local inhabitants in any place where they may have built a community. Similarly the unity of these communities all over the world was also taken for granted. This state of affairs is explainable to a great extent by the religious distinctiveness of the Jews, for the adherence of the Jews to their ancient faith was the apparent reason for their political and social disabilities. Individuals who accepted the religion of their non-Jewish society changed by implication their political and social status. Nonetheless the description of Jewish society as a purely religious unit is not complete. Belonging to the Jewish community was indeed dependent on the acceptance of the Jewish faith. But once an adherent of this faith it entailed much more than mere religious affiliation. The tenets of the Jewish faith are embodied and enmeshed in an old and complicated tradition which abounds in historical reminiscences as well as national aspirations with regard to the future. The destruction of the Temple in Jerusalem by Titus was referred to in the daily prayers and especially remembered at one season of the year which was dedicated to mourning for their lost glory, this mourning culminating in the day of fasting on the ninth of Av, the date of the actual destruction of the Temple. But more frequent yet than the sad remembrances of things past were the prayers for the future redemption. The popular

[2] See the literature quoted in note 1.
[3] The best summary of the history of Jewish nationalism is B. HALPERN, *The Idea of the Jewish State* (Cambridge, Mass., 1961).

version of the messianic belief had it that the redemption would come
about in a miraculous way; some even believed that it would possess
spiritual or eschatological features, such as the renewal of prophecy or
the resurrection of the dead. But even so the political aspects of the deliverance were not lacking either. The expectation of redemption in Jewish
thought has always been bound up with national fate.[4] Acceptance of/or
adherence to the Jewish faith entailed therefore at the same time the
consciousness of being a son of a nation, ill-fated in the present, divinely
endowed in the past and with splendid prospects for the future. While
with respect to the first two factors of prenationalistic conditions in
national movements, territory and language, the Jews were at a dis-
advantage in comparison with other ethnic groups, with regard to their
historical consciousness they were indubitably in advance of them. Their
historical awareness served, moreover, not only to compensate for their
territorial deficiency, but even to correct it. For their memory of the
land of their past served in a sense, as a symbolic substitute for it.

As far as national consciousness is concerned we may reasonably
maintain that on the threshold of modern times the Jews were better
prepared for a national movement than any other ethnic group in Europe.
It is true that before the historical consciousness could become an ingredient of modern nationalism it had to undergo first certain trans-
formations. The miraculous and eschatological elements had to be replaced by realistic concepts. But by the same token all nations had to
undergo equally important changes in their mental attitude before they
could be caught up by a national movement. Jewish society itself achieved
this transformation with the appearance of modern Zionism. In it
Jewish messianic belief was, so to speak, purged of its miraculous elements, and retained only its political, social and some of its spiritual
objectives. But even in this phase of development, modern nationalism
leaned heavily on the old messianism, and derived from it much of its
ideological and even more of its emotional appeal. Yet, all this was accomplished, as is well known, only at the end of the nineteenth and the
beginning of the twentieth century. Thus, in spite of having preceded
other nations in possessing the potentialities of modern nationalism, the
Jewish national movement lagged behind most of the European nations
in its actual development.

The retardation of Jewish nationalism is easily explained by the fact
that the Jewish nation, as we have noted, possessed the pre-nationalistic
characteristics in a symbolic or token form only. In reality Jewish society
was embodied into the structure of non-Jewish societies. Economically
and politically it represented one section of non-Jewish society albeit

---

[4] G. SCHOLEM, "Zum Verständnis der messianischen Idee im Judentum", *Eranos-
Jahrbuch*, XXVIII (1960), pp. 193–198; "Toward an Understanding of the Messianic
Idea in Judaism," in *The Messianic Idea in Judaism* (New York, 1971), pp. 1–36.

one of very special character and one of unusual standing. As mentioned
above the nationalism of other European peoples arose as a by-product
of the disintegration of the estates on which the pre-nationalistic society
of Europe was built. Disintegration meant a loosening of the bonds by
which the individual was tied to his estate, his corporation and his church.
But no such change had occurred in his belonging to an ethnic group.
On the contrary, the displaced individuals continued to be kept together
by their common attachment to their birthplace, their language and their
cultural tradition. The disintegration of the old social structure provided
these national elements with the chance to become an important factor
in the reintegration of the uprooted individuals.

But here the case of the Jews was quite different. The same factors
which led to the disintegration of the other estates affected equally the
position of the Jews. They, like all other individuals, were suddenly or
gradually freed from bondage to legally defined estates. Instead they
were to be regarded as independent citizens of their respective countries.
The so-called emancipation of the Jews is only a special case of the
rejection of the idea of the estates on which the old European society
was founded.[5] But from the standpoint of the old Jewish society this had
more far-reaching consequences than for any other estate. In the case of
the Jews no chance of reintegration on the basis of the ethnic elements
was to appear. Although we observed that national consciousness was
conspicuously developed, the lack of concrete elements of national unity
could not be easily made up for. The tokens and symbols which in the
old days replaced these elements lost their power over the individuals
who by the disintegration of Jewish society came into contact with the
individuals of other estates. The second phase of the development which
followed, the reintegration, did not bring the Jews back to their own
national tradition but on the contrary it led them into the society of those
nations in the midst of which they dwelt. The process of assimilation
which affected the first generations who enjoyed civil emancipation was
strongly supported by the idea of nationalism. Jews became overnight
French, German or Hungarian patriots. This assumption of nationalism
was in the case of the Jews perhaps not as "natural" as with other parts of
the population. But very often it was experienced even more consciously
and was backed by a greater ideological assurance. The Jew who lacked
the elements of autochthonous patriotism acquired his attachment to the
new national movement more through the acceptance of its ideas than
by the possession of its ethnic ingredients. And this led in turn to the
discarding of his own national consciousness.[6] Thus the impact of

[5] S. STERN-TÄUBLER, "The Jew in the Transition from Ghetto to Emancipation,"
Historia Judaica, V. II (1940), pp. 102–119.
[6] B. OFFENBURG, *Das Erwachen des deutschen Nationalbewusstseins in der preussischen
Judenheit* (Hamburg, 1933).

modern Nationalism on Jewish society instead of producing a Jewish variation of the national movements led to the integration of Jewish individuals into the movements of other nationalities.

Put differently, it is a commonplace that the nationalist movement is inconseivable without the age of Enlightenment which preceeded it. It was the corrosive power of rationalism that had undermined the ideological base of the old society as it pointed out the patent absurdity of founding and organizing a society along the principle of the segregation of estates of one and the same nation.[7] But as man cannot live by reason alone and logic seldom serves as communal cement, the societies which arose on the ruins of the old sought new symbols of re-integration, and found them in the elevation of ethnic elements into ultimate values. In the instance of Jewish society this dialectical process was stopped halfway. The old, indeed, dissolved under rational scrutiny, but this did not leave Jews atomized among themselves, but scattered in different gentile societies, bereft of distinctive symbols, and at one with their neighbors in place of birth. Thus no corresponding re-formation of Jewish society took place.

* * *

The old messianic idea did not disappear entirely under the impact of rationalism. The idea was alive in the Jewish masses. As late as 1840 there was a widespread rumour in the Balkans and in Eastern Europe that the Messianic year had arrived which was destined to bring about the great turning point in Jewish history.[8] Many held this belief genuinely and were waiting in a state of mental agitation. For one of these believers, Rabbi Jehuda Alkalay (1798-1878), the messianic expectation of this year became a starting point for the transition from the traditional miraculous messianism to a realistic one. This change of conception was caused by the coincidence of the messianic expectation with the rescue of the Jewish community in Damascus, charged with ritual murder, by the two leading figures of French and English Jewry, Adolphe Crémieux and Moses Montefiori. As the miraculous events of the redemption failed to appear Alkalay inferred that the rescue of this one community is a model for the messianic procedure. The further stages of redemption were supposed to be achieved through similar activities of outstanding Jews.

Alkalay was an undistinguished preacher of a little Sephardic community in Semlin near Belgrade.[9] Until the year of his newly-found con-

---

[7] On the social ideals of rationalism in Jewish society see J. KATZ, *Tradition and Crisis* (New York, 1961, 1971), chap. 24.

[8] H. G. DUKER, "The Tarniks," *The Joshua Star Memorial Volume* (1953), pp. 191-201.

[9] See my article (in Hebrew) in B. DINUR (ed.), *Shivah Zion*, V. 4 (1956), pp. 9-41.

viction he was hardly known or wished to be known outside his limited circle. But after having convinced himself of the truth that the era of the Messiah had arrived and that the redemption would have to be achieved by human action, he felt himself compelled to convey this message to his fellow nationalists. Not only did Alkalay in the remaining thirty-seven years of his life publish numerous pamphlets and articles to spread his ideas but he travelled on two occasions to Western Europe and later on settled in Palestine in order to convince Jews and non-Jews of the truth of his mission. He tried to induce people to implement the practical conclusion of his belief. This amounted indeed to an organized resettlement of Jewry, or some part of it, in their homeland and their equipment with the attributes of a united modern nation. For although Alkalay started as a preacher imbued with the traditional and especially kabbalistic sources he gradually acquired the elements of a fully-fledged national *Weltanschauung*. He propagated the idea of national unity. The instrument of unification was supposed to be an over-all organization which should have included the whole of world Jewry. Alkalay conceived national unity to be based on a common language which should be Hebrew after undergoing modernization. Religion, it was understood, would play its part in the new national life in Palestine. But as at that time the controversy between orthodox and reform Jews appeared likely to lead to a schism Alkalay characteristically sought in the idea of national unity the remedy for this. Therein we may recognize the sign that nationalism was becoming with him the leading and all-embracing idea. If the expression Prophets should indeed be found adequate to describe the men who strove to awaken the national consciousness in modern nations (as indicated in the title of the well-known book of Hans Kohn), Alkalay, who wrote in the language of the ancient prophets and often let himself be carried away by their pathos, should certainly have a place among them.

Alkalay does not stand alone as the originator of Nationalism by linking it up with the old Messianic belief. On similar lines developed his ideas Z. H. Kalisher (1795-1874), a German rabbinic scholar of Polish origin who however refused to accept any position in communal life.[10] Imbued with Jewish tradition but keeping himself free from any communal engagement, he was free to contemplate the events which had befallen Jewish existence in his life-time. The great experience of his youth was the emancipation of the Jews in France and in the German countries at the time of Napoleon. He explained these events not as a part of the general political and social processes in their respective countries, but exclusively in terms derived from Jewish tradition. The emancipation and even more the ascendance of Jewish individuals,

---

[10] On Kalisher see my article *ibid.*, V. 2–3 (1953), pp. 26–41.

as, for instance, the Rothschilds, to unheard of economic and political influence appeared to him to be the fulfilment of the old prophecy of liberation which according to Jewish tradition was to terminate the exile. It is true, this was not the whole fulfilment. For such a fulfilment entailed the ingathering of the Jews in their homeland. But neither could the social and political freedom which the Jews achieved in their respective countries be without significance. By interpreting events of emancipation in terms of Messianism, Kalisher transformed at the same time these very terms. From the first stage of deliverance which was brought about by human activity he inferred the nature of the next stages. These next steps were also to be achieved by human agency. Out of this interpretation of the emancipation arose the demand for the ingathering of at least some part of Jewry in Palestine.

In order to appreciate these nationalist theories and place them in the correct historical perspective one has to keep in mind the underlying motives of their promoters. These theories were derived from the reinterpretation of the old Messianic tradition in the light of the new historic experiences. In view of later developments it is well to remember that modern antisemitism was not amongst these experiences. The activities of Alkalay and Kalisher took place during the flourishing period of Middle European Liberalism, i.e. between 1840-1875 when optimism as to the possible integration of Jews into the life of European nations was almost universal. Certain obstacles which were sometimes put in the way of achieving full civil rights as well as certain signs of reservation in social rapprochement were interpreted as residues of waning prejudices. Alkalay and Kalisher were among the optimists. Until the seventies they never used the argument that Jews needed a country for securing their physical existence, which was to become one of the main planks of Zionism proper. To explain, therefore, early Jewish Nationalism as a mental expression of material needs would mean only the transference of a preconceived theory to a special case. The data of the case itself do not bear out the truth of this theory.

The same can be stated about the motives of the third representative of early Jewish Nationalism, the socialist Moses Hess (1812-1875). The Nationalism of Hess is different from that of the two others in its terms of reference and the basic beliefs on which it was founded.

Hess was not an orthodox Jew but a social revolutionist and philosopher with a Hegelian tinge.[11] His switching over to Jewish Nationalism in the sixties can be understood as the result of both personal disillusionment and despair of the social revolution which was expected at an earlier date but which failed to materialize. But the psychological prompt-

---

[11] On Hess see his recent biography by E. SILBERNER, *Moses Hess, Geschichte seines Lebens* (Leiden, 1966).

ings of any social theory are of little concern in their historical evaluation. The relevant question to be asked is what reasons and arguments were put forward in support of the theory. Hess bases his Jewish Nationalism on the concept of a "National Spirit" which in the ancient Jewish state permeated the entire life of the Jewish people. Since the dispersion, the "Spirit" was supposed to be embodied in the Jewish religious institutions. As these institutions were at that time rapidly disintegrating the gradual disappearance of the Jewish national spirit was the most probable, and from the standpoint of a Jewish patriot the most lamentable, prospect. In order to rescue this Spirit and give it the chance of revival, the only solution was the reconstruction of a fully-fledged national life in the ancient homeland. The argument of Hess is phrased in terms of social philosophy, while the resentment against the non-Jewish contemporary society which had not fulfilled the expectation of treating the Jews as equals provided the emotional climate. But any criticism of the political standing of Jewry which could have led to a diagnosis excluding emancipation as a possible solution to the Jewish problem is absent from the theory of Hess as it is absent from those of Alkalay and Kalisher. More obvious than in the case of Alkalay and Kalisher is the dependence of Hess's theory on the general trend of Nationalism in Europe. The use of such terms as Nationality, National Renaissance, creative genius of the Nation indicate the source of influence, i.e. Romanticism which provided all the national movements with their respective ideological tools. Hess's book *Rome and Jerusalem,* as its title also indicates, was written under the impact of the events which had led to the unification of Italy in 1859. Hess refers expressly to this fact giving the Jewish cause the name "The Last National Problem" after Italy had solved its own.

But on this point there is no basic difference between Hess and his two nationalist contemporaries. It can easily be proved that they received impulses of thought and promptings of feelings from non-Jewish sources also in the cases of Alkalay and Kalisher. Both of them use one characteristic argument in their appeal to those who are nationally indifferent: Jews who are the descendents of a holy and ancient nation should not be behind the newly created nations of the Balkans.

The real difference between Alkalay and Kalisher on the one hand and Hess on the other is the spiritual background from which their respective nationalist drive stemmed. While the first two were originally steeped in the sources of Jewish tradition including the Bible, Talmud and Kabbala, the latter had only a faint idea of all this. He acquired some knowledge of Jewish institutions and concepts from his contact with religious life in his childhood. But for precise information he had to rely on second hand sources. In his knowledge of Jewish history and its evaluation he was strongly influenced by the historian Heinrich

Graetz (1817-1891). Graetz can be fairly characterized as being intentionally liberal minded, but in his actual presentation of facts he displayed a very strong national bias.[12] With Hess it was this last feature of Graetz's History which asserted its influence. Anyhow, the fabric of Hess's philosophical outlook was woven out of strands which were of modern European, primarily Hegelian, origin. He was far from being a religious Jew in any traditional sense, and judged by his activities and writings until his national phase he must be counted as one of those of Jewish race who were absorbed by European movements and systems of thought. That such a Jew should have rediscovered his own Jewish past and was able to erect upon Jewish tradition a new prospect for the future was a strange phenomenon.

Hess is the first figure of Jewish Nationalism who did not grow directly out of Jewish tradition. His Jewishness came back to him after a period of estrangement.[13] Thus Hess and his two contemporaries Alkalay and Kalisher prefigure the two main types of Jewish Nationalism: one which had to overcome the unrealistic elements of traditional Messianism; the other which after having forsaken the tradition altogether had to recover its cultural and political implications.

* * *

That a change of heart such as Hess's was possible is related to the process of secularization which Jewish tradition had to undergo before it could be channeled towards Nationalism. Even after having achieved to a great extent integration into the respective nations of their birth places, the Jews, so long as they were recognized as a distinct group, could not have denied their past. Except in the case of joining the alien religious community, the neglect of Jewish tradition was not tantamount to total negation of nor to complete indifference to one's Jewish origin and background. And in so far as they had any intention of reintegrating themselves as a religious minority in separate communities it was incumbent upon them to take cognizance of the main ideas which clung to the name of a Jew. Messianism which was a common concept of Jewish and Christian religion was one of the ideas which Jews had to give an account of. For the interpretation of this concept was one of the dividing points between Judaism and Christianity. Christianity maintained that the Messiah had arrived in the person of Jesus. The Jews expected the advent of the Messiah in the future.

Indeed even the conception of Jewish liberalism did not merely forsake the old traditional Messianic belief. It had only reinterpreted it.[14]

[12] S. W. BARON, *History and Jewish Historians*, pp. 266, 271.
[13] SILBERNER, *ibid.*, pp. 395-403.
[14] On the Messianic idea in the transition period see B. MEVORAH, "The Problem of the Messiah in the Emancipation and Reform Controversies, 1781-1819," Doctoral dissertation (in Hebrew) (Jerusalem, 1966).

First of all it severed the Messianism from the idea of returning to the ancient homeland. Secondly it detached it from the expectation of a personal redeemer. Instead, the liberal thinkers identified the Messianic belief with a hope for a better future for mankind. Liberalism had conceived an era of political and religious freedom. And Jews had actually experienced a turn for the better in their destinies. The prevalence of tolerance and freedom on a world-wide scale was visualized for the future and this was equated with the Messianic Age. The similarity of this conception with that of Kalisher is striking. The liberals as well as the nationalist Kalisher started from the fact of the political and social liberation of the Jews in the Western European countries. Where they do differ fundamentally is in the following up of the consequences. Kalisher retained in his nationalist conception the idea of regathering the Jews in their homeland as the ultimate stage of Messanism. But this could be achieved only by transcending the given political and social status of the Jews in the present. The Liberals on the other hand used the messianic idea only to justify the political achievement which Jewry had reached or was to reach in the near future, i.e. the integration of the Jews into the life of their respective countries. These two contradictory conceptions growing out of the same tradition represent a striking example of the way differing intellectual matrices condition the adaptation of an identical idea. In modern sociological terms we may call the conception of liberalism an ideology and that of the nationalists' an Utopia in the sense defined by Karl Mannheim.[15] The Messianic idea of liberalism had no other social function but to further the aims of the individuals in the community to which they wished to belong. Contrary to this, the nationalist conception could only succeed by the renouncing of prospects on the part of individuals which were in the sphere of possible achievement. It was an utopia, i.e. an image of the future, which people were called upon to strive for not for the satisfaction of their immediate needs but out of a belief that by doing so they would fulfil a preordained course of historical development.

Through the above statement about the utopian character of Jewish Nationalism we seem to have arrived at its main feature which gives it a unique place among the national movements. Every national idea which served a national movement envisaged a prospective change in the political structure of the country concerned. Sometimes it aimed at the elimination of foreign rule and in any case at the taking over of government by other groups than those which were in power at the time when the movement started. The national movements were also tied up with social changes. Certain strata of the society which were connected with national movements hoped for better positions and brighter prospects.

[15] K. MANNHEIM, *Ideology and Utopia* (New York, 1946).

National movements found their supporters mainly in the strata which were on the move, so to speak, and which hoped to find satisfaction in a new order of things. Thus the national idea seems explainable in terms of class ideology and indeed attempts at just such an interpretation have been often made. Even if future research should vindicate this theory, it has no right, yet, to be offered as a total explanation of Nationalism, for the case of Jewish Nationalism shows its inadequacy. Here the idea of Nationalism emerged not as an ideology covering the interest of any distinct class but rather as a national utopia to be followed because of its being prefigured by traditional Messianism.

By attributing the emergence of Jewish nationalism to the re-vitalization of the messianic utopia we do not mean to say that the mere suggestion of regathering of the Jews in their homeland was instrumental in initiating the national movement. The idea was, indeed, repeatedly aired and propagated also in the pre-nationalistic era. The historical connection between the Jews and their ancient homeland being a conspicuous feature in Jewish as well as Christian tradition, the inference that Jews should return to it dit not need too much ingenuity. The idea of the Restoration of the Jews gained currency especially in England where the awakened interest in the Old Testament in the wake of the Puritan revolution strongly stimulated the concern in the concrete history of the Jewish nation.[16] Most of the adherents of the Jewish Restoration, it is true, connected the return of the Jews to Palestine with their hopes for conversion to Christianity. Some of them however separated the two ideas and presented the plan of the Jews' return of their fatherland as the realization of the Jewish national aspiration—the novel by George Eliot *Daniel Deronda* written in 1874 being the best example of such an anticipation of modern Zionism grown out of the English restorational tradition.[17]

Among Jews too imaginative writers and social projectors came over again forward with the idea of establishing a Jewish commonwealth, either in Palestine or elsewhere, with the view of solving the Jewish problem. A case in point are the efforts of Mordecai M. Noah, one-time consul of the United States in Tunis, who in 1825 issued an appeal to European Jewry to establish a Jewish state named "Ararat" on the Grand Island of the Niagara River.[18] Later Noah fostered the idea of the Restoration in Palestine.

---

[16] See N. SOKOLOW, *History of Zionism* (London, 1919); N. M. GELBER, *Zur Vorgeschichte des Zionismus* (Wien, 1927); FR. KOBLER, *The Vision Was There, A History of the British Movement for the Restoration of the Jews to Palestine* (London, 1956).

[17] KOBLER, *ibid.*, pp. 89–93; L. STEIN, *The Balfour Declaration* (London, 1961), pp. 15–16.

[18] A. B. MAKOVER, *Mordecai M. Noah* (New York, 1917); J. GOLDBERG, *Major Noah, American Jewish Pioneer* (Philadelphia, 1936).

Historians of Zionism were very zealous to collect such early expressions of Nationalism conceiving them to be fore-runners of Zionism.[19] In the original historical setting these utterances of a new approach to Messianism were of no consequence. The propagators of these ideas had never succeeded in realizing any of their plans. No organizations or societies were set up for the propagation and advancement of their ideas. The general Jewish public took almost no cognizance of these ideas and their promoters, and if it did so its attitude was expressed in mockery and derision. The suggestions and their originators were indeed very soon forgotten. They left no mark behind them and scarcely ever influenced the course of coming events. Their historical significance is in something else. In the case of the Christian promoters, it shows how deeply the name of the Jews and the land of Israel were associated also in the mind of Christians. Without this association the comparative success of Zionism, dependent as it was on the support or at least the understanding of the gentile world, would have been unconceivable. In the case of the Jews the recurrent revival of the idea is a proof of the potency of modern Nationalism which was inherent in the Messianic tradition.

Forerunners of modern Zionism, meaning those who initiated and influenced the movement in a real historical sense, we are only entitled to call the three figures mentioned above together with several contemporaries of theirs who were active from the sixties of the nineteenth century. Alkalay who began his activities twenty years earlier succeeded only in the sixties in finding any substantial and lasting support. From this time on one can see a connection between the activities of the various nationalists. The three great figures whom we have described not only knew of each other but also supported each other mutually. They succeeded in founding a more or less interconnected society among themselves together with some other less conspicuous personalities who were influenced by them or who had reached the same conclusions independently. Moreover from the sixties onwards there is an uninterrupted development, and we may speak clearly of historical causation as we witness the ideas and activities of these early nationalists leading the way to the full-fledged national movement, which was founded in the 1880's under the impact of the Russian pogroms and the rise of modern antisemitism in Germany.

The difference between the earlier times when nationalist ideas were kindled only to be extinguished very soon and that of the sixties of the nineteenth century when they were caught up in a strain of historical development is not difficult to explain. The sixties represent the com-

[19] Kobler in his above-quoted book confessedly intended to write the history of the movement "as an integral part of British religious, social and political history" (p. 9) and not as an annex to the history of Zionism, but he cannot be said to have lived up to his intention.

pletion of Emancipation in most Western European countries. Where it was not yet wholly accomplished it was thought to be just round the corner. So long as the struggle for political equality was going on the idea of a Jewish Nationalism could not be tolerated. For the argument that the Jews are a national entity in itself was one of the main weapons of the enemies of emancipation. The Jewish answer to this was the declaration and indeed the manifestation of willingness to integrate themselves into the ranks of the other nations. The acceptance of an idea of Nationalism on a new basis was apt to belie the validity of the Jewish answer. Small wonder that wherever the idea was suggested it met with an adverse response and it was disregarded or suppressed. From the sixties on, when the Emancipation was as good as completed, the idea of Nationalism could be propagated as the next phase. Sometimes as in the case of Kalisher this was suggested to be the natural continuation of the emancipation itself. The successes of the sixties brought about in this way the first success in the development of Jewish Nationalism.

But what was the nature of this success? The colonization of Palestine started only in the eighties after the upheavals in Rumania and the bloody pogroms in Russia. There was an abortive attempt at colonization in 1879 by local Jews in Jerusalem who were strongly influenced by these forerunners, especially Kalisher. The first agricultural school Mikweh Yisrael near Jaffa was founded already in 1870. But this was done by the Franco-Jewish organization the "Alliance Israélite" which was not prompted by any national ideology although some of the forerunners tried to influence it in this direction. By and large one cannot say that the forerunners had succeeded in realizing something of their chief aim, i.e. the ingathering of Jews in their homeland.

The forerunners could have boasted of success but this was of a different kind. This was the uniting of the adherents of their idea through their mutual contact. These first nationalists were widely scattered but they succeeded in keeping some communication between themselves. The common idea became a basis of social unity.

From the standpoint of a relation between social needs and ideas the connection is apparently this: not the need created the idea but the idea created the social unit. We were unable to detect a social need corresponding to the emergence of the messianic-nationalist ideologies. There was no problem of Jewish disability or social discrimination to be solved. These Nationalists believed in the possibility of integration of Jews into the society of their respective countries. They certainly did not see any need for a place to emigrate to. Until the seventies when the troubles in Rumania started there had been no Jewish exodus from any country in Europe. The first Nationalists instead of producing an idea in order to satisfy a need were looking for a need which would correspond to their ideas. Kalisher hit upon any rumours which reached him of Jews wishing to emigrate as a Godsent opportunity to prove that there can be found people who are ready to go to Palestine. In this way he tried to refute the argument that his idea had no hold on reality. He never descended to the level of pragmatism to prove the truth of his idea from its necessity and usefulness. If there were anywhere an idea which preceded its social utility it was here.

* * *

As our case in point demonstrates that ideas at times do appear in advance of their need, it conversely shows the limited power of any idea so long as it is not linked up with a social necessity. We have noted above the failure of the first Nationalists to achieve even a fraction of their ultimate aim, namely, the gathering of the Jews in their homeland. The reasons for this are quite obvious. The re-establishment of a Jewish Commonwealth or even only the resettlement of the homeland demanded more than the creation of a movement similar to the movements which were flourishing amongst other nations. The achievement of the real aims entailed in this case the uprooting of people out of their surroundings and replanting them in another country under new conditions. The history of the Jewish National movement bears out the statement that this was beyond the strength of the National idea in itself. It could only accomplish its task when other forces were linked up with it. The first real objectives were realized only in the eighties when political and economical factors—persecutions and defamation in Rumania and bloody pogroms and civil disqualifications in Russia—set in motion a good many European Jews. The uprooting was now brought about by other factors and the idea of Nationalism had only a secondary task, that of reintegration and resettlement in the right place. In this it has succeeded though not on a very large scale. Out of the two and a half million people who emigrated from Rumania and Russia between the years 1880 and 1914 only some 70,000 settled in Palestine. In this relation between the possible and actual number of emigrants to Palestine we find a quantitative expression of the power of the national idea. It demonstrates its strength as well as its limitations. The emigrants who went to other countries instead of Palestine followed the line of economic and political pressure though, admittedly, a few may have been drawn by the idea of a land of liberty where Jewish suffering would finally be ended. They settled wherever entry was granted and where conditions offered a chance of making a livelihood. No idea of collective purpose was attached to the emigration. With some notable exception at its initial stage the whole process of emigration was accomplished by private initiative. Public agencies such as Jewish and non-Jewish philanthropic societies looked after them only on a humanitarian basis or on that of Jewish solidarity. Those who went to Palestine, on the other hand, followed an ideal and were conscious both of their self-sacrifice for the common goal and of the historic role which they were playing.

The historical task conceived by the pioneers was, it is true, no more the mere fulfilment of the Messianic promise, nor even its nationalistic derivation. During the last but decisive phase of the emigration before the First World War between 1904 and 1914 the so-called Second Aliyah arrived. This consisted mainly of former students, graduates of the Talmud-academies (Yeshivoth), "externs", who privately prepared themselves for entrance examinations to the universities but rarely succeeded, in short intellectually minded young men imbued with a variety of social and socialistic ideologies. Most of these pioneers had been at odds with their traditional Jewish background and maintained some contact with the modern social and philosophical trends prevalent in society at large and which had penetrated at least the periphery of Jewish society. Despairing of the realization of their personal as well as social aims they set out to create a new society. They brought with them a spectrum of ideologies ranging from orthodox Marxism to near anarchism, and a kind of Tolstoyan quest for the natural, pristine state of Man. Some of the pioneers evaluated these ideologies as being of primary importance and in theory even outweighing the national considerations, which however were never discarded. Much intellectual effort went into the attempts of harmonizing between these respective ideologies and the Jewish nationalism which seemed to be unrelated to or even inconsistent with them.[20] In whatever fashion the conflict was intellectually resolved, the fact is undeniable that both emotionally and practically nationalism prevailed. For attachment to the national objectives alone could promote all these to prefer Palestine to other countries of possible emigration. Those in whom the Jewish national renaissance was not a component of their ideology went elsewhere, or, if the attachment to this ideal was not strong enough, they left the country often having encountered the usual hardships of pioneering. Those who remained drew strength to endure the hardship out of their conviction that it is done in the service of their cause. Individually the devotion for the special non-national objectives might have been as strong as the affection for the national ideal or perhaps even greater. But with regard to other objectives the pioneers were divided while in the adherence to the national revival they were united. The attachment to the national cause united the pioneers also with their precursors, the settlers of the early eighties from whom socially and religiously they were divided as widely as possible. The commitment to the ideal of national renaissance

---

[20] I. KOLATT-KOPELOVICH, "Ideology and the Impact of Realities upon the Jewish Labour Movement in Palestine, 1905–1919," Doctoral dissertation (Jerusalem, 1964).

appeared to be a stronger force than all the social or ideological differences.

The idea of nationalism proved itself unable to uproot *en masse*
people out of a well balanced social setting. But it proved strong enough
to reintegrate those who were uprooted. And this was a formidable task
in the case of Jews. For as we have seen above the elements of nationalism were here almost entirely lacking. The settlers had to create not only
the material conditions for their existence but also the very means of
their national reintegration. The idea of national unity preceded the
means of unification. The first settlers had scarcely a common language,
in any case no language they could consider as a medium of social cohesion. Neither was there a real attachment to the landscape of their new
country. The concept of the Holy Land and the belief in the greatness of
the ancient fatherland were no more than ideas. The actual confrontation
with the new country demanded an adaptation to new conditions with regard to climate and even had to accustom themselves to a new and
strange physical environment. Only through a special effort did they succeed in finding poetic expression for the attachment to the scenery and
surroundings of the country.

All this was accomplished in its fundamental stages already in the
first decade preceding the First World War. This period, the time of the
second Aliyah, was politically an unsuccessful time. Nevertheless during
this time the foundations were laid for the new nation to develop. The
utopia began to become a reality. That the idea of Zionism was con-
ceptually nothing more than an utopia was recognized by none other than
by its greatest exponent, Theodor Herzl. In the preface to his *Judenstaat*,[21] in which he outlined the scheme of action for implementing his
idea, he anticipated the criticism that he is expounding a mere utopia.
His answer was that it is indeed an utopia with a qualification. Other
utopists set forth the design of a machine but their plans failed to provide for the driving force that would set the machine in motion. He, on
the other hand, had only to suggest the scheme, the driving energy,
namely, the Jewish distress had been there before. The *Judennot* will
set the machine in motion once it has been constructed. Therein Herzl
proved himself a prophet with a limitation, for he foresaw well the
future but not the course of events which would lead to it.

For the feat was not accomplished as Herzl had claimed through the
pressure of Jewish suffering. The Jewish suffering as Herzl experienced
it, namely the defamation in the West and the pogroms in the East had
other immediate effects. In the West it prompted some individuals like
Herzl himself to heart-searching resulting in some cases of actively

---

[21] TH. HERZL, *Der Judenstaat, Versuch einer modernen Lösung der Judenfrage* (Leipzig,
1896); English translation *A Jewish State* (London, 1896).

joining the national movement. But on the whole it brought about only apologetics and the organization for self-protection. In the Eastern countries it brought about a flight and started a stream of emigrants to overseas countries. It has not produced, as Herzl imagined it would do, a voluntary exodus from any country. At the crucial point of development when the nucleus of the nation was created it did not contribute to the solution of the Jewish problem. Palestine of that time was not considered as a possible country for emigration by those who sought only peace and livelihood. The sixty or seventy thousand people who were absorbed in Palestine in the formative years of the new nation represent a negligible percentage of the emigrants of those years. They could have easily found their way to some other country where the bulk of the Jewish emigration was absorbed.

The driving force which indeed was there when Herzl appeared on the scene was modern Jewish Nationalism, drawing its strength from the old but transformed messianism. Of this Herzl, while conceiving his plan, had not had the slightest knowledge. Being brought up in the atmosphere of assimilated Jewry of Budapest and Vienna, Herzl was unaware of the existence of the national movement when in the wake of the Dreyfus affair in 1896 he arrived at the idea of solving the Jewish problem by the creation of a Jewish state.[22] The idea would have indeed fallen into the dustbin of unredeemed utopias were it not for the enthusiasm of the nationalists who hailed Herzl as the Godsent leader arriving as it were from another planet. By the force of Nationalism deriving its strength from the deeper sources of Messianism, Herzl's utopia became ultimately a reality.

[22] A. Bein, *Theodor Herzl, a Biography* (Cleveland, 1962).

MOSHE MISHKINSKY

THE JEWISH LABOR MOVEMENT AND EUROPEAN
SOCIALISM

ROM its beginnings, the Jewish labor movement was bound up with the history of European socialism. Its continuous organizational existence dates from the end of the 1880s, at the time of the formation of the Second International at the Congress of Paris in 1889. But its origin goes back practically to the time of the official dissolution of the First International. In May 1876, there was established in London the Hebrew Socialist Society (it called itself in Hebrew: *Agudat ha-Sozialistim ha-Ivrim*). This was the first socialist association of Jewish workers. It is worthwhile to dwell on this society in particular, not so much because it was the first but because it showed a number of symptoms of substantive problems which were to manifest themselves fully in the Jewish labor movement when it came of age. Fortunately, the list of its members has been preserved, together with its constitution and program (written in the original in Hebrew and Yiddish) and the minutes of its meetings during the eight months of its existence. All these have been compiled under the title, *Pinkas*, in accordance with the best traditions of Jewish 'societies' (Hevroth).

The leading spirit in the formation of the society was A. S. Lieberman (1844[1842?]–1880), who is considered as the pioneer of Jewish socialism and in a sense also a precursor of the Jewish labor movement, although there were many contradictions in his thought. At the beginning of the 1870s Lieberman was part of a secret, revolutionary-socialist circle of Jewish youth in Vilna, Lithuania. There the idea crystallized that it was necessary to preach socialism to the Jews in their own languages, Yiddish and Hebrew. To escape imprisonment, Lieberman fled the country, and for several years he was active in London, Berlin, Vienna, and again London in an effort to establish a Jewish socialist organization. His main practical achievement after the dissolution of the Hebrew Socialist Society was the publication of a few issues of the first socialist periodical designed for Jews (in Hebrew): *Ha-Emeth*—The Truth. In London, Lieberman was connected with the Russian social revolutionary journal, *Vpered*. He was given encouragement by the editor, P. Lavrov,

the well-known theoretician of Russian Populism, while the managing
editor, V. Smirnov, played an important role in initiating the founding
of the Hebrew Socialist Society.

Of the society's 30–40 members, apparently not a single one had been
born in England. The members were Jewish immigrants from various
countries, most of them from different parts of Russia: Poland, Lithuania
and the Ukraine. They were workers, craftsmen, particularly in the
clothing trades. There were also a few intellectuals, like Lieberman, who
became workers when they immigrated. The society tried to form trade
unions of Jewish workers, but it is characteristic that the declared purpose of the society was not local, but the uniting of the Jewish workers
"to fight their exploiters" and the preaching of socialism among them
wherever they were to be found. The platform and the discussions, as
reflected in the minutes, reveal a hodgepodge of ideological elements
coming from a number of socialist streams, echoes of ideas that had been
bandied about at the First International, laudatory remarks about
Bakunin and his merits as a socialist, together with views which had their
origin in the ideational world of his unmitigated rival—Lavrov. Of the
name, Karl Marx's—a London resident—the minutes make no mention,
although the influence of his thinking is easily seen. Far removed from
the English labor movement and permeated with Russian-style revolutionary socialism, they understood, albeit unwillingly, that London was
not Russia, and they showed a tremendous interest in German Social
Democracy.

At the same time, we find the members raising the basic question of
whether the society really had a *raison d'être*. The salvation of the Jewish
people would come about only as part of the salvation of mankind, we
read in the society's platform. Was it in the spirit of socialism, which
proclaimed the equality of all mankind, to maintain a special Jewish
association? Perhaps this was not in conformity with the class principle?
Would the socialists in the various countries evince sympathy for the
society and its objects? Both the questions and the answers given to those
who expressed doubts and reservations reflect different viewpoints with
respect to the nature of the connection between a socialist world-view
and the methods of activity and organization to be adopted by Jewish
workers, and between the ties with the general labor movement and the
consciousness, however thin, of Jewish belonging and identity and of
what this entailed in practice. The explanation of one of the members
is narrowly empirical: the Jews are living in London among themselves;
therefore, and for the time being, one should work among them. Another
member (he, too, a former member of the above-mentioned revolutionary circle in Vilna) goes beyond the utilitarian position and gives
subjective expression to the feeling of self-respect, to the natural aspiration
for equality, and even to a certain grasp of the essence of the Jewish

collectivity: socialist societies exist in every nation, and socialists of the Jewish nation likewise want a society that bears their name. Lieberman touched on these questions at a number of meetings, and he broadened the picture. True, the class division was what counted, and for socialists there were no national distinctions. But the complete brotherhood of all men would come about only under the socialist banner; so long as the existing system prevailed the Jews would always be persecuted, they would always constitute an abnormal group. It was the Jewish bourgeoisie that was the enemy of the Jewish workers, but precisely for that reason the later had to unite and organize themselves, for they alone and no one else could and should fight against their enemies. In other words, it is precisely the idea of class auto-emancipation that gives rise dialectically (Lieberman does not use the term) to the justification for a special Jewish cohesion within a socialist framework. There is also something common to all Jews. In answer to the argument of one of the members (in the course of a debate on the holding of a meeting on *Tisha b'Av*, a day of fasting and mourning) that Jewish socialists should have nothing to do with any part of the old tradition, Lieberman said that that was not necessarily so. Until the advent of the socialist revolution, the political freedom of every nation was a matter of importance. *Tisha b'Av* commemorated the loss of independence by the Jewish people, which had been mourning this for over 1,800 years. For the time being, its value for Jewish socialists was no less than it was for the rest of their people. As for international solidarity, Lieberman described the program (unfortunately this is not given in the minutes) the Jewish workers in each country ought to adopt in order to unite among themselves, on the one hand, and to work in harmony with the socialist parties in all countries, on the other.

These ideas and viewpoints do not add up to a systematic philosophy, and owing to the paucity of the sources we do not know whether there was one. Probably not. But closer examination may enable us to detect here the beginning of a new chapter in a historical development, which opened with the period of Jewish emancipation in Europe. The question was: how would the Jews be incorporated in the general society—by gaining equality (civil or social) with the loss of their independent national identity, or through equality which allowed for difference? In the seventies this was mainly a matter of ideational difficulties for a few Jewish socialists of the type of Lieberman and his colleagues. With the appearance of a mass Jewish labor movement the question assumed new aspects—political and organizational—and in effect constituted the chief background for the *reciprocal relations* between European socialism in all its branches and the Jewish labor movement.

In surveying the problems involved in the influence of European socialism on the Jewish labor movement and of those by which European socialism was faced as a result of this development, two semantic explanations will be of help. One of them has to do with the adjective "Jewish" in the expression "the Jewish labor movement". The other concerns the geographical-territorial scope of the movement, which was an international in miniature, as it were, and the explanation of the significance of this fact in the context of our subject.

The adjective "Jewish" as used in "the Jewish labor movement" has two connotations, corresponding to two stages in the history of the movement or, perhaps it is more correct to say, to two tendencies which frequently operated side by side. Actually, we can make a terminological distinction and say that in the beginning this was a movement of "workers-Jews"—a definition which applies both to Russia and the United States. Jewish workers established their own organizations because they lived together, worked together, and spoke the same language; and by organizing they wanted to satisfy various needs, whether economic-occupational or cultural-educational. Neither the workers themselves nor the intellectuals who were connected with the Jewish environment, who joined the workers and frequently served as organizers and guides, intended at the beginning to establish an independent Jewish labor movement. The influence of socialism was decisive in these organizations; most of them arose to begin with under the inspiration of its ideas. In Russia this inspiration assumed the coloration of a blatantly revolutionary mood. The Jewish labor organizations received socialist doctrine as revelation, as a messianic vision which had been nourished to some extent by Jewish eschatological traditions and universal ideas of redemption. The universal ideal was the vision, and the workers' international was the method of achieving it. The idea of the common struggle of the toiling masses of all nations and tongues abolished, as it were, the reality of national differences and of the particular national aspirations, not only potentially—in the future order of things—but also actually, by the force of the image of the spiritual and even organizational fusion of the workers of all lands in one world movement, of which the International was both bearer and symbol. The second legacy—alongside universalism—of European socialism to the Jewish labor movement was the theory of the class struggle. This idea instilled in those who accepted it first of all a feeling of self-esteem, the motivation for organization and activity, and a new world view. The theory was acquired mainly from popularized pamphlets explaining the ideas of Marx, Lasalle and others. But the rather weak abstractions necessarily sought support in actual life. And in actual life the Jewish workers generally worked for Jewish employers, although usually not for big capitalists (as described in the pamphlets), but—especially in eastern Europe—for medium-sized and petty enterprises. In this actual life there was also truly a large measure of endless hours of work, low wages, degradation, and all sorts of exploitation. Against this background, the concepts of "capitalist exploitation," "class enemy" and "the class struggle," assumed the form of a belief in an unbridgeable conflict between Jewish workers and Jewish capitalists. In real life there was also a great mass of Jews who did not fit in either of these two categories. This problem was solved by the conception of the structure of society which declared that anything outside of "bourgeoisie" and "proletarian" was destined by the "historical process" to disappear and so need not be taken into account. According to these ideas, the reality of the existence of the Jewish people seemed to melt away, the inner ties within Jewry were severed, and they would not be restored—particularly since religion was losing its significance as a factor lending uniqueness to the Jews as a whole.

Such an approach emerges from the first document of the first Jewish labor movement organized in Russia—*Four Speeches of Jewish Workers* (in Russian) at the clandestine May Day rally in Vilna in 1892. We read:

> "And we Jews, too, 'Russian subjects', renounce our own holidays and fantasies which are useless for human society; we join the socialist ranks and we adher to their holiday ... which will exist forever, for its goal is to raze to the ground the pillars of the old world ... and to establish on their ruins a world of peace for all ... And as for our holidays which were bequeathed to us by our fathers, they are destined to disappear together with the old régime."

And an echo of these words seemed to resound from across the ocean. An editorial in honor of the first of May, 1894, published in the Yiddish socialist monthly, *Zukunft* (which had first made its appearance in New York two years before), had this to say: "Adieu, holidays of religion, and adieu, national festivities... let us raise a glass to the freedom, equality and happiness of a nation whose birthplace is the world, whose religion is brotherhood, and whose Torah is science." According to this approach, the Jewish origin of the workers in their organizations is an objective fact which in no way determines their aims or goals. When Abraham Cahan came as a delegate to the Congress of the Second International in Brussels in 1891, it was as the representative of "Yiddish-speaking workers' organizations" in the United States. For many years thereafter most Jewish socialists in that country took pains to designate themselves in that fashion, in order to emphasize that their organizations had nothing to do with Jewish identity in the broad sense. And Jewish Social Democratic circles in Vilna by 1891–1892 no longer regarded the Jewish labor movement as an independent factor with equal rights in the general labor movement but rather as a sort of appendix to it.

Only in its second stage did the movement of Jewish workers become a "Jewish labor movement," that is, it saw specific significance in the

Jewishness of the movement, and it laid out for itself special tasks on the strength of this fact—not only social, political and economic tasks, but also those of national significance. In the United States this was a long drawn-out process, which we shall refer to in another context. In Russia this tendency developed gradually but steadily until it crystallized fully in the period of the first Russian revolution. The growth of the new consciousness was linked up with the patterns of European Marxist thought as formulated by Plekhanov. But essentially it constituted an independent attempt to comprehend the special situation of the Jewish working class within Jewish existence in general. The new standpoint was put forward in a little pamphlet by S. Gozhanski that appeared at the end of 1893, "A Letter to Agitators," and more fully in a lecture delivered by V. Martov (later the leader of the Menshevists and sharp opponent of the Jewish labor movement) at a secret meeting in Vilna on the occasion of May Day, 1895.

The premise is that the jewish working class has special tasks of its own, and that to achieve them it must establish an organization of its own. The reference is to a struggle for equal civil rights for the Jews in Russia. This aim would be achieved only if the Czarist regime were over-thrown and a constitution obtained, and only if indissoluble ties were maintained with the general labor movement. There was no automatic connection, however, between the solution of the question of general freedom in Russia and the insuring of this special aim. For it was not inconceivable that the Russian proletariat, if circumstances required, might sacrifice those demands that applied to the Jews alone, such as freedom of religion or equality of rights. The Jewish proletariat therefore had to constitute a power in its own right and to wage a "political-national struggle". The fostering of the socialist class consciousness of the proletariat was combined with the fostering of its national self-consciousness. These in effect were the main ideological assumptions of the *Bund,* whose founding convention took place in the fall of 1897 in the same city of Vilna. They expressed a realistic revision of the abstract internationalist approach which brushed aside the tangible significance of differences and contrasts between nations, including contrasts between workers of different nations. The essence of the revision lay in the awareness of the difference and the special interests of the Jewish workers—both as workers and as Jews—and of the fact that these must find clear and organized expression in the general labor movement. Internationalism is not perceived here as something fixed and definite, but as a yearned-for goal, with the factors that make for separation not ignored, but with an effort being made by both sides to overcome them. There is a limit to the degree of confidence that the Jewish proletariat can have in the general labor movement with respect to the satisfaction of its special needs and the fulfilment of its special ambitions, and that is the extent of its self-confidence and the cultivation of its independent power. This would facilitate the fostering of internationalism—in a partnership of equality—in the general labor movement, which in the face of reality is obliged to act not only in accordance with principles but which is also influenced by extraneous considerations.

It is not our purpose here to consider all the factors that led to this development. But as far as our subject is concerned, we can say without hesitation that if the rise of the labor movement among the Jews was ideologically a product of the influence of European socialism, this is not true of the crystallization of the Jewish labor movement as a force in itself. The most important piece of evidence on this point is to be found at the congress of the Second International in Brussels in 1891. A. Cohen, a representative of organizations of "Yiddish-speaking workers" in the United States, moved the following question for the agenda: "What shall be the attitude of organized workers in all countries to the Jewish question?" The stimulus for this question was the intensified persecution of the Jews in Russia and particularly the expulsion of the Jews from Moscow. The congress decided to strike the question from the agenda. It did not resolve that it was the duty of the socialist parties to fight against anti-Semitism or to put forward as a programmatic demand the equality of political rights for all citizens without regard to religion or nationality. Instead, the congress denounced both "anti-Semitism" and "philo-Semitism". The resolution also included the following statement: "The Jewish-speaking workers have no other means of liberation except unity with the Socialist-labor parties in the countries they inhabit." That sentence can only be understood as meaning that there is no place for a Jewish labor movement with goals of its own, and that in fact is how it was interpreted (with approval) by *Vorwärts*, the German Social Democratic organ. The resolution in general—according to the testimony of the leader of one of the groups there—caused resentment in Vilna. Perhaps they took some comfort from the sharp criticism of it by Plekhanov. Meanwhile there occurred the pogrom against the Jews of Lodz, a concomitant of the strike of May 1892 in that city. There were also recollections of the positive attitude evinced by the executive committee of the revolutionary organization, *Narodnaya Vola* ("The People's Will") towards the pogroms in Russia in 1881–1882. The ideology of the Jewish labor movement thus appeared, from the historical aspect, as an expression of the need and the desire for self-defence through organizing, and for independent activity to fight discrimination and persecution, out of a feeling of being somewhat isolated from the environment. This task was destined to assume a new expression after the Kishinev pogrom of 1903 and in the wave of pogroms in 1905 and 1906, when organizations of Jewish workers became the leading element in the armed "self-defence" against the pogromists. The International

never repealed the Brussels resolution, but after 1900 both the Bureau of
the International and its congress in Amsterdam (1904) denounced the
Russian government's persecution of the Jews and discrimination against
them in the law.

The Jewish labor movement in Russia took on its full significance at
the turn of the century when it arrived at the distinct recognition of the
need to combine the national with the socialist element in its ideology
and program. There is no single model here, but a wide variety of
organizations, streams and views, and even with sharp struggles being
conducted between them. This testifies not only to how deeply the
national idea had penetrated Russian Jewry, but also to the great spread
of socialist ideas and revolutionary activity among broad classes of the
people. The *Bund*, which had played a cardinal role in the founding
of Russian Social Democracy and which constituted the strongest
organized force within it, in 1901 put forward the demand for cultural-
national autonomy for the Jews. In 1898 Nahman Syrkin published a
pamphlet, *Die Judenfrage und der sozialistische Judenstaat*, in which he
establishes the basis for socialist Zionism. In 1905–1906, a series of new
parties arose. There was Poale Zion, which stood for the establishment
of a socialist Jewish society in Eretz-Israel. There was the Socialist
Zionist Workers Party, which advocated a Jewish territorial concentration, but not necessarily in Eretz-Israel. (It also played an important
rôle in the revolutionary period of 1905–1906.) The Socialist Jewish
Workers' Party (known by its Russian initials, SERP) put forward the
demand for personal-national autonomy. All these parties recognized
the need to take part, in practice, in Russian political life. From the
ideological aspect, Poale Zion and the "Socialist Zionists" (the Territo-
rialists) based themselves on Marxist axioms. The analysis of Jewish
economic life and, in particular, the study of the special situation of the
Jewish proletariat, served as the point of departure for their programs.
In SERP, the majority tended towards the socialist conception of the
Socialist Revolutionary Party.

But the idea of Jewish nationalism, not only in its Zionist and territorialist versions, but even as formulated by the *Bund*, met with sharp
opposition in the socialist movement. The *Bund* (and SERP too) based
its program on the theoretical works of the leaders of Austrian Social
Democracy, Karl Renner and Otto Bauer. Yet Bauer—an assimilated
Jewish socialist—objected to the application of the principle of autonomy
to the Jews, since in effect he denied the national character of the
Jewish communities. The toughest struggle took place within the Russian
Social Democratic Party, a struggle that reached its climax at the
second convention, when the *Bund* left the party, to return after three
years. Here too particular weight attached to the opposition of assimilated Jewish Social Democrats (e.g., Martov, Trotsky) to a national

conception of the Jewish question. But it was Lenin's position that was of special significance. Much has been written on the subject, and here we shall only note a few points. The *Bund* proposed a federative structure for the Social Democratic Party. Lenin, who favored extreme centralism in the party, objected. But the debate on the structure of the party was linked up with a dispute on the Social Democratic program on the Jewish question, on national-cultural autonomy, and on the Jewish national idea. A draft resolution which Lenin prepared (not later than July 30, 1903) for the second convention of the Social Democratic Party speaks of "national culture" in connection with the Jews. According to elementary logic, it would thus appear that the Jews were a nationality. But less than three months later, in an article entitled "The Position of the Bund in the Party" (published in *Iskra* on October 22, 1903), Lenin declared that the idea of Jewish nationalism is reactionary and false, and he puts the concept of Jewish "nationality" in quotation marks. In his article, "Concerning the Bund's Decision" (February 1, 1903), he says that there is no "greater foolishness" than to determine in advance whether the evolution of the Jews in free Russia would be as it had been in Western Europe, or not. But in the other article mentioned, "The Position of the Bund in the Party", Lenin no longer has any doubt that in Russia too the assimilation of the Jews is both necessary and desirable. There are more contradictions and zigzags that can be discovered here, but what stands out is the utilitarian and capricious approach in deciding the nature and future of a national group, with reliance on quotations from Renan, Naqker, Kautsky, and, in a later period, Bauer. Gozhanski never dreamed that the eventual renunciation of the special demands of the Jews which he advocated would ever be applied to the right of their group existence as such. The struggle over the *raison d'être* of the Jewish labor movement, which in this case was represented by the *Bund*, took the form of a struggle over the right of the Jews and the Jewish proletariat to determine for themselves the question of their continued national existence.

A second semantic explanation is called for here, namely, the *geographical* concretization of the concept, "the Jewish labor movement". Technically this can be done very simply, by giving a concentrated itemization of the countries in which all sorts of workers' organizations arose, developed and crystallized in the period between 1880 and 1939: trade unions, political parties, mutual assistance societies, cooperatives, kibbutzim, cultural and educational organizations, newspapers, schools. An almost complete list (and one quite impressive in its scope) for the period before World War I includes Czarist Russia, England, the United States, Rumania, the Austrian Empire (particularly Galicia), France, Canada, Bulgaria, Ottoman Turkey (mainly Salonica), Holland,

Argentina, and Eretz-Israel. For the period between the two World Wars, that map would have to be brought up to date, to take account of the geopolitical changes that occurred following the break-up of the Habsburg Empire, the revolutions of 1917 in Russia, the achievement of independence by Russia's border areas (Poland, Lithuania, Latvia), as well as the growth of new Jewish settlements in South American countries.

The details of the history of the Jewish labor movement in each of these countries were of course bound up with the social and political texture of the particular country, and was influenced by developments in the general labor movement there and, more particularly, by the developmental trends of the various Jewish settlements as units in themselves and from the aspect of their relations with non-Jewish society. At the same time, we are likely to err, it would seem, if we take the fact of the geographical fragmentation as our sole guide when we come to consider comprehensive questions of the type which become focused in the dynamic contact with European socialism, from the ideological, programmatic, and even institutional points of view. For an examination of the genesis of the territorial-geographical diffusion in the end leads us back to the recognition of the need for some degree of integration, that is, of conceiving the Jewish labor movement as a *universal* historical phenomenon. There exists a real, material background against which the multi-faceted unity of the movement took shape: the process of Jewish migration, which practically assumed the dimensions of an exodus. The mass Jewish migration began in the 1880s and it grew greater and greater as World War I approached. The countries abandoned were Rumania, Galicia, and Russia. The driving force was economic distress, but no less important was the influence of political pressures and legal discrimination: in Russia—the pogroms, restrictive laws, official persecution and the spread of public Judaphobia; in Rumania—the legal status of the Jews, who were considered "aliens"; and even in Galicia there were many indications of political and economic anti-Semitism. The emigrants made their way westward to England, to Argentina, to Eretz-Israel, but mainly to the United States. The number of Jewish immigrants to the United States alone in the period between 1881 and 1910 is estimated at 1,560,000, and only a relatively small proportion— in comparison with other ethnic groups—returned to their country of origin. The decisive fact was that the Jewish immigrants retained their group identity. They concentrated mainly in certain cities and neighborhoods (New York's East Side and London's East End are today only a historical reminder of this fact). They made a special place for themselves in certain branches of industry or even created them (the clothing industries), and they developed different forms of communal life. The process of adaptation to the new environment, which continued steadily, took place concomitantly with the cultivation of a network of independent institutions—and this too served to prevent assimilation. Nor were the Jewish workers dissolved in the "American Melting Pot". The Jewish labor movement in the countries of absorption was thus, in effect, an immigrants' movement, both from the aspect of its social theme and from that of the composition of its leadership and the continuity of the immigration. For two generations it preserved both its distinctiveness in regard to the American labor movement and its attachment to the labor movements in the countries of origin. The Jewish labor movement in the United States was in fact a channel of influence of European socialism. Most of the pioneer organizers of the Jewish workers in the United States were intellectuals who left Russia after the pogroms and who had been influenced there by the revolutionary Populism of the seventies and eighties. Among them were those who before coming to the United States had been active in Jewish labor organizations and in Jewish socialist newspapers in England, which in general served as a way station for immigrants to the United States. Some of these became workers themselves, while others resumed their studies but did not sever their ties with the movement. Among the first arrivals were members of the *Am'Olam* group, which had been organized back in Russia. In the spirit of the agrarian socialism characteristic of the *narodniki*, they tried in America to establish agricultural communes, which did not last very long. This group later contributed many active workers to the Jewish labor movement. Some of them were attracted to anarchism, which as a result of the conditions of immigrant life exerted considerable influence during a certain period among the Jewish workers in general, both in England and the United States. The activity among the Jewish workers was influenced by the trade unions of the German workers in the United States. The German socialists also held a decisive position in the Socialist Party. With its help the United Hebrew Trades was established in New York in 1888, with a socialist program. This combination of trade unionism and socialism was also a feature of the Jewish labor movement in the United States later on, and distinguished it from the dominant trend in the American labor movement, as embodied in the American Federation of Labor whose slogan was "pure and simple unionism". The large wave of immigration from the period of the first revolution and the pogroms in Russia brought immigrants who, unlike the previous wave, included many skilled workers who had already gone through the experience of activity in the *Bund* and other labor parties, and of participation in the revolutionary movement. These brought with them something of the militant spirit of their country of origin as well as a broader grasp of the Jewish content that should be instilled in the labor movement. Revolutionary activity did not have much chance of success in the United States, but ideological and social radicalism left their mark on the movement even after trade union militancy had dissipated, leaving its traces by bequeathing liberal and reformist tendencies even to the second and third generation of immigrants who, as a result of the social mobility and the economic opportunities, were able to abandon manual labor.

Similarly, the Eretz-Israel labor movement (the development of which requires separate treatment), whose foundations were laid in 1904–1905, bore many signs of the European socialist heritage.

The link of the Jewish labor movement with the immigration process impressed on it a special character, from the ideational aspect, such as is not found in any other labour movement. In the first place, the very existence of the process of immigration and the evaluation of its nature and prospects served as basic premises of the Zionist and territorialist parties in various countries (England, Argentina, the United States, and others). Poale Zion also organized a world union. Even the Jewish labor movement in the United States, owing to its special interest in Jewish immigration, generally took a stand different from that of the American labor movement in general, which favored immigration restriction. The *Bund*, too, which was represented in the International as part of the Russian Social Democratic section and which enjoyed a prestigious position there, could no longer ignore the immigration question, and at the congress of the International at Stuttgart in 1907 succeeded in blocking an extreme resolution advocating immigration restrictions.

Both the immigration question and the efforts of the Jewish labor parties to get the International to admit a world Jewish section helped to put the Jewish question as an international question before socialist public opinion. Likewise, the ground was prepared for a change in the attitude of the Socialist International towards the end of World War I and thereafter with respect to the subject of the national rights of the Jews in the countries where they were living and even with respect to the Zionist-Socialist ideal.

European socialism in its different varieties tended, when it penetrated the Jewish environment, to serve first of all as the inspiration for cosmopolitan and assimilatory tendencies among a good part of the Jewish intellectuals. Yet the socialist vision and the humanitarian aspirations which derived from socialism aroused broad sections of Jewish society to social consciousness and public activity, advanced the democratization of Jewish internal life, and varied and intensified the forms of organization within it.

When the Jewish labor movement became a mass movement and spread to different countries it in effect evinced specific forms of the forces of constancy which have operated in recent generations to preserve the group distinctiveness of the Jewish people. At first, the Jewish labor movement drew its ideological inspiration from the different trends of European socialism, but once it became independent, it began to participate in shaping the latter's character. This applies first of all to questions directly connected with Jewish life. But the Jewish labor movement also made a unique contribution to socialist ideology and to the methods of realizing it in the spirit of social progress—and this contribution was made in particular by the experience of the labor movement in Eretz-Israel.

SELECT BIBLIOGRAPHY

[1] M. EPSTEIN, *Jewish Labor in U.S.A.* (New York, 1950, 1953), volumes 1–2.

[2] A. L. PATKIN, *The Origins of the Russian Jewish Labour Movement* (Melbourne, 1947).

[3] B. SAPIR, "Liberman et le Socialisme russe," *International Review of Social History*, III (1938), pp. 25–88.

[4] "The Early Jewish Labor Movement in the U.S.", *YIVO* (New York, 1961). Ed. by E. TCHEVIKOVER. Trans. and rev. from the original yiddish by A. ANTONOVSKY.

[5] L. P. GARTNER. *The Jewish Immigrant in England* (London, 1960), chap. III-IV.

[6] W. PREUSS, *The Labour Movement in Israel* (3rd ed., Jerusalem, 1965).

LLOYD P. GARTNER

IMMIGRATION AND THE FORMATION OF
AMERICAN JEWRY, 1840-1925

T HE Jews of the United States form today the largest Jewish group of any country in the world, as they have since the break up of Czarist Russia in 1918. Their number is estimated at 5,720,000 persons.[1] Although they have lived since the mid-seventeenth century in the territories which now compose the United States, only since approximately 1880 has the Jewish population attained great size. Historians generally accept that perhaps 2,000 Jews lived in the Thirteen Colonies at the time of the American Revolution, and fifty years later, about 1825, the number was still no higher than about 6,000. Sharp increase began from then, however, for in 1840 there were about 15,000 Jews, and at the outbreak of the American Civil War in 1861 an estimated 150,000 lived there.[2] When the first rudimentary survey of American Jewry was undertaken in 1877 by the Board of Delegates of American Israelites, the total was put at 280,000.[3] From this point, the Jewish population multiplied with astonishing rapidity, owing almost entirely to mass immigration from Eastern Europe. Contemporaries estimated that 1,000,000 Jews dwelled in the United States in 1900, 3,000,000 in 1915, and 4,500,000 in 1925, when drastic immigration laws took effect.[4] The rate of Jewish population increase between 1840 and 1925 was thus far higher than that for the United States as a whole. While

[1] *American Jewish Year Book, 1966*, ed. Morris FINE and Milton HIMMELFARB (New York and Philadelphia, 1967), pp. 81 ff. (abbrev. *AJYB*). The statistics of American Jewish population for all periods are unreliable. For the earliest known head count of an American Jewish community, taken by a Milwaukee rabbi in 1875, see Louis J. SWICHKOW and Lloyd P. GARTNER, *A History of the Jews of Milwaukee* (Philadelphia, 1963), pp. 65–67. There have been, however, numerous quite exact population surveys of local communities during recent decades, based on careful sampling rather than actual count. Portions of this paper were delivered before the Organization of American Historians at Chicago, April 29, 1967.

[2] Salo W. BARON and Joseph L. BLAU, eds., *The Jews of the United States 1790-1840: A Documentary History*, 3 vols. (New York, Philadelphia, London, 1963), I, pp. 85–86, 255 n. 1; Bertram W. KORN, *American Jewry and the Civil War* (Philadelphia, 1951), p. 1.

[3] David SULZBERGER, "The Growth of Jewish Population in the United States", *Publications of the American Jewish Historical Society* (abbrev. *PAJHS*), VI (1897), pp. 141-149.

[4] The growth may be seen from the annual estimates in the *AJYB*, "Statistics of Jews" section.

the country's 11,000,000 inhabitants multiplied over tenfold to 115,000,000 during this period, the Jews increased more than three hundred times over. Since 1925, however, Jewish population growth has been reversed. With 200,000,000 persons now (November, 1967) living in the United States—an increase of 85,000,000 since 1925—the Jewish increment has been a relatively small 1,250,000. This disproportionately small growth has occurred notwithstanding the fact that, despite immigration laws, American Jewry has received a proportionately greater accession to its numbers since 1925 from foreign immigration than has the general American population.[5]

Between 1825 and 1925, therefore, the increase in American Jewry was owing to immigration from abroad. Since 1925, the relatively small increase seems due to the great decrease in that immigration.

These immigrants became transformed into Americans in culture, language, and loyalties, yet the vast majority also remained distinctly Jewish in consciousness, by desire, and in formal affiliation. It is of great interest, therefore, to examine the sources and character of Jewish immigration, and its adaptation to American life.

Well before substantial Jewish immigration began to flow, the highly favorable terms by which Jews, and others, could enter and accommodate themselves in American life were fixed. Early America was a land of Protestant Christians, whose bugbear in religion was not the near-legendary Jews but recognizable Catholics—a bitter heritage of Reformation struggles. Gradually, however, religion in America was permeated during the eighteenth century with philanthropy and humanitarianism, the belief that the truest Christianity was man's fulfillment of his purpose to do good on earth. These ideas tended to slice through Protestant denominational walls, and very slowly to flatten them. The denigration of the historic dogmas of Christianity opened the chance that the ancient "synagogue of Satan" might be granted rights nearly equal with the church of Christ on American soil. Moreover, the emphasis upon good works was to have very far-reaching consequences for the character of Judaism in America during the nineteenth century.[6]

Thinking about religion during the eighteenth century also helped to produce a change of fundamental character in the relations between Church and State. Most Protestant sects in America stressed the utterly individual nature of human sin and conversion and salvation, and vigor-

[5] United States Department of Commerce, Bureau of the Census, *Historical Statistics of the United States: Colonial Times to 1957* (Washington, D. C., 1963), Series A 1-3, p. 7; Series C 88-114, p. 56; Mark WISCHNITZER, *To Dwell in Safety: The Story of Jewish Migration since 1800* (Philadelphia, 1948), p. 289; the *AJYB* contains an annual report on Jewish immigration to the United States.

[6] H. Shelton SMITH, Robert T. HANDY, Lefferts A. LOETSCHER, *American Christianity: An Historical Interpretation with Representative Documents*, 2 vols. (New York, 1960), pp. 374-414.

ously opposed any coercive ecclesiastical intervention, particularly the Church linked to the State. Members of State churches in Europe, such as Lutherans and Catholics, were generally small, little loved minorities in Colonial America which also became accustomed to maintain their religious institutions unaided and unhampered.

The power of the Protestant left thus combined with its spiritual opposite, the secular, anti-clerical bias of Enlightenment thinking, to bring about the separation of Church and State. Religious tests and sectarian oaths of office were abolished and prohibited, and the First Amendment to the Federal Constitution virtually completed the process by forbidding Congress to establish or support any religion. State Constitutions made similar provisions.

These momentous developments during the latter half of the eighteenth century were of invaluable importance for the Jews who were destined to come to America. Except for an occasional religious qualification for public office in a few State constitutions, all of which were presently removed, the Jews enjoyed full civil, religious, and political equality with other religions from the time of American independence. This was full emancipation in the European sense, and it was acquired with barely any reference to the Jews as such, but rather as a matter of broad principle.[7] The separation of Church and State also meant that no one was required to profess religious belief or maintain religious affiliation; churches, and religious societies generally, were private associations which established rules as they wished. Religious sects and institutions could be established at will; schismatics enjoyed unlimited freedom alongside orthodox communicants. How deeply Judaism was affected by this pattern may be judged from the fact that most Jewish religious institutions in the United States are synagogues which have deviated more or less from the Jewish canon, and nearly nothing could be done by traditionalists to restrain them While the Constitutional deliberations were in progress, the Jews seem to have remained indifferent to them. They were mainly interested in the abolition of religious tests and oaths,[8] not in the separation of Church and State. But then, these Jews were newcomers, and probably still retained the historic Jewish wariness of intruding into the political affairs of the Gentile nations.

[7] Alan HEIMERT, *Religion and the American Mind from the Great Awakening to the Revolution* (Cambridge, Mass., 1966), pp. 128–129, 136–137, 524–527, 537–539; Anson Phelps STOKES, *Church and State in the United States*, 3 vols. (New York, 1950), I, pp. 133–149, 240–253, 519–552, 731–744, 744–767; for the exceptions to the generalities, see *ibid.*, pp. 428–432 (New Hampshire), 865–878 (Maryland). A useful review is Abram Vossen GOODMAN, *American Overture: Jewish Rights in Colonial Times* (Philadelphia, 1947).

[8] STOKES, *op. cit.*, pp. 286–290, 528–529; Edwin WOLF 2nd and Maxwell WHITEMAN, *The History of the Jews of Philadelphia from Colonial Times to the Age of Jackson* (Philadelphia, 1957), pp. 147–149.

Thus, even before European Jewry began its historic struggle for emancipation which was not consummated until the end of World War I, the entire question was settled quite casually in America. The issue of the enfranchisement of Jews specifically, and the terms of Jewish entry into the general society, never existed here. Jewish immigrants also found that no formal, legally established Jewish community existed here with its traditions, controls, and taxes. They could be or not be Jews, as they pleased, and if they preferred not they did not have to become Christians—an act repugnant to most of the reluctant Jews. They could occupy the neutral ground of enlightened secular humanism or religious indifferentism. The possibilities of Judaism and Jewish life in America under the regime of free option, State aloofness, and automatic emancipation were to be explored by every generation of Jews who came to America. Such a regime had no precedent in the entire millenial history of the Jews.

The first Jews in America were Sefardim, descendants of Spanish and Portugese Jews. It has long been known that many of these pioneers were not actually of Spanish culture. By the eighteenth century, formally Sefardi congregations consisted mainly of Ashkenazi (Central and East European) congregants, who accepted the strange liturgy and customs of what was then the single synagogue in the town.[9] In fact, the Philadelphia synagogue, founded only a few years after the first recorded appearance of Jews in that city in 1735, had no Sefardi members, yet adopted the Sefardi rite.[10] The continuance of the Sefardi form of worship, despite the minority of Spanish and Portugese Jews in the little Colonial communities, was assisted by the characteristically Sefardi rule of prohibiting the separate local congregations which proliferated among Ashkenazim, and of centralizing local Jewish affairs in the Mahamad (executive) of the single established synagogue.

Colonial Jews who were not Sefardim were mainly recently arrived Central Europeans. The differences between them and the Sefardim lay deeper than in ritual. The latter were for centuries naturalized in Iberian culture, spoke Spanish or Portugese, and had fused their Judaism with Spanish culture. To that extent they could be called modern Jews. Their Judaism was not learned or passionate, but polite and urbane. The comparative success of this combination of contemporary culture and Jewish tradition, although it was rather superficial, suggests the principal reason why no Sefardi synagogue abandoned Orthodoxy for Reform Judaism during the nineteenth century. On the other hand, the Central European Jewish majority consisted largely of Jews of traditional culture. They were not of learned of wealthy stock, nor had they

---

[9] David de SOLA POOL, *An Old Faith in the New World* (New York, 1955), pp. 437,461.
[10] WOLF and WHITEMAN, *op. cit.*, pp. 7, 32, 41-42, 122, 228; correspondence was conducted in Yiddish (p. 226).

moved in the small circles of German Jews which were reaching out ultimately to create the memorable synthesis of German culture and Judaism. These Bavarian, Posen, or Silesian Jews came to America from the villages and small towns of their native land, generally knew and observed the rudiments of Judaism and little more, and spoke and wrote Yiddish rather than German. In their great majority they were tradesmen, ranging from country peddlers to merchant shippers, and many were independent craftsmen. Apprentices and indentured servants could be found, and rarely a physician, a lawyer, or a leisured gentleman.[11] The main cities were New York City, Philadelphia, and Charleston, South Carolina, with outlying settlements in inland or "fall line" towns like Lancaster, Pa., Albany, N.Y., and Richmond, Va.

The 6,000 Jews of 1826 began to increase rapidly from that year. The impulse to emigrate was strongly felt in German Jewry, which by the 1830's and 1840's was more different from its eighteenth century ancestors than those ancestors had been from sixteenth century German Jews. Young Jews of the day uniformly received a German education, and even university study was not uncommon. Great political events also had their influence. During the Napoleonic years bright hopes for emancipation and full entry into German society soared, as Prussia and other duchies and cities freed their Jews from venerable restrictions on marriage, settlement, occupation, and from special taxes. But the period of political reaction and economic depression after 1815 brought the deepest disappointments to expectant Jews. Political restrictions were reinstituted, and the restored powers of Christian guilds denied access to some occupations for skilled Jews. The Christian State theories by which these measures were justified were subscribed to by influential politicians and intellectuals, and increased the Jews' sense of deprivation and exclusion. Apostasy was one escape from the predicament, and emigration was another. If the German homeland would not have them as faithful subjects, a new homeland could be found in free America. Land hunger, which drove millions of Germans across the Atlantic, played no role in Jewish emigration.[12]

German Jews had known and idealized America during the eigh-

[11] Jacob R. MARCUS, *Early American Jewry*, 2 vols. (Philadelphia, 1951-1953), II, pp. 395-428; WOLF and WHITEMAN, *op. cit.*, pp. 165-186; Leo HERSHKOWITZ, *Wills of Early New York Jews, 1704-1799* (New York, 1967), supplies unique, fresh data.
[12] Mack WALKER, *Germany and the Emigration 1816-1885* (Cambridge, Mass., 1964), pp. 42-102; Marcus L. HANSEN, *The Atlantic Migration 1607-1860* (new ed., New York, 1961), pp. 120-171; Selma STERN-TAEUBLER, "The Motivation of the German-Jewish Emigration to America in the Post-Mendelssohnian Era", *Essays in American Jewish History* (Cincinnati, 1958), pp. 247-262; Rudolf GLANZ, "The Immigration of German Jews up to 1880", *YIVO Annual of Jewish Social Science* (abbrev. *YAJSS*), II/III (1948), pp. 81-99; *idem*, "Source Materials for the History of Jewish Immigration to the United States 1800-1880", *YAJSS*, VI (1951), pp. 73-156 (invaluable gathering of sources, mostly from German Jewish press).

teenth century. The Constitutional Convention of 1787 received a puzzling but ardent petition from anonymous German Jews about settling in America, and periodic talk of the New World was not rare.[13] To the economic and psychological background of immigration could be added the steady improvement in the safety, speed, and regularity of trans-Atlantic travel. Between the 1820's and 1870's perhaps 150,000 Jews from German lands came to the United States, mainly from Bavarian towns and villages, German Poland, Bohemia, and Hungary.[14] Their geographic diffusion in America was wider than any Jewish immigrant group of earlier or later times. During these mid-nineteenth century decades of newly founded Western frontier cities, California gold, and the peak of the Southern cotton economy, German Jews scattered throughout the United States. Probably the majority settled in the Northeast, but a large number made their way to newly opened California, centering in San Francisco; a string of Jewish settlements appeared at the ports down the length of the Mississippi River; numerous Jewish communities arose in the cities along the Ohio River and the Great Lakes, centers of commerce and heavy industry; in dozens of small towns in the South, Jewish merchants kept store and traded in the freshly picked cotton.[15]

Jews from German lands took pride in their German culture. They were pillars of American Germandom, contributing and participating heavily in the advancement of German in the United States. They maintained German social and charitable societies, were subscribers and writers for German newspapers, singers and instrumentalists in German musical societies, impresarios, performers and faithful patrons in the German theatres. It appears also that Jews enjoyed access to the Turnverein athletic societies and German social clubs in many cities. German fraternal orders included many Jewish members. Indeed, Jews were included among the American Germans who articulated the idea

[13] BARON and BLAU, op. cit., III, pp. 891–893; Morris U. SCHAPPES, A Documentary History of the Jews in the United States 1654-1875 (3rd ed., New York, 1971), pp. 159–160.

[14] Rudolf GLANZ, "The Immigration of German Jews...", loc. cit.; idem, "The 'Bayer' and the 'Pollack' in America", Jewish Social Studies, XVII, 1 (January, 1955), pp. 27–42; Guido KISCH, In Search of Freedom: A History of American Jews from Czechoslovakia (London, 1949), pp. 13–58.

[15] Allan TARSHISH, "The Economic Life of the American Jew in the Middle Nineteenth Century", Essays..., pp. 263–293; Rudolf GLANZ, The Jews of California from the Discovery of Gold until 1880 (New York, 1960), pp. 18-91, 106-109; Harris NEWMARK, Sixty Years in Southern California 1853-1913 (3rd ed., Boston and New York, 1930); Jacob R. MARCUS, Memoirs of American Jews 1775-1865 (3 vols., Philadelphia, 1955), contains dozens of useful and interesting autobiographical statements, typically by immigrant businessmen of the times; SWICHKOW and GARTNER, op. cit., pp. 12–18, 93–110; W. Gunther PLAUT, The Jews of Minnesota: The First Seventy-Five Years (New York, 1959), pp. 9–30, 61–68; Stephen BIRMINGHAM, "Our Crowd": The Great Jewish Families of New York (New York, 1967), is a gossipy social chronicle, occasionally useful.

that they had the mission of diffusing a higher, philosophic culture among the Yankees.[16]

For some German Jews, the German milieu in America was so fully satisfying that they more or less abandoned their ancestral Judaism. One might mention in this connection Abraham Jacobi (1830-1919), the father of American pediatrics, the socialist leader Victor Berger (1860-1929), or Oswald Ottendorfer (1826-1900), who published the leading German newspaper in New York. The great majority, however, remained within Judaism and created a version satisfying to their desire for a religion which harmonized intellectually with contemporary liberalism, rationalism, and historical scholarship. This was Reform Judaism. On the surface, it meant that the old informality and intensity of Jewish worship was replaced by a liturgical model suggestive of Protestantism, housed in a Temple which often imitated intentionally the "Golden Age" architecture of Spanish Jewry. All Jewish laws and customs which enforced a social gulf between Jews and Christians were abrogated, with the single, critical exception of Jewish-Christian marriages. The transition from inherited Orthodoxy to new-style Reform took place with astonishing speed. After a false beginning in Charleston during the 1820's, Reform actually began about 1850. By 1890 nearly every synagogue founded by German Jews had overturned the traditions of centuries and taken up the new way. The Orthodox and proto-Conservatives survived as small groups, individual rabbis, and a few congregations.[17]

In any of dozens of American Jewish local communities during the 1880's and 1890's, the typical scene was a representative leadership of prosperous merchants, sometimes bankers and lawyers. By coming to America, they had not left a bitter for a gentler exile, where they would await messianic redemption; the Messiah was the millenium of all mankind, and their own future lay entirely in America. To these Jews, "Jew" meant only to profess the Jewish religion. All that was suggestive of "ghetto" had to be discarded, now that the physical ghetto was a

[16] Rudolf GLANZ, *Jews in Relation to the Cultural Milieu of the Germans in America up to the Eighteen-Eighties* (New York, 1947); SWICHKOW and GARTNER, *op. cit.*, pp. 13-27; John A. HAWGOOD, *The Tragedy of German-America*, (New York and London, 1940), is a penetrating analysis.

[17] David PHILIPSON, *The Reform Movement in Judaism* (new ed., New York, 1967) (originally published in 1907 and somewhat revised in 1931; this rather partisan work is quite antiquated but has not been superseded as a whole); James G. HELLER, *Isaac M. Wise: His Life, Work and Thought* (New York, 1965) (a voluminous, compendious biography of the most important leader); SWICHKOW and GARTNER, *op. cit.*, pp. 32-51, 171-192; Morris A. GUTSTEIN, *A Priceless Heritage: The Epic Growth of Nineteenth Century Chicago Jewry* (New York, 1953), pp. 57-92, 139-208; (these studies exemplify local developments); Moshe DAVIS, *The Emergence of Conservative Judaism: The Historical School in 19th Century America* (Philadelphia, 1963), pp. 149-228 (on the opposition to Reform); the *Dictionary of American Biography* includes Berger, Jacobi, and Ottendorfer, as well as most major nineteenth century Jewish religious figures.

thing of the past and Jews no longer wished to live in segregation. Their Judaism contained nothing mystical or contemplative; it was formulated as an optimistic, reasonable American religion, with happiness and salvation attainable by human effort. The essence of Judaism was only moral and ethical, while the externals of the traditional way of life were classified among changeable outward observances and consequently abandoned. Yet persons who did not practice or believe in any Jewish religious principles were still regarded as Jews. The ethnic basis of Judaism remained alive among the German Jews, but subdued, until vigorously thrust forward by the new arrivals from Eastern Europe.[18]

Germanic Judaism declined in America from the 1880's. The Second Reich founded by Bismarck disappointed the liberal traditions cherished by '48ers and hastened their American assimilation, while the anti-Semitic trends in Imperial Germany did not encourage Jews.[19] Germanness in the United States was preserved longest not among urban German liberals, but in the conservative, rural and small city German Lutheran churches. Yet it was inevitable that children and grandchildren finally ceased to speak and study German and finally forgot it. The close, comfortable association of Germanness with Judaism ended when East European Jewish immigrants inundated the 280,000 Jews of 1880. Although German was still spoken in the privacy of many families, the German age was past at the close of the nineteenth century.

Once again, numbers tell much of the story which began in the 1880's. By 1900, there were 1,000,000 Jews in the United States, and about 3,000,000 in 1915. When free immigration to America ended in 1925, there were probably 4,500,000 Jews; this was the point when Jews reached their highest proportion in the American population— about 4%. The climactic years of East European immigration came after the pogroms of 1881, again in 1890 and 1891, and above all during the years of war, revolution, and reaction in Russia which began for Jews with the notorious Kishinev pogrom of 1903. From 1904 through 1908, 642,000 Jews entered the United States.[20]

It would be an error to take pogroms as the main cause of emigration. Galicia, with its Jews emancipated from 1867 and without pogroms, showed perhaps the highest proportion of emigration from Eastern

[18] This paraphrases SWICHKOW and GARTNER, op. cit., pp. 169-170.

[19] GLANZ, Jews in Relation to the Cultural Milieu..., pp. 34-37; SWICHKOW and GARTNER, op. cit., pp. 133-136; Carl F. WITTKE, Refugees of Revolution: The German Forty-Eighters in America (Philadelphia, 1952), pp. 344-373; two small tales recounted in BIRMINGHAM, op. cit., pp. 159, 191-192; HAWGOOD, op. cit.

[20] On East European Jewish immigration, in addition to sources cited supra, note 5, see Samuel JOSEPH, Jewish Immigration to the United States 1881-1910 (New York, 1914) (useful for statistics) and the massive collective work: Walter F. WILLCOX, ed., International Migrations, 2 vols. (New York, 1929, 1931), which contains a useful conspect on the Jews by L. HERSCH (II, pp. 471-521). Lloyd P. GARTNER, The Jewish Immigrant in England 1870-1914 (London and Detroit, 1960), may serve for comparative purposes.

Europe. It was the fivefold increase of East European Jewry during the nineteenth century and the failure of the economy to keep pace with this multiplication, which must be considered the most deeply rooted cause. Repressive Russian laws restricted economic opportunities still further, and drove Jews to a feeling of hopelessness about their future in Russia. With railroads and steamships fully developed into instruments of migration, there were widely advertised and regularly scheduled departures of emigrant ships from such major ports as Hamburg, Bremen, Rotterdam, and Liverpool. Human movement could proceed in massive proportions. Russia also took a passive attitude towards emigration, by unofficially permitting hundreds of thousands of Jews to cross its border. After 1905, the Jewish Colonization Association was permitted to maintain emigrant offices in several cities. Above all, entrance into the United States continued to be nearly unhindered, although immigrants feared the examination at the port of entry (usually Ellis Island, in New York harbor) which disqualified for entry perhaps 1 per cent of arrivals.[21]

Between East European and Germanic Jews there are marked contrasts. The newer arrivals were almost exclusively of traditional Jewish culture. They had no Polish or Russian education—although the Galicians had been required to attend a government school—and few knew the languages of Eastern Europe. A significant illustration is furnished by the Russian Jewish revolutionary refugees who came to America especially in 1882 and during the post-revolutionary reaction in 1906, 1907, and 1908. Before they could assume leadership in the Jewish labor movement, they had to learn or relearn Yiddish. East European Jewry was undergoing a period of extraordinary ideological development, but most immigrants came from the small towns and villages, far from the centers of thought and agitation. Their ideological experiences were to take place in huge urban colonies in America.

The earlier Jewish immigrants had not much intellectual dynamic. They developed a Judaism which they found suitable and believable, and then tended to hold to it with little change. Well-conceived philanthropy was their strongest urge as Jews. The East Europeans, on the other hand, tended to be intellectually mobile and innovative, in keeping with their regional traditions of intense piety and arduous, sharp-witted Talmudic study. This intellectuality had a pervasiveness rarely equalled in Jewish history. Even quite simple Jews lay under the spell of these traditions, and those who broke with them to pursue newer causes—Zionism, Russian revolutionism, Hebrew or Yiddish revival, entry into Russian, Polish, or American culture—rarely lost the quality of intensity and mobility.

[21] John HIGHAM, *Strangers in the Land: Patterns of American Nativism 1860-1925* (New Brunswick, N. J., 1951), pp. 87-105.

There is a third important contrast. Germanic Jews had spread pretty thin across the United States, although, like their Christian neighbors, they later left the smaller towns for large cities. The vast majority of East European Jews settled at once in the largest cities, above all New York, and Chicago, Philadelphia, Boston, Baltimore, and Cleveland. If seven or eight smaller metropoli are added, over 90 per cent of East European Jews are accounted for.[22]

American Jewry has been shaped by the numbers and traditions and aspirations, and also the envies, jealousies, and mutual dependence, of Germanic and East European Jewries. This will not deny the awareness of their common Jewishness, nor the overwhelming force and attraction of American life in shaping a Jewish group different from any previously known. How old and new American Jews encountered each other merits closer notice.

> My dear Russian brethren, who have done so much
> to cast a stigma on the Jewish name, are now adding
> this new sin to their long list of offenses
> which we are asked to stand responsible for.[23]

Thus a Reform rabbi in the Middle West; the sin on this occasion was the founding of a Jewish political club for Bryan in 1896. Nine years earlier, Benjamin F. Peixotto addressed a New York City audience:

> I would say here to those who say "send them back;
> let them stay at home; we don't want them here",
> I would say you might as well attempt to keep the
> waves of old ocean from rushing on our shores, as
> to keep those from seeking the refuge which this
> country offers.[24]

The speaker had spent five years in Roumania during the 1870's. Few, if any American Jews had seen Jewish immigrants in their lands of birth or better appreciated why they sought to quit them. Fifteen years, more or less, passed before American Jews—themselves near immigrant origins—appreciated Peixotto's insistence that a high proportion of the 5,000,000 to 6,000,000 Jews of Eastern Europe was bound to leave for America. Since the emancipation and modernization of German Jewry beginning in the eighteenth century, there had been a

[22] Moses RISCHIN, *The Promised City: New York's Jews 1870-1914* (Cambridge, Mass., 1962), pp. 19–47; Elias TCHERIKOWER, *Geshikhte fun der Yiddisher Arbeter Bavegung in der Faraynikte Shtatn*, 2 vols. (New York, 1943), of which Volume I contains invaluable material on this background (there has been an unsuccessful English translation, abridgment, and revision: Elias TCHERIKOWER and Aaron ANTONOVSKY, *The Early Jewish Labor Movement in the United States* [New York, 1961], pp. 3–74).

[23] SWICHKOW and GARTNER, *op. cit.*, p. 151.

[24] Benjamin F. PEIXOTTO, *What Shall We Do With Our Immigrants?* (New York, Young Men's Hebrew Association, 1887), pp. 3–4, quoted in Zosa SZAJKOWSKI, "The Attitude of American Jews to East European Jewish Immigration (1881-1893)", *PAJHS*, XL, 3 (March, 1951), p. 235.

scornful or condescending attitude to backward, impoverished, persecuted Polish and Russian Jews. For their part, Polish and Russian Jews
admired and envied their German fellow-Jews and, like other intelligentsia of their time, some acquired German language and culture at a
distance. But there were also many who feared and deprecated the de-
Judaization of these favored brethren.[25] All of these heritages were
brought to America. Now, German and East European Jews found
themselves living next to each other, inhaling and exhaling, one may
say, each other's attitudes.

Through the voluminous literature of the decades of large scale
Jewish immigration from the 1880's into the 1920's, several motifs are
to be easily discerned in the "uptown" and "downtown" views of each
other. To Russian immigrants, the German Jew was hardly a Jew, but a
"yahudi", a "deitshuk". His Reform Judaism was a sham as Judaism,
little more than a superficial aping of Christianity meant to curry
Christian favor. Not only the minority of unswervingly Orthodox
among immigrants thought so, but also the much larger mass which
failed to recognize anything but old-time Orthodoxy as real Judaism.
Probably more damning than the Reform Judaism of the German Jews
was the seeming absence among them of folk-feeling, that sense of
mutuality, of common fate and kinship, so well developed among poor,
oppressed Jews. The immigrants were acutely conscious of the native
American Jews' social distance from them, and of their haughtiness
and condescension. Even their vaunted charities were cold and im-
personal, miscalled "scientific", vacant of sympathy and kindness. It
grated them that Jews should hold aloof from other Jews. Among
Jewish socialists, this feeling was expressed in a detestation of the
Jewish uptowners as capitalist oppressors, although one has the impression that the immigrant Jewish socialists really disliked a much
closer target—the climbers to fortune among their own Russian and
Polish Jews.[26]

The native German-American Jews had perceptions of their own.
The new immigrants were primitive and clannish, unwilling to take
on American ways, insistent on maintaining "Asiatic" and "medieval"
forms of religion and social life. "Culture" and "refinement" could

[25] Cf. S. ADLER-RUDEL, *Ostjuden in Deutschland 1880-1940* (Tübingen, 1959),
pp. 1-33. The attitudes of some German Jews to first encountering Jews in Eastern
Europe are suggestive; e.g. Franz ROSENZWEIG, *Briefe* (Berlin, 1935), pp. 320-322;
Alexander CARLEBACH, "A German Rabbi goes East", Leo Baeck Institute *Yearbook*,
VI (1961), pp. 60-121.

[26] RISCHIN, *op. cit.*, pp. 95-111; Harold M. SILVER, "The Russian Jew Looks at
Charity—A Study of the Attitudes of Russian Jewish Immigrants Toward Organized
Jewish Charitable Agencies in the United States in 1890-1900", *Jewish Social Service
Quarterly*, IV, 2 (December, 1927), pp. 129-144; Arthur GORENSTEIN (Goren), "The
Commissioner and the Community: A Study of the Beginnings of the New York City
'Kehillah', " *YAJSS*, XIII (1965), pp. 187-212.

not be found amongst them. They demanded charity as a matter of right without any appreciation for what they received. They were unduly aggressive and assertive, and embarrassed the painfully acquired good name of the American Jew. They had a disturbing penchant for unsound ways of thought, especially political radicalism, atheism, Zionism, and held to a form of speech which could not be called a language.[27] Only slowly did it come to be understood why they were coming en masse, and that pleas to stay home were fruitless. Well into the 1890's, Western—not only American—Jewry pleaded for Russian, Polish, Roumanian, Galician Jews to stay home and await the better times which would surely come in an age of inevitable human progress.[28] Benjamin F. Peixotto was nearly isolated. The few natives who welcomed immigration seem mostly to have been traditionalists who expected reinforcement of their small numbers by Jews arriving from the East European reservoir of religious piety.[29] For those who did come, the policy preferred by native Jews was to develop a class of respectable workingmen. Skilled manual trades in the city and farming on the countryside were to replace peddling and tailoring.[30] How remote this was from the explicit as well as the buried hopes of the immigrants may be seen from the widely known outlines of their social history during the last fifty years.

The real change in the native Jews' attitude occurred around 1903. The Kishinev pogrom of that year, in which high Tsarist officials were notoriously implicated, followed by the Russo-Japanese War, the Revolution of 1905 and the pogrom-ridden counter-revolution, proved that the condition of Russian Jews would only deteriorate, not improve. Reluctant American Jewish sympathy replaced the earlier dislike as greater numbers of immigrants than ever poured into the United States during the decade before World War I.[31]

This decade also marks the coming of Jews to the political and

---

[27] SZAJKOWSKI, op. cit., pp. 221-293; Irving A. MANDEL, "The Attitude of the American Jewish Community toward East-European Immigration as Reflected in the Anglo-Jewish Press (1880-1890)", American Jewish Archives, III, 1 (June, 1950), pp. 11-36; HELLER, op. cit., pp. 583-586; David PHILIPSON, "Strangers to a Strange Land", American Jewish Archives, XVIII, 2 (November, 1966), pp. 133-138 (excerpts from his diary); Selig ADLER and Thomas E. CONNOLLY, From Ararat to Suburbia: The History of the Jewish Community of Buffalo (Philadelphia, 1960), pp. 227-231.

[28] This theme is treated in Zosa SZAJKOWSKI, "Emigration to America or Reconstruction in Europe", PAJHS, XLII, 2 (December, 1952), pp. 157-188.

[29] DAVIS, op. cit., pp. 261-268.

[30] Herman FRANK, "Jewish Farming in the United States", The Jewish People Past and Present, 4 vols. (New York, 1948-1955), II, 68-77; Moses KLEIN, Migdal Zophim (Philadelphia, 1889).

[31] HIGHAM, op. cit., pp. 106-123; Zosa SZAJKOWSKI, "Paul Nathan, Lucien Wolf, Jacob H. Schiff and the Jewish Revolutionary Movement in Eastern Europe (1903-1917)", Jewish Social Studies, XXIX, 1 and 2 (January and April, 1967), pp. 3-26, 75-91; Morton ROSENSTOCK, Louis Marshall, Defender of Jewish Rights (Detroit, 1965), pp. 79-89.

intellectual forefront among the defenders of free immigration. Of course, other immigrant groups also staunchly defended the right of their families and countrymen to come to America, but of the more recent immigrant stocks the Jews had the best established native element which would press the case effectively. Behind the political and communal leaders were a group of intellectuals both demonstrating and advocating the anthropological and intellectual equality of Jewish and all other newcomers—Israel Zangwill, Mary Antin, Israel Friedlander, Franz Boas, Horace M. Kallen, and others. Moreover, immigrants at the ballot box were now effectively enforcing the doctrines of human equality expounded by these intellectuals.[32] The most favored and seemingly innocuous aid to immigrants remained the dispensing of charity. The old-time charitable societies founded during the 1850's and 1860's—dozens of them named "Hebrew Relief Society" and "Hebrew Ladies Benevolent Society"—took on masses of new clients. How bread and coals and warm clothing developed around the 1920's into family budgets, mental health, and vocational guidance is a story vaguely but widely known in its barest outlines. Again, how the disparate relief societies, orphanages, homes for the aged and the like united their fund-raising and then began to spend and plan in unison, is another story of wide significance. These forward-looking "scientific" institutions were not at all the first resort of the distressed immigrant, who had his own "home town" societies, mutual aid groups, and "lodges" in the hundreds. The tendency to resent charitable patronage was one of the reasons which brought immigrants to found separate institutions. It was stressed that only in their own hospitals and orphanages and homes for the aged was kosher diet and an intimately Jewish atmosphere fostered. Yet it is revealing how "downtown" unconsciously flattered "uptown" by accepting the institutional network founded by the natives and attempting to rival it.[33]

The evolution of other, much more sophisticated institutions is instructive. The Educational Alliance was built on New York's Lower East Side in 1889. During its first years, no Yiddish or immigrant cultural expression was permitted within its walls, and the regime was one of an often artificially imposed English culture. By 1914, however, it had become a cultural and social center where young artists and musicians, as well as athletes, trained, where Yiddish was publicly

[32] HIGHAN, op. cit., pp. 123-130, 304-305; Arthur GORENSTEIN (Goren), "A Portrait of Ethnic Politics: The Socialists and the 1908 and 1910 Congressional Elections on the East Side", PAJHS, L, 3 (March, 1961), pp. 202-238.
[33] A useful historical anthology is Robert MORRIS and MICHAEL FREUND, Trends and Issues in Jewish Social Welfare in the United States 1899-1952 (Philadelphia, 1966); SWICHKOW and GARTNER, op. cit., pp. 53-54, 211-212, 215-234; PLAUT, op. cit., pp. 140-146; GUTSTEIN, op. cit., pp. 334-360.

used, and where even youthful Hebraists practiced the reviving language.[34]

The case of the Jewish Theological Seminary suggests still more subtle problems. Jewish natives worried over the young people who rejected the religion of their fathers in favor of radical social doctrines or militant atheism, or drifted into hedonism and seemed criminally inclined. It was virtually postulated that Jewish immigrants would not take to Reform Judaism (actually some of the younger ones became interested in Ethical Culture). In the eyes of native leaders, a traditional but modern form of Judaism for immigrant or immigrants' children was needed, and so the moribund Jewish Theological Seminary was re-founded to train "American" rabbis at an institution of higher Jewish learning. A substantial building, considerable endowment, and an outstanding Library and Faculty were quickly brought together. Yet tensions were never absent between the eminent Solomon Schechter, head of the Seminary, who desired before anything else an institution of learning, and some of the Board who seemed to want religiously inspired "Americanization" work.[35] A suggestive contrast is furnished by the immigrants' yeshiva on New York's East Side. With very meager resources, it was solely a full-time non-professional school for advanced Talmudic study by young men. Long controversy within Yeshivat Rabbenu Yizhak Elhanan preceded the introduction of very modest secular studies. But before 1920, however, the Yeshiva provided full secular secondary training within its own walls, and later established Yeshiva College. This was much to the displeasure of most native Jews, who considered general education under Jewish auspices "ghettoizing". On the other hand, the modernist Jewish scholarship fostered by Schechter at the Jewish Theological Seminary was religiously unacceptable to the Yeshiva's contemporary leaders. Secular study could be taken in and by some welcomed, but not the modernized, historical study of the sacred tradition.[36]

Immigrant Jews began to acquire uptown esteem. For one, they exhibited an intellectual elan and interest in ideas—especially unconventional ideas—which younger members of staid society found exhilarating. For some Jewish members of proper society the Jewish immigrants seemed to show a more authentic, passionate, somehow appealing way to be a Jew. A second source of esteem derived from the immigrants' greatest short-term achievement, the Jewish labor movement. After

[34] RISCHIN, op. cit., pp. 101–103; In the Time of Harvest: Essays in Honor of Abba Hillel Silver, ed. Daniel Jeremy SILVER (New York, 1963), p. 3.

[35] Norman BENTWICH, Solomon Schechter (Philadelphia, 1938), pp. 187–197; Louis Marshall: Champion of Liberty, ed. Charles REZNIKOFF, 2 vols. (Philadelphia, 1956), II, pp. 859–894.

[36] Ibid., II, pp. 888–894; Gilbert KLAPERMAN, The Story of Yeshiva University (mimeographed, ca. 1966, to be published).

a full generation of unsuccessful fits and starts, the movement's surge of vitality and success attracted bourgeois liberals, and drew wide respect and attention. Native Jews repeatedly attempted to mediate strikes of Jewish workers against Jewish employers, on the grounds that they washed Jewish linen in public. The Jewish labor leaders, generally committed to revolutionary rhetoric, refused to regard the strikes as an internal Jewish quarrel but quite often accepted "uptown" mediators anyhow.[37]

World War I was an intense, even decisive experience for both the old and new Jewish stock. Immigrants or their sons wore military uniform in large numbers, and Army egalitarianism and patriotic fervor proved a superlative "Americanizing" experience. Native Jews were more vigilant than ever in defending immigrants at a time of patriotic xenophobia, against the imputations of disloyalty to which they were vulnerable on account of revolutions and political complexities in their lands of origin and widespread Socialist anti-war sentiment among them. But during World War I also, native Jews became persuaded and in turn became advocates of causes once distasteful to them. Thus they took up the cudgels for Jewish national minority rights in Eastern Europe, toning it down to "group rights" as a more palatable term. The Jewish National Home promised in Great Britain's Balfour Declaration was the other cause. The relief poured out for European Jewry came from "uptown" and "downtown", and was distributed mostly by the well-named American Jewish Joint Distribution Committee.[38]

The problems of the 1920's lie beyond the scope of these remarks. By that time, the influence of the two segments upon each other was, or should have been, long evident. The old stock's staid conception and practice of Judaism was outmatched and altered by the newcomers' intellectual vigor in that and in other spheres. Indeed, two generations of native Jews, gradually joined en masse by acculturated and prospering immigrant families, focussed practically the whole of their communal life and concerns upon the East European immigrant and his

[37] RISCHIN, op. cit., pp. 236–257; Louis LEVINE (Lorwin), The Women's Garment Workers: A History of the International Ladies Garment Workers Union (New York, 1924), pp. 360–381; Hyman BERMAN, "The Cloakmakers' Strike of 1910", Essays in Jewish Life and Thought Presented in Honor of Salo Wittmayer Baron (New York, 1959), pp. 63–94. The slowly rising interest in Yiddish literature may be seen through Morris ROSENFELD, Briv, ed. E. LIFSCHUTZ (Buenos Aires, 1955), pp. 34–105.

[38] Oscar I. JANOWSKY, The Jews and Minority Rights 1898–1919 (New York, 1933), pp. 161–190, 264–320; ROSENSTOCK, op. cit., pp. 98–127; Zosa SZAJKOWSKI, "Jewish Relief in Eastern Europe 1914–1917", Leo Baeck Institute Yearbook, X (1965), pp. 24–56; Naomi W. COHEN, "An American Jew at the Paris Peace Conference: Excerpts from the Diary of Oscar S. Straus", Essays... Baron, pp. 159–168; for a view of World War I on the local Jewish scene, see SWICHKOW and GARTNER, op. cit., pp. 268–285; see also E. LIFSCHUTZ, "The Pogroms in Poland of 1918–1919, the Morgenthau Committee and the American State Department" (Hebrew with English summaries), Zion, XXIII-XXIV, 1–2 and 3–4 (1958–1959), pp. 66–97, 194–211.

transformation. It was the older Jewish stock which long and effectively defended the Jewish newcomers, while chastising them not too privately, and above all helped to keep immigration virtually free before 1925.[39] For the East European immigrants, the example of their predecessors provided a model—for many the model— of the way to be an American and a Jew. Adaptation and change were extensive, but those who came first showed those who came later this most significant of lessons. The still sizeable numbers of Jews who came after 1925, especially from Germany and Austria during the 1930's, and after 1945 as survivors of the European Jewish holocaust, found a fully formed American Jewry. Their limited influence on American Jewish life, with the possible exception of its Orthodox religious sector, also shows that the formative years had ended.

[39] HIGHAM, *op. cit.*, pp. 264–330; ROSENSTOCK, *op. cit.*, pp. 214–233.

S. N. EISENSTADT

ISRAELI SOCIETY — MAJOR FEATURES AND PROBLEMS

THE Jewish community in Palestine (the so-called *Yishuv*) and the State of Israel developed out of the activities of the Zionist groups emerging in the late 1890's in Eastern and Central Europe.[1] This rebellion denied that a compact and viable Jewish life and tradition could be maintained within the framework of a modern society outside of Palestine. Zionist ideology maintained that within any such framework the Jews would be torn between spiritual and cultural annihilation, the undermining of their traditional and communal life by modern economic, political, and cultural forces on the one hand and physical annihilation due to incomplete assimilation and the inability of modern society to digest this alien element on the other. Zionist ideology assumed that only in Palestine could a new, modern, viable, Jewish society and a new synthesis of Jewishness and universal human culture between tradition and modernity be established.

The aim of the first pioneers was that the Yishuv should become not only a modern society in every sense of the term but also one that embodied wider values and meaning and some transcendental significance. This aim developed, in a transformed way, from the legacy of traditional Jewish society, which combined an ardent yearning for universal meaning with the realities of an oppressed minority. As long as this minority remained closed within itself, the tension between this yearning and actuality produced considerable creative activity within its own framework, while relegating any hope that its universal claims would be accepted in the distant future. When the gates of European society were—at least partially—opened, many of its members succeeded in entering fields of general social and cultural activity in which they could be highly creative. But at the same time, they faced the problem of losing their collective Jewish identity and/or of not being fully accepted into the broader European society.

---

[1] The present analysis is mostly derived from S. N. EISENSTADT, *Israeli Society* (London, 1967).

The Zionist movement aimed at providing the opportunity for cultural and social creativity of universal significance within the framework of a free, modern, self-supporting Jewish society; and it is this combination which accounts for the tremendous emphasis placed on socio-cultural creativity and for its strong elitist orientations. This emphasis was further heightened by the external circumstances prevailing in Palestine—the conditions of the country, the absence of capital reserves and suitable manpower resources, as well as the lack of a long tradition of an orderly civil society.

These orientations were borne mostly by the first pioneer groups which consisted mostly of intellectual youth who rebelled against their parental background in the Diaspora (especially in Eastern and Central Europe), who organized themselves into small sectarian-pioneering groups which went to the old homeland in Palestine in order to establish there a new, viable, modern Jewish society.

It was these characteristics of the first waves of immigration (*Aliyoth*) which shaped some of the most important features of the Yishuv—and especially its being an ideological society—i.e., a society whose basic collective identity was couched in ideological terms. And it was the encounter between these ideological orientations and the reality of Palestine and the continuously new waves of immigration that shaped the major institutional features of the Yishuv.

Perhaps the most outstanding characteristics of the Yishuv was that its center developed first. Its central institutions and symbols crystallized before the emergence of the "periphery", made up of broader, less creative, social groups and strata. This center—built up through the elitist and future orientations of the pioneering sects—was envisaged as being capable of permeating and absorbing the periphery which, it was hoped, would develop and expand through continuous migration.

The ideological and elitist orientations of the first pioneering groups, the strong transcendental orientations and the strong sense of personal responsibility for the fulfilment of the ideal inherent in the image of the pioneer guided the initial development of this center, its symbols and institutions.

Far-reaching attempts to develop a specific modern structure were implied in the pioneering ideology. These attempts combined the positive aspects of modern technology with the maintenance of basic human and social values and were oriented especially to their implementation in the fields of economic and social organization. However, these economic orientations were not purely social or ideological. They were closely related to national effort and were conceived not in utopian terms but rather as part and parcel of the building of a new nation.

The encounter between these orientations and the tasks encountered in their implementation in Palestine during the Ottoman and Mandate periods constituted the focal point of the development of the Israeli social structure.

As the development and maintenance of a high standard of living for existing and future waves of immigrants was implicitly assumed, it necessitated a partial separation from the local, traditional Arab economy.

Among basic initial factors which influenced the implementation of these ideals were the lack of adequate capital resources and manpower for primary occupations, combined, however, with a high initial educational potential. This latter attribute eventually ensured a relatively smooth transition to a fairly high level of technological development.

These basic exigencies, together with the ideology of the pioneering groups, caused the initial heavy concentration of public capital in the major development sectors while, at the same time, permitting the continuous expansion of the private sectors. They also gave rise to the specifically Israeli form of socio-economic organization—above all, to the communal and co-operative settlements—and to the proliferation of co-operative enterprises in the urban sector, a feature also found to some extent in other sectarian and colonizing societies. However, most of these co-operative and colonizing bodies were to some extent incorporated into the more unitary framework of the Histadrut to a degree unparalleled in other countries, thus going beyond the initial agrarian orientation of the first pioneering groups. It was here that the major characteristics of the urban social structure of the Yishuv developed. Most important was the attempt to combine unified large-scale organizational frameworks, designed for implementing collective goals, with the more totalistic and closed sects or social movements on the one hand and with the differentiated, functionally specific, organizations on the other.

The second aspect of the emerging social structure of the Yishuv was the strong emphasis on equality and deprecation of specialization. It showed itself in two ways: in the strong egalitarian trend in the distribution of rewards allocated to major occupational roles, and in the minimization of differences between them and the presumption of an easy transition from one to the other.

Another aspect of egalitarianism was that of general accessibility to various occupational positions. This aspect was, however, much less explicitly emphasized in the initial ideological tenets. This was due to the fact that in the beginning access to these positions did not constitute a problem; it was assured by the comparative homogeneity of educational and cultural facilities and by the dependence of all groups on external economic and political resources.

The Yishuv did also develop some specific characteristics in the cultural field and especially in the relations between tradition and modernity. Here two features have to be singled out. One is the spectacular revival of the Hebrew language as a modern language which, on the one hand, became the common national language of the community, the language of kindergarten, schools and of daily discourse, while on the other proved capable of coping with the problems of modern, scientific, literary and technological demands.

In this it occupies probably a rather unique place among traditional languages, and this in turn had important repercussions on the cultural format of the community.

The fact that the "traditional" religious language became the common, national language and means of discourse of a modern community minimized the possibility that within that community there would develop strong rifts or symbolic cleavages between "traditionalist" and "modernist", as well as minimized the cultural dependence on foreign outside centres as sources of modernity.

In a similar direction worked also another factor in the cultural sphere—the attainment, early in the history of the Yishuv, of a *modus vivendi* between the secular and the religious groups.

Characteristics of the Yishuv and of the Israeli Society from a Comparative Point of View

It might be worth while at this point to summarize the comparative indications implied in the preceding analysis and to see what characteristics Israeli society shares with other societies in which some of its analytical components may also be found.

Israeli society shares important characteristics with some non-Imperial, colonizing societies (especially the United States and the British Dominions). First, a strong emphasis on equality, at least among the initial settler groups, and the consequent lack of any strong hereditary, feudal, aristocratic landowner class. Second, the development of a strong concentration of various types of economic and administrative activities within broad, unified, organizational frameworks in common with other sectarian, colonizing societies. And last, and again in common with other colonizing societies, Zionist settlement emphasized the conquest of wasteland through work—as shown in the expansion of productive, primary occupations and in the expansion of the colonizing frameworks and frontiers.

Such combinations of co-operative endeavours and economic-colonizing enterprise could be found also, for instance, in the settlement of wasteland by the Mormons. The combination of trade unions with the industrial and financial activities of the entrepreneur could also be found in other politically-oriented labour movements, especially in Scandinavia and—to a lesser extent—in England.

However, the fusion of these features as developed within the Histadrut seems to be unique and is explained by the Histadrut's political character and outlook. This also explains its political power although it is, economically, by no means the largest sector of the country.

These characteristics became closely interwoven with other components of Israeli society, such as the sectarian or social movements which are evident in the totalistic outlook of the pioneering sects with their strong internal ideological cohesion and in the institutionalization of ideology in the face of growing social differentiation.

Unlike many other sects, the pioneering groups aimed from the beginning at being the trail blazers of a modern society and committed themselves to many institutional frameworks and organizations which might serve as the forerunners of such a development and through which these broader groups of Jewish society could participate in the economic, ideological and political life of the Yishuv.

Unlike most modern social and nationalistic movements, however, the Zionist pioneers did not plan for the immediate seizure of power and a new, unitary, political framework. Their primary emphasis was on broad rural and urban colonization which, in itself, weakened the political implications of totalistic orientations.

It was only at the end of the mandatory period, with the intensification of the external political struggle, that some conception of a self-governing polity developed.

It was out of the sectarian and social movement elements of the Yishuv that another crucial trend developed—the strong elitist ideological bent, aiming at the achievement of a new society through the implementation of an ideological program.

In this, Israel was akin to some revolutionary societies, such as the U.S.S.R., Yugoslavia, or Mexico, which attempted to mould relatively traditional societies into a specific modern pattern. However, the ideologies which were developed within the Zionist movement contained more variegated and heterogeneous elements than either those of closed religious sects or of revolutionary political movements. This ideological diversity was greatly reinforced by the coexistence of many different groups within the federative structure of the Yishuv, creating new institutional nuclei with orientations to broader, more universalistic, cultural and social values.

Israeli society also shared many features and problems with other countries which had large-scale immigration. It had to deal with continuous waves of immigrants and with their integration into its emerging institutional framework. But it also developed specific characteristics of its own, rooted in the basic motivations and orientations among the immigrants and their strong emphasis on national and social goals.

As pointed out, Israeli society contained also many elements and problems similar to those of other developing countries. This similarity could also be found in the establishment of a new political framework by the élite of a colonial ruler and the consequent transformation of this élite into a ruling class. However, several important differences stand out.

Unlike many contemporary developing societies, the initial institutional framework in Israel was established by modern élites and along modern lines. These élites had a large pool of educated persons committed by ideology, outlook or creed to the creation of a modern society. The traditional elements were only taken into these frameworks much later, and the process of their modernization was quicker and more intense than in many other newly independent developing countries. Further, and again unlike most New States, the attainment of independence did not create a sharp break with the past, since the Yishuv and the Zionist movement had already developed manifold political, administrative, and economic organizations. The emphasis on the "Political Kingdom" was therefore much smaller.

Israel, the United States and the U.S.S.R.—Comparisons in Modernity

The combination of characteristics listed above was almost unique, as can be seen from a comparison with two major industrial societies: the Puritan colonization in the United States and the ideologically orientated political revolution in the U.S.S.R.

Some of the similarities with these societies, such as settlement by sectarian groups in the American colonies and the strong social-ideological emphasis in Russia, though striking, should not obscure the major differences. With regard to the United States there were, of course, the obvious differences in external environment—the differences between a large, sparsely populated, potentially open continent and a small, barren, densely populated country, surrounded by other countries which soon became hostile to the colonizing efforts made and thus created immediate security problems and considerations in the development of the new society.

But beyond this, there were also some important differences between the Puritan groups on the one hand and the Zionist and socialist pioneering sects on the other. Unlike the former, the latter were mostly secular; and it was not within the religious sphere that they were most inventive or revolutionary. Hence, while American society had to face continuous secularization which had to be related to its initial religious value orientations, Israeli society faced almost opposite problems. It had to transform its totalistic secular ideologies into a value-system of a more differentiated and partly de-ideologized society, and later faced the possibility of erosion of these values by many factors—among them the growing militancy of the newly growing non-Zionist religious groups. On the social and economic side, there was the great difference between the collective orientations and organizational form of the predominant Zionist groups and the more individualistic emphasis and individual recruitment of the American pioneers.

Next came the great difference in the development and expansion beyond the initial phase. Although both cases deal with societies which had to absorb waves of immigrants whose social orientations differed from those of the first settlers, there were basic differences in these problems and the framework in which they were set. In America the major common motivation of new immigrants—especially during the second half of the nineteenth century and the beginning of the twentieth—was the attainment of personal security and economic advancement, while in Israel it was more a common national orientation. Thus, while some of the differences between the newer, traditional immigrant groups and the initial settlers were perhaps smaller in Israel than in the United States, they were perceived as more crucial for the unity of the nation.

The differences with the U.S.S.R. are even more striking. Beyond the obvious differences of scale and the relative backwardness of Russian society, was the fact that in Russia attempts to mould society to an ideological formula came by a highly unified and closely organized élite after the Revolution and after the establishment of a new political framework and that the ideologists were therefore caught up in the establishment and maintenance of a totalitarian regime bent on quick industrialization of a relatively backward country.

In the Yishuv and in the State of Israel, attempts to implement the ideology came long before the establishment of a unified political framework and were mainly concerned with economic, colonizing, and social fields. The establishment of the State continued this process of selective institutionalization in a pluralistic setting and weakened the effectiveness of the monolithic elements in the ideological orientation of the élite. Not only were these attempts set in a pluralistic-constitutional setting but, paradoxically, the emphasis on the pioneering ideology also gave rise to claims for some political influence by some of the older pioneering groups, against those of the State, thus reinforcing the pluralistic tendency. Moreover, these groups were comparatively successful in absorbing new elements which did not, as in Russia, have to be coerced into the new central framework.

Processes and Problems of Israel's New Stage of Development

The differences between the societies mentioned above and the Yishuv help to illuminate the latter's specific structural characteristics and the ways in which it was able to deal with the various problems which it had to face at the new stage of its development which it entered into when the State of Israel was established. It was at this stage that the Yishuv's capacity to grow, to absorb new elements and to deal with new kinds of problems was to be severely tested in many ways.

These problems developed out of the three broad trends which brought about the structural transformation of the Israeli society and which, as it were, ushered in the new stage of development or modernization.

The first of these was the growing differentiation and specialization in all major spheres of society, but especially in the occupational and economic fields, culminating in the "situation of irreversibility" in occupational mobility—a development which was, to some extent, opposed to the initial pioneering ideology.

The second trend was the transformation, with the establishment of the State, of the élite into a ruling group and the concomitant changes in the structural placement and orientation of all other major groups.

Third, was the large-scale influx of new immigrants, which was one of the major sources for the growing expansion and differentiation of the Israeli social structure but which also brought some of the hardest problems Israeli society had to face. Here there developed risks of lowering the level of economic, technical, and educational performances and the possibility of creating a whole gamut of new social and cultural tensions and conflicts, leading to the possible cleavage between "Orientals" and "Occidentals" and thus giving rise to the possibility of creating "Two Nations" within Israel.

These three coinciding trends accentuated the problem of the extent to which the existing élites and center are able to absorb the new broadened periphery within the framework of its basic institutions and symbols.

As in all other modern or modernizing societies which enter a new stage of development and face new problems, the attempts to solve these problems could develop either in a way which could assure the further growth of the society or in a more stagnant and conflict-ridden direction.

In Israel each of these possible developments was based on some combination of the older ideologies and institutions combined with new orientations and organizations.

These encounters created varied possibilities of developing new, broader, universalistic, cultural orientations and patterns of social organizations, and integrating those organizational and institutional

nuclei which were the bearers of such orientations into the new organizations developed in the State period. Conversely, there could develop a stronger emphasis on the particularistic and ascriptive framework, thus reinforcing the tendencies in the society towards stagnation and contributing to the possible lowering of levels of social, economic, and cultural activity.

Such tendencies towards stagnation could become reinforced by the transformation of many social movements into more constricted interest groups, by the development of restrictive orientations within the 'older' movement groups (the settlements, the Histadrut, the political parties), and by the development of such orientations within several new sectors of the society, such as the new ethnic and religious groups and the various professional organizations.

In the following section we shall point out briefly the major ways in which new problems—and varied attempts to deal with them—were developed in the major fields of Israeli society.

Major Economic Problems

In the economic field, many difficulties developed in the transition from an economy in which the main emphasis was on the mobilization and investment of capital for physical expansion to an economy in which much investment has to be put into technological development.

The social and economic structures of the Yishuv were originally geared to the continuous physical expansion of both agriculture and industry and to the mobilization and investment of capital through collective and private channels.

The influx of new immigrants from societies with lower educational and technological levels and the internal dynamics of the economy, with its pressure towards higher standards of living, gave impetus to the growing differentiation and specialization in the occupational and economic sphere, resulting in the establishment of new enterprises and in the continuous physical expansion of the economy, according to the existing pattern and framework.

Within this framework the partial social security provided by the Histadrut, provided important facilities for initial absorption of immigrant manpower, both in agriculture and in industry, to a degree probably unparalleled in most other developing countries.

But these policies were not enough to ensure the attainment of new levels of economic and technological development, and the ability of the élite to deal with continuous economic development and differentiation was severely tested.

Problems and difficulties were on two levels. On the central political level, they became evident in the attempts made by the government to maintain its overall control of major processes of growth and development, while at the same time attempting to use all available entrepreneurial groups in order to assure the physical expansion of the economy.

This gave rise to the paradoxical development of a strong upsurge of speculation both in the private and public sectors, and the consequent attempts by the élite to control the symptoms (such as conspicuous consumption), though not the deeper causes of such speculation. It also created great difficulties in curbing growing consumption, and in putting Israeli economy on a technological level which could compete in the international market.

On the more sectorial level the main impediments to structural transformation were rooted in the conservatism of many of the trade unions which, being somewhat similar to those in England, did not have the flexibility of the Swedish unions. This conservatism constituted an obstacle to the mobility of labour and to progress towards higher levels of technical and professional competence.

Similarly the policies of the government tended to discourage the development of relatively new types of entrepreneurs not dependent on the protection in the local market given to them by government subsidies and customs policy and of a higher level of economic specialization.

Here also many developments, connected with the highly politicized electorate which developed continuous pressures for growing consumption, gave rise to possible waste of resources needed for economic development.

In contrast to the older non-specialized roles which claimed to be the only legitimate bearers of such wider orientations, it became vital in all these spheres to find new or differentiated, occupational roles, and to find ways of how to connect the more technical aspects of such roles with wider collective and value orientations.

Here also, the problem of the adequacy of the educational system in providing for the needs of a variegated social structure and for higher technical development became very acute.

As in other countries with a strong tradition of humanistic, elitist education, a homogeneous educational system tended to develop, offering a predominantly humanistic education with relatively little variety. This created some rigidity with regard to technological and professional orientation and accentuated the necessity of finding ways of combining general, broad cultural values with more specialized tasks, rejecting both a rigid adherence to the general orientation of the preceding period and an indiscriminate system geared only to the changing, specialized technical needs.

Reinforced by the over-emphasis on public service and the expansion of academic educational facilities, this trend could contribute to the rigidity of the educational system, to the growing bottlenecks within it, and to the possible lowering of general standards of education.

However, it also helped to crystallize the more dynamic possibilities of development, of establishment of new centres of potential creativity in the cultural, scientific, professional and technological spheres.

Major Changes and Problems in Social Organization

Similar problems and dilemmas arose also in the broader sphere of social organization and stratification. Growing differentiation fundamentally changed the Israeli social organization, destroying the relative equality of different occupational positions and disturbing the homogeneity of status. It also changed the bases of accessibility to various new—and especially higher—occupational positions and created new cleavages and tensions around these avenues of access.

As in most other countries, the increased importance of educational achievements underlined the problems of differential access to educational facilities and institutions.

The establishment of compulsory general State education led to the absorption of strata groups which did not share the social orientations of the originators of the system. At this stage the educational system became an important instrument of occupational selection.

In Israel the most crucial aspect of these problems was the "ethnic" one, i.e., the problem of the so-called Oriental groups.

In all the spheres of social organization the problem of the possible cleavage between the new Oriental groups and the European old timers became very important. This is evident mostly in the fact that the Oriental groups tended to become concentrated in the lower occupational and education echelons. Both the economic and the educational systems, while very successful in the initial stages of absorption were very much less successful in transforming themselves in ways that would cut across this distinction and create new levels of specialization and new frameworks and organizations that could be common to old and new, "Orientals" and "Europeans" alike.

With the possibility of perpetuating their deprivation through continued failure in the educational sphere, a feeling of frustration developed among these groups—not least among their more successful middle echelons.

This problem was to some extent similar to the problem of adjusting traditional groups in other developing societies to modern educational and occupational tasks. However, the acuteness of this problem in Israel was accentuated by the high initial success (as compared with other underdeveloped or immigrant communities) in absorbing traditional groups into modern surroundings and by the society's overall commitment to their full integration and to the creation of one common nationhood.

The search for solutions to these problems developed, as in other societies, in two different directions—towards increasing flexibility and growth in the social and economic structures on the one hand and towards insoluble tensions and stagnation on the other.

The more growth conducive policies were connected with the development of new specialized and universalistically oriented and organized social, educational and economic enterprises and frameworks which tended to cut across the different social and ethnic groups. The more stagnant possibilities were connected with the perpetuation of existing frameworks within which the differences between these groups became more pronounced and with the concomitant symbolization of these differences. These in turn gave rise to attempts to overcome these problems, not by helping the relatively deprived groups to obtain the qualities needed for achievement in various (old or new) universalistic frameworks, but mainly by making membership in various particularistic sectors of the society—political, ethnic or religious—the major criteria of access to different positions and to the emoluments attached to them.

Repercussions on Values and Ideologies and the Continuity of Israel's Identity

All these problems, indicative as they were of the ability of Israeli society to deal with the extension of its periphery and with the problems of a new stage of development or modernization, were very closely connected with the transformation of the pioneer image.

This image combined, as we have seen, both asceticism and this-worldliness, together with some broader, potentially transcendental qualities which went beyond any concrete situation and setting. However, it also contained other more stagnative orientations. In this it was not unlike the ideological and religious orientations connected with the famous Protestant Ethic, as well as many other ideological orientations of modern or modernizing countries.

Here also, as in many of these cases, the initial ideology evinced strong totalistic and restrictive orientations which were initially minimized and transformed through the institutionalization of the religious or pioneering groups within the wider social setting.

But here, as in other cases, the more restrictive and stagnative orientations could reappear or become reinforced in later stages of development—especially when they became embedded in various institutional structures which tended to become foci of vested interests and which tended to restrict and impede the adequate perception of new problems.

As the initial phase of the Yishuv's modernization developed a strong ideological emphasis, this transformation was largely concerned with the transition from predominantly ideological goals to more concrete, variegated and realistic goals, while yet maintaining commitments to broader values and to collective responsibilities.

Thus, in this context, the continuity of Israel's growth centered round the transformation of the image of the pioneer and of the initial symbols of its collective identity.

The major concepts of Israeli collective identity were forged out of several components. Its present exact boundaries or limits are not fixed, although its elements may be easily discerned. One such element is a very strong local patriotism. At the same time some reference to wider values and groups continues to be an important ingredient of this identity. Second, for most Israelis, Jewishness is a crucial part of their identity. At the same time, and particularly in the older strata of the population, there is an awareness of the fact that the stigma of being an Israeli or a Jew goes beyond mere local patriotism. It refers also to wider values, traditions, and orientations, however inarticulate or undefinable these orientations may be.

Whatever the exact contours of Israeli self-identity in relation to the broad framework of Jewish tradition and Jewish communities, it no longer defines Jewish identity in terms of a minority group or culture. Being a Jew in Israel does not necessitate the definition of one's self-identity in relation to a majority group or culture and does not involve the various problems, uncertainties, and anxieties which have constituted such an important aspect of Jewish life and identity throughout the modern world.

Another crucial element in this identity is the strong emphasis on individual and collective self-defense, rooted in the tradition of the first "watchmen" and developed since then through the traditions of the "Haganah" and the Israeli army.

Many attempts were made to re-define the concrete elements of this pioneering image. Claims made by the various groups that specific new tasks and activities contained certain elements of the collective commitments of the pioneer are significant as attempts to maintain such commitments in the new setting, even though such claims continuously contributed to changing the image of the pioneer and to making it more diffuse.

As against these there developed the possibility of the expansion of amorphous mass culture and the possible resurgence of so-called Levantinism and provincialism could greatly weaken the wider cultural and social horizons and erode their institutional bases and nuclei. This could become evident in diminishing orientations towards other centres of culture in the West, in loosing contact with other Jewish communities and, accordingly, in increasing the narrow provincial identity and growth of purely instrumental orientations to collective commitments.

A similar range of dilemmas and problems developed around the symbols of collective identity with regard to the possibility of the absorption by the central symbolic sphere of the society, of new elements, traditions and orientations. Here several areas of potential conflict developed which could easily become very disruptive.

The first of these was in the sphere of secular-religious relations. The conflict in this sphere has lately intensified and the growing militancy of the religious groups may well restrict the flexibility of the collective identity and its ability to deal with modern problems. Another was the conflict between over-emphasis on ideology on the one hand, and a more flexible commitment to broader values on the other.

A third area of conflict was that in the "ethnic" sphere, in the possibility of the development of "Two Nations", of the intensification and symbolization of the cleavage between "Orientals" and "Europeans", and in the development of this cleavage as a major divisive element in the sphere of central social, political and cultural symbols.

Against these constricting and conflict-ridden possibilities we also find the continuous expansion and recrystallization of the Israeli collective image, its ability to incorporate many new ethnic, traditional and modern (technical and professional) elements, and to adjust the centres of its creativity to new problems and changing situations.

Summary

In the preceding pages we have briefly summarized some of the major problems which Israeli society faces at this stage of its development, their historical and sociological roots as well as the different directions in which solutions to them are being attempted.

All these varied problems tend to converge into the central problem of whether Israeli society will be capable of maintaining some of its major premises and especially of combining the maintenance of a self-supporting modern Jewish society together with the development of social and cultural creativity which has some significance beyond its own confines.

We have seen that many of the problems are largely due to a convergence of expectations and demands for creativity on the one hand and of conditions of development in a small new country with limited population and resources on the other hand.

As we have seen, this society perceived itself as a "centre" which has its "periphery", to a large extent, outside itself. Although the establishment of the State helped to develop a growing "natural" internal differentiation between centre and periphery, Israeli society continuously attempted to maintain its "central" and "elitist" characteristics and the concomitant specialized institutional arrangements that emphasize its commitments to the creation of a cultural and social order of wider significance.

However, these orientations inevitably face the problems created by the growth of a modern but small society, where the smallness of its population may limit the ability to develop differentiated specialized roles and activities and the means by which such roles and activities could be maintained.

This problem has become even more acute with the mass immigration since 1948 which brought in its wake not only a wider but also a different kind of periphery—namely, many groups from relatively lower educational and technical levels, with many of the characteristics of underdeveloped, "traditional" societies, and above all with but little initial commitment to these new, modern traditional types of social-cultural creativity.

These groups grew, as we have seen, into almost half of Israel's population, creating both new types of demands on the central institutions as well as the possibility of a cleavage between the "Oriental" and the "European" parts of the society and the development of a situation of "Two Nations".

All these trends tended to produce various structural pressures liable to lower the creative characteristics and tensions of the society. These pressures are manifest in the development of various particularistic orientations and organizations.

These particularistic trends seem to have developed from three roots. The first was the traditional, closed, Jewish-European society from which the veteran half of the population came, and many of whose characteristics could have become perpetuated in the setting of Palestine once their original revolutionary fervour abated and the revolutionary ideology became more and more routinized and institutionalized. Second were the parallel particularistic orientations of the new immigrants which became transformed in the new setting into new types of demands for political and social participation and for economic rewards based on particularistic criteria. But particularistic tendencies could also, thirdly, have developed from the basically elitist orientations of the pioneering groups themselves—rooted as they were in small sects and social movements which could easily become transformed into relatively narrow interest groups and organizations attempting to claim for themselves the right to be the sole bearers of the "pioneering", social and cultural creativity inherent in the Zionist ideology.

All these tendencies could, of course, become easily reinforced by the smallness of the country and its population and by the attempts to create within it a "normal" modern economic structure with a differentiated role-structure.

But these new developments could also serve as starting points for new directions of creativity, challenging the existing centre to find, together with the new groups, new ways of creating various nuclei of social and cultural creativity with broader universalistic orientations and attempting to continue to overcome the various limitations inherent in its background and in its setting.

As, due to lack of appropriate social traditions and environmental conditions, it seems doubtful whether Israeli society can develop as a normal small or medium-sized modern country, these problems become even more important and crucial for its future. Israeli society faces now in all its sharpness the dilemma either of declining to a local stagnant structure, lacking both internal and external forces of attraction, or of overcoming this possible stagnation by finding new ways of developing social and cultural creativity which has some significance beyond its own confines.

Beyond this, there looms the more fundamental question of the extent to which it will be possible for a social and cultural tradition which maintained strong orientations to such broader social and cultural creativity throughout its history to maintain them under new conditions. As we have seen, such orientations were maintained by this society both when it was an oppressed or segregated minority in a traditional-religious society and when its members began to enter into the various fields of the majority society or societies when these became modernized. The problem which it faces now, and which constitutes its greatest challenge, is whether it will be able to preserve and develop such orientations now that it has ceased to be embedded only in a situation of a minority but became also transposed into an autonomous modern society, which has to develop its institutional frameworks and organizations within the confines of a relatively small country.

H.H. BEN-SASSON

DYNAMIC TRENDS IN MODERN JEWISH THOUGHT AND SOCIETY

I

THE question of Jewish unity still lies at the heart of the way Jews think about themselves, and the way others think about them, both in Israel and throughout the Diaspora. Whether such unity is felt to be good, bad or non-existent, it raises questions that touch us on the quick. Are the Jews a nation, ask individuals, or is it only religion that unites them? Have Jews today any real unity at all? Some would answer it no. The label "Jews" (they say) is merely a label, stuck on a group of people lumped together by a certain ancestral past and by other people's hostility. Such "identity", in their opinion, is artificial. The holders of this view have become socially and culturally part of the country where they are settled. Others feel that their lives and loyalties belong not to any nation but to some general human cause that has won their hearts, be it social, humanitarian or cultural. To think about these questions at all is to think about the nature and roots of Jewish identity. Is it dead and gone, or is it a dynamic part of modern life? If, after all, Jewish identity no longer exists, how can it legitimately be the subject of this article? The author's answer to this crucial question is definitely a positive one.

That the Jews do in fact possess an identity is the conclusion of many students of Jewish history and modern Jewish society, particularly scholars living in Israel. They are led to this conclusion by a study of Jewish history, and by observing Jewish experience in our time. They see how the Jews have lived among the nations and they see clear signs of internal vitality in specifically Jewish thought and life, not only in the past but in the present. The author proceeds from the often-contested assumption that the Jews today are a people in all respects with a fate and struggles of their own. Another fundamental assumption here is that the fate the Jews had to endure and the identity this impressed upon them shaped their attitude to reality and their ways of thought far more than they themselves realised. Jewish history and Jewish culture, the values which were formed and are being formed specifically

for the Jewish people—these, in the author's opinion, pervade all branches of the Jews' life and thought, even among those whose minds and
feelings most violently reject the unwanted yoke. What is more, the
rebellion of these latter, their search for a new bond and a new mission
in life outside Judaism, is the product of that same heritage that they
see as a dead end, a slavery alien to them. The dialectics of Jewish
assimilation teach us the essence and meaning of Jewish national culture no less than the vitality and tenacity of that culture today.

II

The lives of the Jews in our time seem at first glance to be nothing
but change. As in a kaleidoscope, new patterns constantly appear.
Sometimes the changes are the result of hostile forces; sometimes they
are brought on voluntarily by the Jews themselves. Sometimes a combination of the two produces an unexpected situation. Only thirty years
ago Europe was the centre of Jewish settlement, culture and society; it
possessed, in Eastern Europe, the main reserve of tradition and the
main source of conscious devotion to Jewish national continuity. The
Nazi holocaust finished Eastern Europe as a centre of Jewish settlement
and cut away the creative ground in most of the countries concerned.
The political and social changes that followed the fall of the Nazis in
some countries still further limited the possibilities of independent
cultural activity on the part of the Jews. Some of the nationalist Jewish
elements, chiefly young people, had left for Eretz-Israel even before
the holocaust; there, and in the new state of Israel that arose, new creative horizons opened and a new focus of Jewish culture took shape in
the ancestral homeland. The largest Jewish population bloc today is in
the United States of America. Another centre is the Soviet Union. In
general, the map of Jewish settlement, the distribution of Jewish population in the world and the location of its creative centres have all
changed somewhat. The cultural climate has changed too. Anglo-Saxon
culture formed the background of Jewish existence and creativity to a
very considerable extent. Today, within less than a generation, a difference is felt in spiritual content, conventions and subjects of controversy. The whole tone has changed among Jews, as their manners and
social customs have changed.

However, at a second and more searching glance, we see that within
this continuing change, in the professional and social configurations
that seem so utterly foreign to those who knew the previous Jewish
society, behind and moulding the changes are certain constant forces.

Not only has the map of the Jewish diaspora changed: in the process
(which far predates the holocaust but belongs entirely to the modern
period) the type of place where Jews settle in the Diaspora has changed

too. Jews settle today all over the world, except in Israel, in large cities. The city of New York, for example, is a centre of Jewish population no less important than the State of Israel, both in numbers and social strength. Moscow and Leningrad also contain large numbers of Jews; one recalls that until 1917 these cities were forbidden to Jews. This tendency to gravitate to large cities is relatively new, but in essence it is only the climax of an ancient tendency, dating at least to the beginning of the Middle Ages, for the Jews to be an urban people par excellence. Of course the roots of this tendency lie in past persecutions and decrees which cut the Jews off from the land, but the results of this forcible separation from the land became a basic fact of their life, and except in modern Eretz-Israel and the State of Israel efforts to move the Jews from town to country have had little real success.

Yet, even within this long urban perspective, megapolitanization is revolutionary. The grandson of an eastern European immigrant from the *shtetl* lives in a real and human environment utterly different from that of his grandfather, and the same is true even if the grandfather hailed not from a townlet but from a large town. The town Jews of eastern Europe retained their connection with the Jewish townships and these townships were very close to the rural life around them. Whereas the grandchild lives today among the skyscrapers of New York, Chicago, London, Paris and Leningrad, cut off from the naturalness of that life. Nonetheless, the fact that his grandparents came to the city from a rural environment is not completely blotted out of his ways of life. It still registers. Whenever and wherever possible, for example in the towns of Western Europe and the United States, the Jewish immigrant has known how to preserve with some success the forms of communal life and the signs and symbols of unity that came from the town and the townlet of eastern Europe. Even the immense charitable activity of western Jewry (of which more will be said below) serves as a focus and bond of great strength between the donors themselves and between the donors and those they help, a bond all the more meaningful for its association with old Jewish traditions.

In these years of Jewish megalopolitanization, the State of Israel arose. Many, many of the big-city dwellers love her, cherish her achievements and borrow dignity from her. Israel, however, arose from a social process diametrically opposed to the trend that drew these people to the skyscrapers. The motive that drew Jews to Israel was to a very considerable extent rebellion against Jewish town life. Jewish Eretz-Israel, and later Israel, arose from the initiative of pioneers, *Halutzim,* who responded to the call for the Jew's return to nature and to mother earth; they felt an absolute human and cultural obligation to themselves and to their people to return to the historic land of their fathers. Manual labour they valued and esteemed, especially agriculture. The strength of these opinions and feelings renewed and fertilized the land of Israel. Out of them arose the *kibutzim*—the collective agricultural settlements or communes founded by young people, overwhelmingly from the middle and upper classes of their native towns and townships in Europe, who had left town life by deliberate intent. The ideas still keep going the kibbutz way of life; the settlements are central to the quality of Israel life, not to speak of Israel's "image" in the eyes of the world. Thus, over against the trend to the big cities we must place the rural experience, so important a part of the State of Israel. Numerically, the first trend is immeasurably the stronger; in quality and spiritual attraction the latter would seem to outshine it in the eyes of Jews everywhere.

The social evolution of the Jews in modern times is marked both by the rush to the "liberal professions" and the arts, and the idealization of higher education, with determined efforts to get more of it. The respect felt by Jews for those engaged in the arts and the liberal professions is well known. So many of these occupations were barred to Jews until the beginning of modern times. In fact the Jews' entrance into universities in various countries begins with their emancipation there, and is part of it. This phenomenon was conspicuous in all the social and political regimes under which Jews have lived, regardless of general social and economic forms. United States Jewry "pulled itself up by the bootstraps"; from a community of tailors, pedlars and small shopkeepers, it became in 80 years or less a community outstanding for its academic intelligentsia, its managerial executives and its practitioners of the arts—a communal elite in its own eyes and in the eyes of others. This revolution was not simply the result of a desire to get rich—not even mainly that, for the road to big business (which was flourishing at the time) lay equally open before them, and might have been thought to be the easier way for the sons of pedlars and shopkeepers. After all, it is only very recently that members of the free professions have made much money. The story of the superhuman efforts made by "green" immigrants and their sons to acquire education and culture, seeing the university as the pinnacle of their hopes—this is in essence the story of the great Jewish immigration into the United States from the eighties of the nineteenth century onwards. It is one of the best known stories and needs no documentation here; it is told, described and analysed as much in literature as in historical and sociological research.

In Soviet Russia the Jews turned to exactly the same professions, and chose the same set of ideals of education. That is to say, the difference in the social and ideological structure, the differences in the economic and social rewards available in the east and in the west, did not deflect the Jews from their course. The trend remained, wherever it was allowed to find expression. Some may condemn that trend as "social-intellectual", out of hostility to the trend itself or to the Jews, or from a conviction that too much intellectual occupation does society and the Jews no good. But whether one praises it for its own sake or for the sake of the growing Jewish contribution to intellectual, human, creative and professional life and to various national cultures—the fact itself remains unchanged. It actively exists in our own time, growing all the time in volume and quality.

The existence and persistence of this phenomenon demands an explanation arising from itself, not from external circumstances. It is in fact explained from within the Jewish tradition since as far back as the days of the Second Temple. From that day to this traditional Jewish society has seen the study of the Torah as the *highest religious and social value*, a commandment in the fullest sense of the word. "Thou shalt study in it day and night" was an ideal close to realization by many, and those who achieved it were admired. Everything attests this. In the Middle Ages even hostile Christian monks noticed it. In modern times Ḥayim Nakhman Bialix has expressed in his poem *ha-Matmid*—a song of praise and a piece of documentary evidence more compelling for its social criticism or the very phenomenon it praises—the unbounded devotion of Jewish youth to study; the poem expresses the Jewish public's boundless admiration of one who gives himself to study.

The rush to the universities in the twentieth century, the respect for learning and the learned among modern Jewry, are thus merely a secularization of an ancient, sacred ideal. The value attached to the study of Holy Writ has been transferred to secular subjects.

The prestige of the ideal of learning was enhanced in Jewry by the social distinction acquired by devotion to study, by whoever evinced intellectual talent. In the days when the Talmud was being compiled in the 3rd century C.E., Jewish sages asked "Who are kings?" They answered: "teachers (rabbis)". In Babylonia, in the 9th to 12th centuries of the present era, a sort of permanent aristocracy emerged among the sages in the religious colleges; a rash, even desperate, attempt to make wisdom and knowledge hereditary. In the families of these Torah sages it was assumed that wisdom is transmitted hereditarily from father to son. At the end of the Middle Ages the sage and scholar, learned and acute of mind, had become the aristocrat of Jewish society. In modern times, this social position belongs not only to those learned in religious lore but also to their modern extension, people of intellectual attainments and holders of secular academic degrees—acute of mind and learned in mathematics, philosophy, medicine and the like.

At first Christian society evinced lack of understanding and active opposition to the stream of Jews into spheres where they had been hitherto unknown. During most of modern times, and in some countries right down to the present day, the Jews have to overcome obstacles placed in the way of academic study and careers in the liberal professions. There were diverse ways of keeping Jews out of universities and technical schools; methods and arrangements of great ingenuity were invented to prevent Jews from enjoying the full benefit and profit that non-Jews got for the same achievements, degrees and services. Nothing succeeded in holding the Jews back from following the main highway of their tradition.

This noted phenomenon frequently amazed governments that failed to appreciate the nature of the inward urge to study. In the sixties of the nineteenth century, the Czarist government of Russia opened the secondary schools and institutions of higher learning to Jews, and even promised that Jewish graduates would enjoy more rights than other Jews. The stupendous flow of Jews to these schools appalled the government to make entrance requirements for Jews more and more severe; it then turned out that many Jews were successfully meeting the special requirement for hyper-excellence in study in high school, which was a condition of their entrance into universities. At this point the Russian government decided on cruder weapons and introduced a *numerus clausus* for Jews. The result was an exodus of young Jewish men and women in their thousands to the universities of Germany and Switzerland, and the creation of great colonies of "Russian students" there.

As the sciences, in particular the pure and applied sciences, grew in importance to modern state and society, to their industry, their national defence, and their prestige among the powers, the Jews found themselves well placed to serve the state and in a national, social and functional position of prime importance. The ever-growing need for scientists weakened the desire to oppose the entrance of Jews into institutions of higher education (in some countries the proportion of Jews in such institutions far exceeds their proportion in the population). And in some countries, particularly those in the forefront of scientific and technological advance in the world, this opposition is now almost entirely silent. Throughout these fluctuations in the fate of the Jewish student, loved and hated by turns, he and his parents were and are still drawn to study by an inner force planted in their people generations ago, whether they know this and admit it or not.

At the period we are speaking of, the Jewish people also revealed creative gifts in forming, developing and using language in widely differing circumstances and with impressive success. Platoons of Jews in those generations took as their province languages unknown to their forefathers. In the United States of America, in England and in the British Dominions English became their language; in South America, Ashkenazi Jews from Eastern Europe made Spanish and Portuguese their own. In a remarkably short time, considering the magnitude and delicacy of the task, the Jews became creators in these literatures and languages, stylistic artists and literary critics. But the main achievement from the point of view of national Jewish culture was within the Jews' own languages, Hebrew and Yiddish. The first of these, Hebrew, belongs to all Jewry, the second to Jews of east European origin. Ancient Hebrew, language of the Bible and the Mishnah, had always been, from before the Middle Ages, the language of literature and of holiness. They prayed in it, wrote ceremonial documents in it, wrote books of *Halakha,* homiletical interpretation and morals. But in the field of creative literature other languages at times tended to push it out: Aramaic, in which most of the Talmud is written; Arabic, in which Maimonides wrote most of his works. Even as late as 1912, Jews prepared to help establish a technical college in Ḥaifa, Eretz-Israel, were opposed to the introduction of Hebrew as the language of instruction, because they thought that its vocabulary was inadequate for the teaching of modern technology. Within 60 years at most, Hebrew has become a living language, *spoken by the people in Israel,* by ignorant and learned alike, by children and old people. A rich secular Hebrew literature has been created. Except for the Arabic used in Israeli Arab schools, Hebrew is the universal language of instruction in every branch and every subject; it is used in universities and technical colleges, in kindergarten, in industry and in business; it is the language of political propaganda and the language of instruction and command in the Israel Defence Forces. In their language at least, the Jews have done what the Irish and Welsh are still wistfully longing to do.

Soon after the revival of the Hebrew language, Jews in eastern Europe tried to turn Yiddish from a purely spoken dialect, whose scanty written literature consisted of songs, popular plays and of moral tracts for the people, into a language of literature and science. This revolution too they accomplished; the secular modern literature that has arisen since then in Yiddish is rich and wide. All branches of modern science can be taught and expounded in Yiddish.

Within about two generations, a "dead" language, Hebrew, had come to life among the Jews, growing and developing with and from their lives; while they changed a popular dialect, Yiddish, and raised it to the level of a literary and scientific language. The Nazi holocaust has made most of their Yiddish achievement seem transitory today. Brute force has wiped out the human vessels of that culture and language. Nevertheless, from the point of view of creative effort and practical cultural implementation, transformation of Yiddish deserves to be mentioned by the side of the living, present success of Hebrew.

The Jewish community in modern times has consciously continued the tradition of mutual help and charity of Jewish communities in previous generations. The scope has grown with the need; the financial and organisational effort among the Jews, especially the American Jews, was often both hard and impressive in its material achievements and the organisational structures set up to collect money and give help. Disasters raining on the heads of whole communities demanded great aid; witness the needs of Eastern European Jewry through wars, revolutions, pogroms, years of famine and pestilence; witness the rehabilitation needs of Nazi concentration-camp survivors and the problems of moving and resettling Jewish refugees from many countries today. Above all, help was needed for the immense constructive work that modern Jewry took upon itself, the crown of which was the settlement of Eretz-Israel and after this the upbuilding and defence of the State of Israel. But there were also settlement activities in Argentina and the well-known attempt to set up autonomous Jewish agricultural centres in the Soviet Union, first in Crimea, then in Birobidjan. To all these causes the Jewish public responded. Being scattered over distant continents and living in big cities (which might have been thought unlikely to foster altruistic feelings) these could not cancel what Jewish history had built in. The old medieval life in which the community was close-knit and relatively classless, where the differences were more in property than in class, where the surrounding sea of hatred made help to the weak and support for communal needs a commandment—all these made aid a deep-rooted part of Jewish life. It remains part of Jewish life today, even though class distinctions have cut deep into Jewish society with the entry of Jews into new and varied fields of occupation and changed their attitude to each other. The feeling "I must help" pervades the Jewish attitude to all weak and needy people.

These examples chosen from the reality of Jewish life today—the change in the map of the Diaspora, the move to big cities, the building of a unique society in Israel, the hunger for learning and the idealisation of it, the revival of Hebrew and the transformation of Yiddish, the immense works of Jewish construction and of Jewish charity—all these are examples that illustrate, in the author's opinion, continuity within change; the outward and visible face of old values may have changed— not their essence.

Thus the Jewish people stands today, alive in its continuity, though wounded and mutilated in many of its limbs. Yet this continuity and even the Jewish people's right to its own life are in some circles subject to question and controversy. This nation, after two thousand years, has a state of its own, the State of Israel, which unites those of its sons who wish to be joined together within it with a validity and reality lacking from Jewish life for generations. On the other hand, the very existence of Israel is an irritant to those who would deny the unity of the Jews, those who feel and express the bitterest anger at the national, political element in Jewry. Hebrew is more and more becoming the language of Diaspora Jews. They make efforts to learn it, to get to know it at least as a living language, even if they do not succeed in mastering it as they

MODERN JEWISH THOUGHT AND SOCIETY

would like. The Jews have not lost or let drop their old values—the aristocracy of learning and the holiness of wisdom, the value of social cohesion, the duty to give aid and build collectively. All are part of the nation's historic dialectic. There are signs of dialectical tension in the desire to assimilate on the part of some of its sons; in many, the sense of mission, messianic, historic, is preserved in the feeling of a duty to act in the general cause of human justice and order. The same sense of mission inspires the best sons of the State of Israel both in work and defence. All in all, in its social reality, the Jewish people is a nation whose ideas and ways of social life are new, sometimes even rebellious. But much of the strength that activates its individuals, ways and institutions comes to it from past tradition, from the ancient fires of the past and from the strength of values and trends that have become immanent in it through the deeds, thoughts and feelings that form its historic heritage.

III

A good deal of the thought of Jews in recent generations does not belong in this discussion, remembering our basic assumptions. Many Jews have contributed and do contribute much to human thought. But their work is informed intellectually and culturally by forms and languages showing that the creators voluntarily regard themselves as part of cultural patterns that are non-Jewish. The fruit of these Jews' thought is therefore a contribution by them to the world surrounding Jewish culture and thought. In what they contribute, many Jewish intellectuals and thinkers belong to the innovating camp in culture and society. You find them at the head of the fighters for equal human rights and for the abolition of anything that diminishes the dignity of any part of mankind. Many Jews are leaders in the boldest forefront of experimental literature, philosophy and art. In art, the work of Marc Chagall marks the boundary line in terms of our present discussion, and suggests how difficult it is to draw such a line.

From the standpoint of his artistic life and the locus of his creativity Chagall belongs to the wider circles of Russia and France, and he is a product of French modernist schools. But in associative, mythical content, in the thoughts his work embodies and brings before the eyes of modern man like a folk-legend, Chagall is conspicuously a Jew from the land of the Jews in Eastern Europe. The township, its joys and sorrows, its Jewish beauties, its goats and cocks hovering in an intoxicating riot of colour and in wondrous imaginary conjunction, are nearly all mostly taken from Jewish teachings, the earthy wisdom and folk-tales of the people and they are exhibited so in the museums and galleries of Europe. The stained-glass windows that Chagall created for the synagogue of Hadassah hospital in Jerusalem express in extremely experimental modern European artistic terms motifs of great historic antiquity and legends of the people of Israel, in which again we find lines and figures from the township in Eastern Europe—all this drawn and painted for the glory of the reborn State of Israel in the artist's workshop in France.

In truth, Chagall is from this point of view a distinguished representative of a whole Jewish spiritual approach and a treasure of Jewish scenes and associations which entered modern European art after the Jews had come to play an important part in the plastic arts, especially in modernistic movements; for until the middle of the 19th century there were virtually no Jewish creative artists in that sphere. It is unnecessary to say that the same phenomenon appears elsewhere as well. There are many creative movements among the Jews in various fields of Eastern and Western European culture: Jewish motifs recur and their expression is irresistibly demanded, the response being sometimes unconscious on the part of the artist, philosopher or scientist.

The readiness for a righteous war and the search for new values to create and follow, wherever they lead the thought or imagination of the creator, are found among many Jewish intellectuals who attached themselves to the mainstream of non-Jewish creation. It seems for all that that their contribution tends more and more to be to the upbuilding of society, and the once-characteristic bitterness of this type of Jewish nonconformist is disappearing. They see themselves now—despite the grim experience of what happened in modern Germany—as responsible leaders and teachers who are called upon to spread enlightenment among the masses and to educate their own and succeeding generations; they want to draw the public nearer to a positive constructive outlook on life. With the spread of education in the world and the rise of science to a position of central importance to humanity, the Jewish thinker and scientist sees himself as the bearer of the most important tools of his society; by virtue of them he speaks as one who expresses the trend leading the society of his time towards its hoped-for future, and from his speech disappears the bitter sense of being a lone voice, the upholder of values that nobody of intellectual decisive importance in his world wants to listen to. Where we still find this bitterness, it is a deposit from an earlier situation, from the days before science and education acquired their present strength; or it is the result of struggling in a cause that even the prestige of the intellectuals cannot make palatable to the opposition, and this depresses the Jewish fighter for the cause. In some cases, there is a bitterness springing from the frightful disappointment suffered by the modern Jewish intellectual, by nature an individualist (we shall have more to say of this below), when he clashes with the will of the social and historic forces around him to form violent collective patterns. In this respect Boris Pasternak of the period of "Dr. Zhivago" represents typically the friction of the Jewish individual who flees his people and himself and is disappointed in political and social experience in the nation and culture he chooses to belong to. His angry call to the Jews to "disperse" and give up their national bond, as uttered in the book, seems to reflect his own struggles and soulsearchings on the social bond in general, and his grudge against his blood-brothers' success in finding voluntary, not compulsory union, unlike his adopted brothers.

Another important part of modern Jewish creative thought is the elucidation of questions on the nature of the Jews today, on the trends desirable for Jewry to develop or suppress, on the paths of religion or secularity most likely to advance the culture of the people. The teaching of A.D. Gordon for instance, on "the religion of labour" and on the value of the return to nature and work on the land in the ancestral homeland, is the foundation of the kibbutz in Israel. The teachings of Rabbi A.I.H. Kook, first Chief Rabbi of modern Jewish Eretz-Israel, is the focus of thought on the sanctity of deeds in national revival; a meeting-point of mystical ideas of God's will with modern national assumptions. If one turns to the views of Dr. M.M. Kaplan on the reconstruction of Judaism, one finds a system of ideas that seeks to offer the religious man a concept of Judaism as a society and civilisation in whose development religion finds its place. There are also a number of systems of ideas that put forward national assimilation and religious existence as their conclusion about the world and Judaism. In this spectrum there is one view—that of R. Joel Teitelbaum in the U.S.A.—which is far from proposing assimilation but rejects with violence and disgust the idea that Jews exist today as a nation. He loathes the secular State of Israel. The utter dismissal by Rabbi Teitelbaum of the unity of modern Jewish society in Israel (and not only in Israel), his rejection of its symbols, its institutions and its struggles, reads unwittingly like the apostle Paul's denunciation of the national Judaism of *his* generation; the difference is that in this case the hatred of national unity goes out in the name of Torah law, not antinomianism, and the teachings of the "Satmar Rebbe" (as he is known) contain no message for the Gentiles... We may mention here, by way of contrast, the various proposals that the Jews should exist as a nation but drop their religion. This is the line taken, for example, by the Socialist "Bund", and it underlies some of the movements in Zionism. Among the latter there has even appeared a "Canaanite" movement which proposes that the Jews in the State of Israel should cut themselves off from the historic continuity of Judaism and regard themselves as a new-old nation, different from Diaspora Jewry and "blending with the background" of the present-day Middle East; from this standpoint the "Canaanites" regard themselves as chiefly related to the Biblical period—or rather to the distant pre-Biblical period.

Here I should like to dwell on two phenomena that have been discussed within Judaism as meaningful ideas, but which also have significance and roots in the wider cultural and social world of which they are part. The influence of each and the solutions found have their implications for the whole of Judaism, and both have resulted in a widening of the modern significance of Jewish thought, and the bringing of Judaism into the mosaic of international cultural and social thought.

Jewish thought in recent generations has been both disturbed and fertilised by the growing individualization of important circles in Jewish society. It is city-dwelling that has brought this individualization about. Intellectual tension and mental power have produced it, the results of the meeting between the old world of Jewish education and the new world that values and esteems the individual who shows personal talent and intellectual achievement. What, above all seems to have made the individual Jew realize the value of his personality was the Jews' experience and the feelings that accompanied it—that the individual, especially if he is a Jew, stands alone now, exposed to himself, facing man and God in a present-day social world growing ever crueller and more complex. The individualization of the Jews produced acute crises to individuals and to the patterns of unity; on the other hand it enriched more and more their intellectual and social world, and strength was found among Jewish thinkers to build up frameworks of unity out of the individualization, on the basis of its peculiar merits and values.

The confrontation of the individual with another individual who is his equal, human relations opening out of equality or being blocked by the other person's shutting himself off, has been discussed by a very great Jewish thinker; to him the equal opening out is the principal virtue of being human in natural surroundings, as well as the way to a meeting between man and God. It is not by chance, and there is much symbolism in this, that the modern Jewish philosopher who has most gained the ear of the world, Martin Buber[1], whose life encompassed almost the entire period discussed here, and whose width of interests embraced every problem that faced the Jews in his time, was the man who set in the centre of his system, especially in its later stages of development, the dialogue and "dialogueness" as a vision of all. Buber thought that humanity and truth worthy of the name are created and arise only when and where individuals "see each other", when each listens to what the other has to say with open thought and feelings,

---

[1] Cf. now : G. SCHOLEM, "Martin Bubers Auffassung des Judentums", *Eranos Jahrbuch*, XXXV (1966), pp. 9-55.

when each comes to know the other in a dialogue of "I" and "Thou". He also thought that the "dialogue life" was the great discovery made by the people of Israel. In his own words: "Israel hat das Leben als ein Angesprochenwerden und Antworten, Ansprechen und Antwort empfangen und verstanden, vielmehr eben gelebt" (Schriften, Vol. III, p. 742).

In his opinion, the "dialogue" is the foundation and essence of the inclusive monotheism of Judaism. As he says: "Die Einzigkeit im Monotheismus... ist die des Du und der Ich-Du Beziehung... Der 'Polytheist' macht aus jeder göttlichen Erscheinung... ein Gotteswesen; der 'Monotheist' erkennt in allen den Gott wieder, den er im Gegenüber erfuhr" (ibid., I, p. 629). Whoever takes part in this "dialogue" automatically assumes the duty or commandment of putting into practice his proclaimed ideals—the ideals he has proclaimed to the open ears of the "Thou", God or man. Hence in Jewish martyrdom of the Medieval type, the supreme sacrifice of life, Buber heard the last and highest note of the dialogue between the Jew and his Maker: "Nicht im Bekenntnis allein, sondern in der Erfüllung des Erkenntnisses, keineswegs im pantheistischem Theorem, sondern in der Realität des Unmöglichen, in der Verwirklichung des Ebenbildes, in der imitatio Dei. Das Geheimnis dieser Wirklichkeit vollendet sich im Martyrium, im Sterben mit dem Einheitsruf des 'Höre Israel' auf den Lippen" (Der Jude und seine Judentum, p. 189). That is to say, the Jew who suffers for his faith "responds to" his God in a last self-determining answer in this phase of the continuing, perpetual dialogue, in which his personality and the "personality" of his God stand open, face to face. Son of a people despised and rejected by many, a people whose individuality many sought to blot out of existence, Buber claimed that his people had taught humanity to know the contact of open recognition: individual facing individual, and he taught this as the crux and the way that all humanity should follow for human completeness and as the true way to God.

The theory that the individual is free to decide according to the light of his own reason has been heard in an original form from a very conservative source. A Lithuanian Rabbi, one of the greatest Jewish Talmud scholars of the beginning of the twentieth century, R. Meir Simkha Hacohen of Dvinsk, Latvia, expounds the biblical phrase about man, "in the image of God created He him" (Genesis I, 27), as follows: "The image of God is free intellectual choice, unforced free will... this we know, that free choice is a limitation of divinity: that the Lord leaves His creatures (i.e., men) room to act as they choose; and does not decide the details of their actions. Therefore He said to Himself 'Let us make man in our image' (ibid., 26); this means that the Torah speaks in the language of men, saying: let us leave man room to choose, that his acts may not be forced nor his thoughts imposed... that he may be able to act against his own nature and against what is right in the eyes of the Lord... Man is not (human) by nature but by choice, and his choice changes, (even) evidence shall not compel him" (From his commentary on the Pentateuch, *Meshekh Hokhma,* section on Genesis). Now this is an interpretation of *Be-Zelem* "in the image", taking as the real image of God his absolute freedom, which allows him to dictate to all creatures, making them obey the laws of their own natures which he has planted in them, and ordering strictly their fate. Only to man has God given his "image", the freedom of decision by pure reason. Thus "in our image" means within our image, having contracted it to "make room" for the coming into being of the human-divine image. The starting-point of this exposition is necessarily the recognition by the rabbinical commentator that freedom must be dictatorial or anarchic unless for the sake of freedom it limits itself voluntarily to permit co-existence with other freedoms "in its image and form". The sovereignty of the free-born individual really and truly can never permit dialogue with a creature of equal worth, unless he voluntarily limits his prerogatives. This is the ground of the religious views of R. Meir on man, God and their "image". His views have deep and ancient roots in Jewish thought, but his recognition of the dialectical tension of mutually competing freedoms, the making of man an ikon of divine freedom, and God, "human", this agreement by God to "push himself out", as it were, to let a creature on his world be his equal, the emphasis on human freedom—all these not by chance answer the spiritual needs of modern isolated man.

Despite the gulf between the two views, between the world-famous Jewish philosopher, writing in lofty, philosophic German, and the modest Talmud sage in his Latvian town, immersed in the holy scriptures, and setting down his views in the old midrshic-homiletical style—both in their teachings give profound utterance to individualization. Their teachings spring from their search for God's presence, their yearning to encounter or enter it, to do His will in truth yet not to renounce the independence of individuality. We have seen the strength of this individualizing approach among Jewish God-seekers of many hues, and we see it again, intensely, in the thought of other Jews who have left off the search for God but have not ceased to seek truth and the social mission of the sovereign individual. Such people sought and still seek a sublime secular ideal, to which they can give themselves because *they* have chosen to serve it.

In recent times the thought and the whole being of the Jews has been shocked by the forcible confrontation with bestial human cruelty—with the crimes of the Nazis. The terror of the deeds committed by one of the world's most cultured peoples, the atrocity of silence on the part of many bodies that the Jews assumed might react to the most systematic and complete murder of non-combatants in history, murder in the name of Race theory, which utterly denies humanity and God's image in man,—all these might have been thought to constitute a spiritual danger to the Jews. The attack on them from the forces of moral anarchy was a feat of the highest organizing technique using all the accepted instruments and terms of state and society. It might have been thought that the Jews would respond with a moral anarchy of their own, by a declaration of no confidence in man and disbelief in humanitarianism as a real possibility. But the immense inner force of the Jewish heritage, of a people long schooled in suffering inflicted from outside, saved them from a moral crisis. The appalling shock brought them together—those who survived—and fertilised their thought.

The shock drew these people into Judaism: individuals and groups of Jews who had fought with messianic fervour for social revolution, for the freeing of oppressed classes and peoples, now saw their own people humiliated and ground into the dust in the name of racial hatred, inescapably. Moreover, the national and social upheaval in the world after the Second World War showed many of them that classes and societies today prefer their own leaders, from their own ranks; and that it matters little to them whether the Jew identifies himself with their interests and will work for them wholeheartedly in a cause he has made his own; it became clear that the virus of Nazism had not left the body politic unaffected. At the same time the distress of their own people demanded relief from them as a matter of common humanity, while the great constructive work begun by the Jews in the State of Israel demanded more concretely that they should do their share in realizing the messianic dream by building Israel in its land.

The shock also found relief in extensive works of aid and rehabilitation for the survivors of the holocaust. Yet all the while, within the people, moral tension continued to grow, as they took a new look at reality. The Polish writer Czeslaw Milosz has suggested to westerners the essential difference in the feel of life between those who underwent the horrors of Nazi occupation and those who did not: "A man is lying under machine-gun fire on a street in an embattled city. He looks at the pavement and sees a very amusing sight: the cobblestones are standing upright like the quills of a porcupine. The bullets hitting their edges displace and tilt them. Such moments in the consciousness of man *judge* all poets and philosophers... In the intellectuals who lived through the atrocities of war in Eastern Europe there took place what one might call the *elimination of emotional luxuries.*" *(The Captive Mind* [New York, 1955], p. 39).

As far as the Jew was concerned, such "elimination of emotional luxuries" was far sharper and more drastic—for even if he himself had not lain in the body at the edge of the pavement, he knew well that the brothers with whom he felt inward and outward solidarity—for they were spiritually himself and physically the same in the eyes of the oppressor—his brothers were thrown daily into the gutter; self-respect must be taken from the Jew because he is a Jew, before you take his life. Today the Jew knows that to stand upright facing the enemy and to look straight into the eyes of the aggressor means the salvation not only of the body but of the soul.

So it was that the holocaust engendered a willingness for supreme sacrifice. The seed of courage, which has flowered among the youth of Israel in heroic deeds, was watered by the blood of the martyrs. We have heard Buber speak of the ancient tradition of martyrdom from a human and religious standpoint. In the Middle Ages, from the first Crusade onwards, the Jews clave to traditions of enduring torture and facing death that reached back to the days of Antiochus Epiphanes and the first revolt against the Romans; they laid down a way to die for their faith, and more than that, to kill themselves and their dear ones when they saw that active resistance was no longer possible, and they feared that not all of them would face enemy weapons bravely. The techniques of deluding the victim and breaking him down psychologically prevented most of the Nazis' victims from taking this way out. Yet the heroic and doomed rising of the Warsaw ghetto and the deeds of Jewish partisans, dogged by quislings in the forests and underground, are a mass martyrdom in different circumstances. Now a change has come over this ancient value; it seems to have become merged in the consciousness of the Jewish fighting youth with the active heroism they so boundlessly display.

This short survey of modern Jewish thought, thought bubbling with life in different channels, takes as the crux of the social and mental situation in the Jewish people the question of endurance, of autonomy, the question how free man should meet God and man face to face. It emerges that even in old patterns of thought and expression the question still most actual is that of the sovereignty of individual freedom and the need to limit it voluntarily, in order to live with other free men, equal "in image of God", that is in freedom. The results of the holocaust too, the miraculous moral unity and human courage it begot among the Jews, seem central to the Jews, and they are of value to all humanity. The individual, freedom, open dialogue, the ability to endure humiliation and to come out of it with a straight back—by these things not the Jews alone will be tested.

INDEX